ANSWERING AUSCHWITZ

Answering Auschwitz

Primo Levi's Science and Humanism after the Fall

Edited by

Stanislao G. Pugliese

Fordham University Press

New York 2011

Library of Congress Cataloging-in-Publication Data

Answering Auschwitz : Primo Levi's science and humanism
after the fall / edited by Stanislao G. Pugliese.—1st ed.
        p.   cm.
Includes bibliographical references and index.
ISBN 978-0-8232-3358-8 (cloth : alk. paper)
ISBN 978-0-8232-3359-5 (pbk. : alk. paper)
ISBN 978-0-8232-3360-1 (ebook)
 1. Levi, Primo—Criticism and interpretation.
I. Pugliese, Stanislao G., 1965–
PQ4872.E8Z562   2011
853'.914—dc22
2010052417

Printed in the United States of America
13 12 11   5 4 3 2 1
First edition

CONTENTS

PREFACE

In April 1987, as my classmates and I were preparing to graduate from college, word arrived that the Italian writer and Holocaust survivor Primo Levi had died, presumably a suicide. Like millions of people around the world, I was stunned. Having read only his first book, *Survival in Auschwitz*, I had formed an image of Levi as calm, serene, a beacon of hope in a postwar Europe, a writer informed by the traditional legacy of humanism and the Enlightenment. If anyone had shown us how to live in a post-Holocaust world, surely it was Primo Levi. And yet . . .

Haunted by that death, I eventually found Levi's other books, then his science fiction, poetry, essays, and two novels, *The Monkey's Wrench* and *If Not Now, When?* When Hofstra University asked me to organize a conference on the writer, I readily agreed, hoping that an academic atmosphere would banish that ghost. In fact, the reverse was true. Unable to exorcise that perplexing, complicated, and sometimes frustrating figure, I (perhaps foolishly) agreed to organize a second conference to commemorate the twentieth anniversary of his death. The essays published here were first presented at that three-day international conference at Hofstra University in Hempstead, New York. I am indebted to the administration of Hofstra University, especially President Stuart Rabinowitz, his charming wife, Nancy (a devoted admirer of the Italian writer), Provost Herman A. Berliner, and Dean Bernard J. Firestone of the Hofstra College of Liberal Arts and Sciences. The conference was a success in large part because of the dedication and professionalism of the staff of the Hofstra Cultural Center, especially its director, Natalie Datlof; the associate director, Athelene Collins-Prince; and conference coordinator Deborah Lom. Colleagues from Scotland, Italy, England, Israel, Belgium, and the United States participated to ensure a fruitful and collegial exchange of ideas. I am grateful for their dedication and their acceptance of editorial guidance with good grace and cheer. Thanks also to three anonymous readers whose suggestions made this a better book. This publication was made possible, in part, by a grant from the Elmer Kirsch Memorial Endowment for the Hofstra Cultural Center.

Some essays deal directly with Levi and his work; others tangentially use Levi's writings or ideas to explore larger issues in Holocaust studies, philosophy, theology, and the problem of representation. These are included here in the spirit that Levi described himself: proud of being "impure" and a "centaur," cognizant that asymmetry was the fundamental structure of organic life.

I am grateful to Terri Bowman for permission to reproduce artwork she completed while taking a course with me on Primo Levi during the spring 2006 semester, and to Rene Burri and Magnum Photos for permission to use one of his fine photos of Levi for the cover. Readers should note that some authors refer to Levi's first book as *Survival in Auschwitz* (the common American translation of *Se questo è un uomo*), while others use the more telling and correct British translation *If This Is a Man*.

Finally, a word of thanks to Jennifer Romanello and our children, Alessandro and Giulia. Over the past few years, as I was working on another project concerning Carlo Levi, the children often cautioned me to avoid confusing the two Levis. I hope we have not failed Primo Levi in remembering him here.

ANSWERING AUSCHWITZ

Answering Auschwitz:
Levi's Science and Humanism as Antifascism

Stanislao G. Pugliese

> It is very unhappy, but too late to be helped, the discovery we have
> made that we exist. That discovery is called the Fall of Man. Ever
> afterwards we suspect our instruments.
>
> RALPH WALDO EMERSON, "Experience" (1844)

In April 1987, the Italian chemist, writer, and Holocaust survivor Primo
Levi fell to his death in the stairwell of his apartment building in Turin.
Within hours, a debate exploded as to whether his death was an accident
or a suicide and, if the latter, how this might force us to reinterpret his
legacy as a writer and "survivor." Elie Wiesel, Cynthia Ozick, Philip Roth,
Diego Gambetta, Alexander Stille, and Susan Sontag, among many others,
weighed in with thoughtful and sometimes provocative commentary, but
the debate over his death has sometimes overshadowed the larger significance of his place as a thinker "after Auschwitz."

"It is barbaric," thundered Theodor Adorno, "to write poetry after
Auschwitz."[1] Adorno's dictum has perhaps been misunderstood. He was
not arguing for a taboo to be placed on any representation of the Holocaust, but instead that the Shoah represented a break in the ontological
status of *Homo sapiens* that resulted in the impossibility of a traditional
aesthetic. "After Auschwitz," Adorno argued, "events make a mockery of
the construction of immanence as endowed with a meaning radiated by an
affirmatively posited transcendence."[2] Levi himself hints at this in commenting on the "simple and incomprehensible" stories the inmates tell
each other in the evenings: "Are they not themselves stories of a new
Bible?"[3]

We are forced, after the Fall of contemporary humanity, into an impossible double bind: the necessity of recording, reflecting upon, and representing an event for which we do not have the proper conceptual or
linguistic tools. "Then for the first time," realized Levi, "we became aware

that our language lacks words to express this offense, the demolition of a man."[4] Levi, while recognizing our linguistic and hence conceptual poverty, might have argued that after Auschwitz, there could be no poetry (nor art) that was not—in some sense—about Auschwitz.

His own response can be found not only in his memoir of the concentration camp universe, *If This Is a Man*, but also in his subsequent *The Truce* as well as his poems, essays, and science fiction. For if science had been corrupted—first by social Darwinism, racism, and imperialism, then harnessed to the cause of genocide by National Socialism—and if humanism seemed to be an inadequate bulwark against moral and political bankruptcy, Levi still insisted that science and humanism were our only hope against a recurrence of madness.[5] Here I conceive of "science" not so much as the "hard" or natural sciences (much has been written about Levi and his chosen profession of chemistry) but rather the Latin *scientia* (knowledge or understanding). And we embrace a new variant of humanism, no longer naïve, tinged with tragedy and wary of the future. Perhaps thinking of his situation in Turin in the early days of fascism and war—similar in some ways to that described by Giorgio Bassani in his novel *The Garden of the Finzi-Continis*—Levi admonished us: "After Auschwitz," he wrote, "it is no longer permissible to be unarmed."[6]

Closely related to Levi's intellectual, philosophical, and cultural position was a political stance of consistent, fervent, and ongoing antifascism and left-wing politics. He often spoke and wrote for antifascist partisan organizations in Italy, such as the ANED (Associazione Nazionale ex-Deportati Politici nei Campi Nazisti, the National Association of Former Deportees to the Nazi Camps) and the ANPI (Associazione Nazionale Partigiani d'Italia, the National Partisan Association of Italy). On other occasions, I have remarked on this political legacy of Levi's.[7] Here I would simply ask the question: why has his political thinking been all but erased from the critical commentary in the United States? This erasure is revealing of the flaws of a certain cultural critique that either could not or would not engage Levi at a political level because his ideas did not conform to "acceptable" interpretations.

It was only thirteen years after the end of World War II that Levi already discerned a disturbing reality: the naïve illusion that fascism was dead. Instead, he sensed that it was "very far from being dead; it was only hidden, encysted. It was keeping quiet, to reappear later under a new guise, a little less recognizable, a bit more respectable, better adapted to the new world that had issued from the catastrophe of World War II which fascism itself had provoked."[8] Levi's analysis of the Holocaust did not stem from a counter-Enlightenment critique but from a deeply felt humanism. Auschwitz was the logical culmination of fascism, "its most monstrous manifestation,"⁹ but one could also have fascism without the camps. Fascism begins by denying the fundamental freedom and equality of human beings, proceeds to burning books, and, as foreseen by Heinrich Heine, ends by burning men, women, and children. (Many know Heine's famous 1823 aphorism "Where they burn books, they will also, in the end, burn men," but few know that he was referring to the burning of the Koran by the Spanish Inquisition.)

Lest we pride ourselves on having escaped this malediction, Levi has some sobering words. "Every age has its own fascism," he darkly warned in an essay of 1974,

> and we see the warning signs wherever the concentration of power denies citizens the possibility and the means of expressing and acting on their own free will. There are many ways of reaching this point, and not just through the terror of police intimidation, but by denying and distorting information, by undermining systems of justice, by paralyzing the education system, and by spreading in a myriad subtle ways nostalgia for a world where order reigned, and where the security of the privileged few depends on the forced labor and the forced silence of the many.¹⁰

I would argue that Levi recognized the Holocaust as "a second fall of man" in that we could never again conceive of human beings in the same way as before. "Consider that this has been" he writes in the poem "Shemà" on January 10, 1946. This event has erupted into history; we have witnessed what men can do to other men; if it has happened, it can happen again, and we can never return to an imagined state of innocence, no matter how fervently desired. On a more personal note, he recalled the days in the transit camp at Fossoli as "a condemnation, a fall, a reliving of the biblical stories of exile and migration. However, it was a tragic fall in which despair was tempered with the surprise and pride of a rediscovered identity."¹¹

The conceit of the Holocaust as a second fall has now become so accepted that we might easily fail to grasp its significance. "At Auschwitz, not only man died," laments Elie Wiesel, "but the idea of man."¹² The title of Eva Hoffman's meditation on the post-Holocaust world, *After Such Knowledge*, explicitly argues for our changed moral status.¹³ Emil Fackenheim predicted that "all authentic future philosophers and Christians would be sick with permanent fear."¹⁴ The critic George Steiner equates the Holocaust with an act of suicide, "inspired by hatred of the condemning best that is in man. The Holocaust signifies a second Fall of Man, one that is chosen in full awareness of the consequences; and we have burned the garden behind us."[15] Ironically, Martin Heidegger, considered by many to be the greatest philosopher of the twentieth century, also spoke of "a second fall of man," but for the German thinker, perhaps haunted by his own tainted relationship with National Socialism—which he never explicitly condemned, even after the Second World War—this was a fall into banality, not brutality. The only similarity with other post-Holocaust thinkers is that for them and for Heidegger, this was a fall from which no redemption is possible.

This rendering of the Holocaust as a "second fall of man" has not gone unchallenged. Harold Kaplan critiques the literature of the Holocaust that "has been dominated by demands for meaning as if the world faces an eternal day of judgment focusing on a new more drastic version of 'original sin,' a second fall of man."[16] Yet I imagine Levi, the secular Jew, would have agreed that humankind's ontological status has been irrevocably altered.

When Primo Levi was born (July 31, 1919) the Jews of Italy had already assimilated into Italian social, cultural, and political life. As has often been pointed out, two Italian Jews (Sidney Sonnino and Luigi Luzzati) became prime minister, and the most highly decorated officer in World War I was a Jew, Emanuele Pugliese. There was anti-Semitism, often cultivated by the Catholic Church, but not to the extent found in Poland, Russia, or even France. Zionism found only a small foothold in Italy. Typical was the historian Nello Rosselli, younger brother of the more charismatic Carlo.[17] A member of the Federazione Giovanile Ebraica Italiana (Federation of Young Italian Jews), Nello spoke at a Zionist conference in Livorno in November 1924 and eloquently explained his ties to Judaism. Confessing that he did not attend the synagogue on Saturday, that he was ignorant of Hebrew, that he did not support the Zionist cause, and that he did not observe any of the religious practices demanded by his religion, Nello asked, "How then can I call myself a Jew?

> I call myself a Jew . . . because . . . the monotheistic conscience is indestruc-
> tible in me . . . because every form of idolatry repels me . . . because I
> regard with Jewish severity the duties of our lives on earth, and with Jewish
> serenity the mystery of life beyond the tomb . . . because I love all men as
> in Israel it was commanded . . . and I have therefore that social conception
> which seems to me descends from our best traditions.[18]

When Fascism came to power in 1922 it carried with it no innate anti-Semitism. But an alliance with Nazi Germany laid the foundation for tragedy. Levi—as well as most Italians, Jew and Christian alike—was shocked when the Fascist regime published a "Manifesto of the Racial Scientists" in the summer of 1938. The following autumn, the regime promulgated a series of anti-Semitic laws patterned on the Nuremberg Laws in Nazi Germany. In the chaos of the Second World War, Levi joined the militant underground Resistance but was captured in December 1943. In February 1944 he was sent to Auschwitz, managing to survive through a fortuitous combination of his extensive knowledge of chemistry, the humanity of a precious few other prisoners, and simple luck. His memoir of life in the extermination camp, *Survival in Auschwitz*, has claimed its rightful place among the masterpieces of Holocaust literature. When the camp was liberated by the Red Army in January 1945, Levi began a picaresque odyssey as recounted in *The Truce*. His last work, *The Drowned and the Saved*, is arguably the most profound meditation on the Shoah.

Although best known for these works on the concentration camp universe, Levi did not want to be known as a "Holocaust writer"; he aspired to the simple title of "writer" without any adjective ("Holocaust," "Italian," or "Jewish"). Besides his Holocaust masterpieces, Levi also wrote poetry, essays, science fiction, and a novel concerning Jewish partisans in World War II. His testimony was not only, as he stated, "to bear witness," but to search for an ethical line of conduct and moral reasoning based on classical humanism but cognizant of humanity's changed moral status after Auschwitz.[19]

In their search for a common definition of "fascism," historians and political philosophers from Benedetto Croce to John Rawls have sometimes adopted the metaphor of disease.[20] Fascism, they write, was a virus, a virulent malady, a political affliction, a moral disorder, an ethical sickness. It attacked all that was healthy in European civilization (the Enlightenment tradition, rationality, humanitarianism, and all the freedoms associated with classical liberalism) and ended with the deaths of tens of millions of innocents and the rotting corpses of Benito Mussolini and Adolf Hitler.

As with other forms of totalitarianism, fascism sought to strip away the private sphere from the individual and turn it over to the state. On another front, it inflated language to its own ends so that rabid nationalism and distorted history became the common tongue of empire. For many, the antidote to the bombastic, inflated rhetoric of fascism was the seemingly

plain and simple language of American literature; it was no coincidence
that the antifascist writer Cesare Pavese and others spent the 1930s translating Whitman, Melville, Thoreau, Anderson, and other great American
writers of the nineteenth and early twentieth centuries.

In the face of the grandiose (and often ridiculous) claims of fascist rhetoric, writers and others took refuge in the simple pleasures of the quotid-
ian. To combat the attempt of the fascist state to seize control of the family
through social legislation (preventing abortions, outlawing contraception,
taxing bachelors, granting stipends to large families) some writers, such as
Natalia Levi Ginzburg, whose husband, Leone, was killed by the Gestapo
in Rome, fell back to the familial and domestic scenes of the hearth. Primo
Levi instead turned to science.

"Every age has its own fascism," Levi warned, and it would be facile to
imagine that our age is immune from such temptations. As Isaiah Berlin
perceptively noted:

> Few things have done more harm than the belief on the part of individuals
> or groups that he or she or they are in sole possession of the truth: espe-
> cially about how to live, what to be and do and that those who differ from
> them are not merely mistaken, but wicked or mad, and need restraining or
> suppressing. It is a terrible and dangerous arrogance to believe that you
> alone are right; have a magical eye which sees the truth, and that others
> cannot be right if they disagree.[21]

Another extraordinary Levi from Turin, Carlo, had written of the
perennial danger of our "fear of freedom" in a powerful and provocative
1939 essay as World War II was beginning.[22] And it was in his anthropo-
logical masterpiece of empathy and understanding, *Christ Stopped at Eboli*,
that he warned of an eternal attraction to fascism:

> We cannot foresee the political forms of the future, but in a middle-class
> country like Italy, where middle-class ideology has infected the masses of
> workers in the city, it is probable, alas, that the new institutions arising
> after Fascism, through either gradual evolution or violence, no matter how
> extreme and revolutionary they may be in appearance, will maintain the
> same ideology under different forms and create a new State equally far
> removed from real life, equally idolatrous and abstract, a perpetuation
> under new slogans and new flags of the worst features of the eternal
> tendency toward Fascism.[23]

How might Levi's analysis of fascism, a political phenomenon of a particular place (Italy) and time (1922–1945), be employed to understand

contemporary events? In interviews three-time Prime Minister Silvio Berlusconi solemnly intones, "Only I can save Italy from communism."[24] Is it possible that an Italian politician could utter that line without knowing that Benito Mussolini said the very same thing eight decades ago? By then (1922), the threat of a communist revolution in Italy had already dissipated. Similarly, today there is no threat to the Italian Republic from communists, and it is arguable that such a threat never really existed, even at the peak of the Italian Communist Party's popularity. Under siege by what he perceives to be a politically motivated judiciary looking into allegations of his corrupt business practices, Berlusconi has resurrected the specter of communism, but in reality he is the embodiment of another ghost, that of fascism.

There can only be two possibilities regarding Berlusconi's public remarks that only he "can save Italy from the perils of communism": either he is deaf to the irony of his own rhetoric or his hearing is pitch-perfect and his comments are really a not-so-subtle reference to his own brand of "benign" fascism. Controlling most of the mass media in Italy (from private and public television stations to newspapers, radio, publishing houses, and magazines), Berlusconi has acquired—with the help of influential but corrupt politicians—a stranglehold on popular culture. He now wishes to stifle intellectual dissent by rewriting the nation's history books (since he considered them too lenient on the antifascist partisan movement) and prosecuting anyone who "insults the office of the prime minister." And let us not forget that the vice prime minister is Gianfranco Fini, neofascist (or postfascist, as he likes to say) and that Umberto Bossi is a key member of the governing coalition. Bossi, in his own farcical and theatrical political theater, marched through the Veneto to Venice with his followers a few years back. Italians seem to have forgotten to be wary of politicians who "march" on their cities. One is reminded of Marx's observation, "History repeats itself: first as tragedy, second as farce."

Not content with merely "saving" Italy from communism, Berlusconi has developed a Christ complex as well. In interviews, he has lamented that his responsibilities are so overwhelming that he no longer has the opportunity to enjoy the fruits of his labor (such as sailing on his yacht or visiting his many vacation homes). "Italians simply do not realize how much I've had to sacrifice to be prime minister," he laments, conveniently neglecting that most Italians do not have a villa on the Emerald Coast of Sardinia. In January 2007, in a perfectly brilliant synthesis of fascism and Christianity, in which Berlusconi morphs into a combined Duce and Christ, he "anointed" Fini his "heir apparent" in what amounted to a symbolic "investiture." (In a 1994 interview with the Turin newspaper *La Stampa*, Fini hailed Mussolini as "the greatest statesman of the century," a judgment he has since modified.) And if the reference to his own Christ-like essence were not clear enough, Berlusconi remarked that he would happily pass to others such as Fini "the bitter chalice" of political power.[25]

It was not the first time that Berlusconi had (ab)used the fascist past. In an interview with the British journal *The Spectator*, Berlusconi claimed that "Mussolini never killed anyone" and that in the practice of *confino*, the Italian dictator merely sent his political enemies "on holiday" to such idyllic locales as the islands of Lipari and Ponza or quaint hill towns in the Italian south,[26] conveniently forgetting the deaths of Antonio Gramsci in prison, Piero Gobetti in exile, and the double assassination of the Rosselli brothers, which became the basis for Alberto Moravia's novel *The Conformist* and Bernardo Bertolucci's film of the same name.

As anyone who travels frequently to Italy can attest, Berlusconi's brand of unfettered consumerism has done more damage to the country's traditional way of life than that supposedly inflicted by Communist Party members.

Although the manipulation of the media in Italy has generated considerable scrutiny (see, for example, the work of Alexander Stille) in our attempt to guard against contemporary variants of fascism, the assault on the archive has been less conspicuous but perhaps more pernicious. An episode from the Nazi occupation of Naples illustrates an early attempt to rewrite history:

He's lucky.

He's a young partisan who has been captured, not by the German SS, who have just arrived at the outskirts of Naples, but by the Fascist police.

He undergoes the usual beatings. The police commissioner holds an adjunct professorship in the university law school, and after a few hours, hearing that the young partisan is a university student, he steps in and personally takes over the interrogation. After three days of questioning, the young partisan still remains silent, so the police commissioner makes him an offer. He tells him that this will be his "final examination." To complete it, he must choose between two alternatives. One: if he betrays the hiding places of his comrades, he will be sentenced to death. But the sentence will not be carried out; he will live, and eventually have his freedom. If the young partisan chooses this alternative, the police commissioner promises to plant false documents in the files proving that the information came from other sources. In this way, his reputation will remain untarnished, and in an anti-fascist victory, he will be in line for all the honors due a hero of the resistance.

On the other hand, if the young partisan refuses to give him the information about his comrades, the police commissioner tells him he is confident that in a few days, as a result of the terror caused by the arrival of the German SS, all his comrades will be rounded up. After which, they will be shot. Then the commissioner will plant "proof" that it was information from him which had betrayed his comrades and thereafter everyone will look upon him as a traitor and spit on his grave.

It is for him to choose. Which will it be? The young partisan asks for a day to consider, and goes back to his cell.

Sixteen hours later, he hangs himself.[27]

Here we are reminded of Levi's deepening despair over the rise of Holocaust denial and, more insidiously, Holocaust revisionism toward the end of his life.

In a speech delivered at the Casa Italiana at Columbia University (today the Italian Academy for Advanced Studies) on April 25, 1995, to commemorate the fiftieth anniversary of the liberation of Italy, Umberto Eco traced a typology of what he called "Ur-Fascism."[28] Here, I would like to place Eco's Ur-fascist into dialogue with Levi, using the latter's essays from *The Periodic Table*.

As Eco points out, the Ur-fascist insists on *a cult of tradition*, while in "Uranium" Levi praises "the boundless freedom of invention of one who has broken through the barrier and is now free to build himself the past that suits him best" (199). The fascist stands on the *rejection of modernism*, where Levi, in "Potassium," suggests that "the truth, the reality, the intimate essence of things and man exist elsewhere, hidden behind a veil" (56).

Fascism embraces *irrationalism*, whereas Levi, in "Iron," was filled with "disgust at all the dogmas, all the unproved affirmations" and felt a "dignity" in chemistry and physics which were "the antidote to fascism" (42). The Ur-fascist insists on *action for action's sake*; Levi recounts his decision to join the Resistance in "Gold": "extremely insecure about our means, our hearts filled with much more desperation than hope, and against a backdrop of a defeated, divided country, we went into battle to test our strength" (130). For the fascist, *disagreement is treason*; and Levi confessed in "Gold" that while they proclaimed themselves antifascists, "Fascism had its effects on us, as on almost all Italians, alienating us and making us superficial, passive, and cynical" (128).

Fascism has an innate *fear of difference*; Levi instead sings the praises of difference in "Zinc": "In order for the wheel to turn, for life to be lived, impurities are needed, and the impurities of impurities in the soil, too, as is known, if it is to be fertile. Dissension, diversity, the grain of salt and mustard are needed: Fascism does not want them, forbids them, and that's why you are not a Fascist; it wants everyone to be the same, and you are not" (34). Fascism makes an *appeal to a frustrated middle class*; Levi noted with the astuteness of a sociologist in "Nickel" the "ironic gaiety of a whole generation of Italians, intelligent and honest enough to reject Fascism, too skeptical to oppose it actively, too young to passively accept the tragedy that was taking shape and to despair of the future" (63).

The fascists live in fear of being *humiliated by the ostentatious wealth and force of their enemies*; in "Nickel," Levi embraces Cesare Pavese's dictum to embrace "the two experiences of adult life": success and failure. "We are here for this: to make mistakes and to correct ourselves, to stand the blows and hand them out" (75). The fascist rants that *pacifism is trafficking with the enemy because life is permanent warfare*; Levi, in "Vanadium," argues that "the enemy who remains an enemy, who perseveres in his desire to inflict suffering . . . one must not forgive him: one can try to salvage him, one can (one must!) discuss with him, but it is our duty to judge him, not to forgive him" (222–223). Whereas the fascist has nothing but *contempt for the weak*; Levi, in discussing the village simpleton in "Argon," writes in biblical fashion that "the simple are the children of God and no one should call them fools" (7). Under fascism, *everyone is educated to become a hero in the cult of death*; Levi defuses this decadent cult in "Gold," writing of his own seemingly impending death: "I harbored a piercing desire for everything, for all imaginable human experiences, and I cursed my previous life, which it seemed to me I had profited from little or badly, and I felt time running through my fingers, escaping from my body minute by minute, like a hemorrhage that can no longer be stanched" (137).

For Eco, the Ur-Fascist *transfers his will to power to sexual matters*; Levi is frank and remorseless in recounting his failures with women. Besides the memorable image of "feminizing" his pistol—an object notorious for its phallic connotations—("it was tiny, all inlaid with mother of pearl, the kind used in movies by ladies desperately intent on committing suicide" [131]), he laments in "Phosphorus" that his "inability to approach a woman was a condemnation without appeal which would accompany me to my death, confining me to a life poisoned by envy and by abstract, sterile, and aimless desires" (125).

Fascism must be *against "rotten" parliamentary governments*; but the antifascists, emerging "out of the shadows," men "whom Fascism had not crushed," spoke to them of others—of Antonio Gramsci, Gaetano Salvemini, Piero Gobetti, Carlo and Nello Rosselli—and told Levi and his companions that "our mocking, ironic intolerance" of the old order "was not enough" (129–130). Finally, according to Eco, *Ur-Fascism speaks Newspeak*; but Levi saw through the veil of sanctity with which the regime wrapped itself: "Fascism was not only a clownish and improvident misrule but the negator of justice; it had not only dragged Italy into an unjust and ill-omened war, but it had arisen and consolidated itself as the custodian of a detestable legality and order, based on the coercion of those who work, on the unchecked profits of those who exploit the labor of others, on the silence imposed on those who think and do not want to be slaves, and on systematic and calculated lies" (129–130).

And in language that echoes Levi's 1974 essay, Eco concludes:

> Ur-Fascism is still around us, sometimes in plainclothes. It would be so much easier for us if there appeared on the world scene somebody saying, "I want to reopen Auschwitz, I want the Blackshirts to parade again in the Italian squares." Life is not that simple. Ur-Fascism can come back under the most innocent of disguises. Our duty is to uncover it and to point our finger at any of its new instances—every day, in every part of the world. Franklin Roosevelt's words of November 4, 1938, are worth recalling: "If American democracy ceases to move forward as a living force, seeking day and night by peaceful means to better the lot of our citizens, fascism will grow in strength in our land." Freedom and liberation are an unending task.[29]

Levi was willing to problematize the categories of traditional humanism, as is evident in his concept of the "Gray Zone," the second chapter of his last work, *The Drowned and the Saved*. Since much has been written on this, I would here like to approach the idea through a tenuously related work, Tim Blake Nelson's 2001 film, *The Grey Zone*.

Just as Levi refused to embrace an easy Manichean division of the concentration camp universe into evil Nazis and innocent victims, Nelson rejects sanctifying the victims. Levi was one of the first to point out the moral contagion that infected the inmates and focused on the extreme situation of the Sonderkommando (SK, Special Forces) at Auschwitz. Both the Italian writer and the American filmmaker were struck by the moral choice made by Miklos Nyiszli, a Hungarian doctor who "volunteered" for the SK in exchange for the safety of his wife and daughter (both of

whom survived the camps). On clearing out a contingent of Jews from one
of the gas chambers, SK troops discover a young girl who has miraculously
survived the Zyklon B. The discovery of the girl changes the SK's moral
calculations. Although not depicted in the film, an episode recounted by
Nyiszli and mentioned by Levi deserves mention here because it accurately reflects the sense of moral corruption institutionalized in the camps,
even away from the gas chambers or crematoria. One evening a soccer
match is organized between the SS and the SK. "The teams lined up on
the field," recalled Nyiszli. "They put the ball into play. Sonorous laughter filled the courtyard."[30] Levi not only paints a grim portrait of the event
but also points out its larger moral significance, hearing in this episode
only satanic laughter for the Nazis have won the game before it is even
played: "it is consummated, we have succeeded, you no longer are the
other race, the anti-race, the prime enemy of the millennial Reich. . . . We
have embraced you, corrupted you, dragged you down to the bottom with
us . . . dirtied with your own blood. . . . You too, like us and Cain, have
killed the brother. Come, we can play together."[31]

Yet even in this modern Inferno, there are the lessons of humanism.
One is taught to Levi by the Austrian veteran of the Great War, Steinlauf,
who convinces Levi that

> precisely because the Lager was a great machine to reduce us to beasts, we
> must not become beasts; that even in this place one can survive, and
> therefore one must want to survive, to tell the story, to bear witness; and
> that to survive we must force ourselves to save at least the skeleton, the
> scaffolding, the form of civilization. We are slaves, deprived of every right,
> exposed to every insult, condemned to certain death, but we still possess
> one power, and we must defend it with all our strength for it is the last—the
> power to refuse our consent.[32]

Compare Levi's passage with that of the Catholic noblewoman Pelagia
Lewinska, also a prisoner at Auschwitz:

> At the outset the living places, the ditches, the mud, the piles of excrement
> behind the blocks, had appalled me with their horrible filth. . . . And then
> I saw the light! I saw that it was not a question of disorder or lack of organi-
> zation but that, on the contrary, a very thoroughly conscious idea was in
> the back of the camp's existence. They had condemned us to die in our
> own filth, to drown in mud, in our own excrement. They wished to debase
> us, to destroy our human dignity, to efface every vestige of humanity, to
> return us to the state of wild animals, to fill us with contempt toward

ourselves and others. But from the instant I grasped the motivating principle . . . it was if I had awakened from a dream. I felt under orders to
live. . . . And if I died at Auschwitz it would be as a human being. I was not
going to become the contemptible, disgusting brute my enemy wished me
to be.[33]

One of the most commented upon passages of Levi's work is the chapter "The Drowned and the Saved" in his first book. Yet sometimes over-
looked is a ringing manifesto in defense of humanism on its first page:

> We are in fact convinced that no human experience is without meaning or
> unworthy of analysis, and that the fundamental values, even if they are not
> positive, can be deduced from this particular world which we are
> describing. . . . We do not believe in the most obvious and facile deduction:
> that man is fundamentally brutal, egotistical and stupid in his conduct once
> every civilized institution is taken away, and that the Häftling is conse-
> quently nothing but a man without inhibitions. We believe, rather, that the
> only conclusion to be drawn is that in the face of driving necessity and
> physical disabilities many social habits and instincts are reduced to silence.[34]

Whereas the other inmates have scratched their numbers onto the bottom of their tin soup bowls, and Clausner has written *"Ne pas chercher à
comprendre"* (Don't try to comprehend), Levi and his friend Alberto have
insisted on carving their own names.

Tzvetan Todorov has perceptively called our post-Holocaust humanism
"an imperfect garden."[35] Indeed, while science and humanism may permit
a precarious return to the garden, it is a garden we must share with the
serpent. But there are other beasts in the garden that are not as pernicious:
the centaur, for example. As both a chemist and a writer, Levi felt the
divorce of science from humanism as the tragic flaw of the twentieth century. He reveled in his stance straddling two worlds. "I am a centaur," he
once wrote enigmatically, as all men and women are centaurs: "a tangle of
flesh and mind, divine inspiration and dust."[36] He insisted that his roles as
a scientist, chemist, and technician were complementary and not contradictory to his status as a writer and humanist. As he remarked in an interview with the American writer Philip Roth: "In my own way I have
remained an impurity, an anomaly, but now for reasons other than before:
not especially as a Jew but as an Auschwitz survivor and an outsider-writer,
coming not from the literary or university establishment but from the
industrial world."[37]

He was an essayist and a prolific writer for various Italian newspapers; today we might recognize him as a "public intellectual." It was in this "other" work, such as *The Monkey's Wrench* and *The Periodic Table*, which Levi did not perceive as divorced from his Auschwitz experience, that he offered a possibility of living in a post-Holocaust world. Here, Levi redeemed the idea of work for us, transforming it from a curse to a blessing. He would reverse the perverse irony of "Arbeit Macht Frei" and insist that indeed, work—productive, humane, creative work—could make one free. Work well done; work as the expression of techné, of craft, of the intellect. The Italian bricklayer Lorenzo Perrone, finding himself in the camp as a slave laborer and befriending Levi, refuses to build shoddy walls. Not only does he slip Levi and Alberto extra rations of bread and soup for six months, but in his example of *lavoro ben fatto* ("work well done"), he also teaches Levi an important lesson: "Lorenzo was a man; his humanity was pure and uncontaminated, he was outside this world of negation. Thanks to Lorenzo, I managed not to forget that I myself was a man."[38] These were paeans to the dignity of work, "especially," Levi insisted, "the work of the craftsman as modern analogue of the search for adventure and creativity . . . a theme valid for all times, all places and all social structures."[39]

Yet, he suffered from depression most of his life, and this could not all be blamed on Auschwitz. Sometimes he could find respite in writing, but the completion of a work or a specific task, such as the translation of Kafka's *The Trial*, could thrust him into the darkest despair. Toward the end of his life, with the appearance of Holocaust deniers and historical "revisionists," he was again haunted by the shadow of Auschwitz. He is often compared to Elie Wiesel, but there is one major difference: Wiesel had the gift of faith, however tormented by the reality of the Shoah. Wiesel has spent the last sixty years in a continuous dialogue and debate with his God; Levi, the atheist, had the benefit of no such interlocutor. Instead, he had only the foundation of classic humanism: "I was helped by the determination, which I stubbornly preserved, to recognize always, even in the darkest days, in my companions and myself, men, not things, and thus to avoid that total humiliation and demoralization which led so many to spiritual shipwreck."[40]

"I became a Jew in Auschwitz," he once wrote, comparing the concentration camp to a "university" of life. Yet he could also paradoxically admit in an interview late in life, "There is Auschwitz, and so there cannot be God."[41] Rather than seek to untangle these contradictions, Levi embraced them. It was perhaps his last lesson to us.

PART ONE

Psychology, Theology, and Philosophy

CHAPTER I

"Warum?"

Joram Warmund

During his initiation into what one survivor labeled the "Holocaust King-dom"[1] and others would describe as the "Anus Mundi,"[2] the young and naïve Auschwitz prisoner Primo Levi reached outside a window for an icicle to quench his thirst. A guard patrolling outside rudely slapped it away, prompting Primo to ask, "*Warum?*" Why? The reply was, "*Hier ist kein warum.*" Here there is no why. In Levi's words: "The explanation is repugnant but simple: in this place everything is forbidden, not for hidden reasons, but because the camp has been created for that purpose."[3]

Indeed, more than sixty years later, the "*Warums*" have not been answered but have only been multiplied: Why the killings? Why the bru-tality connected with the killings? Yes, we know the racial rationalizations, and, yes, we also know that the demolition of human beings—their humil-iation and debasement—went part and parcel with the killings within and outside the Lagers. The "process," particularly at the execution sites and in the extermination camps, was almost mechanical and impersonal, as in a factory conveyor belt system; yet we also know that the perpetrators were more than robotic executioners. Many of them made sport of their jobs, humiliating and debasing men, women and children, and performing incredible acts of cruelty. We also know that the hands-on killers came from all walks of life and were transformed into enthusiastic murderers.

They very often carried out their duties in sadistic ways that challenge human comprehension.

Two of the still unanswered whys remain: How was it possible to transform everyday people into rabid murderers? Why did apparently normal people become avid killers? These are some of the most essential questions driving the continuing explosion of Holocaust publications. Addressing these questions requires a synopsis of the current status of contemporary approaches to Holocaust studies.

The Holocaust is most often presented chronologically, in book form or in classroom curricula, in order to provide a developmental context and to facilitate explanatory analyses. The literature has varied widely, but can be reduced to two major approaches: top-down, from the perspective of the perpetrators, and bottom-up, from the point of view of the victims. Within these approaches, some studies explain the Holocaust as a primarily German historical event; others broaden the scope to include the non-German initiatives.

These four broad perceptual combinations provide useful insights into the studies of the Holocaust; they also create large gaps between them. This essay begins to bridge some of those gaps. Using primarily historiographic, not archival, material, it delineates the diverse roles of the perpetrators, then narrows its focus to those who perceived themselves as victims of forces beyond their control, and to those who participated in acts of brutality and mass murder but still appeared and acted as ordinary people. A larger work, now in progress, will eventually expand the scope to include the victims and bystanders.

What is needed is some functional framework that will weave together the various human components. One very useful construct that avoids the organizational pitfalls of most Holocaust literature is introduced in Raul Hilberg's *Perpetrators, Victims, Bystanders: The Jewish Catastrophe, 1933–1945*.[4] It provides a workable model that can be applied across nations while also greatly—but not entirely—resolving the top-down/bottom-up perceptual limitations of most other works. However, Hilberg's approach loses the sense of chronological development and, by placing individuals and groups in rigid categories, it tends to harden their distinctions at the expense of recognizing their commonalities. The dynamics and fluidity of human behavior within and across these categorizations is thereby submerged or lost.

It was the radically contradictory behavior demonstrated by people in the "Victims" category that led Primo Levi to describe a phenomenon he labeled the "Gray Zone."[5] Similarly, in explaining the behavior of a subcategory of perpetrators, Robert Jay Lifton suggested that the Auschwitz doctors exhibited a psychological phenomenon of "doubling."[6] Neither the perpetrators nor the victims were monolithic groups. There were differences between and among them reflecting internal distinctions; but the existence of extreme paradoxical behavior within the categories of perpetrators and victims suggests that a behavioral dualism operated on both sides of the demarcation.

The combining of Lifton's "doubling" and Levi's "Gray Zone" into one concept of behavioral dualism provides us with a more continuous and broader behavioral spectrum that functioned on both sides of the enclosures (camps or ghettos), and, to varying extents, was also manifested in the wider social settings of war-torn Europe. The demarcation lines between (sub)categories were not set concretely. Individual actions varied with real and/or imagined pressures. What surfaced were contradictory, sometimes radically paradoxical, instances of human conduct within each category. There may even have been some symmetry of responses on both sides of the perpetrator-victim divide. In its most extreme form some individuals could simultaneously act and perceive themselves—and be perceived by others as well—as both abusers and victims.

In developing a new working paradigm it becomes necessary first to refine the broad categories of perpetrator, victim, and bystander. Raul Hilberg has already identified some useful distinctions among the perpetrators. He begins with Hitler as the "supreme architect of the operation"[7] and then continues with the progression of "a vast establishment of familiar functionaries and ascending newcomers."[8] Within this "conglomeration," Hilberg writes, "some men displayed eagerness, while others had doubts. . . . When the process was extended to the four corners of Europe, the machinery of destruction became international as Germans were joined" by non-Germans.[9]

Hilberg's diagram of the perpetrators proceeds as follows: "Adolf Hitler"; "The Establishment"; " Old Functionaries"; "Newcomers"; "Zealots, Vulgarians, and Bearers of Burdens"; "Physicians and Lawyers"; "Non-German Governments"; and "Non-German Volunteers."[10] This organization is primarily functional in its design and therefore is only partially adaptable to the creation of a behavioral spectrum. For this study, borrowing Hilberg's language, the progression might be better designed from "zealots" to "vulgarians" to "bearers of burdens." Such a behavioral mode cuts across career and national identities and connects to situational conditions of proximity or opportunity. Thus, the closer the perpetrators came to the targeted victims, the more defined their roles became, and the less room existed for them to exercise alternate courses of action. At that point the phenomenon of "doubling" became increasingly more evident. Under the pressure of fulfilling expected roles most did their "duty"; some (the zealots) enjoyed their roles more than others, while others proceeded with a sense of misgiving; a few opted out, requesting transfers to other duties and functions.[11] Still others exhibited a duality of responses that vacillated from occasion to occasion or operated concurrently, as in the Lifton "doubling" examples.

Christopher Browning refines Hilberg's organization by referring to different levels of perpetrators. Within the "lower echelon" he introduces a spectrum from "sadists" to "killers without remorse" to "passive executors of orders" and to "abstainers" who nevertheless contributed in other ways to the killing activities.[12] He concludes that a "significant minority" of the Order Police squads he studied were "eager killers." Some were transformed into that role by the situation, while others—he now concedes, contrary to his earlier assessment in *Ordinary Men*—were already ideologically preconditioned for the task. He further concludes that still another ten to twenty percent of these squads evaded direct involvement. They chose to opt out of the hands-on killings for alternative assignments—such as assisting in the roundups and guarding the prisoners—which were still necessary for the successful administration of these "actions"; and these evasions were accepted. In Browning's words, "evasion was easily tolerated but protest and obstruction most emphatically were not."[13]

Browning connects those engaged in the face-to-face executions with those who were involved in the other stages of the extermination process into a wider hierarchy of perpetrators. In this compartmentalized manner, each segment was connected with the others. In his words, "On the local level, they [the eager killers] formed a crucial nucleus for the killing process in the same way as eager and ambitious initiators at the middle echelons and Hitler, Himmler and Heydrich at the top. Their influence was far out of proportion to their numbers in German society."[14]

The local-level perpetrator subcategories are seen on a continuum. At one end was a group of people who were thoroughly committed to the most extreme aspects of the Nazi agenda; in between were those who sought some form of evasion from the more brutal part of the operations but assisted in the various supportive activities needed to accomplish the "Aktion"; and at the other end were those (a very few) who approached the opposite extreme of protest and obstruction. Browning's top-down view is primarily focused on the perpetrators, as is this essay, and does not satisfy the need to examine events from the perspective of the victims. He begins to provide such an approach in the case of the Starachowice Jewish workers, but primarily with the intent to explain better the varieties of perpetrators.[15]

Browning's interconnected grouping provides a useful model for analyzing each segment individually. By such an approach it may become possible to find points of commonality traversing the entire perpetrators hierarchy. One such attempt was undertaken by four prominent psychologists: Eric Zillmer, Molly Harrower, Barry Ritzler, and Robert Archer. They analyzed the Rorschach protocols of the Nazi leaders who were tried at Nuremberg in 1945–1946 and compared them to Rorschachs taken by 148 rank-and-file Danish Nazi collaborators who were also placed on trial right after the Second World War, with suggestive but inconclusive results.[16] In comparing the two groups, the four psychologists noticed no distinctive set of characteristics that would define a Nazi personality. In fact, although some were diagnosed as pathological sadists, most of those tested exhibited characteristics considered within the range of regular members in society; they were basically ordinary men.

Perhaps the most vexing, and crucial, subgroup to understand is not the sadists but those who were indistinguishable from everyday people, that is, the "ordinary" persons who were transformed into the face-to-face killers. Two primary dilemmas emerge from studying this subgroup that are implicit within Primo Levi's *"Warum?"* First, why did apparently "ordinary" people—who before and after the war had belonged to what we might call "normal" society, who were good neighbors and law-abiding citizens—transform into brutal murderers of defenseless men, women and children? Second—and this dilemma is not confined to the rank and file—why did many of these perpetrators later, paradoxically, describe themselves as victims of circumstances?[17]

In response to the first dilemma, a wide variety of explanations has been proposed, relying on the perspectives of a broad spectrum of academic disciplines, each one plausible with specific subgroups or in specific instances. In summary, Holocaust analysts have consistently referred to a mixture of psychological, ideational, and situational conditions to explain the transition. They have differed on the degree of emphasis each ingredient played in the overall mix. So, some argue the impact of the environmental context: that the proximity of the target population, the opportunity to undertake an initiative without a negative repercussion, the prior preparation of the individual in group training sessions (both in functional/organizational as well as in opinion-forming preconditioning), and the development of group pressure to be "hard" enough to do one's duty, all were situational conditioners that turned normal people into energetic executioners. Other scholars—while usually accepting situational factors—have nevertheless stressed the primacy of ideational conditioning, that a prior cultural-ideological immersion into the rationale for undertaking such activities had taken place that created the mentality that objectified the victims into a threat; still others would argue further that a degree of personal predisposition toward violence must have also existed that facilitated the conversion of a large minority of ordinary people into mass murderers.

Christopher Browning, in his *Ordinary Men*, originally belonged closer to the situational school. The members of Reserve Police Battalion 101 were mostly working-class, middle-aged police reservists from the city of Hamburg. In early 1940 they were assigned tours of duty that became incrementally more brutal and deadly. Browning provides the predominant explanations that have already been proposed in other similar situations to explain the battalion's behavior. In his words, "wartime brutalization, racism, segmentation and routinization of the task, special selection of the perpetrators, careerism, obedience to orders, deference to authority, ideological indoctrination, and conformity. These factors are applicable in varying degrees, but none without qualifications."[18]

Browning proceeds to deal with each of these factors and finds them all partially valid, and therefore also partially invalid. Without clearly selecting one set of explanations over others, Browning nevertheless is far more categorical in limiting the influence of ideological—that is, racist and anti-Semitic—indoctrination. He prefers instead the argument of the irresistibility of group pressure and conformity. Again, in his words: "To break ranks and step out, to adopt overtly nonconformist behavior, was simply beyond most of the men. It was easier for them to shoot."[19]

Sharply contradicting Browning's explanations for the transformation of ordinary Germans into enthusiastic killers, Daniel Goldhagen's *Hitler's Willing Executioners* ascribes primacy to ideational factors—that is, to a special form of German anti-Semitism that had created a broad consensus within German society to remove the Jews. It was therefore relatively easy to find the needed killers who would put into action what was already a commonly held set of beliefs. So, the perpetrators were a representative sample of German society; they were "willing executioners," faithfully actualizing the wishes of their society.[20] In short, the virulent, "eliminationist" anti-Semitism had been so deeply ingrained, had so thoroughly permeated German society that the actions of the perpetrators were not really the result of a situationally induced transformation but, instead, were the logical result of prior years of intensive indoctrination.

Goldhagen's book became an instant best-seller, but it also attracted widespread criticism from Holocaust scholars. Browning felt compelled to add a special "afterword" in his 1998 edition to respond to Goldhagen's numerous direct challenges. Yehuda Bauer, the former director of the International Institute for Holocaust Research at Yad Vashem and a pre-eminent Holocaust historian, devoted substantial space, two chapters out of eleven, in his *Rethinking the Holocaust* on the current state of Holocaust historiography.[21] In his presentation, he does not provide the usual synopsis of the main schools of Holocaust literature. Instead, he analyzes some of the more prominent Holocaust interpretations of the last two decades. The works of Zygmunt Bauman, Jeffrey Herf, Goetz Aly, Daniel Goldhagen, John Weiss, and Saul Friedländer are carefully scrutinized.

In each case—other than with Friedländer, whose considerable contributions are not germane to this specific topic—Bauer assesses the strengths and weaknesses of their arguments and provides some salient conclusions of his own. Thus, Bauman's and Herf's stress on the rate and type of modernization experienced in Germany, and Aly's argument that the "Final Solution" was the result of the Nazi middle management's Malthusian obsessions with effecting a favorable population shift in accordance with the priorities of "Lebensraum," are all carefully stated and then challenged with specifics that obviate the stated theses. The main deficiency of all three, Bauer contends, is that the ideological influences are undervalued. In his judgment, "all those who want to divorce the Holocaust from anti-Semitism arrive at a dead end."[22] And, again, "we have to see that the motivation was not bureaucratic but ideological."[23]

So, having disposed of the more recent proponents of the various situational arguments in one chapter, Bauer spends the next one dealing with the internal variances within the ideational school. Although he prefers an ideational perspective and credits Goldhagen with a timely redressing of a previous imbalance that had favored the situational models, Bauer is no supporter of the Goldhagen thesis. In fact, aside from some kind words in support of Goldhagen, Bauer's analysis of *Hitler's Willing Executioners* amounts to a dissection. Goldhagen's central thesis, to Bauer, is a simplistic, monocausal, and erroneous treatment of a complex historical issue. Indeed, Bauer contends, the John Weiss book "provides a much more cogent answer to the problem of anti-Semitism in Germany and Austria."[24] Bauer juxtaposes the Weiss and Goldhagen treatments of anti-Semitism to illustrate the flaws in the Goldhagen position. Bauer also rejects Goldhagen's assertion of a unique form of German anti-Semitism in light of the existence of similar outbreaks of murderous anti-Semitism in other European regions, including Romania, Ukraine, and the Baltic, where the mass murder of the Jews was frequently initiated and conducted by local, non-German, perpetrators.[25] Still further, Bauer argues, even when he had a good opportunity to make his case, Goldhagen undermined his own argument by using the wrong examples. In Bauer's words: "did not Goldhagen promise to present us with proof that ordinary Germans, and not the Nazi S.S. elite, were willing executioners? He took the wrong examples and flunked his own test."[26] Yet, despite all of these criticisms, Bauer remains well entrenched in what might be described as a modified version of the ideational school; and Browning has meanwhile moved closer to a moderated situational viewpoint that recognizes a greater degree of ideological influence than he had originally accepted in his *Ordinary Men*.[27]

The third, and perhaps oldest, school of interpretation of perpetrator behavior relies on psychological perspectives and investigations conducted as early as the late 1940s, which continued through the 1960s and 1970s. It is within this category that we find the often cited works of Theodor Adorno, S. E. Asch, Philip Zimbardo, and Stanley Milgram, which Christopher Browning individually examines and finds of limited value to explain the behavior of his police reservists.[28] Richard Rhodes, in his treatment of the killing squads that were especially selected for their extermination assignments—clearly, one would have to assume, not ordinary people—goes beyond the earlier psychological studies to rely on the more recent research of criminologist Lonnie Athens on the development of the violent criminal personality. Apparently, the "violent socialization" process of any individual passes through four distinct stages from "brutalization" to "belligerence," "violent performance," and, finally, "virulency."[29] Thus it can be inferred, as Rhodes seems to do, that even ordinary men could be conditioned—by a combination of ideational indoctrination and experiential, trauma-inducing training sessions—to pass through these stages of transformation. The process was not limited to individuals who already had predispositions toward violence; it applied as well to ordinary men who served in various organized German services, such as the police and military units studied by David Goldhagen and Omer Bartov respectively.[30]

Yet, addressing the atrocities from a primarily German historical perspective does not properly explain the actions of non-German, or non-Austrian, perpetrators. Hilberg, for example, describes the many thousands of non-German volunteers throughout Europe, and particularly in the Baltic, Ukrainian, and Byelorussian regions alone, who actively joined the Nazi cause in military units and as concentration camp guards and as initiators of mass murder. They were usually organized into auxiliary police units assigned to support the activities of the notorious Einsatz-gruppen. Some of them roamed far beyond the confines of their national boundaries, actively and enthusiastically fulfilling their objectives of killing Jews.[31] These anti-Jewish actions were not limited to organized, native paramilitary or police units. Early in the invasion of the Baltic states, for example, they were also conducted by recently released Lithuanian convicts and by less formally organized groups of civilian volunteers, often in open squares where local women were seen holding up their children for a better view of the slaughter.[32]

In the Polish town of Jedwabne, on July 10, 1941, approximately 1,200 Jewish men, women and children were massacred by their neighbors. Many of them were first tortured and then clubbed or knifed to death; others were drowned. Most of the victims were eventually herded into a barn and burned alive. The perpetrators were men from that town.[33] Clearly, the widespread active participation of non-German hands-on killers cannot be explained by an exclusive concentration on German history.

The emergence of the various psychological experiments dealing with the transformation of ordinary people into assorted types of abusers up to the level of murderers has certainly obligated historians to investigate their applicability for explaining perpetrator behavior. What complicates full reliance on these psychological studies is that they are themselves limited by the population samples studied. None of the experiments were conducted in a war environment, nor did they deal with ordinary Germans or ordinary Europeans. The Adorno investigation of an authoritarian personality, the Asch experiments on social conformity, the studies of Milgram on obedience to authority, the Zimbardo studies of prison life, and the more recent work of Athens on the development of the criminal mind have all been reviewed by historians of the Holocaust with varying degrees of acceptance; but underlying all of these studies, and what makes them problematic for convincingly explaining the behavior of the perpetrators, is the fact that the people investigated were ordinary Americans. Therefore, acceptance of any of the psychological findings must presuppose, on the part of the historian, a commonality of behavioral patterns that may include but must transcend any unique cultural characteristics. Any historian who stresses the existence of peculiar or special national or cultural historical paths is limited in his use of most of the psychological material so far produced. The same also applies to proposals of a unique process of social acculturation—such as with the development of the concept of the existence of a life not worthy of life—that prepared German society for what ensued.³⁴ The Holocaust cannot be fully explained from an exclusive study of any one national history. The existence of incontrovertible evidence of an active, widespread non-German participation in the killing process and the concomitant acceptance of postwar psychological studies conducted with American subjects therefore require the historian to relent on the issue of a uniquely German—or uniquely regional—explanation for the atrocities of the Holocaust and to broaden his scope of inquiry.

Of course, the alternative to a generic psychological interpretation of perpetrator behavior that would augment the unique ideational, situational, and cultural explanations would require psychological investigations of subjects who operated in the historical and cultural environment in which the atrocities took place. At the very least, the kind of tests originally conducted in the United States would have to be repeated with randomly selected ordinary Europeans. Examinations of the criminals themselves would have certainly been the best option. Unfortunately, that opportunity was lost at the time; very few of the captured perpetrators were ever psychologically tested.

One rare attempt to create a psychological profile of an actual and particularly vicious and cold-blooded murderer was published in Germany in 2003. It recounted the life, capture and execution of "SS-man" Josef Blösche. Blösche was a policeman who used to take human "hunting" and "target shooting" expeditions through the Warsaw ghetto, shooting pedestrians on the streets or unsuspecting people sitting by the windows of their apartments. He also entered various living quarters and shot babies in their beds. During the Warsaw ghetto uprising, he was active in its suppression and in the subsequent roundup of the residual population, a large number of whom were randomly selected out of lines of prisoners and shot by Blösche and his colleagues. Some of the more famous photographs of the period—one of a roundup, showing him in the background pointing a rifle at a young boy with raised hands, and another where he is accompanying General Jürgen Stroop during an inspection of the ghetto at the end of the uprising—have become world-famous. After the war, he settled in East Germany, married, had children, and led an uneventful life. He kept his prior life a secret from all those around him, including his wife and children. His neighbors considered him an especially good person who could always be relied upon to help out when extra hands were needed to push a car that was stuck or to accept extra duties when someone was sick at work. Eventually the Stasi, the German state police, discovered him. He was arrested, interrogated, and then tried on some twenty-five separate counts, ranging from participation in actions that killed more than a thousand people (he admitted to "only" three hundred) to the murder of one or two children at a time on the open streets of the ghetto. Finally, twenty-four years after the end of the war, on July 29, 1969, Blösche was executed, and his remains were disposed of in an unmarked grave.

The story was revisited in 2003 by two German writers, Heribert Schwann and Helgard Heindrichs, who dedicated large sections of their book to creating a psychological profile of Blösche. What emerges from the findings of the various experts who examined the relevant available material is a man who had been influenced by the group mentality of his unit. He soon changed from a follower of the men in his group into an example for them. The psychological studies conducted some thirty years after his death analyzed his family history, the commentaries from his postwar co-workers and neighbors, the available testimony of wartime eyewitnesses, even his handwriting, and concluded that Blösche was a deeply disturbed personality. He was a sadist who, by the circumstances of his time, had gained a position of control over helpless and unprotected people. Yet, his upbringing in the Sudetenland was not radically different from that of millions of other ordinary Germans, and although he wound up in Einsatzgruppe B, by age and background he fits the profile of the reserve policemen described by Browning and Goldhagen, whom Edward Westermann has recently restudied.[35] At one point, during his time in Russia, these inner tendencies were released by the unfettered opportunity to exercise unlimited power over defenseless people.[36]

Another psychological study of assorted Nazi war criminals came out in 1995 but has received relatively little publicity or recognition. Four psychologists—already mentioned earlier—revisited the previously poorly analyzed and difficult to obtain Rorschach tests of two distinct groups of Nazis: the leadership group that was tried at Nuremberg in 1945–1946, and a large group of rank-and-file Danish Nazi perpetrators who were tried in Copenhagen in 1946. Their book, *The Quest for the Nazi Personality*, engaged these four professional psychologists in a mighty effort but apparently resulted in proving very little. They concluded that they could not identify such a thing as a Nazi personality. Yet, this work may still prove to be more valuable than one may assume at first reading.

The subjects scrutinized were indigenous Europeans. They were either prominent members of the German regime or members of the rank and file. Soon after the end of the war, they all took Rorschach exams that could be empirically—that is, nonsubjectively —evaluated. Their original responses were now recalibrated in accordance with the latest Rorschach assessment guidelines. In all of these ways, these samples differ fundamentally from the psychological experiments conducted with American subjects, some of them over two decades after the conclusion of the war. Thus, these Nazi protocols provide an important component that was previously missing from the psychological school of interpretation. These tests of actual participants in Holocaust violence—which involved individuals at different levels of participation—were assessed with special care to cultural and national characteristics. It was also recognized that the responses were being compared with a normative sample compiled in the United States four decades later. Thus, accommodations were made to restrict their findings to include only the most reliable "conclusions"; these were presented as "descriptive" and "tentative," pending further test samples.[37] Still, despite all of these evaluative restrictions and although limited in the total number of subjects tested, these protocols provide insights into what the perpetrators were really thinking at the time, rather than what others who were far removed in time, geography, and culture might do under simulated conditions. The Nazi Rorschach evaluations have taken into account both the cultural distinctiveness and the common human characteristics of those tested. Thus, the gap between the American simulations and the tests of some of the actual perpetrators is narrowed; and, consequently, the insights gained from both sides of the Atlantic may indeed be pertinent and make the psychological school of interpretation more valid. Then, the implicit separations of the situational, ideational, and psychological perspectives can also be reconciled.

The findings of the four psychologists may also suggest a possible new glimpse into one of the enigmas raised earlier: the curious fact that so many of the postwar defendants—even after their fates had been sealed and they had nothing to gain from obfuscations—still persisted in describing themselves as victims of circumstances. These perpetrators could exhibit behavioral dualism—what Lifton labeled as "doubling" and Primo Levi described as the contradictory behavior of some prisoners in the "Gray Zone"—which allowed them at the same time to exhibit the diametrically opposite behaviors of brutal killers and empathetic, even model, members of a community. One of the psychologists, Barry Ritzler, compared the Rorschach tests of the Nazi leaders with those of the Danish rank and file and noticed a higher than usual incidence of chameleon characteristics in both groups. The data were not sufficient to draw any firm conclusions. Chameleons are abundant in Europe, and they often figure in the responses to the inkblot cards used in these tests. Still, to Ritzler, in his words: "The content of a chameleon presents a tempting speculation for the personality of a rank-and-file Nazi."[38] The finding is suggestive but inconclusive. Many more Rorschachs of ordinary Europeans are needed to establish whether or not the chameleon tendency of large numbers of the rank and file and of the leaders tested was representative of Europeans in general or was a distinguishing characteristic of the Nazis, and especially of the perpetrators.

The three schools of interpretation each offer plausible—but not exclusive, nor complete—responses to Primo Levi's "Why?" It seems that no one reason by itself would, or could, apply in all cases. Once the killings started, a desensitizing followed—usually reinforced with pep talks from unit leaders and with a concomitant increase in alcohol consumption—which facilitated and habituated the daily process. Still, the impetus for the first killings remains an enigma.

Certainly, Bauer is correct to assert that without anti-Semitism there can be no Holocaust; but anti-Semitism existed before and after the war and does not, by itself, explain the conversion of the rank and file, even of racists, into mass murderers at this specific point in time. Anti-Semitism was a historical constant throughout the regions involved—the equivalent of gravity or of air. To argue that it was the cause—in the case of Goldhagen, as the primary cause—is the equivalent to explaining someone's drowning to the existence of water. It is too generalized to be used as a cause. In many cases, it may have been a rationalization, or an after the fact explanation, but not the trigger that impelled individuals to act.

The situational argument offers the context and opportunity necessary for the commission of the crimes; but again, by itself, it does not explain why the Jews were especially targeted for destruction. Segments of other social, ethnic, and national groups were also mistreated, abused and killed; but the Jews were selected for total annihilation. This distinction requires the retention of the ideational school, at the very least, as an important component in a multicausal explanation. A refinement of the situational argument does in fact depend on incorporating some of the ideational and psychological perspectives. The inner dynamics—that is, the special culture—at work within the killing groups seem to have combined the situational, ideational, and psychological impulses into the potent potion necessary to fortify most of the individual members with the resolve to get on with the job at hand.[39] In such an environment, the real exceptions were those who could not find the inner strength to participate in the killings. They were excused without risking more than a loss of face with their "buddies."

The psychological reasons, which should be the most persuasive, suffer from internal difficulties. Testing ordinary people from another time and place is a poor substitute for not having examined the actual perpetrators, especially since the opportunity to do so existed when they were first captured at the end of the war. Still, if we accept the obvious, that there is such a thing as a human commonality—that Europeans, despite their varied cultural and historical identities, are nevertheless members of the human community who share certain similar characteristics with other humans—we may then apply many of the psychological observations derived from samples in the United States, at least partially, to understand better the behavior and motivation of the German and non-German perpetrators.

One final observation still remains: In none of the main literature dealing with this dilemma of the conversion of ordinary people into sadistic killers is there any serious treatment of an incontrovertible fact: the existence of a radical imbalance in power between the perpetrators and the victims. The atrocities could be, and were, carried out with total impunity. No restraining force—be it an inner restraint or an external one—was present to inhibit the killing of defenseless human beings. In terms of real power, no one fought for the Jew. No fear of retaliation existed to stay the hand of the masters. Whether it was the physicians who sat at the crossroads of life and death, the common soldiers and policemen, or the non-German volunteers in the various regions of Nazi occupied Europe, none of them needed to fear the usual consequences to be expected from committing acts that clearly would not be accepted in normal society. In fact, the sadists who would be shunned in a civilized society now had free rein.

It would take extraordinary qualities to resist the temptation of acting like a god, possessing intoxicating power over life and death. In the East, "euphoria of empire," or an "intoxication with the East," an "*Ostrauch*," seemed to prevail.[40] The very fact that today Yad Vashem honors the "Righteous Among Nations" who protected—rather than turned over or persecuted—the victims is a recognition of their exceptional behavior, which, on further reflection, should have been the prevailing mentality.[41]

So, in response to Primo Levi's "*Warum*?"—even while accepting some, or any, combination of the explanations already considered—perhaps the answer may be far less complicated—and more disturbing—than previously considered. Like a childhood bully who responds to a victim's "Why?" with a "Because," the most nakedly honest response that Primo's guard could, and should, have given was: "Because I can!"

CHAPTER 2

Guilt or Shame?

Amy Simon

Primo Levi's corpus of writings has become an important part of a larger discussion in trauma, emotion, guilt, and shame theories. Because he is the Holocaust survivor who most articulately, poignantly, and openly discusses his own experiences during the Holocaust and his own relationship to survivor guilt and shame, many have used his writings to promote their own interpretations of these theories. Ruth Leys has outlined recent trends in these fields in her 2007 book *From Guilt to Shame: Auschwitz and After*. As the title suggests, this book claims that the past twenty years has seen a change from a focus on survivor guilt to survivor shame. She traces the discussion from the 1960s through the present, concluding that "whereas in the past the theorization of survivor guilt remained within an intentionalist or cognitivist paradigm of the emotions, current shame theory shares the positivist ambitions of the medical sciences by theorizing shame in anti-intentionalist (or anticognitivist) terms."[1] In other words, those who used to speak about survivor guilt argued that guilt originates in an action or a fantasy of action, suggesting that Holocaust survivors were either themselves guilty, guilty by association with the Nazis, or guilty through mimesis identification with the perpetrators. Conversely, those who now speak of survivor shame are concerned not with actions and mimesis, but with "an experience of the self when the individual becomes aware of being exposed to the diminishing or disapproving gaze of another."[2] Thus, these new theories of shame take responsibility away from the victim and suggest that their feelings of "guilt" are really feelings of shame stemming from their sense of self's being diminished by another's viewing.

My project here is to conduct a close reading of Levi's manifold interpretation of the specific shame experienced by victims of the Holocaust as outlined in his essay "Shame" from his 1986 collection entitled, *The Drowned and the Saved*, as well as in *If This Is a Man* and *The Truce*. Though Leys uses Levi herself, taking special notice of Giorgio Agamben, Lawrence Langer, Sue Miller, and Emmanuel Levinas in her analysis of his works, she nowhere examines his works in depth. As opposed to Leys's, my project seeks to understand specifically how Levi understood shame and guilt and represented them in his writings rather than to speak of these concepts more generally. Rather than bringing literature to theory, I seek to bring theory to literature. Thus, I will examine Primo Levi's interpretation of shame and guilt for its own sake, only in the end fitting it into the larger picture of guilt and shame theory.

The theme of shame in Primo Levi's writings holds a place of central importance. Levi defines shame as "a feeling of guilt during the imprisonment and afterwards,"[3] thereby conflating the two states of mind. As the psychologist Sue Miller suggests, "the victim experiences a mix of both guilt and shame, according to whether he focuses on guilty recollections of what he did or imagines he did, or on the moral shame he feels for being a weak or inferior person."[4] I propose, however, to keep the emotions of shame and guilt separate as much as possible in my analysis in order to examine Levi's use of the term "shame." This essay will demonstrate that his descriptions do point to a distinction between the two sentiments even though he does not personally address this divergence. That shame and guilt are not exactly the same and should not be read as such in Primo Levi's works is essential given the importance of both to the psychological well-being (or lack thereof) of many survivors after the Holocaust, including Levi himself. Thus, my reading fits into the larger trend of moving the discussion away from the notion of survivor guilt to shame. Although Levi himself does feel guilt and does feel shame, I agree that the future of Holocaust studies would do better to focus on shame as an emotion that imparts less responsibility to the victims of atrocity. While not negating the ideas of victim complicity and mimesis, I suggest here a reading that allows the postwar, non–Holocaust survivor reader a stance of neutrality. That is, a switch from guilt to shame lessens the impulse of those who have come after to judge Holocaust survivors from our own moral perspectives. Perhaps this change will help mollify the "judgment that the survivor believes he sees in the eyes of those (especially the young) who listen to his stories and judge with facile hindsight, or who perhaps feel cruelly repelled."[5]

As defined by the online edition of the Merriam-Webster dictionary, guilt is "the state of one who has committed an offense especially consciously," or "a feeling of culpability for offenses," while shame, somewhat different, is defined as "a painful emotion caused by consciousness of guilt, shortcoming, or impropriety," or "a condition of humiliating disgrace or disrepute." The main difference, then, is that guilt almost always includes a real or imagined offense while a feeling of shame can exist without such offense. Levi uses the word *culpa*, which can also mean "blame," to refer to guilt, and the word *vergogna*, which is very often translated as "embarrassment," to refer to shame (these mirror the English translations exactly), suggesting his own basic acceptance of this definition. The question so often posed by Levi and other survivors, "Are you ashamed because you are alive in place of another?"[6] involves the question of guilt (actually surviving at the real or imagined expense of another person's life) and represents a good example of Levi's own conflation of the two terms. Lawrence Langer, among others, has already dealt with this kind of guilt at length. Thus, this essay will focus instead on other types of shame with no real *or* apparent moment of guilt.

In *The Drowned and the Saved*, Levi identifies four different types of shame (relatively separate from guilt) caused by the Holocaust as experienced by survivors. First, he points to the shame "one suffered because of the reacquired consciousness of having been diminished."[7] This suffering occurred only after liberation, when survivors could look back and see their dehumanization in the camps and feel that emotion of shame toward themselves. This relates to Leys's discussion in which shame appears only after the individual experiences the outside gaze of another. Here, Levi suggests that it is his own seeing of himself that causes shame. Perhaps the "other" here is the man living again outside of the concentration camp universe, able to look back and evaluate his past. Second, Levi discusses the shame felt at not having done anything to resist. He recognizes this shame as an irrational feeling because of the sheer impossibility of resistance within the camps, but he insists on the feeling of shame that this inaction nevertheless brought. Third, Levi addresses the shame felt at having had "failed in terms of human solidarity"[8] In following the rules of the

Lager which clearly stated that a prisoner must put himself above all others, Levi sees a breakdown in human interaction and compassion for which he, in retrospect, feels shame. Last, Levi insists on a feeling of "the shame of the world."[9] He describes this as shame felt by the "just" because of the Holocaust, which proved that man could "construct an infinite enormity of pain."[10] The shame of the Holocaust involved not only its immediate victims, but by proxy, the entire human world. These examples of shame all originate in moments of failure rather than in moments of action. The victims feel shame at these instances in which they recognize their own helplessness.

Here I will discuss these aspects of shame by using examples from *If This Is a Man* and *The Truce*, focusing specifically on three different perspectives—shame described by Levi as affecting everyone alike, the shame he experienced personally, and shame as he observed it in other people. Shame, one of the enduring evils of the Nazis, was felt long after Auschwitz; hence its continued interest to us today. Levi's discussion of it both in his early works and later years proves this point and demonstrates the importance of yet another dimension of the many atrocities committed during the Holocaust. As Anthony Rudolf writes in *At an Uncertain Hour: Primo Levi's War Against Oblivion*, "That such a man should feel shame and guilt at surviving is not the least indictment of the Germans."[11]

The best-documented aspect of this shame in Levi's writings appears as the general shame of all survivors at having lived (and survived) at such a base level within the camps. Though the victims did not choose this state of being, this imposed dehumanization, the fact that they endured it nonetheless brought a feeling of shame. As Levinas suggests, "shame appears to be reserved for a phenomena of a moral order: one feels ashamed for having acted badly, for having deviated from the norm. It is the representation we form of ourselves as diminished beings with which we are pained to identify."[12] This echoes also Miller's suggestion that the victim's shame can come from his or her perception of the self as weak or inferior. Throughout *If This Is a Man* and *The Truce*, Levi makes reference to experienced degradation almost unconsciously. Because living like an animal was such an essential part of the camp system, in most of the instances in which he describes these debasements, he adds no additional commentary. In *The Drowned and the Saved*, however, he looks back and remarks on the shame felt at having "endured filth, promiscuity, and destitution" in the camps.[13] The entire second chapter of *If This Is a Man* describes the initial humiliation of the victims at having to undress, having everything they owned taken away, and being shaven upon arrival in

Auschwitz.[14] This degradation was the initiation into the bestial life they were to lead during the entirety of their incarceration. Levi continues to give examples of the way in which all dignity and pride were stripped from the prisoners and replaced by shame. Descriptions of being called by a number rather than a name, having to empty the toilet bucket at night in the snow, and using the word *"fressen"* instead of *"essen"* to mean eating (which indicates an animal rather than a human), all describe ways in which the Nazis imposed this feeling of shame on their victims. In his descriptions of these events, Levi discusses the victims not individually, but rather by using "we." or "us." In this way, the reader understands that these examples of the shame imposed by the Nazis applied to all of their victims and are dealt with by Levi in the general sense.

However, in certain instances, Levi looks at the shame of others from the outside. He sees their shame while not experiencing it himself. At the beginning of *If This Is a Man*, when he describes his first encounters with people already caught up in the camp system as walking "in squads, in rows of three, with an odd, embarrassed step, head dangling in front, arms rigid," and again later when he describes the ordeal of the dysentery patients having to prove their illness, Levi steps outside his own shame and comments on it as he observes it to be felt by others.[15] In the first case—that of the already interned camp inmates—Levi observes their "embarrassed step" and "dangling heads." These gestures typically describe people suffering some sort of derision or shame. Either they have been reprimanded by someone else or have reprimanded themselves. These inmates have clearly yielded to the dehumanization of the Nazi camp system and are feeling either beaten down or ashamed of their appearance in front of the new arrivals. The situation involving the dysentery patients also suggests a high degree of shame. Though having little choice, these men must physically perform acts of degradation (displaying their unhealthy, bloody bowels), which produces, by default, both shame and guilt. These men feel guilty at having actually committed an unclean act and are also immensely embarrassed by what is required of them by the Nazis. Having to prove intestinal illness in a public and vulgar way is something unthinkable in the world outside of the concentration camp.

In other cases, however, Levi speaks about the shame he experienced personally simply by living through the camps. When he refers specifically to his own sense of shame, he usually describes it in reference to women. Just as many survivors could not feel shame while in the camps because of the continued need for survival, Levi feels shame first when juxtaposed

with women. The gazing "other" discussed earlier, these women represented to Levi the complete opposite of the concentration camps. While
in the Buna laboratory, Levi feels an acute pain: "Faced with the girls of
the laboratory, we three feel ourselves sink into the ground from shame
and embarrassment. We know what we look like: we see each other and
sometimes we happen to see our reflection in a clean window. We are
ridiculous and repugnant."[16] This shame in front of women comes back
again in *The Truce* when Levi meets the young Galina. Here he feels
"weak, ill and dirty" and is "painfully conscious of [his] miserable appearance, of [his] badly shaved face, of [his] Auschwitz clothes."[17] For Levi,
seeing women in the concentration camp universe and directly thereafter,
especially because of his lack of contact with them during his time in
Auschwitz, brings him back to the sane world he knew before his imprisonment. Just as the nonworking Sundays in Auschwitz gave prisoners time
to reflect on their former lives and how far away they suddenly were physically and emotionally from these lives, Levi's contact with women gives
him the impetus to look inside and realize his distance from his former
world. Perhaps the reentry of this aspect of the outside world forces him
to realize the difference between that world and this, between his human
life before and his dehumanized life within. This shame in relation to
women also seems to be more specific to Levi. Neither the general shame
of all prisoners nor the observed shame of others, this shame is intensely
personal. This is not just the shame inflicted by an outside viewer, but
specifically by a female viewer. His troubled relationship with women
becomes a theme in Levi's later writings, and it is not surprising that these
women should be the lens through which he most poignantly describes
his own shame.

Another aspect of shame outlined by Levi in his essay by the same name
finds its origins in an experience that he felt at a personal level, but which
certainly resonates among other survivors. This shame comes from not
having physically resisted while in the concentration camps. While many,
including Levi, resisted in "small" ways such as remaining clean, not stealing from other prisoners, not becoming "collaborators," and maintaining
a determination to live and be human, very few risked or were able to risk
armed physical resistance. This lack of clearly defined resistance to the
Nazis within the camp system is the lasting shame of many prisoners.
Despite the near impossibility of such action, Levi explains the feeling
clearly when he says, "Therefore, on a rational plane, there should not
have been much to be ashamed of, but shame persisted nevertheless."[18]
He goes on to elaborate that this feeling of shame continued to haunt him

in the form of judgment. Because of his inner feeling of shame and the different moral codes of those who never experienced the Holocaust, Levi describes the feeling of being judged by all who hear his story. He sees in their eyes disapproval at his lack of resistance and incorporates it into his own persistent feeling of shame. This aspect of shame first and most importantly appears in the chapter "The Last One" from *If This Is a Man*. After the hanging of a man supposedly involved in an Auschwitz revolt, Levi remarks:

> Alberto and I went back to the hut, and we could not look each other in the face. That man must have been tough, he must have been made of another metal than us if this condition of ours, which has broken us, could not bend him. . . . We lifted the *menaschka* on to the bunk and divided it, we satisfied the daily ragings of hunger, and now we are oppressed by shame.[19]

Here, he expresses shame at having allowed Auschwitz to have its natural effect on him. When compared with someone who had the remarkable ability to keep a spark of life and to use that in order to attempt material resistance, Levi feels ashamed. He feels ashamed at not having been stronger and ashamed at not having had the power to resist. He experiences the feeling that "you too could have, you certainly should have" done something to resist or revolt.[20]

Another form of shame felt by Holocaust survivors more generally concerns the self-accusation "of having failed in terms of human solidarity."[21] Levi experiences this shame personally, as described in his essay from *The Drowned and the Saved*, but relates it in *If This Is a Man* on a broader level. There he describes this feeling that the Nazi concentration camp system broke down human interactions between fellow victims vividly. He informs us, "here the struggle to survive is without respite, because everyone is desperately and ferociously alone. If some Null Achtzehn vacillates, he will find no one to extend a helping hand; on the contrary, someone will knock him aside."[22] Instead of helping each other with advice, compassion, and human warmth, the inmates of the concentration camps took the attitude of putting themselves before all others. This harm could take the form of anything from stealing from a neighbor to simply turning a blind eye to someone else's suffering. To have survived Auschwitz "with . . . moral conscience not destroyed and not subdued by the Germans" as Gian Paolo Biasin claims of Levi in his article "Our Daily Bread," was a rarity in the camps.[23] Even such survivors as Levi who did nothing ostensibly "wrong" during their imprisonment could look back and see the everyday instances of selfishness and lack of collective compassion as at least a partial breaking down of this "moral conscience," causing a great sense of shame; a sense of one's own human diminishment. Levi himself ruminates on an instance in which he failed to share a few drops of water from a two-inch pipe with his fellow inmates. He bitterly regrets having only shared the water with one close friend instead of dividing it up among many others, especially when another of his squad saw and made a point of bringing it up to him after liberation.[24] This was enough to indict Levi to the position of the "guilty" within the concentration camp universe.

Furthermore, upon first arrival at Auschwitz, one typically received no helping hand and thereafter gave none to the new arrivals. Shame at this behavior, felt by survivors after liberation, endures. The principle of putting oneself first, second, and third, as Levi mentions in reference to Ella Lingens-Reiner's *Prisoners of Fear*, demonstrates a rule which was relevant at the time, but seems, in retrospect, cold and unfeeling.[25] No wonder that survivors living once again within a "normal" moral code feel shame at this remembrance. Instead of blaming the Nazis who created the entire world in which they lived, survivors feel instead this self-accusation at how they acted. Levi expresses a shame at his actions, or more precisely his "inaction," which haunted him still forty years later.

The last aspect of shame outlined by Levi in his essay from *The Drowned and the Saved* is perhaps the most interesting. More than a personal feeling at the behavior of an individual or an observation of somebody else's shame, this sense of shame concerns something much larger. Levi describes this shame as "another, vaster shame, the shame of the world."[26] With its roots in John Donne, who emphasizes the entire world as one community, this shame either does or should affect every living being. Levi's memorable description of his Russian liberators at Auschwitz personifies this feeling of universal shame:

> They did not greet us, nor did they smile; they seemed oppressed not only by compassion but by a confused restraint, which sealed their lips and bound their eyes to the funereal scene. It was that shame we knew so well, the shame that drowned us after the selections, and every time we had to watch, or submit to, some outrage: the shame the Germans did not know, that the just man experiences at another man's crime; the feeling of guilt that such a crime should exist, that it should have been introduced irrevocably into the world of things that exist, and that his will for good should have proved too weak or null, and should not have availed in defence.[27]

Greater than the shame at having lived like an animal, having not resisted, or having failed to help someone, this is the shame not only of survivors who witnessed the event, but of every person with a feeling heart because each one knows about the breakdown not only of human solidarity within the camps, but of the entire human race toward one another that occurred during the Holocaust. Perhaps this break with humanity is the most fundamental level of evil that the Nazis perpetrated. More than any of the other aspects of shame described by Levi, this feeling of the shame of the world has no roots in a definable offense. There is no point at which an individual survivor or liberator can look back and feel guilt at having done something wrong which led to the Holocaust. Even countries implicated in the crime experienced complicated political and historical situations that make it hard to place blame and to find a real offense. Perhaps only the Nazis and Germans who either perpetrated or turned their backs on this occurrence have the right to feel this kind of shame, while the people who most often do (the "just") are those who were powerless to stop it. This shame represents the diminishment of the entire world after the knowledge of the Holocaust. Here Levi uses both the words shame and guilt, suggesting their inextricability.

After the hunger and physical pain and work and harsh conditions were over, survivors nonetheless continued harboring these feelings of shame foisted on them by the Nazis. Though they had done nothing wrong, and though most survivors realized this fact logically, they continued to feel this shame. As Dori Laub explains in his description of a Holocaust survivor's testimony, "the untold events had become so distorted in her (the survivor's) unconscious memory as to make her believe that she herself, and not the perpetrator, was responsible for the atrocities she witnessed. If she could not stop them, rescue or comfort the victims, *she* bore the responsibility for their pain."[28] Herein lies the crux of the issue. The fact that each survivor "is tormented by an ongoing regret for something that he or she may have done or failed to do"[29] reveals the reality that no true moment of guilt exists. In the case of the survivor mentioned before, the psychiatrist Laub recognizes that the survivor is actually not guilty of anything, but the survivor herself cannot understand that. Too many years of viewing the memory of her experiences as guilty keeps her from realizing her own innocence. One most often feels shame in this way—introduced by an outside source, here the Nazis, then perpetuated by internalization. Thus, what remains is perhaps better described as shame. The shame of having witnessed the event and having been unable to stop it requires no actual fault on the part of the victim. It requires no actual or imagined action at all and appears most often in moments of inaction. Guilt requires some perceived misdeed, while shame can come from a feeling of helpless-ness—the shame of being helpless. Whether viewed from the outside by another person or from within by oneself, the Holocaust victim's sense of self is diminished by experiences of degradation to the point that he or she can no longer distinguish between guilt and shame. Our duty as postwar intellectuals is not to judge actions through a discussion of survivor guilt (which by definition imparts blame), but to try to understand the possible moments of action and inaction in the concentration camp universe and the ways in which survivors have interpreted their experiences and negoti-ated their resulting emotions.

CHAPTER 3

Primo Levi and the Concept of History

Johan Åhr

The chronicler who narrates events without distinguishing between major and minor ones acts in accord with the following truth: nothing that has ever happened should be regarded as lost to history.

Every age must strive anew to wrest tradition away from the conformism that is working to overpower it.

There is no document of culture which is not at the same time a document of barbarism.

WALTER BENJAMIN, "On the Concept of History"

The God That Failed

After World War II, which wreaked havoc on a Europe still in shock and bleeding from the great war before it, a distrust and rejection of "historicism"—skepticism toward any abstract, imposing generalization about the character and trajectory of society and history except in defense of individual liberty and personal responsibility—sank deep into Western thought.[1] Intellectuals in Europe and America professed a loss of faith in formulaic, all-embracing theories; they sensed danger in the sort of anonymous, collective identification that had guided the philosophy of Georg Hegel.[2] This zeal for individual matters and wariness of grandiose doctrines liable to demonize and annihilate entire classes of people finds expression in the works of Hannah Arendt, who, born in Hanover, Germany, fled to France upon Adolf Hitler's assumption of power.[3] In magisterial defiance of historicist presumption, moved by Hungary's revolt against Communism, addressing doctrinaire apparatchiks and their intransigent sycophants, this critic of totalitarianism bitterly writes about the century in which she lived: "To our modern way of thinking, nothing is meaningful in and by itself, not history nor nature taken as a whole, and certainly not particular occurrences in the physical order or specific historical events." That is, we have allowed supposedly sacrosanct processes to shape and pattern our comprehension of the world, degrading "every tangible thing, every individual entity," into functions of a deterministic chain of being passing for an ideology of liberation.[4] She would later dedicate a revised and expanded version of this essay in title and spirit to Walter Benjamin's memory.[5] German and Jewish too, this philosopher of alienation, likewise disturbed by historicism's ambition of totality, denied that history was a science, causal and logical.[6] Imagining himself a flâneur and ragpicker, he saw meaning, essences, in fragments—catching colorful but transient hints of society's dialectical intricacy (its plural, liminal debt to the past and hold on the future) in the windows and topography of commercial Paris.[7] It was his mantra, gleaned from Aby Warburg, the iconologist, that "the greatest is revealed in the smallest"—that "the size of an object was in inverse ratio to its significance," or "graphicness (*Anschaulichkeit*)."[8] In this there is an aspect of the close and alert commentary by digression that in the Talmud and Midrash governs study of the Tanakh.[9]

Primo Levi (1919–1987)

The resistance to historicism was understandably tough and livid among Jewish European intellectuals, wherever the fates of war had pushed them. An abhorrence of this sort, though nobody has yet looked for it there, certainly agitates the writings of the Italian Primo Levi. His memoir, *Il sistema periodico* (1975), presents no cradle-to-grave account of the life that he lived, but is rather an allegory in fractions, culled from flashes of memory, with each section centered (if also on the author) on the properties and behaviors of a specific chemical element.[10] But it is not here that this survivor of Auschwitz-Birkenau dwells tellingly on historicism: on the practice of history, what its objectives, categories, terms, and bounds ought to be.[11] His atomistic, historical particularism—an argument that people do have causal agency on the basic phenomena explaining them[12]—shows best elsewhere, in the last book that he wrote, the grim and edgy *I sommersi e i salvati* (1986), or *The Drowned and the Saved*.[13] In this text on the hardship of survival, written in agony over the continuation of genocide, no one person is reducible to another.

The Holocaust nearly took his life and put a gloom over him, but Levi still exuded curiosity about the world. He read always and variously, if with an eye for the serious and solemn, following attentively the international nuclear arms race and the wars in Vietnam (1946–1975) and Lebanon (1982)—condemning all three. But it was the history that Levi himself had lived, the epoch of totalitarianism, that especially consumed him. He showed interest in the *Historikerstreit*: the dispute over whether the Soviet Union's record of crime can be productively compared with that of the Third Reich. And Levi evinced concern over the vulgarization of the Holocaust by media bent on producing spectacles for profit, sanitized and redemptive pictures of a conquering human spirit.[14]

In opposition to such vulgarity, Levi's own writing was marvelously varied and specific in style.[15] He would say that it was his duty to bear careful and complete witness—to honor the millions of victims who did not live to speak for themselves about their tribulations. But his fascination with detail was also a way of setting the record straight, against glossy interpretation and exploitation. According to the historian Stuart Woolf, the history that Levi wrote shows clearly, in addition to a passion for the Old Testament and classic literature, an anthropologist's fascination with the discrete and concrete: "the lesser history of individual experience."[16] Tendered but not tested, this thesis—that Levi purposely spurns the greater history of collective experience, its summary, schematic code of analysis—calls for elaboration, application, and context. The claim here is that it concerns not only a humanist impulse but also an historical critique.

Levi strove to record everything about his experience in the Holocaust; as Anthony Rudolf remarks, "He lived every minute in order, later, to tell. And then, later, he would tell every minute in order to live."[17] First, Levi wrote about Auschwitz, where this prisoner (*Häftling* #174517) languished terribly for nearly a year, until the Red Army liberated him. Also vivid and urgent in Levi's memory were other miseries, endured before and after these months of captivity: Italy's prewar anti-Semitism, initially subtle, then legal, threatening his education in Turin; the failure of the partisan unit he joined, its capture by fascist militia; the internment of the Jews, their deportation to camps, the trip itself a nasty, often fatal ordeal; and Europe's postwar turmoil, in which his return home took him into Russia and beyond, a long, hard journey through thefts, scams, hunger, and illness. These are the trials that he ordered more or less chronologically in his oeuvre, episodes that he recalled with vigilant attention to descriptive detail—afraid that his view may seem an exaggeration, the truth warped by self-pity and a desire for revenge.[18]

Because he was a man of science raised to value education and achievement, Levi knew how to craft articulate, purposeful prose. His writing is never just a list of facts, a mere catalogue of events. When he wants to, Levi shapes narratives that move gracefully through a beginning, middle, and end. As a rule, his digressions lead to fascinating insights (often into chemistry's ways and means) and rarely obscure the guiding themes. These skills and Levi's patience with the pains of testimony explain why his reputation as a witness and writer is broad and strong—see the rapidly growing critical literature on him.[19]

So least of all in Levi, striving for objectivity and coherence, does a reader expect to find a subjective if irregular theory of history, based on profound, combative suspicion. But *The Drowned and the Saved* reveals the thinking of a once-proud young man rendered dependent, helpless, subject to random, ludicrous orders, daily under threat of death, aged beyond his years, who miraculously finds a way to repair himself, recovering a power to act in meticulous testimonial writing. Informed by trauma, a bewildered feeling of virtually unbelievable pain and loss, this is a philosophy of life founded on mistrust of any scheme in which individuals lose the positions and functions they may make for themselves.[20] Empirically grounded, it cautions against the thinking characteristic of historians who privilege the importance of immense, diachronic systems, like industry or the climate, all but ignoring the plain plebeians who built the gates of Thebes, the modest masons of the world.[21]

The Drowned and the Saved *(1986)*

The narrative here is heterogeneous, disjointed, for *The Drowned and the Saved* is fundamentally a study of exceptions; seemingly of pieces, its composition lacks a center. Looking at our past and present, Primo Levi warns, "one cannot say that each turn follows from a single why" (150). For a complete, truthful understanding of who we are, he insists on the deviations and aberrations. Levi calls attention to how "historical and natural phenomena are not simple," but often frustratingly complicated (37). In such sporadic statements, by the sum of its eight chapters, *The Drowned and the Saved* urges its audience to make distinctions, not to paint people and their communities with one brush only, but to look for their different and contrasting features and aspects. In effect, it models a concept of history, honed in Italy, that shuns teleological theorems, a "microhistory" (*microstoria*) of singular incidents, seen from a qualitative rather than quantitative perspective.[22] To use the language of Francis Bacon, who lived for experimentation and in 1626 died from it, Levi—who swore by his microscope—favors wary induction over bold deduction, reasoning from facts, not ideas.[23]

To the degree that the sections of *The Drowned and the Saved* contain a distinctive unifying theme, it is this compulsive concern for the disparate peculiarities of life in Auschwitz III (Monowitz-Buna), our subject's prison from February 26, 1944, to January 27, 1945. Perhaps a play on the failure of reason, or a hint at memory's elusiveness, the idiosyncrasy of the book is likely in part a result of it coming from the hand of a writer at the end of his career. Levi died on April 11, 1987, at the age of sixty-seven, likely from suicide.[24] By this time he had already given us noble lessons, duly grounded in pages of deep evidence, in other works on Germany's war on the Jews. Levi's *Se questo è un uomo* (*If This Is a Man*; 1947, 1958) demonstrated how survival in the *Konzentrationslager* (concentration camp) was on the whole a matter of fortune, and few were those who found it.[25] And his *La tregua* (*The Truce*, 1963) established that for the survivor the torment of the Holocaust persists horribly, beyond the experience of the evil, in paralyzing guilt and nihilistic doubt.[26]

"No historian or epistemologist," claims Levi in *The Drowned and the Saved*, "has yet proven that human history is a deterministic process," linearly or cyclically patterned and therefore predictable (150). The Europe of 1933, Germany included, could not have foreseen what was soon to become of it (161–166). Even so, suggestively contradicting himself, he fears in his conclusion that genocide is an eternal threat, a madness endemic to humanity (198–203). This notion of a human capacity for virulent cruelty, even a special unruly tendency toward it, is also to be found elsewhere in his work—notably in articles and interviews. For Levi continually worried over systematic mass murder in Europe, Africa, and beyond.[27]

History's Miscellany

From start to finish, *The Drowned and the Saved* dwells on history's miscellany: consider "Letters from Germans" (Chapter 8), comprising notes sent to Primo Levi about his writing—from points west, the East being in the grip of censorship. (From the dates on these letters he conjectures that the wall raised in 1961 to separate *Westie* from *Ostie* provoked deliberation on history, retrospection [175].) In this correspondence, Levi felt it his duty to discover an explanation for the Holocaust. And so he perused, however skeptically, every message sent to him, answering many in an effort to correct errors and dispel myths. "My task was to understand them," he explains, "those from among whom the SS militia were recruited, and also those," in the crowd, "who did not . . . throw us a piece of bread, whisper a word" (168–169). To his satisfaction, what Levi generally finds, despite a heap of qualifiers, are expressions of responsibility and contrition, and, as from a clerk in Wiesbaden, commitments to education about genocide and promises of vigilance against any temptation to excuse it (189–197). Yet he accentuates too the conceited, obsequiously officious spirit of *"Deutschtum"* in many of these missives, the sort of apathetic and craven deference to authority that enabled Germany's officially organized mass murders (not to mention the awful sadism analyzed in "Useless Violence" [Chapter 5; 105–126]). But Levi counsels that "it is dangerous, wrong, to speak about 'the Germans,' or any other people, as of a single, undifferentiated entity, and include all individuals in one judgment" (183). He expounds, "save the exceptions, they were not monsters" (202).

Indeed, Levi elaborates, not every German supported Nazism— curiously assuming it to be our belief that all of them did. Some courageous and enterprising souls among them opposed the Nazis. One such agitator he knew well, a translator of his who feigned illness to avoid recruitment into the Wehrmacht and, finding his way to Padua, where he studied literature, fought for "Justice and Liberty" against Benito Mussolini's Republic of Salò (170–175). Levi notes further that after the war many Germans actually renounced the Führer and expressed chagrin over their contributions to his totalitarianism. But never resting from his leeriness, he asks us to bear in mind the others, who like a doctor in Hamburg not only relativized these atrocities, but also denied them (175–180). There was no telling what people would do, or disclose that they had done.

It is the point of "Stereotypes" (Chapter 7) that this multiplicity of experience applies not only to Gentiles. Between 1933 and 1945, Levi stresses, Jews did fight their oppression, despite claims that they were a cowardly, subhuman race (*Untermenschen*). Some struck back against their tormentors even within the confines of the Lager, where organization and resistance were enormously difficult and perilous. Rebellions may have been scarce and limited in size, but Levi cites examples at Birkenau, Sobibor, and Treblinka, undertaken in part to alert the world to the fact and scope of the Holocaust. The trouble that the insurgents caused in the camps achieved much against the odds, not the least of their victories a sense of worth before dying (158–161). Levi himself had dared to battle

Fascism; that was why he was arrested on December 13, 1943, in the mountains of Val d'Aosta, north of his home, a member of a group of partisans plotting to overthrow Il Duce's Repubblica Sociale Italiana.[28]

Very few ventured to flee the Lager, Levi concedes, citing the deterrent of capture and its corollary, death by hanging. But prisoners of war had other reasons not to attempt escape, especially if without money, fluency in the local tongue, and connections in the territories under the swastika. Imagine yourself, Levi bids us, Russian and a captive in Germany. Should you manage to break out and get through foreign, hostile territory to the front (which was in flux), you were there—tattered, tattooed, bruised, and blistered—likely to meet with revulsion and chariness, even scorn. To have surrendered on the battlefield deserved anathema, and stragglers were usually taken for spies and shot (151–152). But any Jew on the run was likely to fare worse, having no ready refuge anywhere on the continent (154–155). As always, there were the exceptions, sanctuaries among the armed Jewish partisans hiding out in dense and remote woods (151–152), which Levi portrayed in his 1982 novel about the resistance, *Se non ora, quando? (If Not Now, When?)*.

Much as Levi admires the rebels who combated the Nazis, he avoids speaking loosely of heroes and villains—finding it a challenge to separate "victims and persecutors" into two tidy groups of actors (37). In "The Gray Zone" (Chapter 2), Levi explores the role of a minority of Jewish inmates who chose to serve the SS as Lager auxiliaries—as translators, for instance—in return for privileges such as special medical attention, not to mention a feeling of "power and prestige" (69). Some such functionaries even operated the gas chambers and crematoria ovens; it was their task "to pull gold teeth from jaws" (50). He speculates that many of them, in "imitation of the victor," but only aggravating their slavery, found catharsis in the infliction of violence on the living and dead (43). Oddly, here, "masters and servants" thus both "diverge and converge" (42). This pact was of course not for everyone's fair and equal benefit. It eased the conscience of the oppressors, likewise their load, relieving them of petty chores and dirty jobs; and it simultaneously humiliated the prisoners, except those so invigorated by a feeling of control that they knew no shame. Jews helping to kill their own kind, brothers and sisters, this auto-genocide the Nazis deemed proof of an essential lack of humanity, a radical animalism (50–55). But Levi warns, "no one is authorized to judge them" (59), these men and women of "ambiguity and compromise" (67), for they were but cogs in the machine fueled by Zyklon-B (the cyanide-based poison gas), instruments of Nazism's power of degradation and

destruction. Instead, he concludes, with a certainty otherwise missing in
The Drowned and the Saved, "responsibility lies with the system" (44).

Anyone, Levi holds, who did survive to speak from experience of an
inferno like Auschwitz must have compromised himself, herself, taken
advantage of others, even friends. In *The Drowned and the Saved* he cites
himself as an example of such behavior. "Shame" (Chapter 3) addresses
the aching, ceaseless ignominy of having traded honor for survival. And
"The Memory of the Offense" (Chapter 1) probes the survivor's need for
normalization, the desire, reasonable but futile, to exist only in the present, oblivious to the past, innocent of baseness: "Reality can be distorted"
(33). The prisoner who was abnormally valiant and virtuous seldom lived
to bear witness. For standing up to terror, these heroes and heroines would
usually die soon after arrival in the *Lager*. Levi worries: "I might be alive
in the place of another" (82).

Other than luck and opportunism, what allowed Levi to survive the SS
and their henchmen was his higher, specialized education. A measure of
Levi's learning were the languages that he knew, much French and some
German ("Communicating" [Chapter 4]), which at the *Bunawerke* helped
him understand orders and—as when trading goods—negotiate with others. "I soon understood that my extremely meager *Wortschatz* [vocabulary]
had become an essential factor of survival" (95). In "The Intellectual in
Auschwitz" (Chapter 6), Levi further observes that his mind kept him both
optimistic and disciplined. Rigorous schooling and an ardent love of literature had created in Levi an internal, cerebral refuge, to which he could
retreat when under duress—a reservoir of chapter and verse on which this
youth drew for comfort and relief (138–140). When depressed, Levi qui-
etly recited *La Divina Commedia*, anything (but especially this story of the
afterlife, about heaven and hell) to evade the pain of reality and yet also,
paradoxically, to keep himself alert. "Can I," he wonders, "foresee the
blow, know from which side it will come . . . elude it?" (141). However
much the Nazis tried to beat and bore his wits out of him, they could not
do it.

Levi's classical and humanist culture reached far and deep, giving him
"a link with the past, saving it from oblivion" (139)—and so too did his
science, especially since at Auschwitz he worked as a chemist for IG Farben. At this factory, which put him under a roof, sheltered from heat, cold,
rain, and snow, Levi lent his hand to the production of synthetic gasoline
and rubber (composed of butadiene and sodium, hence the acronym
"Buna")—also to the making of dyestuffs and other basic by-products of
coal.[29] The position allowed Levi to preserve his identity. However lowly

and servile—ragged, shaved, beset by lice—he remained a species of scientist who could occupy his mind with pipettes and burettes (140–141).

Levi thought the intellectual at an advantage in the Lager, but he realized that the opposite was also the case—as asserted by Jean Améry in *Jenseits von Schuld und Sühne: Bewältigungsversuche eines Überwältigten* (*At the Mind's Limits*, 1966). Here, from experience, this philologist (born Hans Mayer) contends that almost any learning was a worthless and painful burden in a place like Auschwitz. He lacked not only the worker's brawn and stamina, but also his way with a pick and shovel.[30] Moreover, Améry, like Levi both Jewish and agnostic, or not willing to seek an answer to the Holocaust in religion (145–147), found his own attempt to fathom Nazism and its illogical, immoral horror stupefying: "Reason, art, and poetry are no help in deciphering a place from which they are banned" (142). He laments, "beauty, that was an illusion."[31] As Améry saw it, the simple man was a realist who did not care to ask questions of his condition if there were no answers (143). The complex man, on the contrary, was an idealist prone to implosion for lack of an existence worth contemplating (132–133). "In Auschwitz the intellect," lacking stimuli, "was nothing more than itself."[32]

Like his argument in *The Drowned and the Saved* about systems and individuals, Levi's case for the significance of culture comes with qualifiers, its application always subject to restrictions. Neglect these, and his message no longer applies. Levi is not saying that the prisoners who succumbed to terror did so because they had let their minds go, dying from apathy.[33] Alarmed that he might be read as adamant and arrogant on this matter, Levi often humbly refers his reader elsewhere for a fuller and finer picture of the kaleidoscope of pain that was the Holocaust. He especially recommends studying the historian Hermann Langbein, a survivor of more than one Lager (45–46, 190). In his opus on Auschwitz, an edition of which opens with an ode by Levi,[34] that veteran of the Spanish Civil War, a Communist from Austria, examines some fifty different diagnoses of the *Musselman* ("Muslim"), descriptive but derogatory slang for the prisoner, lethargic, limbs numb, staggering on the brink of death.[35] To him these documents do not suggest that a surrender of wit or will led internees, the ashen and gaunt, to expire. What ruined them was fundamentally famine and disease, spiraling physical decline, hastened by a daily regimen of hard labor and cruelty. They spent every hour of each day fantasizing about food. Eugen Kogon, who lived to tell of Buchenwald, offers a dismal glimpse of related despair there: "There were hundreds who time and again tried to ransack the garbage pails in search of edible

offal, who gathered and boiled bones. . . . There were even cases of canni-
balism." These were the acts, Hans Marsálek regrets, citing conditions at
Mauthausen, of people living erratically on scraps of turnips and potatoes,
in an acute deficit of necessary calories.[36]

The Facts of the Holocaust

In *The Drowned and the Saved*, Primo Levi finds the objective (never mind
the subjective) facts of the Holocaust so diversely intricate that, for fear of
inductive and deductive logical fallacies, he advocates against their use in
any generalization, "a trend against which I would like here to erect a
dike" (157).[37] In part it is the summa-cum-laude scientist in him speaking;
he knows that in the laboratory one gram more or less of a substance, one
degree Celsius up or down, can mean a world of change, the difference
between success and failure, understanding a problem or not. In the chapter of his autobiography linked to "Potassium," he asks us to watch what
lack of knowledge and experience—not only a shortage of instruments
and materials—can produce, the spoiling of a quiet distillation by loud
explosion. However close one thing is to another, you may lose your life
confusing or substituting them. "One must distrust the almost-the-same
. . . the practically identical, the approximate, the or-even, all surrogates,
and all patchwork. The differences can be small, but they can lead to radically different consequences, like a railroad's switch points," one track
leading, for example, through night and fog to Auschwitz-Birkenau, the
extermination camp, another to Auschwitz-Monowitz, the industrial
plant.[38]

Levi repeatedly cautioned against what can happen when we start to
guess, trusting in routine: "Theory is one thing and practice another," he
opines in *La chiave a stella* (*The Monkey's Wrench*, 1978).[39] It is the lesson
that guides a story of his appropriately titled "The Molecule's Defiance"
(1980), in which a tiny error by an otherwise diligent and scrupulous technician ends in a huge mess, with the gelatinization of tons of resin—and in
humiliation, since not only have egos taken a beating, but also a powerful
motorized reactor. The tale concerns the sudden, looming possibility of
chaos and death, even in a world ruled by educated minds and elaborate
machines; in its own way it is a parable of Nazism and the Holocaust.
Innocuously, on the surface, a fickle thermograph—so predictably erratic
that it was deemed reliable—appears to have led its monitor astray. And
from there the situation began to spiral out of control. "It was not like

beer, where the foam subsides, and rarely overflows the glass. This mass kept rising," until it ruined everything.[40] In a 1986 essay, Levi admits to having nightmares about spoiled, anarchic batches of varnish—and that at some point or other, for better or worse, such obsessive dreams of failure began to crowd out his menacing dreams of the Lager.[41]

So we must resist generalizing about Levi's grief, for as he taught his reader, each and every casualty of Auschwitz was one of a kind. This is why *The Drowned and the Saved* features Améry, also a Jew and an intellectual, to allow us to compare and contrast the experiences of individuals. The lesson is that whatever similarities may be manifest between them, no two fates are exactly alike. Fail to understand as much—the hazard of abstraction—and you risk viewing the universe in rigid, finite categories, as did the Nazis.[42] To think only of "we and they, Athenians and Spartans, Romans and Carthaginians," is an error both facile and grave, writes Levi, because it denies critical, formative "half-tints and complexities" (37). Hence his *Lilìt e altri racconti* (1978), which delights in the eccentric. Every part of it illustrates what makes a particular individual, be that person a Jew, Gypsy, German, or Pole, strange and therefore special and alluring, whether in deed basically good or bad. Its stories are partly studies of survival, how in the *Lager* a sense of humor could—like the recitation of a poem—provide a precious if fleeting break from reality. But they express humanism too. Dwelling on fiddlers and jugglers, Levi pays respect to life's bizarre surprises even in situations so terrible as to beggar the imagination.[43]

Levi's refusal to see life in terms of black and white ("as if the hunger in Auschwitz were the same as that of someone who has skipped a meal" [158]), his stubborn insistence on its flickering shades of gray, tells who he was: not only a professional in the laboratory and a writer of witness, prudent and observant, but also, while something of an atheist, Sephardim by birth and spirit. Born on July 31, 1919, he was raised to respect Judaism. Members of his immediate and extended family in Turin, though spiritually liberal, still observed religious holidays; they were only a generation or so removed from rigorous orthodox practice of their faith. As was expected of him, Levi celebrated his bar mitzvah at the age of thirteen. And yet he only became Jewish, Levi would confess, as a result of being so classified by Fascist Italy's Racial Laws of 1938, which segregated the country into arbitrary ethnic groups, one privileged, the other deprived— and forced Levi to matriculate in his city's Hebrew school, where, timid but curious, he quickly made acquaintances over discussions of everything from Fascism to the Torah. From whatever source, Levi in time came to practice a positive, cultural Jewishness. He would take interest in the state of Israel, Ashkenazi culture, and Talmudic discourse, its searching and dia-logical mode. This composite, incomplete assimilation, being hybrid, both Italian and selectively Jewish (by biology, choice, and force), was not a condition that Levi could negotiate easily. It is no wonder that he habitu-ally viewed the world as complicated, an often confounding amalgam, a palimpsest of sundry linked peoples and cultures.[44]

Although Levi's biographers disagree on several major questions about him, they do confirm that on religion he was a skeptic first, and then, not a man of faith, but something of a casual yet ever curious student, mindful and appreciative of Judaism's rich complexity and brave tenacity. He was not simply one or the other, but both. Ian Thomson tells us that Levi on occasion felt guilty, oddly conflicted, when he broke commandments, though he usually acted as if they amounted to no more than quaint, cher-ished conventions.[45] Carole Angier relates that "the sacred and solemn flight of biblical Hebrew" intrigued Levi greatly, not in isolation, but as the root of "the rough, laconic, earthy speech of Piedmont," what is known as *ebraico piemontese*.[46] And as Myriam Anissimov reports, Levi was enough of a Jew to be buried on the eve of Passover (in a coffin of walnut decorated with white irises and pink orchids), and by a rabbi, Emanuele Artom, in the old Jewish cemetery of the Corso Regio Parco—this to the sound of the communal, sonorous Kaddish, the ode to God's glory, and *El Mal'e Rachamim*, a prayer for compassion in memory of the deceased.[47]

For all its concern with difference and emphasis on doubt, *The Drowned and the Saved* is not a stock philosophical treatise that assigns history to particulars and philosophy to generalities. Levi is a proponent of measure and perspective, yet he puts no credence in chaos.[48] His own personal anthology to a general education, *La ricerca delle radici* (*The Search for Roots*, 1981), includes selections from Homer, Lucretius, Jonathan Swift, Her-man Melville, Bertrand Russell, the physicist William Bragg (mentor of Francis Crick and James Watson), and equally varied others. According to Levi—who credits his father, Cesare, an engineer, with teaching him to think of print as "a sort of fairy wand bestowing wisdom"—these authors were confident that they inhabited an intelligible and manageable cosmos, not something "infinitely, fruitlessly, tediously divisible."[49] But it may be that with age, sickness, and sorrow over a world continually torn by vio-lence, he was losing his sense of history's capricious, captivating vitality, seeing instead mostly a muddle, no possibility of synthesis and progress.[50] It has been said that what at once energizes and enervates *The Drowned and the Saved* is nothing other than a potent, naked furor.[51] This may be to exaggerate. But Levi was feeling increasingly anguished over life's absurdity, fatigued and parched by it. In a poem of January 2, 1987, he speaks forlornly of the egotistical, competitive impulse that, despite our intelligence, at once moves us forward and back, toward extinction: "Very soon we will extend the desert."[52]

The Poverty of Historicism

Primo Levi, the empiricist, writing about the deluded, harmful construct that was anti-Semitism, did not take kindly to heroic paradigms—"the grand revealed truth" (199)—that dismissed humble particulars as insignificant because allegedly inconvenient or irrelevant. Indeed, his hostility to normative, universalist assumptions about history went beyond an aversion to the Aryanism of which he was a victim; Levi would not accept sweeping assertions of any sort, whether progressive or conservative. "Right-left asymmetry is intrinsic to life," he held, musing on the shape of matter.[53] Levi was in his particularism a thinker as unconventional and nonconformist as Hannah Arendt, who refused to bear any flag, including ultimately that of the burgeoning nation of Israel, writing, "I have never in my life loved any people or collective."[54] In writing about himself, Levi shows a fondness for baffling, obdurate inconsistencies and contradictions. "Bereft not of ideals but of certainties," he feared that we may rush to judgment and miss either the whole truth or part of it, in the process creating false hierarchies, bogus groupings of strong and weak (199).

To help himself with his own testimony, for corroboration, Levi read widely in books on Nazism written for general, educated readers, if not usually in specialized scholarly monographs and journals.[55] Nonetheless, the attention to anomaly that characterizes *The Drowned and the Saved* calls to mind the philosopher Michael Polanyi's thinking on science. Born in Budapest, Polanyi, like Levi, was a Jew, a chemist, indeed a professor of chemistry, and a writer at large, writing in the course of his career on everything from crystal structures and reaction kinetics to economics and politics. And he, too, was dramatically displaced and transformed by Nazism and the Holocaust. A researcher at the Kaiser Wilhelm Institute for Chemistry in Berlin when the Nazi Party seized the Reichstag, Polanyi promptly took flight to the University of Manchester, England. In exile, he developed an ardent personal religiosity and became a variety of Christian—a blend of Catholic and Protestant.[56] And there Polanyi crafted theses against the tenets of mechanical, positivist science, arguing that all

knowledge is at its core personal and peculiar, affected by experience—
"For we live in it as in the garment of our own skin."[57] Liberal and inventive but neither a secularist nor a deductivist, he considered learning to be
the result not only of detached or objective study (insofar as such empiricism was genuinely feasible), but also of guesses and hunches—of evident
creativity and obscure intuition, not to mention the fruit of customary
apprenticeship and international cooperation on one hand, chance on the
other.[58] To Polanyi, hypotheses based on quantifiable sense data were necessary and valuable. But it was his contention that they regularly functioned as restraints on the imagination.[59] Levi was not a mystic like
Polanyi, whose work was translated into Italian, but they would likely have
agreed on the complexity of knowing and being.

The loathing of reductionism in *The Drowned and the Saved* also evokes
Karl Popper's polemic on "the poverty of historicism," in which, defend-
ing free will, this philosopher attacked deterministic history. "The belief
in historical destiny," Popper declared, "is sheer superstition."[60] With the
fervor of a missionary, he swore (again, in translation, maybe to Levi's
knowledge) that historicism could not meet the test of falsifiability or veri-
fication. Born Jewish in Vienna but raised Lutheran and on account of
Nazism an émigré to Christchurch, New Zealand, in 1937, Popper
believed that the historian's business is strictly the study of actual, specific
events and their causes—not prediction, or looking for immanent constan-
cies and fatalistic patterns.[61] Doctrines tend to beget fatalities, he held, and
the more absolute the doctrine, the less moderate the follower. His critique of the utopian social engineering that had fueled both revolutionary
Marxism and corporate Fascism was tinted by a sense of loss, carrying this
dedication:

> In memory of the countless men and women
> of all creeds or nations or races
> who fell victims to the fascist and communist belief in / Inexorable Laws of
>   Historical Destiny.[62]

Whether aware of this address or not, Levi, though not a zealot like
Popper, would surely have appreciated its censure of awful cruelties committed in the name of illusory commandments.

Although Polanyi and Popper disagreed on how science happens, they
shared faith in its value and trust in progress. Both of them also believed
strongly in the virtue of classical, Western liberalism.[63] Neither of them
expressed any sympathy for Walter Benjamin's kind of incredulous thinking, the angst of which sprang from the realization that no transcendent

truth—religious, secular, or scientific—orders experience. Nor did they therefore show enthusiasm for the kindred, doleful concerns and problems that trouble Levi, whose *The Drowned and the Saved* tenders no absolution or redemption, champions only skepticism and tolerance—taking liberty and pleasure for a kind of miracle, given our penchant for brutality.

CHAPTER 4

Kenosis, Saturated Phenomenology, and Bearing Witness

Marie L. Baird

Any appreciative reading of Primo Levi's *The Reawakening* is experienced, at least in part, as an avid cheering on of Levi and his assorted companions as they wend their way homeward to Italy (via Russia) in a circuitous meandering that is somewhat reminiscent of a picaresque adventure. Indeed, to read of his safe arrival in Turin fills one with a special satisfaction born of the sense that justice is sometimes permitted to prevail against even the worst of odds. But *The Reawakening* does not end there, as is well known. It ends with a dream, or rather "a dream within a dream,[1] in which Levi, caught in the cruelest of reversals, discovers that his putative recovery of a beloved home, family, and friends is itself the dream, and that the only reality is Auschwitz: "nothing is true outside the Lager" (207). It is perhaps the relentlessness of this haunting that may have first forced Levi to pick up the pen and recount the tale of his survival. I believe we can say with relative confidence that Auschwitz created Levi the "writer-witness" (230). He writes: "if I had not lived the Auschwitz experience, I probably would never have written anything" (230). In this sense, Auschwitz can be said to have literally given Levi to himself as a writer.

It is this realization that provides a direct link between Levi's Auschwitz-bestowed vocation as a writer and the thought of French phenomenologist Jean-Luc Marion. Such is the case because Marion's philosophical analyses of "saturated phenomenality" delineate the process whereby an overwhelming historical event such as Auschwitz can indeed be understood as having positioned Levi as a writer, a vocation to which he had not previously aspired.[2] Provisionally, Marion characterizes certain phenomena, including some historical events, as "saturated" "in that [conceptual] constitution encounters there an intuitive givenness that cannot be granted a univocal sense in return. It must be allowed, then, to overflow with many meanings, or an infinity of meanings, each equally legitimate and rigorous, without managing either to unify them or to organize them."[3] The contention here is that the searing unmanageability of what Levi had experienced overwhelmed his attempts at rational mastery and control, thereby casting him into the hitherto unanticipated vocation of "writer-witness" as a way of coping with the psychological and emotional aftereffects of his ordeal. Although one might argue that psychological analyses of trauma provide an adequate key to understanding this kind of experience, I contend that such analyses are less able to account adequately for the creative blossoming forth of Levi's literary oeuvre after his homecoming. One is left with the question of *how* it is that experiences of trauma are able to form the basis for a successful literary career. Marion's analyses of saturated phenomenality, on the other hand, can offer an explanation of Levi's authorial vocation *if* such a vocation can be shown to have emerged, seamlessly, from Levi's experience of incarceration—as he held to be the case. In this essay, I will attempt to demonstrate that such an explanation is possible from a philosophical perspective.

I also contend that Levi's status as a "writer-witness" is relatively resistant to a more traditional metaphysical analysis of writer as transcendental subject because such an undertaking is unable to explain as adequately as Marion's analyses of saturated phenomenality do Levi's seemingly obsessive need to write about his ordeal upon his return to safety—a need that literally took hold of him at the time of his arrival back in Italy and that held on throughout the rest of his life.

More specifically, invoking Marion's delineation of the saturated phenomenon, I will argue that what we might call the "self" of the Lager casts Levi into the position of a more or less pure recipient of what Marion would call the "self" of the Lager's phenomenality as a historically overwhelming event. Such positioning relativizes Levi's pre-Lager capacities as an autonomous, self-constituting agent as typically understood by modern philosophies, especially those with a traditional metaphysical foundation. It is in this sense that I characterize Levi's ordeal as a form of *kenosis*, or self-emptying, in order to accept the position of witness-recipient even as his acute powers of observation and memory are heightened exponentially. From a phenomenological perspective, any claim to transcendental subjectivity is relinquished in favor of a now historically empirical "me": in this case, Levi the prisoner, intent on observing, remembering, and ultimately, writing. Marion theorizes that a saturated phenomenon, given the fact of its ability to "saturate" intuition and thereby overwhelm it—even as the conceptualizing capacities of intentional consciousness remain in place, although relativized—asserts its own "selfhood" and simultaneously repositions its witness as a pure recipient of the phenomenon in question, rather than as its actively constituting agent.[4] In this sense, Auschwitz literally gives itself to Levi and in turn, gives Levi to himself as a writer.

Thus invoking Marion's analyses of saturated phenomenality, with evidence provided by Levi's writings, I will first characterize Auschwitz as a historical event that meets all of Marion's criteria for "saturated phenomenality": unforeseeability, unbearability, absoluteness, and increasing complexity of form and function in its reception, analysis, and consequences (anamorphosis).[5] Understood in this way, Auschwitz indeed functions as the sole reality of Levi's dream, for again "nothing is true outside the Lager."

For the rest, my essay will analyze the means by which Auschwitz can be said to have given Levi to himself as a writer, as provisionally described earlier. It will probe the contours of Levi the writer-witness whose "reawakening" consists, in an important sense, of taking on the vocation of communicating the "truth" of Auschwitz that he has been given. Again, as will become evident, receiving the "truth" of Auschwitz goes hand in hand with receiving the self as its observer and amanuensis—initially, the former prisoner with quasi-secretarial duties who, prompted by "those memories [that] burned so intensely inside me that I felt compelled to write as soon as I returned to Italy" (209) inscribes the "truth" as dictated by the "self" of Auschwitz as a saturated phenomenon.[6] Levi writes in the same vein: "It seemed as if those books were all there, ready in my head, and I had only to let them come out and pour onto paper" (230). Given the anamorphic nature of Auschwitz as a saturated phenomenon, the increasing complexity of its "truth" with the passage of time will transform the amanuensis into the writer-witness whose work will transcend the boundaries of the "truth" of Auschwitz he felt initially called to articulate. His oeuvre will become correspondingly multifaceted, flowering forth into fiction and poetry. And yet it will remain inspired, or so I will hope to have demonstrated, by the dream of the sole reality of Auschwitz, the saturated phenomenon whose "truth"[7] will have given Levi to himself as a writer-witness. This newly discovered vocation will thus help to initiate Levi's "reawakening" to life that the cruelest of reversals had sought to obliterate, the one that had reduced the world to "a grey and turbid nothing" (207) and had subjugated his existence to the "feared and expected" "dawn command of Auschwitz" (208).

The Event of Auschwitz as a Saturated Phenomenon

It is a fair assessment to state that "saturated phenomenality" is a centrally important concept in the thought of Jean-Luc Marion. As previously noted, a phenomenon that is rightly termed "saturated," for Marion, is one that overwhelms the conceptualizing capacities of the individual who experiences it; unlike trauma, however, a saturated phenomenon thus opens up myriad potentially positive, as well as negative, meanings that may be assigned to it.[8] This capacity to overwhelm conceptualizing consciousness requires, however, that the human capacity to intuit, rather than to merely conceptualize, what Marion calls the "givenness" of a saturated phenomenon must be in the ascendancy, otherwise the phenomenon in question would remain the "great blooming, buzzing confusion"[9] famously coined by William James. This last point is important, for it heralds the primacy of "givenness" over "manifestation" in Marion's thought.[10] Specifically, the degree of manifestation that a phenomenon exhibits is directly contingent on the degree to which it "gives" itself or *makes itself available to be rendered manifest or apparent to consciousness.*[11] From this perspective, we do not constitute saturated phenomena conceptually; rather they make themselves apparent (give themselves) to our intuition, prior to conceptualization. What renders a phenomenon "saturated" is that it "gives" itself (and thus shows itself) to intuition in a degree that overwhelms the conceptualizing capacities of representational consciousness, thus releasing a bounteous potentiality of meanings that may be assigned to it.[12] Auschwitz functions as such a phenomenon, and Levi's writing bears witness to that fact.

Marion ascribes saturated status to historical events because they saturate the Kantian category of quantity by undoing it first of all, given their impermeability to any sweeping, exhaustive, or definitive categorization.[13] Such events cannot be quantified because they are more than the sum of their parts in a way that cannot be foreseen in advance.[14] They lie resolutely outside of conceptual mastery, in other words; they defeat such mastery by overwhelming it with significatory possibility. They exhibit a "teleology without end" that invites an indeed endless generation of knowledge and commentary about them, producing a "historical community" that itself generates a further history—the history of the original event's reception and analysis of which Levi's work forms a part.[15] Most notably, however, historical events such as Auschwitz give *themselves* and render *themselves* manifest from a phenomenological perspective; they are not constituted by the conceptualizing consciousness of a transcendental ego. Those swept up in their maelstrom are, at best, their witness-recipients.

Marion delineates four criteria that saturated phenomena must meet in order to be designated as such: unforeseeability, unbearability, absoluteness, and anamorphic quality. The historical event of Auschwitz fulfills the criterion of unforeseeability as commonly understood not only because the technologization and bureaucratization of genocide was accomplished on a scale never before seen or anticipated, but also because its very occurrence is not exhaustively explained by the causes advanced to do so. Marion notes that the "partial causes" of historical events "are only discovered once the fact of their effect has been accomplished."[16] I would suggest that such discovery is still ongoing in relation to Auschwitz.[17] To the extent that such is the case, as yet unidentified causes could help to produce other events that could be currently unforeseen precisely because these causes have yet to be understood as such.

The unforeseeability of saturated phenomena also arises from the intuition's inability to master or control the quantity of parts that the phenomenon in question gives to be rendered manifest because saturation nullifies any controlling conceptual parameter that would allow for such mastery.[18] The experiential result is amazement: "Every phenomenon that produces amazement is imposed on the gaze in the very measure (more exactly, in the excess of measure) to which it does not result from any foreseeable summation of partial quantities."[19] Or, as Levi recounts in *Survival in Auschwitz* upon his arrival there:

> two groups of strange individuals emerged into the light of the lamps. They walked in squads, in rows of three, with an odd, embarrassed step, head dangling in front, arms rigid. On their heads they wore comic berets and were all dressed in long striped overcoats, which even by night and from a distance looked filthy and in rags. They walked in a large circle around us, never drawing near, and in silence began to busy themselves with our luggage and to climb in and out of the empty wagons.

> We looked at each other without a word. *It was all incomprehensible and mad*, but one thing we had understood. This was the metamorphosis that awaited us. Tomorrow we would be like them.[20]

The unbearability of Auschwitz as a historical event is commonly understood in its intolerability,[21] which can be demonstrated on any number of levels and perspectives: from the truly appalling conditions prisoners were forced to endure—Levi writes of "total humiliation and demoralization which led so many to spiritual shipwreck" (231)—to the murderous abdication of even the slightest degree of ethical responsibility by its administrators and guards. One can extend the range of intolerability surrounding Auschwitz exponentially by chronicling all the known circumstances that led to the political rise of Hitler in the first instance. In this sense, the unbearability of Auschwitz is perhaps the most immediately self-evident criterion that satisfies Marion's requirements for the status of saturated phenomenality.

Marion, however, understands unbearability in terms of the intensity with which an intuition "saturating a phenomenon attains an intensive magnitude without measure, or common measure, such that . . . the intensity of the real intuition passes beyond all the conceptual anticipations of perception."[22] The eyewitness accounts of camp liberators are also appropriate in this context: "The things I saw beggar description . . . the visual evidence and the verbal testimony of starvation, cruelty and bestiality were . . . overpowering."[23] Or, as Levi notes in describing the first liberators he encountered:

> They did not greet us, nor did they smile; they seemed oppressed not only by compassion but by a confused restraint which sealed their lips and bound their eyes to the funereal scene. It was that shame we knew so well, the shame that drowned us after the selections, and every time we had to watch, or submit to, some outrage: the shame the Germans did not know, that the just man experiences at another man's crime; the feeling of guilt that such a crime should exist, that it should have been introduced irrevocably into the world of things that exist, and that his will for good should have proved too weak or null, and should not have availed in defense. (16)

In such accounts, the unbearability of that which is seen saturates the gaze of the eyewitness to the point of unsustainability and conceptual paralysis. Marion regards the result of such unbearability to be the gaze's "bedazzlement,"[24] that is, the flooding and simultaneous undoing of the

Kantian category of quality, or degree of intensity with which a phenomenon gives itself to intuition.[25] In this context, Auschwitz can literally not be borne.[26] With the testimony that Levi provides us, I propose understanding unbearability in a register more attuned to his account: as a saturation of quality that does not bedazzle so much as it *shames* in the face of intuition's confrontation with absolute moral depravity.[27]

Marion defines the absoluteness of saturated phenomena as being "outside all relation and all analogy (even that of causality)."[28] An event such as Auschwitz qualifies for him as the saturation—which in this context once again means the undoing—of the Kantian category of relation because it breaks with the "unity of experience" by means of its aforementioned unforeseeability, its unavailability to exhaustive comprehension or reproduction, and its "purity" as an occurrence that is "absolute," "unique," and thus without analogy on the experiential level.[29] More prosaically, this means that Auschwitz as saturated phenomenality is absolute and without relation to any other phenomenon. An event such as Auschwitz is indeed absolute and therefore without analogy because it has abdicated or undone the very phenomenality of relation, which is the bedrock of lived experience. Not only is Auschwitz as saturated historical event without analogy, but the experience of incarceration there also assaults the capacity for relation-building that is vital to normal human commerce. Terrence Des Pres cites the testimony of Auschwitz survivor Dr. Ella Lingens-Reiner, who offered the following observation about one of her medical colleagues:

> Ena Weiss, our Chief Doctor—one of the most intelligent, gifted and eminent Jewish women in the camp—once defined her attitude thus, in sarcastic rejection of fulsome flattery and at the same time with brutal frankness: "How did I keep alive in Auschwitz? My principle is: myself first, second and third. Then nothing. Then myself again—and then all the others." This formula expressed the only principle which was possible for Jews who intended—almost insanely intended—to survive Auschwitz.[30]

Or, as Levi asserts, "in the Lager things are different: here the struggle to survive is without respite, because everyone is desperately and ferociously alone."[31] The ultimate outcome of the utter abdication of relation to which Lingens-Reiner and Levi bear witness is the *Muselmann* (literally, Muslim), "an emaciated man, with head dropped and shoulders curved, on whose face and in whose eyes not a trace of a thought is to be seen."[32] For an individual who has arrived at this penultimate state of life in extremity, the destruction of relationality takes place from two perspectives, that of the prisoner him or herself, and that of his or her fellow inmates:

> Whoever has not himself been a *Muselmann* for a while cannot imagine the depth of the transformations that men underwent. You became so indifferent to your fate that you no longer wanted anything from anyone. You just waited in peace for death. They no longer had either the strength or the will to fight for daily survival. Today was enough; you were content with what you could find in the trash. . . .
>
> What's worse than a *Muselmann*?
>
> Does he even have the right to live?
>
> Isn't he there to be stepped on, struck, beaten?
>
> He wanders through the camp like a stray dog.
>
> Everyone chases him away, but the crematorium is his deliverance.
>
> The camp infirmary does away with him![33]

Here, it is the utter abdication of even the capacity for relation that places the *Muselmann* "outside all relation," as mentioned before, and hence establishes the *Muselmann's* phenomenality also as saturated, as those who are "submerged," the "complete witnesses," those who have "seen the Gorgon."[34] And given the conditions of extremity that produced them, what experience could ever approach it analogically except that which is suffered under the same conditions of extremity? As Giorgio Agamben asserts, "The sight of *Muselmanner* is an absolutely new phenomenon, unbearable to human eyes."[35] The *Muselmann* is the penultimate outcome of the saturated phenomenality of Auschwitz, second only to the victim of the gas chamber or phenol injection to the heart.

Marion argues that saturated phenomena "exceed their horizon,"[36] meaning the phenomenological context within which they give themselves; an event such as Auschwitz becomes endlessly available to an "infinite hermeneutic"[37] in which Levi's work participates. It follows that the final saturation the historical event accomplishes—the undoing of the Kantian category of modality—finalizes its anamorphic character as "irreducible to the I"[38] because it cannot be constituted as an object by a transcendental ego who would control every aspect of its appearing under the auspices of said ego's conceptual parameters.[39] Again, somewhat more prosaically, Auschwitz exceeds our ability to conceptualize it and hence to gain representational mastery over it. Such being the case, it becomes available to a veritable cornucopia of interpretive strategies—the "infinite hermeneutic" to which Marion refers and in which at least part of Levi's literary oeuvre participates. A brief contemplation of the sheer vastness of Holocaust writings—both scholarly and otherwise—demonstrates the truth of Marion's claim.

We recall once again Levi's dream in which Auschwitz functions as the sole reality, for "nothing is true outside the Lager." Given the characteristics of unforeseeability, unbearability, absoluteness, and anamorphosis that define saturated phenomena as such, we arrive at Marion's concluding evaluation: "The saturated phenomenon in the end *establishes the truth of all phenomenality* because it marks, more than any other phenomenon, the givenness from which it comes."[40] If Marion's conclusion is warranted on phenomenological grounds,[41] then Levi's assertion that "nothing is true outside the Lager" becomes a witnessing to Auschwitz's function as a phenomenon whose saturating degree of givenness commands the intuition's recognition of it as "true." Auschwitz "gives" itself as saturated phenomenality because it undoes our capacity to foresee it in advance even as it overwhelms, and thus undoes, our capacity to bear it. It gives itself as an absolute event without analogy, and it destroys the capacity for human relationality; the *Muselmann* is the very symbol of the abdication of relation. Auschwitz gives itself by forever eluding, finally, the mastery which our conceptual parameters would exert in an attempt to control it by conferring upon it—*ex cathedra*—a final, exhaustive, signification. If "nothing is true outside the Lager," then this is the brutal face of truth that gave itself to Levi, and still gives itself to all of humanity.

From Witness-Recipient to Writer-Witness

We have already seen that Marion's thought situates givenness as the prerequisite for the degree to which any phenomenon will render itself manifest. Givenness indicates a phenomenal self-giving, rather than the phenomenon's constitution by a transcendental ego according to the conceptual categories of representational consciousness. The phenomenon literally "gives itself" for Marion and in so doing dethrones the "I" from its transcendental status as constituting agent.[42] The phenomenon is now in control, to put it more prosaically, thus repositioning the "I" as the "receiver" of the phenomenon's self-giving gesture: "The 'self' of the phenomenon . . . transforms the I into a witness."[43] The transcendental, nominative "I" has been transformed into the dative "me" who undergoes, in Levi's case as victim, the pure experience of that which gives itself relentlessly. We see here further confirmation that Levi's statement "nothing is true outside the Lager" functions as a witnessing to Auschwitz as a saturated phenomenon. Such being the case, it follows that Auschwitz indeed gives Levi to himself as the witness to its phenomenality as an event: "It was the experience of the Camp and the long journey home that *forced* me to write" (230, emphasis added).

Since Marion's thought thus invites us to discard the traditional metaphysical notion of a free, autonomous subject who constitutes both the fact and meaning of an event on the basis of the conceptual categories of representational consciousness, we can designate this "dethroning" of the transcendental "I" as an instance of *kenosis*, or self-emptying.[44] It is in this sense that I propose understanding Levi's strong desire to take up his pen upon his safe arrival home in Turin. It is no longer a question of Levi deciding freely and autonomously to record his experiences of incarceration; it is rather the recognition that the degree of givenness the experience of Auschwitz thrust upon him also consigned him to take up actively the position of witness that he had already received as a prisoner: "onto my brief and tragic experience as a deportee has been overlaid that much longer and complex experience of writer-witness" (230). The complexity that he alludes to is not entirely reducible to trauma undergone; it includes the forcefulness and relentlessness with which Auschwitz as saturated phenomenality gave itself to Levi as its witness-recipient and in turn, gave Levi to himself as its writer-witness.[45]

It is important to point out that the shift from transcendental "I" to historically empirical "me" as occasioned by exposure to the saturated phenomenon of Auschwitz as event does not strip Levi of what Marion calls the "privileges of subjectivity,"[46] keeping intact those qualities that would make Levi one of the twentieth century's greatest writers. Indeed, Levi as writer-witness is precisely the one called upon by the saturated phenomenon of Auschwitz to render its givenness—its "truth"—visible to all. This task forms the basis for Levi's vocation as a writer and his dream as recorded at the end of *The Reawakening* may be an indirect recognition of this task for, yet again, "nothing is true outside the Lager."

Upon his return to Italy and his resumption of a "normal" life, the trajectory of Levi's professional career was increasingly forced to accommodate this vocation of writing to which Auschwitz had called him; he finally gave himself over to the practice of writing altogether. That the givenness of Auschwitz as a saturated phenomenon continued to remain with him is evident in the following assertion:

> Well, it has been observed by psychologists that the survivors of traumatic events are divided into two well-defined groups: those who repress their

past *en bloc*, and those whose memory of the offense persists, as though carved in stone, prevailing over all previous or subsequent experiences. Now, not by choice but by nature I belong to the second group. Of my two years of life outside the law I have not forgotten a single thing. Without any deliberate effort, memory continues to restore to me events, faces, words, sensations, *as if at that time my mind had gone through a period of exalted receptivity*, during which not a detail was lost.[47]

The writer-witness of Auschwitz, whose oeuvre begins as "the dolorous itinerary of a convalescent," subsequently becomes "the veteran who tells his story," and who discovers in the telling, "a complex, intense, and new pleasure, similar to that I felt when penetrating the solemn order of differential calculus."[48] Surely this observation suggests an experiential outcome of his "two years of life outside the law" that is not solely attributable to trauma. And as we have already seen, the "infinity of meanings" that saturated phenomena are capable of giving are not limited to traumatic ones and can therefore not exclude positive outcomes. Most tellingly, perhaps, is Levi's observation that "paradoxically, my baggage of atrocious memories became a wealth, a seed; it seemed to me that, by writing, I was growing like a plant."[49] Correspondingly, his oeuvre flowered forth into fiction and poetry, appearing in print as recently as the February 12, 2007, issue of *The New Yorker*.[50] Yet since his "memory of the offense persists, as though carved in stone, prevailing over all previous or subsequent experiences," he returned repeatedly as a writer to these "two years outside the law." His final work, *The Drowned and The Saved*, is an extended meditation on his ordeal and its long-term aftereffects. Without wishing to enter into the debate surrounding the reasons for Levi's apparent suicide, I think it is fair to assert that the experience and subsequent memory of Auschwitz as a saturated phenomenon, having given Levi to himself as its writer-witness, continued to exert a decisive influence on him to the end, "prevailing over all previous or subsequent experiences."

CHAPTER 5

After Auschwitz: What Is a Good Death?

Timothy Pytell

Suicide brings on many changes. A life ends abruptly and the suicide is interpreted differently depending on circumstances and opinion. Sometimes it is seen as profoundly irrational, absurd and tragic, other times, as a heroic last act of an individual taking action to determine their fate. Often we aestheticize another's suicide with heroism or capitulations. But no matter how we view suicide, a person's death necessarily becomes the capstone that "backshadows" the entire existence of the deceased.

It comes as no surprise that suicide among Holocaust survivors is high. A few of the most recognizable figures are Bruno Bettelheim, Paul Célan, Jerzy Kosinski, Jean Améry, Tadeusz Borowski, and apparently Primo Levi. Since so many survivors choose suicide, it is almost considered a truism that their camp experience led them to make the choice. However, a closer look at the "deaths" of Primo Levi and Jean Améry unveils a great deal of ambiguity.[1]

Although a consensus seems to have emerged that Levi committed suicide, the uncertainty surrounding his death has left the issue open to doubt. For example, Diego Gambetta has investigated Levi's death and provides us with a very clear picture of Levi's "Last Moments":

Sometime after 10:00 a.m., Saturday, April 11, 1987, on the third floor of a late-nineteenth-century building in Turin, the concierge rang the

doorbell of Primo Levi's apartment. Levi . . . opened the door and collected
his mail from the concierge like every other day. He was wearing a short-
sleeve shirt. He smiled, thanked her as usual, and closed the door. The
concierge descended on foot the ample spiral staircase occupied in the
middle by a caged elevator. She had barely reached her cubicle on the
ground floor . . . when she heard Levi's body hit the bottom of the stairs
by the elevator. . . . The autopsy established that he died instantaneously
of a "crushed skull." No signs of violence unrelated to the fall were found
on his body. At 12:00, barely an hour and a half after the event, I heard the
news on the radio in Rome. There was already mention of suicide. The
police inquiry simply confirmed that conclusion.[2]

We are left with a number of questions. Why would a chemical engineer commit suicide by jumping down a narrow stairwell? Why was there
no suicide note? Why was there no will? Was jumping just a spur-of-the-
moment decision (similar to what some have argued about the existentialist philosopher Albert Camus's death in a car crash)? Or did he just
become dizzy? After all, he had recently undergone a prostate operation
and was on antidepressants. Gambetta concludes that the "facts known to
us arguably suggest an accident more strongly than they indicate a suicide." In contrast, all biographers of Levi, Myriam Anissimov, Carol
Angier, and Ian Thomson believe it was a suicide, along with almost all of
Levi's relatives and friends. The one notable exception is David Mendel,
a British cardiologist who befriended Levi late in life.

On some level therefore, the jury is still out on Levi's "suicide." The
ambiguity and subsequent anxiety remains troubling. As Gambetta
describes, the admirers of Levi are left in a state of unease. Did the humanist Levi, who somehow had managed to reaffirm life and hope in the
human condition even after Auschwitz, give up? Did Auschwitz reclaim
him somehow? Did his suicide destroy the humanistic values his survival
and writings testified to? Jonathan Druker provided one response to this
unease. Druker thinks the death was likely accidental and therefore argues
against the "defeatist" version of Levi's death. He also asserts that there is
a "danger of reading suicide into the works of Levi" because we cannot
even know if it was suicide, much less the role of Auschwitz in his death.
Key to Druker's concern is the fear that if we view the death as suicide,
Levi's writings all become interpreted through his survival of Auschwitz,
and therefore, "reading suicide into Levi's texts with undue insistence
tends to reduce their possible range of meanings."[3]

It appears then, that the act and significance of Levi's "suicide" will
remain ambiguous. In trying to solve the riddle numerous commentators

have focused on Levi's reflections in his final work *The Drowned and Saved* on the suicide of the Auschwitz survivor Jean Améry. In his analysis of Levi's reflections on Améry, Druker concludes by calling for a "distinction between what the two writers experienced in Auschwitz and what their agendas were after the fact."[4] This strikes me as a central issue, and this essay intends to fulfill this calling by comparing Améry and Levi's biographical experience in combination with an exploration of the relationship between their attitudes on Nazis, concentration camps, survival, and finally their opinions of each other. The overarching goal is to glean some insight into how their "deaths" shape their "lives."

Thanks to Irene Heidelberger-Leonard's biography *Jean Améry: Revolte in der Resignation*, we have a detailed understanding of Améry's life and his last moments. We also know from Amery's last scholarly work, *Hand Sich Legen*, translated as *On Suicide: A Discourse on Voluntary Death*, that he viewed suicide not as a sign of a social or individual sickness, but rather as a "privilege of being human." Given this thesis, it should come as no surprise that Améry committed suicide at the age of sixty-six on October 17, 1978. However, in a 1976 interview (published in *Der Spiegel* a few weeks after his death), Améry remarked that he came to his notion of a "free death" as a child, and the idea remained with him. In the same interview he also confided that his first attempt at suicide occurred when he was in solitary confinement after being tortured by the SS at Breendonck. He described how he tried to slit his wrists with a piece of a rusty bucket—but "failed miserably." As he remarked, under the conditions of solitary confinement and without communication with his wife, his resistance weakened, but afterward in the concentration camps, he felt a renewed obligation to stay alive against the assault of the camps because his "death should be his own thing."[5]

In February 1974, when he was suffering from a heart condition, Améry first seriously attempted suicide by sleeping pills. After spending thirty days in a coma, he survived.[6] After having failed at an attempted suicide and having long been interested in suicide, it makes sense that Améry would make his one of his last intellectual efforts a phenomenology of the suicidal. In *On Suicide*, Améry attempted to describe those who take their own lives from the standpoint of their own world in order to rescue the suicidal from being "the last of the great outsiders."[7] Following through on this vision, Améry successfully committed suicide at the famous Oesterreichischen Haus in Salzburg on October 17, 1978. At the time of his decision, Améry was in the midst of a marathon book tour throughout Germany promoting his novel *Charles Bovary, Landartz*, when he suddenly broke it off and went to the area of his birth. He killed himself on the opening day of the Frankfurt Book Fair, at which he was scheduled to appear.[8] It is not exactly clear why Améry choose Salzburg. W. G. Sebald remarked that Améry felt no affinity for Austria because the Anschluss, which had forced him into exile, had also taken his Austrian identity from him.[9] Heidelberger-Leonard suggested he chose Salzburg nostalgically because in 1976 he wrote a wistful note to an old friend that in his old age he must return to his homeland stating: "I belong in our Huegelland."[10] On the other hand, many commentators—as we shall see, Levi included— believed that Améry's suicide was a fulfillment of his concept of resent- ment, which rejected any notions of forgiveness for Nazi crimes. He defended his attitude of resentment "in order that the crime of the Nazi becomes a moral reality for the criminal, so that he is swept into the truth of his atrocity."[11] According to Améry, "resentment nails every one of us firmly to the cross of his destroyed past."[12] In this view, it seems that his suicide, along with the choice of Salzburg (which is widely known as the birthplace of *Sound of Music* and subsequently an icon of the postwar myth that Austrians were victims of the Nazis), stemmed from Améry's position of resentment toward his former homeland. However appealing this inter- pretation is on the surface, a close look at Améry's death reveals a great deal of complexity.

Heidelberger-Leonard's portrayal of Améry's suicide begins by describing how depressed he was on Christmas Eve in 1977. He wrote to a friend that he was miserable and had dire concern about the year 1978. He was especially anxious about his fall book tour, where, despite the acclamations and honors, he would have to play the role of the "Auschwitz Clown."[13] Given that his apprehension was occurring months in advance of the actual tour, his choice to abandon it and commit suicide was a deci- sion that clearly had been brewing for a while. In contrast to the scribbled almost illegible suicide note left in his 1974 attempt, the handwriting in a series of farewell letters in 1978 is quite clear and articulates his feelings and sympathies beautifully. He first apologizes to the hotel staff for the trouble, and he explains to the police, "I freely, willingly and in full posses- sion of my mental capacities choose to kill myself."[14] He also informs the police how to contact his wife and leaves a considerable sum of money on the table to pay for his expenses.

He also writes to his editor Hubert Arbogast and his publisher Michael Klett: "Forgive me the inconveniences that I have caused you. Also, Michael Klett, please forgive me, I was a bad investment. . . . However, above all, my cher ami, thanks for so much. I am sad that I cannot change things. I kept myself upright, as long as my energies were enough. Now they shrink, and I must go."[15]

Finally, there was a very moving letter to his wife:

My loved Herzilili, all-loved . . . I am on the way to the free. It is not easy, but nevertheless a release. Think if you can, not with ill will and not too painfully. You know everything that I have to say to you: that I loved you infinitely and that you are the last picture, which stands before my eyes. Schau, my heart's favorite, psychologically I am at the end of my energies and cannot watch my intellectual, physical, decline. . . .

I lived—with the exception of the years of despicableness—upright and want to die upright. My whole concern is you. A tiny comfort for me is that you—on a modest basis—are halfway secured. I am, like poor Charles,[16] "*grundschlect*"; when I think about it I feel miserable. But you always understood me, and so I have hope in this last evening of my life that you will understand also this last position. Please, please, don't grieve for I am now, as you might suspect, with a glow of a soul at peace.[17]

A comparison of the deaths of these two Auschwitz survivors confronts us with a number of troubling issues. Améry's suicide was clearly chosen and planned, almost celebratory, while Levi's remains ambiguous. The question becomes this: How do their deaths shape our understanding of their lives, and what is the role of their survival of Auschwitz in their deaths? Before turning to a comparison of their reflections on the camps and intellectual positions, we first need to describe the key biographical details of their life experiences.

Both Levi and Améry were assimilated Jews and they shared of experience of having a Jewish identity forced upon them by the Nazis. Jean Améry was born Hans Maier in Vienna on October 31, 1912. He was raised in Hohenems, Vorarlberg, one of the alpine provinces of western Austria. Although Améry's great-grandfather was fluent in Hebrew, his father was fully assimilated, while his mother was Roman Catholic. In addition, his father, a Tyrolean imperial rifleman, was killed in the second year of World War I, and therefore Améry never knew him. In these circumstances Améry emerges as something different than a fully assimilated Jew. Although he was fully aware of his origins, he apparently never conceived of himself in any way as Jewish. Or, as he stated bluntly in his essay *Being a Jew: A Personal Account*, "How can I speak of *my Judaism?* It did not exist."[18] However, his family moved from the provinces to Vienna when he was a teenager, and his sense of self underwent a radical transformation. Confronted for the first time with anti-Semitism and the threat of Nazism, Améry recalled, "It was becoming clear to me that in their minds and hearts these people had made all the preparations for plunging me and my kind into ruin."[19] Under these circumstances, he gradually and somewhat begrudgingly began to see himself as a Jew.

Two experiences were central for his assumption of a Jewish identity. The first decisive event was the promulgation of the Nuremberg Laws in 1935. He quickly memorized the laws and accepted "the sentence" that society had "decreed" that he was a Jew. The second was falling in love. He met the pretty, fair-skinned, redheaded and freckled Regine Berger in the summer of 1932, when she was eighteen. Améry described her as someone "who would have cut the best figure as a model for the tourism offices in the *Ostmark*."[20] Much to his surprise and his mother's consternation, Regine "was a full-blooded, professing Jew." However, Améry decided not to "give up the fair-skinned girl, but ignored her background" because he "was not ready to take a Jewish identity upon himself."[21] Heidelberger-Leonard suggests that Améry's development of a "Jewish racial identity" was "accelerated" by his decision to marry Regine Berger on December 12, 1937.[22] We also know Améry had the option to opt out of his Jewish identity after the Anschluss in 1938 because his mother's fiancé was a "flawlessly Aryan gentleman" who was ready to swear that Hans was his child. But this would have required parting ways with his wife. Améry admits that he might have chosen this route if he had "been less passionately attached" to his wife, but in the end concludes, "I vaguely felt nonetheless that a human being cannot exist within a total lie, one that encompasses his entire person, his entire of life. I constituted myself as a Jew."[23]

Améry's biography and story of survival is difficult to reconstruct because, unlike Levi, he never published a detailed account. In addition, his autobiographical work has a phenomenological orientation that focuses on states of consciousness rather than factual events. In Améry's words, he was not "concerned with stories about myself but rather with reflections on existence and the passage of time that would begin introspectively but ascend to ever more abstract and general areas of thought."[24] Thankfully, Heidelberger-Leonard has clarified much of the details of his biography by her careful research along with access to an unpublished text, *Zur Psychologie des deutschen Volkes* that Améry wrote in June of 1945—just three months after his release from the concentration camp.[25] We know that as a youth Améry aspired to be a writer and had already published a manuscript at the age of sixteen in Vienna. Heidel-berger-Leonard also clears up the confusion over Améry's intellectual training. Despite the widely held assumption that Améry studied at the University of Vienna and was connected with the Vienna Circle, it appears that he had no formal schooling after the gymnasium.[26] During the 1930s in Vienna, Améry worked at various odd jobs, including porter, messenger, and bar pianist. His most important job was as a clerk in a bookstore, and his self-education took place there. The bookshop was located at Zirkusgasse 48 and was directed by Améry's mentor Leopold Langhammer, a staunch socialist. Because of his politics, the Nazis imprisoned Langhammer in Buchenwald immediately after the Anschluss in 1938. This experience "legitimized" Langhammer, and in 1945 he became Vienna's director of education. In this position, Langhammer concocted an "official" education for Améry as a lecturer (Referenten, Dozenten und Vortragenden). Langhammer was apparently willing to invent an official education for Améry because at the time Améry was contemplating a return to Vienna. When Améry declined to do so, Langhammer then provided him with a strong letter of recommendation written in December 1946 that claimed, "Hans Mayer from 1934 to 1938 gave lectures at the Volkshochschule on literary, historical, and philosophical topics."[27] Finally, although Heidelberger-Leonard suggests that Améry was influenced by the rational empiricism of the Vienna Circle, and especially Rudolf Carnap,[28] according to the Austrian historian Friedrich Stadler, Améry never attended any lectures. We can assume that part of the reason for this absence of biographical detail in Améry's work stems from this "fiction" about his education. Last, Nazi racial laws did not affect Améry's mother, and she died in Vienna in 1939.

Heidelberger-Leonard has also done an admirable job of reconstructing the details of Améry's survival. After the Anschluss in March 1938, Améry fled to Antwerp, Belgium, with his wife. At the time, the generous Jewish community of Antwerp provided support for Jewish refugees. In Antwerp, Améry was surrounded by a circle of friends that included his wife and the Viennese painter Eric Schmid, along with the woman who would become his second wife, Maria Eschenauer-Leitner. (Regine developed a fatal heart condition that led to her death in April 1944).[29] When the Nazis invaded Belgium in the spring of 1940, the French and Belgium authorities ironically arrested Améry as a "German citizen." As an enemy alien, he was deported to Camp de St. Cyprien. After the rapid "strange

defeat" of the French by the Germans, Améry's status suddenly was transformed from enemy alien to a Jew, and he was subsequently transferred to
Gurs on July 28, 1940. According to Améry, Gurs was "not a concentration camp like Dachau, Buchenwald, or Mauthausen" because in the camp
prisoners were not on "the borders of the spirit as in Auschwitz," and
in addition there were "many cultural activities such as concerts, theatre
performances, language courses and lectures."[30] Further proof that Gurs
was not a concentration camp is evident in the fact that Améry, in order
to reunite with his wife, was able to escape on June 6, 1941. Heidelberg-
Leonard describes how the initial escape was easy compared the difficulties
faced in getting back to Belgium. The treacherous journey took nearly
four months and included a short imprisonment in Bayonne before he
reached his goal of being reunited with his wife. In Brussels he worked as
a language instructor and in furniture delivery, and eventually joined a
communist resistance cell that had about thirty or forty members. Looking
back at his activities in the resistance Améry thought himself and companions naïve, and suggested it was his "last perhaps even only unconscious
attempt to evade the Jewish identity" that he had already taken on intellectually, because he "didn't want to be detained by the enemy as a Jew but
rather as a resistance member."[31] Améry and his companions' resistance
activities focused on spreading anti-Nazi literature amongst the German
soldiers. In hindsight Améry considered his activities almost silly. When
he was arrested Améry had a handbill stating "Death to the SS-Bandits
and Gestapo executioners."[32] The day of his arrest was July 23, 1943, and
after interrogation he was imprisoned in Breedonck. Améry described how
he was initially "interesting" to the SS as long as they thought he was "a
German deserter, soldier, or perhaps an officer."[33] Given the "curiosity"
of the SS, he was tortured "strappado" style by being hung with his arms
tied behind his back until his shoulder sockets were dislocated. Since
Améry had no pertinent information to confess, and once the SS discovered he was Jewish, he was given the "death sentence" of Auschwitz.

   Améry was deported to Auschwitz on January 15, 1944, and arrived
there two days later. In his unpublished manuscript "On the Psychology
of the German People," he describes his horrifying initiation into the realities of Auschwitz when, after the initial selections, a mother who had been
separated from her children beseeched an SS officer. He replied, "Do you
want the child?" Then he calmly walked over to the children and seized
the four-year-old child by the foot, swung him in the air, and smashed his
head on an iron post.[34]

Améry was numbered 172364, and 417 of the 655 people in his transport were murdered. Améry was interned in Auschwitz-Monowitz, which was one of the larger of the forty satellite camps of Auschwitz and had about three thousand inmates. It provided workers for the IG Farben dye factory. At Monowitz, conditions were better because there were showers and a medical department, and no gas chambers or torture rooms on the premises.

Initially, Améry was assigned to a work detail. However, Heidelberg-Leonard has also accessed a second unpublished text titled "Arbeit Macht Unfrei," where Améry describes how in June 1944 he was transferred to work in the offices of IG Farben. This work was obviously less strenuous and dangerous than the labor detail and was also a haven from being beaten by the guards. Améry claimed he worked for "some weeks" for IG Farben, adding that this is where he came to know of Primo Levi. As we shall see, Levi began working in the chemical commando of IG Farben in the fall of 1944. Therefore, if Améry is correct (for Levi said he did not recall him), it appears he would have worked for some months at IG Farben. In the middle of January 1945, Auschwitz was evacuated, and Améry was force-marched to Gleiwitz II and then transported by train to Sachsen. At the beginning of February, that camp was also evacuated, and he was transported to Dora-Mittelbau, which was also evacuated. He was transported via train to the horrendous reality of Bergen-Belsen, arriving on April 5. He was profoundly grateful when the English liberated the camp ten days later. Clearly, Améry's 642 days in the camps were a horrifying experience; Heidelberger-Leonard quotes a fragment he wrote titled "Journey around Death" that describes "the miserable odyssey" of his "poor life since the beginning of the war."[35]

Levi's story of survival has similarities with Améry's, but as we shall see, even Levi suggested that his experience was not as "extreme" as Améry's. Levi was a shy assimilated Italian Jew born seven years after Amery, on July 31, 1919, in Turin. His father, Cesare, was an engineer. For Levi, fascism was simply something he had grown up with. In his teens, though, he became disgusted with the regime, and when he entered the university in 1937 he decided to study chemistry as "a haven of reason against the madness of fascism."[36] While at the university Levi took up mountain climbing as a hobby, and he later described how he learned the virtues of resistance, endurance, and sustenance in the mountains and then claimed without which "no doubt I would have not survived."[37]

Levi apparently never seriously considered emigration, even after the anti-Jewish legislation of September 1938. After receiving his doctorate in

July 1941, and despite the anti-Jewish laws, Levi managed to find employment in a nickel mine. In his spare time, he began writing his first short
stories. When the mine failed to produce, he took a job in June 1942 with
the Swiss pharmaceutical firm Wander in Milan. There Levi found a circle
of friends, and after the Nazi occupation in September 1943, they fled to
the mountains in Piedmont and joined the partisans. On December 13,
1943, Levi, along with two of his friends, were captured by militia of the
Fascist Republic, interrogated, and imprisoned for a month before being
transferred to the internment camp of Fossoli di Carpi on January 20,
1944. Their captors told them that they would not fall into the hands of
the Nazis, but the seven thousand Jewish prisoners at Fossoli di Carpi
were nevertheless transferred to Nazi concentration camps. On February
22, Levi was deported, arriving in Auschwitz on February 26, 1944. In the
face of this Nazi persecution, Levi echoed Améry's experience when he
claimed he felt for the first time a Jewish identity. As he said, "I lived
through the surprise and the pride of an identity."[38]

In terms of the story of survival, both Levi and Améry shared the experience of Auschwitz at approximately the same time. Of the 660 men,
women, and children Levi was transported with, only ninety-five men and
twenty-nine women survived the first selection. Levi was number 174517
and, like Améry, was interned in Auschwitz-Monowitz. When Levi arrived
in Auschwitz, the horrific conditions of the camp were improving slightly,
and his testimony opens with the ironic claim that it was his "good fortune
to be deported to Auschwitz only in 1944."[39] Levi was referring to the fact
that owing to labor shortages, the food ration was a bit higher and life
expectancy went up from three to four months to six and a half months.
In Monowitz, Levi worked in an excavation commando as a laborer. In
the spring, after severely injuring his foot, he spent twenty days in the
infirmary recovering. In June, Levi had his first great stroke of luck: he
met Lorenzo Perrone, an Italian stonemason. Lorenzo was a civilian who
had worked for an Italian firm in France. When the war broke out, the
Germans moved the firm to the outskirts of Auschwitz. Lorenzo took a
liking to his countryman and provided him with an extra ration of food,
some mail, and a sense of humanity, all of which were key to keeping him
alive. Myriam Anissimov sums up Levi's first five months in Monowitz:
"Thanks to Lorenzo, who continued to deliver the daily bowl of soup . . .
his condition was not desperate. He had not yet caught any illness, and
the combination of his small size, natural thinness, and habitual frugality
continued to give him a nutritional advantage."[40]

The work and deprivation of the summer and early fall clearly took a toll on Levi. Nevertheless, in the autumn of 1944, he managed to survive selection for the gas chambers. Then, as winter set in, Levi had his second great stroke of good fortune: he was chosen for the chemical commando's laboratory after passing an exam. This is likely where Améry came to know of him. And we can deduce that without the indoor work and the subsequent protection it gave from the elements, along with the possibility to organize material goods, they would not likely have survived the winter.

Still, such conditions did not prevent Levi from coming down with scarlet fever, and on January 11 he entered the infectious diseases ward of the infirmary. On January 17, the Germans evacuated the camp as the Russians approached, and Levi, along with a number of sick prisoners, was left behind. Thus began the Robin Crusoesque "Last Ten Days" that Levi movingly described in his testimony. With the arrival with the Russians on January 27, Levi's fever overcame him, and he spent most of February in bed. After an adventurous, somewhat treacherous, detour through Central Europe, he managed to get back to Turin on October 19, 1945.

In sum, there is a great deal of similarity between Améry and Levi. Both were assimilated Jews, and both shared youthful aspirations to be writers and a commitment to reason and secular humanism. As youths, they were each confronted with the political phenomenon of fascism, and eventually in the confrontation each had their Jewish identity "forced" upon them by the Nazis, and then in a somewhat haphazard fashion they each joined the resistance. Initially recognized for their testimonies, they were put in a state of unease by the subsequent fame. It appears that for both Améry and Levi the "fame" of survival was a key component of the depression they suffered at the end of their lives. However, they both accepted that the recognition enabled them to pursue their literary aspirations. Finally, as humanists, they both claimed that believers "survived" better in the camps. Most significantly, both experienced the horrifying shock and reality of Auschwitz. For Levi this was summed up in the statement, "There is no why here," while Améry witnessed the previously described atrocity against an innocent child. They both struggled with the intellectual implications of their experiences in Auschwitz. Améry asserted that Auschwitz was a realm beyond all other concentration camp experience when he claimed that as one of the earliest Nazi concentration camps Dachau had "a tradition," while Auschwitz, created in 1940, "was subject to improvisations from day to day."[41] Both of their testimonies move us into a realm beyond sense, a realm where suffering occurs without reason, where innocent life is destroyed on whims. Levi used the term "useless violence," while Améry described it as being "at the mind's limits." Suffering without reason is almost impossible to endure—but somehow they managed. What is almost miraculous is that they both were able to return from such a spiritual abyss and develop a profound lucidity, and each in his own unique way intensely pursued rational clarity. Indeed, their brilliance is their deep humanism. Each faced surreal atrocity and yet managed to create "characters" of astounding strength and depth. Thus, their legacy for us is two of the more profound and insightful testimonies on the realities of Auschwitz. Yet, despite their brilliance, they shed only a dim light onto an incomprehensible reality.

Nevertheless, there are also some key differences between them. Levi was Italian, while Améry was Austrian. As a native German speaker, Améry no doubt had an easier time communicating in the camps, although Levi quickly learned enough to adapt to the conditions. Levi was trained as a chemist, and his expertise was critical to his survival and led to a successful career after the war. He also became a highly regarded writer. Améry was a "self-taught" and self-described "intellectual" who managed to eke out a living as a writer and journalist after the war. Subsequently, there is a class difference between them. Levi's successes clearly made him more of an "haute bourgeois," while Améry, without formal education and at first forced into "exile" and then chose to remain in exile in Brussels after the war, was more of a "petit bourgeois." His provincial background and left-ist political positions also make him appear more alienated and bohemian. These differences are refracted in their testimonies, intellectual perspectives, and interests, in their "disagreements" and their "deaths."

Given these distinctions the tenor of their testimonies is also quite different. Levi's *Survival in Auschwitz* reveals his training as a scientist. His description is meticulous and detailed, and to the best of his ability it renders an exact remembrance of the erosion of human dignity and struggle for survival. One has the feeling that he is dissecting his experiences in Auschwitz. His intent was to make his reader participate in his experience, and he painstakingly reconstructed his imprisonment in Auschwitz over a number of years after he returned to Turin. The clarity of description and detailing makes it perhaps the best testimony we have on Auschwitz.

On the other hand, Améry's perspective developed over a number of years after 1945. Heidelberger-Leonard's analysis of Améry's text "On the Psychology of the German People," which was written just three months after his release, has a startling insight for anyone familiar with *At the Mind's Limits*—especially his discussion of resentment toward Germans. According to Heidelberger-Leonard, after the war Améry initially had an "optimistic belief in the future that was paired with a strong conviction that analytic reason would solve the most complex moral and sociopolitical problems."[42] Heidelberger-Leonard claims that this confidence and commitment was shaped by his experience in the 1930s under Langhammer (and we should recall at the time he was contemplating a return to Vienna) and in addition to a spirit of "revenge." Heidelberger-Leonard also suggests that this optimism and spirit of revenge was connected to an almost utopian expected "healing" through a reeducation of the German people. Heidelberger-Leonard's claim is confirmed by Améry's essay "Wasted Words: Thoughts on Germany Since 1945," which describes his optimism immediately after the war: "I imagined the world belong to us, the defeated who had suddenly become victors, the utopians whose most extravagant dreams suddenly appeared to be surpassed by reality, the visionaries of a future that was now present."[43] This quote reveals that Améry's optimistic outlook was colored by his leftist politics, anchored in Marxism, along with his experience in the resistance. But these utopian energies waned, and Heidelberger-Leonard describes how the spirit of revenge had morphed by 1965 into an attitude of resentment because the expected healing had never come.[44] Then, with the crushing of the Prague Spring in 1968, he was forced to recognize that this radical cultural project had failed. It seems that for a variety of reasons, by the mid-1960s, when Améry sat down to write his testimony, he had become profoundly embittered by his experience.

We know that after the war he had changed his name from Hans Maier and rarely stepped foot in Germany. In order to survive he wrote a copious amount of journalism on famous people, teenage stars, and jazz. In 1964, his life as a writer took a major turn when he grudgingly accepted the invitation of Helmut Heissenbuettel to return to Germany to deliver a radio address on the intellectual in Auschwitz, just at the same time the Auschwitz trial was being prepared in Frankfurt. This address became the first chapter of his testimony *Jenseits von Schuld und Sühne* (Beyond Guilt and Atonement). His address struck a note and was well received. Now in his mid-fifties, Améry began to first gain fame as a writer and a "voice" to be known among the German reading public. The most important thinker for Améry was Jean-Paul Sartre. His testimony reflects this admiration and subsequent existentialism by focusing on revolt, and it is also reflected in his self-description as a "vehemently protesting Jew." Another influence of Sartre's philosophy is how his testimony reads as a phenomenology of victimhood, or what he describes as "a loss of trust in the world." As he stated: "What occupies me, and what I am qualified to speak about, is the victims of this Reich.[45]

Since their testimonies are two of the more significant reflections on the concentration camps and Auschwitz in particular, it is not surprising that Levi and Améry exchanged letters after the war. However, there is a bit of confusion on whether they actually "met" in Auschwitz. Levi, who maintained he had a "total and indelible memory" of Auschwitz, could not remember him.[46] Améry, on the other hand, was certain they knew of each other and even claimed they lived in the same hut for a few weeks. Since IG Farben employed them both, it seems likely that their paths crossed, and even Levi did not adamantly dispute Améry's claim.

In his profound and deeply meditative final book, *The Drowned and the Saved*, Levi dedicated a chapter to a discussion of Améry, "The Intellectual in Auschwitz." The heart of his concern was to discuss their disagreements over the role of the intellect in Auschwitz and also to counteract Améry's verbal slight to a mutual friend that Levi was a "forgiver."

Why Améry came to see Levi as a forgiver is a somewhat convoluted story. In the mid-1960s Levi began a long correspondence with Hety Schmitt-Maas, a German woman whose husband had worked at IG Farben. Schmitt-Maas was driven to understand the Nazi past and was so impressed with Levi's testimony that she felt all Germans should read it. It was through Schmitt-Maas that Levi learned that Améry had called him "the forgiver." The reason why Améry called Levi the forgiver stemmed from his reading of the correspondence between Levi and Dr. Ferdinand Meyer, a chemist who was one of Levi's overseers in the IG Farben laboratory. Schmitt-Maas had arranged the correspondence between Meyer and Levi and then shared it with Améry. According to Levi's biographer Ian Thomson, Améry stated, "Unlike Levi, I have absolutely no sympathy for men like Meyer who were part of the I.G. Farben Auschwitz leading personnel."[47] For his part, Levi was originally interested in Meyer in order to clarify some lingering issues about his remembrances of his time working in the chemical commando. Meyer, on the other hand, saw Levi as someone who could help him come to terms with his own past. According to Thomson, Meyer also saw "Christian forgiveness" in Levi's testimony.[48] It is not clear why Meyer found forgiveness in Levi's book; however, the preface to the German edition does contain some conciliatory comments. For example, Levi states that he has "never harbored a sense of hatred towards the German people" and indeed "that in Germany there is something worthwhile, and that Germany now asleep, is pregnant, a breeding ground, at the same time a danger and a hope for the rest of

Europe."⁴⁹ But clearly Levi was not "the forgiver" because he eventually refused to meet Meyer claiming he "did not want the responsibility" nor did he "feel it was his place—to grant Meyer forgiveness."⁵⁰ However, from Améry's perspective of resentment, Levi's conciliatory remarks—and the very fact that he was willing to have a "human" exchange with someone involved in the camps—are something he could not countenance.

In his chapter on Améry, Levi engages in what he describes as an "obligatory" polemic with a "dead man" who is a "potential friend and most valuable interlocutor."⁵¹ According to Levi, Améry's attitude of "resentment"—that could tolerate no forms of forgiveness or reconciliation—reflected Améry's desire to achieve dignity by "return[ing] the blow." Levi is referencing Améry's confrontation in the camp with a Polish prisoner that led to blows being exchanged. Levi then distinguished himself from Améry when he remarked that he personally had no capacity for "trading punches" or "to return the blow." Although he admired Améry for "his courageous decision to leave the ivory tower and go down into the battlefield," he also claimed that this "choice, protracted throughout his post-Auschwitz existence, led him to positions of such severity and intransigence as to make him incapable of finding joy in life, indeed of living."⁵² Despite the admiration, Levi is misunderstanding Améry on two levels: first, because we know that Améry was never officially in the "ivory tower," and second, because Améry was perfectly capable of finding "joy in life" not only after "trading blows" in Auschwitz, both also in his optimistic, utopian hopes after the war, and at the very end of his life in his suicide—in his words, "on the way to the free."

In his attempt to come to a full understanding of Améry's attitude of resentment Levi focuses on the differences in life experience: "Had I too seen the world collapse upon me, had I been sentenced to exile and the loss of national identity, had I too been tortured until I fainted and lost consciousness and beyond, perhaps I would have learned to return the blow and to harbor like Amery those 'resentments.'"⁵³ Levi recognized that Améry's experience was more extreme on the physical, psychological, and spiritual levels. However, we know that Améry's attitude of resentment did not stem from his camp experience per se, but rather developed over time in the 1950s and early 1960s. We also know that Améry flirted with the idea of returning to Austria, but in a utopian political haze and the élan of survival he ultimately decided to make a life in "exile." No doubt his horrifying experiences shaped his decisions and attitude of resentment, but not decisively. However it is not surprising that Levi read Améry in this way because in his testimony *At the Mind's Limits* (a book

Levi admired and aspired to translate) Améry remarked on the issue of his
exile, saying that his was different from those who chose exile and suggested he could therefore not return because "for us, who in those days
were not allowed to return, and today therefore cannot return, the problem arises in a more urgent and compelling way."[54] It is not clear why
Améry stated this, because he apparently had the opportunity to return to
Austria. Perhaps the poignant truth is contained in Améry's statement,
"one ages badly in exile."[55]

Finally, Levi also differentiates himself from Améry on a spiritual and
philosophical level when reflecting on the role of the intellectual in Auschwitz. Levi diverges with Améry's view of history as essentially catastrophe
and power, or in Améry's words, quoted by Levi, "the SS were entitled to
do what they did: natural right does exist, and moral categories are born
and die with the fashion." Levi frames this attitude as an "intellectual
abdication" and then claims "perhaps my ignorance of history protected
me from this metamorphosis."[56] It seems Levi recognized that Améry's
experience of torture in combination with his existential reality of "an
intellectual in Auschwitz" was a different and perhaps a more profound
type of suffering. This is perhaps the best explanation of why they incorporated their experiences of Auschwitz into their self-identity in contrasting ways. For Levi the camps were a "university" without which it is
unlikely he would have become a writer and late in his life he could even
conclude "in its totality, this past has made me richer and surer."[57] Améry,
on the other hand, seems more spiritually broken by his experience. He
claimed, "It goes without saying . . . that in Auschwitz we did not become
better, more human, more humane, and more mature ethically. . . . We
emerged from the camp stripped, robbed, emptied out, disoriented." He
then concluded on a note that echoed Levi: that he did not "leave Auschwitz wiser and deeper, but we were no doubt smarter."[58] In a way, they
both seemed to have shared the clarity that comes from working through
the extreme experience of being dehumanized and spiritually shattered—
but Améry's life experience (and subsequent social position), in combination with the extremity of his experience, seems to have scarred more
deeply.

Levi's need to come to terms with Améry, to delineate their differences,
to understand why Améry called him a forgiver, and to compare the
extremity of their experience honestly is deeply tied to the thrust of the
Drowned and the Saved, probing the depths of Holocaust issues. At the
heart of his reflection is suicide. Indeed, the concluding sentence in Levi's

chapter is a chilling "antidote" against suicide by which he again differentiates himself from Améry. "Perhaps because I was younger, perhaps because I was more ignorant than he, or less marked, or less conscious, I almost never had time to devote to death. I had many other things to keep me busy. . . . The aims of life are the best defense against death: and not only in the Lager."⁵⁹ *And not only in the Lager.* These concluding lines suggest Levi (at the time of writing) was face to face with his own mortality, and although not "suicidal," he is fully aware that suicide is an option. From this perspective, his "explanation" of Améry's suicide can shed a dim light on Levi's own death. Most of the scholars who have weighed in on the controversy surrounding Levi's death have cited his statement, "Améry's suicide . . . like other suicides admits a cloud (nebula) of explanations." But few commentators focus on the rest of the sentence, which reads, "but, in hindsight, that episode of defying the Pole offers one interpretation."⁶⁰ Levi is referencing Améry's ability—unlike himself!—to trade blows. In Levi's interpretation, Améry's capacity for defiance led him to be bitter and full of resentment, and eventually to commit suicide (and, in addition, was the perspective from which Améry called Levi a forgiver); it was at the heart of the differences. It is interesting to compare this interpretation with Levi's initial comments, which were published at the time of Améry's death in an article titled "Jean Améry, Philosopher and Suicide/Jean Améry Suicidal Philosopher." Levi suggests that his suicide stemmed from having been tortured, and he focuses on Améry's statement, "the man who has been tortured remains tortured."⁶¹ At about the same time, in his private correspondence to Schmitt-Maas he wrote this about Améry's suicide: "Suicides are generally mysterious. Améry's was not. Faced by the hopeless clarity of his mind, faced by his death, I have felt how fortunate I have been, not only in recovering my family and my country, but also succeeding to weave around me a 'painted veil' made of family affections, friendships, travel, writing, and even chemistry."⁶²

For Levi, then, Améry's suicide was determined by his life experience, confrontational character, and subsequent intellectual commitments. However, based on Améry's statements, his suicide note, and his book *On Suicide*, it seems clear that his decision was more of a humanistic affirmation. His conception of a "free death" first occurred to him as a child, and his book was a thorough articulation of his mature position. In a way, it seems the utopian energies that moved Améry as a youth and went unfulfilled after the war were turned inward in a last heroic act of self-assertion. It also seems clear that Levi misunderstood this determining element of Améry's suicide. However, Levi's interpretation is not all that surprising, and when Amery's death is viewed without a deep understanding of the radical humanism that led to his "free death," most commentators would likely draw the same conclusion. What is surprising is that Levi was very aware of Améry's book on suicide. Why, in his reflection on the "Intellectual in Auschwitz," did he not connect Améry's thoughts on suicide with his deed? Was he still too preoccupied with Amery's slight that he was a forgiver and subsequently focused on their divergent opinions about surviving when he reflected upon Amery's suicide? In another odd twist, Levi's biographer Ian Thomson obliquely suggests that Levi's "suicide" is connected to Améry's when he asserts that "it was Améry's introspective defense of 'self-murder' that concentrated Levi's mind in his last days."[63] Thomson does not make it clear how he knows this about Levi, but if it is true, it suggests that Levi might have created his own "free death." He achieved this by making his death a "riddle" capable of a nebula of explanations, by investing it with a dialectic tension of "unintended/intent." And is Levi's death not perhaps best characterized by a "unintended/ intent," the perfect death for a man who used to say, "It has been my fate to be ambiguous?"[64] Does this capstone event, so full of ambiguity, not render mute the issue of whether Levi somehow "gave up" or "succumbed" to Auschwitz? In a similar fashion, Améry as the self-described and self-made "intellectual" was a humanist in the tradition of the enlightenment. He was transformed by his experiences into a "radical humanist," and his decision to "to take life in his own hands" certainly fulfilled his fate perfectly.

PART TWO

Humanism and Politics

CHAPTER 6

The Humanity and Humanism of Primo Levi

Joseph Farrell

In a wide-ranging, polemical lecture in Turin in 1979, Primo Levi discussed the roots and variations of racial prejudice in history, finding early traces of the phenomenon even in the seemingly innocuous biblical verse in the Canticle of Canticles, "*Nigra sum sed formosa*" (I am black but beautiful). Levi's objection was to the use of the conjunction "but" rather than the more neutral "and," something he judged to be "an important clue" to a racist frame of mind.[1] He agreed that certain civilizations, such as the Roman, seemed to have been free of racism, but asserted that the phenomenon had become widespread and adduced examples from the Europe and South America of his own time. However, the views advanced by the philosopher, Norberto Bobbio, that prejudice "is born in the mind of man," was unacceptable to him: his own conviction was that "racial prejudice is something barely human, that it is pre-human, that it precedes man and belongs to the animal rather than the human world."[2]

This dialectical opposition between the "animal" or the bestial and the "human" is a recurrent and deeply significant theme in Levi, while the underlying fundamental, even fundamentalist, reassertion of a basic humanistic credo in the values of being human contained in those words represents his enduring and authentic voice as writer and intellectual. The sentiments expressed are pregnant with deeper philosophical implications than might be immediately apparent. The distinction between what is genuinely human and what is "barely human" or "pre-human" is a statement, even if an inchoate one, of a philosophical dogma to which he tenaciously held all his life, even in the face of the atrocities he himself had endured and had seen perpetrated by human beings. The question, "What does it mean to be human?" is posed by the very title of his most celebrated work, as are also the opposite questions: What forces can undo a man? Or, alternatively: What conduct is incompatible with humanity? The lecture on racial intolerance is, in addition to being an attack on racism, an extended meditation on the nature and potential of the human being, as well as on his or her capacity for embodying or desecrating an ideal. The ideal is part of the complex of ideas that in European culture has gone under the name of humanism. The very title of the work, *If This Is a Man*, implies the same anguished questioning on humanity and humanism that is present in the lecture, and in both works Nazism is presented as the very denial of humanism as well as of the humanitarian spirit and even of shared humanity.[3]

In the lecture, after his venture into history, Levi turned to Hitlerism and the Holocaust, and he invited his listeners to consider the impact of Nazi policies not in the abstract but on frightened men, women, and children, such as those from the Greek city of Salonika, who were rounded up, loaded onto the goods carriages of a train destined for Auschwitz, and transported across Europe in appalling conditions, "all shoved together with no food, no water, with the promiscuity that you can imagine, no sleep, in the bitter cold of winter and the atrocious heat of summer, in freight cars that were never opened." Even before arrival at the concentration camp, inside the wagons themselves, the process of "brutalization," he writes, would be underway, as it had been for the men and women deported from Italy to Auschwitz with him. He explained to his listeners the concept of "brutalization": "that is, there was the precise objective of demolishing the human in man even before killing him. And I believe that, even in the bloody history of our humanity, this is something unique."[4]

What he emphasizes, as he had elsewhere, as being "unique in history" is not the genocide nor even the systematic anti-Semitic campaign, since, deplorably, such murderous pogroms had been known before in European history, but the specifically Nazi program of "demolishing the human." It was this outrage that, as he believed and indeed stated explicitly, had no precedent in history. He rejected the lazy notion that such degradation was an accidental side-effect of Nazi brutality, insisting that it required to be seen as an intrinsic part of the project, "a precise objective," or "act of will," to use the terms employed in the original Italian.

Having given this judgment, Levi illustrated his meaning by outlining to his audience a personal experience in Auschwitz. When he had been almost one year in the camp, he was scarcely "pretty to look at." Like the other inmates, he was filthy, had a long, unkempt beard, and was dressed in clothes that were no more than rags. Just outside the perimeter fence there was a camp of the Hitler Youth, boys of around fourteen years of age, who were one day given a guided tour of Auschwitz by one of their instructors. In Levi's hearing, the escort gave a commentary not of sympathy for the lamentable condition the prisoners were enduring but on their status as human beings. Levi attributes to the instructor the following words:

> You see, obviously we keep them here in the concentration camp and make them work, because they are not men, are they? Their beards are long, they don't wash, they're dirty, they can't even speak properly, they're only good for work with pick and shovel, so we have no choice but to treat them like this, as you would treat a farm animal.[5]

With great magnanimity of spirit, Levi limits himself to mild and moderate objections to the "turning upside down of cause and effect" involved, and on the effects of comparable behavior in every corner of the world where some form of racism manifests itself. He imagines a gloss on those words as it might be spoken by some genteel, perhaps even *soi-disant* liberal, observer who might opine: "Of course, we persecute them, you can see what they're like, can't you? They are like animals, they're worth less than us, they don't have our culture." It is a constant refrain in Levi's work. If this is a man, what makes him different from the animal level? What is it to be fully human, and who is less than human, the victim or the perpetrator-observer? How is the divide between the human and the animal dimension to be maintained? Can a human being be degraded by external forces to the point of losing that inner essence which separates the human state from the bestial? How should such a degraded or degrading creature be regarded? Primo Levi's writings raise the profound questions that philosophy and classical tragedy have debated: on the human capacity for evil, on the nature of friendship, on the question of identity, on the basis of ethics, on the irrepressible hopes for goodness and above all on the problem that for Kant was the culmination of his critical philosophy and moral quest—what is man? The process of undoing a man, of dehumanizing him, of reducing him or her to a lower state, of making him/her in the most literal sense of the word "brutish," *abbruttito*, was one that tormented and obsessed him.

The terms in which he couched this question are a consequence of the education he had received, of the culture with which he was imbued and of the tradition—humanism—he inhabited. Although he would not regard himself as a philosopher *de métier*, there is a philosophy underlying his writing but a philosophy so unobtrusively and lightly worn, so deeply incorporated into an intellectual persona as to be almost invisible, or to have become synonymous with common sense and instinct. It is wholly in keeping with this invisibility, as well as with the responses and attitudes of a modest man, that the one time he applies to himself the term "humanist," it is in tones of self-deprecating irony, when describing the mock-satirical response of a young colleague at Levi's clumsy attempts to make productive use of the computer. A young friend witnessed Levi's awkward uncertainty with manuals after purchasing an early version of the word processor. "You belong," he told Levi, "to the austere generation of humanists who still insist on wanting to understand the world around them. This demand has become absurd."[6] Austere Levi may or may not have been, but a humanist he certainly was, and it was for this reason that he never renounced the impulse to understand the world as he had experienced it, however absurd the impulse may have seemed to some. He was not innovative or original as philosopher, but should be seen as an intellectual who was a willing heir and inheritor of a tradition which has a philosophical basis, and who was at ease inside that tradition. The Western humanist tradition is not some fixed, unchanging corpus, akin to the Golden Book in pre-Napoleonic Venice, but a developing, accumulating, self-reforming accretion of multiple systems of values, of thoughts and of ethics, to which the contribution of Jewish writers and thinkers has been integral. As George Steiner expressed it, the central constitutive element is the "twofold descent" from Jerusalem and Athens.[7] Levi's distinctive, uniquely twentieth-century contribution was to maintain the value of that tradition in the face of the barbaric monstrosity that was Auschwitz. Very recently, Terry Eagleton has written that "everything in this post-Auschwitz world is ambiguous and indeterminate."[8] It is a curious assertion, perhaps no more than a clever piece of wordplay, but Primo Levi had rebutted it years previously from inside the humanist tradition by insisting that Auschwitz requires that everything be reformulated so that humane ethical canons can be not rejected or left "ambiguous and indeterminate," but restated with crisp, precise clarity. He was critical of the lack of this clarity in writers who should have been engaged on the same task and to whom he was otherwise close, such as Paul Celan and Georg Trakl.[9]

That clash between the humanist formation and the brutalizing personal experience of Auschwitz was a permanent struggle in Levi's mind. There is scarcely any need to stress the dehumanizing experience Levi describes as his initiation to Auschwitz. The prisoners are greeted by the words spoken to the souls of the damned in Dante's *Inferno* as they embark on Charon's craft.[10] Each individual is made to realize that he is on the bottom, and that as a human being he has been reduced to the status of a hollow man. The full description of the plight of the inmate of the concentration camp runs:

> Imagine now a man who is deprived of everyone he loves, and at the same time of his house, his habits, his clothes, in short of everything he possesses: he will be a hollow man, reduced to suffering and needs, forgetful of dignity and restraint, for he who loses all often easily loses himself.[11]

Among the attributes lost by the hollow man newly arrived in Auschwitz are dignity and restraint, although the Italian for the second quality is *discernimento*, the more rational quality of discernment. The hollow man has forfeited, or has been deprived of, the sensibility and understanding that are the basis of the dignity of the human being, and that, taken together, form, in the humanist perspective, the central qualities of humankind. Dignity itself, the intrinsic dignity of the human person, is a key word in this culture. It is in the light of the voluntary renunciation of reason, dignity, and selfhood that Levi's otherwise pitiless judgments on the *mussulmano*, literally "Muslim," translated somewhat surprisingly by Stuart Hood in *If This Is a Man* by the German word *Musselman*, must be seen. Depictions of the *mussulmano* recur disconcertingly often in Levi, something which troubled Giorgio Agamben in his monograph on the ethical dimensions of the testimony literature emerging from the concentration camps.[12] Levi insisted on the centrality of this figure in the life of the camps, and in his discussion of the views of Jean Améry on the role of the intellectual in Auschwitz, published after the latter had committed suicide, he criticizes Améry for keeping his glance fixed on supposedly higher matters, so that in consequence "his gaze is directed on high and rarely lingers on the vulgar populace of the Lager, and on its typical character, the 'Muslim,' the worn-out man, whose intellect is dying or dead."[13]

"*Mussulmano*," translated more coherently by Rosenthal by the English word "Muslim," was, in the mysterious, closed codes in use in the camps, the name given to those who had abandoned the struggle for survival and had in consequence accepted defeat and degradation, making themselves objects of contempt and derision rather than of compassion or solidarity. The *mussulmano* is the figure who has reconciled himself to his condition as hollow man. In a scale of values dominated by the Hobbesian war of all against all and by the relentless struggle for individual survival, the *mussulmano* was bereft of dignity, and had forfeited the right to respect. Levi's language toward the "Muslims" has no trace of fellow feeling. He describes them in a footnote to *If This Is a Man* as the "weak, the inept, those doomed to selection," and explains that there is no point in talking to these "men in decay" since within a few weeks there would remain nothing of them but "a handful of ashes in some nearby field."[14] Even more devastatingly, he describes them as "non-men," in whom the "divine spark" has been extinguished and who are in consequence "already too empty to really suffer."[15] Agamben associates himself with Levi's disdainful dismissal of them, writing that the *mussulmano* is "the human that cannot be told apart from the inhuman."[16] The *mussulmano* is, in other words, beyond the pale, outside the remit of ethical requirements, undeserving of humane consideration and, crucially, deprived of the dignity that a humanist philosophy would accord to all humankind.[17] Dignity and status require to be earned.

Resistance to descent to the status of the *mussulmano* could take various forms, such as the insistence on keeping clean shown by the inmate named Steinlauf. Auschwitz was an inhuman mechanism aimed at reducing the inmates to the subhuman status, he reasoned, and precisely for that reason "we must not become beasts."[18] Once again, the antithesis human/bestial is employed. Levi was unsure of Steinlauf's counsel and later chose a different form of resistance after experiencing a sense of deep humiliation at the hands of a camp *kapo*, Alex, who, while escorting him back to his barracks after the interview to test Levi's worth as a chemist, casually used him as a cloth to clean his oily hand. This unthinking, uncivilized, disrespectful gesture became for Levi the touchstone of the entire code of values, or nonvalues, by which he would judge the caste of warders and their sycophants or dupes, but the language in which he couches his contempt for the moronic, bullying *kapo* will be familiar but is arresting in its contemptuous simplicity: "the poor brute Alex."[19] It is the perpetrator and not the victim who by his self-degradation, moronic conduct and casual incivility earns himself the title "brute." However, the chapter describing that incident is followed, famously, by the episode in which Levi recounts to Pikolo Dante's account of the adventure of Ulysses. The juxtaposition of the two episodes is a stroke of structural genius, and it is no more an accident than is the occurrence of the same word, "brute," in the challenging rhetoric used by Dante's Ulysses in calling on his comrades to live up to their divine nature:

Considerate la vostra semenza:
Fatti non foste per viver come bruti
Ma per seguir virtute e conoscenza.

Think of your seed: for brutish ignorance
Your mettle was not made; you were made men,
To follow after knowledge and excellence.[20]

The reiterated antithesis between the human and the animal, between men and brutes is fundamental. The scale of values it implies stands in contrast to the Nazi program to dehumanize their Jewish prisoners, to make them non-men like the *Mussulmani*, thereby demeaning them before slaughtering them.

The distinguishing feature of Levi's account of the Holocaust is the prominence given to the malevolent process of dehumanization. There is in what has come to be known as Holocaust literature or in the wider literature of testimony a surprising variety of analysis of the core and basis of the Nazi genocide project, and even Levi himself expressed some puzzlement over Hitler's anti-Semitic "obsession."[21] Only the most rabid negationist could dispute the anti-Semitic roots of the Nazi savagery, but thereafter moral, philosophical, psychological, political, and ideological conclusions and analyses vary.[22] The attempt to incorporate the chronicle of Auschwitz into some overarching intellectual theory or narrative, even if that narrative aims, as does Giorgio Agamben's, to provide "contemporary relevance" to the history of Nazi slaughter, has had the most varying outcomes.[23] I find it impossible to read Agamben without a sense of deep unease over his patrician attitude toward Primo Levi, most especially over his dismissal of Levi's accounts of survivor shame as "puerile."[24]

Others have chosen different analyses. Levi himself noted that his fellow inmate, Jean Améry, "a political militant," had dedicated himself to a quest for understanding the "disease which plagued Europe and threatened (and still threatens) the world."[25] George Steiner chose to delve into the roots of civilized European thought, even into medieval Scholastic philosophy, to isolate the prime origins of anti-Jewish feeling in Europe. This search enabled him to conclude that "Auschwitz grew out of its [the Church's] own teachings and out of two thousand years of Jew hatred embedded in the canonic books of Christianity."[26] The Dutch novelist

Harry Mulisch, and more recently Norman Mailer, the first obsessively in book after book and the second in a 2007 novel, have focused on the personality of Adolf Hitler to establish if the character of one deviant criminal mind could provide at least the outline of an explanation of the tragedy. Both have, perhaps fancifully and certainly fictionally, suggested that Hitler's rage was occasioned by some personal, emotional contact with Jewish people, Mulisch imagining that Eva Braun was of Jewish origin so that the child of his she was carrying, in the novel, would then be partly Jewish, and Mailer that Hitler himself had Jewish blood.[27] Arthur Miller, after attending the trial of Auschwitz guards in Frankfurt in 1964, came close to suggesting that every man is guilty "even for the murders he did not perform with his own hands," but from which he profited "if only by having survived." Miller's final conclusion seemed to be that the ill lay in German culture and history, or in the "German heart," in his own expression.[28] Others, mainly historians, have emphasized the nature of the SS state or of totalitarianism.[29] To Levi's indignant disdain, Liliana Cavani, with her film *The Night Porter*, proposed the theory that "we are all victims or killers and accept these roles voluntarily:" Levi retorted that he had been a blameless victim and never a killer.[30] These varying hypotheses are ciphers of the efforts of each writer or witness to identify and analyze what led to the undermining of the most fundamental of ethical postulates, "Thou shalt not kill."

Plainly, these questions haunted Primo Levi. He saw Auschwitz as unique in its savagery, but his conclusions from that uniqueness are original and unexpected. In his introduction to Leon Poliakov's historical work, *Auschwitz*, he refused to allow Auschwitz to be explained as a war, not even as "an episode of war," or as "war in its most extreme form," because its origins were fundamentally different.[31] It seemed to him that all that could be known on the "*quia*" (because) of the Holocaust was known, but noted the lack of consensus on the "why." Exactly what had made possible the overturning of the hierarchy of the moral imperatives that had underpinned Western civilization? "The recent or distant causes and motives that spawned a gigantic death factory in this civilized continent of ours, acting with atrocious efficiency right up to the German collapse, remain an enigma."[32] It was in some ways better that the enigma remained, for "the words and works" of the Nazi leaders, as he wrote in the same introduction, should be viewed as "outside of humanity, indeed against humanity, without historical precedent." These words are delphic but underwrite Levi's mindset. The offence was "outside humanity," or of humanity as viewed in a humanist tradition resting on the concept of *dignitas hominis*.

But perhaps it would be appropriate to offer if not a full definition of humanism, at least some tentative attempt at understanding the concept.

Humanism is conventionally considered the distinctive ideology of the Renaissance, although it can equally be viewed as having its roots in ancient Greek philosophy, notably in the thought of Socrates as interpreted by Nietzsche, who saw Socratic philosophy as displacing the Dionysian element of the Greek vision in favor of a more rational, Apollonian, human-centered outlook. Humanism received its definitive formulation from such Renaissance thinkers as Marsilio Ficino or Pico della Mirandola, whose principal work was entitled, significantly, *De dignitate hominis*. The writings and artwork of such masters as Leon Battista Alberti or Leonardo da Vinci offer support to the crucial belief in an innate human dignity. It is this vision that finds expression in the great individual statues, such as the David of Michelangelo or Donatello. *"L'uomo come misura"* (man as the measure of all things) was the formula that underlay the work of the architects, poets, and painters of the Renaissance, while in one of his soliloquies, Hamlet provided another admiring expression of the same outlook with the words, "What a piece of work is man." If humanism is not amenable to precise, exclusive definition, its principal external characteristic could be identified as the belief in the centrality of the human being in the cosmic scheme, but without, at least in the formative period, a denial of God. (The existence of God was something Primo Levi found incompatible with Auschwitz.) It was of the essence of the human being that he was endowed with a spiritual dimension and with reason, a rational faculty that constituted the fundamental distinguishing characteristic between the human and lower spheres of animal life. This gulf of dignity and status between the human and the bestial was intrinsic to Primo Levi's thinking. The classical definition, by genus and difference, was that man was an *animal rationalis*. In consequence, humankind lived in harmony with nature and was even sovereign over it, a situation justified by the biblical account of creation; he or she had as their birthright free will, autonomy, a moral sense, liberty, and responsibility and was therefore endowed with an inalienable, inherent dignity that derived from the very fact of being human. This is not the place to trace the evolution and centrality of the humanist vision in European art and philosophy, but as a code of ideas the vision attained its fullest form with the rationalism of the Enlightenment. It remained in essence unchallenged until the twentieth century, when in their various ways psychoanalysis, Marxism, surrealism, Darwinism, and successive inchoate waves of irrationalism and relativism

pronounced its obituary as a universally accepted creed. Modernism, especially after World War I, was antihumanist to the core, and to that extent
Primo Levi was no modernist.

One of the most forceful modern exponents of contemporary humanism is Tzvetan Todorov, and it is no accident that he has felt compelled to
confront the challenge to the optimistic humanist vision that is the *Lager*
and the Gulag. In such works as *Facing the Extreme*, he searches for practices that uphold the notion of human dignity in such extreme situations
as the 1943 uprising in the Warsaw ghetto, or, in polemical disagreement
with several works of testimony literature, for traces of altruistic conduct
or moral gestures in the darkness of the concentration camps, since only
such conduct could justify the validity of the humanist vision.[33] Although
Levi was one of the writers from whom he took his distance in that work,
in a later book he forthrightly identified Primo Levi as a humanist. "It is
precisely in living through the horrors of the war and the camps that modern humanists, men like Primo Levi, Romain Gary and Vasili Grossman
have made their impact and confirmed their faith in the human capacity
also to act freely, *also* to do good" (author's emphases).[34]

Todorov is surely right in his assessment of Levi's faith. Levi resisted
the nihilism of modernism, and he based his faith in an older view of the
human. This has consequences that are unexpected and startling. The first
is that Myriam Anissimov, in her much-criticized biography, is justified in
drawing attention to the defiant optimism of Primo Levi.[35] The second is
that, however central Auschwitz had been to his biography, Levi refused—
not surreptitiously but forthrightly and heroically—to allow it to become
the determining feature of the philosophy of life to which he gave alle-
giance. Auschwitz was never for Levi the cornerstone of a new ethical
hierarchy or new vision of the world, of reality or of humanity. It was a
tragedy, a catastrophe, a crime without precedent, as he repeatedly
asserted, but therefore not to be judged by established criteria or canons,
and therefore incapable of undermining them. The humanist vision, with
the confidence and faith in humanity that it implied, remained intact after
Auschwitz.

Auschwitz cannot be the basis for new ethical constructs because it is
sui generis. As already stated, Levi will not even permit the normal suspen-
sion of norms and decencies of life in war to be extended to provide an
explanation of Auschwitz, and not simply because the Geneva Convention
is here irrelevant. Levi's reasoning is more troubling. War was, for him, a

"sad fact that has always existed," but he deepens that reflection by adding that war

> is despicable but it is in us, an archetype, its seed present in Cain's crime, in every conflict between individuals. It is an extension of anger and who does not know anger, who has not felt it in himself, sometimes repressed, sometimes mature and pleasurable?
>
> But in Auschwitz there is no anger. Auschwitz is not in us, it is not an archetype, it is outside of man.[36]

War is in human nature, but Auschwitz is not. It is "outside of man." There are references in the subtext of this passage to C. G. Jung's notion of the fundamental archetypes of human behavior as well as to Freud's belief that every human being was motivated not only by the "pleasure principle" but also by darker forces that expressed themselves as love of violence. Even the recall of "Cain's crime" is a biblically authorized admission of brutality that has to be recognized as human. But for Levi, beneath these shadowy realms of the id, there lies another subterranean realm that is beyond humanity: but precisely for the reason that it never was the realm of the human, the recognition of the existence of such a realm can take nothing away from humanity, or from humanism. Levi's assertion is not only a valiantly defiant reassertion of his fundamental trust in the human being but also a consequent dismissal, as not appertaining to humanity, of those capable of crimes whose nefariousness is beyond comprehension. Auschwitz belongs in that realm not of the inhumane but of the nonhuman.

The point seems to him of such importance that he repeats it on the following page, where he links it with a warning that at the time of writing, the moral lassitude and mental servility of the majority and the amoral opportunism of a degenerate minority risked re-creating the conditions which made Auschwitz a possibility: "Auschwitz is outside of us, but it is still around us, in the air."[37]

Levi's critical rationality, his inheritance of, and immersion in, classical European culture, his innate tolerance, his adherence to a code of moderate values were the underpinnings of a mind and conscience which were the repositories of firmly held, variously expressed, humanist convictions. Those who believe that civilization is only a fragile membrane pulled taut over the fundamentally egocentric, brutal, or cruel impulses of human creatures whose barbaric tendencies are kept precariously in check not by culture or civilization but by the repressive mechanisms of the state, so that once these are removed, as allegedly happened in New Orleans after the onset of Hurricane Katrina, the human beast red in nail and claw is released, will find no comfort in Levi. He explicitly denies any such tendency in humankind as such in the chapter titled "The Drowned and the Saved" of *If This Is a Man*:

> We do not believe in the most obvious and facile deduction: that man is fundamentally brutal, egoistic and stupid in his conduct once every civilized institution is taken away, and that the Häftling is consequently nothing but a man without inhibitions.[38]

Time and again, he displays his disdain for those who view Auschwitz as representing the revelation of the previously concealed truth about the inner, innate psyche of humanity. Auschwitz is not for Levi the external symptom of an enduring disease of the human spirit, and therefore not to be compared to the general and seemingly innate human tendency toward violence. Nazism and its more brutal manifestations were a contingent fact, to be explained in political, social, and historical terms, not psychological or existential ones. The Häftling in his primal quest for survival was the exception.

His scientific training meant that Levi could not prevent himself from using even Auschwitz as a laboratory, and from deducing certain conclusions regarding humans, even if he is undogmatic and hesitant as is right to do so in such surroundings: "it should not seem cynical to say this for me, as for Lydia Rolfi and many other 'fortunate' survivors, the Lager was a University: it taught us look around and measure men."[39]

Once again, the emphasis is on the human dimension. Levi's "education" in the Lager led him to use his experience inside the camps to draw up categories of human character and conduct. He was forthright in his condemnation of those who were truly responsible for the outrages of the Holocaust, judicious in his discussion of those who inhabited a "gray zone," and acute in his celebrated distinction between the "Drowned and the Saved." But of greater importance is his insistence on the separation between the abyss of values *inside* Auschwitz and the standards of normal conduct *outside*. The euphemism he employs on several occasions for Auschwitz is the simple word *laggiú*, "down there." Discussing an unusually brutal *kapo*, he suggests that the man's violence may have been a symptom of mental imbalance, but that whereas the normal impulse is to pity those who suffer from such a condition, any such humane reaction "*down there*" would have been out of place.[40] In an essay on the "language of odors," which begins in a lighter vein, he switches tone when he recalls the acrid smells associated with Auschwitz and how *down there* the scents of liberty were almost a reproach to the inmates.[41] While considering Améry's writings, he asks whether reason, art and poetry were of any value "in the daily life down there" and concludes that probably they were not.[42] But this is not the skeptical doubt over the supposedly civilizing impact of culture and art given such trenchant formulation by George Steiner—how can a human being play Schubert and then go and torture people?[43] Levi distinguishes between how people will behave in extreme circumstances— *down there*—and how they will behave in more relaxed times. The world of *down there* is never allowed to become the norm for a permanent philosophy *here*. *Down there* is a temporary state where values are suspended.

This distinction too is fundamental. No theodicy and ontology that sees the world as wholly permeated with cosmic evil tempted Levi, who refused to allow Auschwitz to become evidence to demonstrate that the human being is a creature wholly inclined to malice. He refused to allow Auschwitz to be evidence for anything other than itself. The social and political conditions that had made and could again make Auschwitz possible did not spring from the inner essence of the human being, but were contingent facts. As such they were within the area where humanity exercised choice and responsibility. The extermination camps had, Levi wrote in the same piece, "extinguished a civilization," but he did say *a* civilization, not that they had shown civilization itself to be a sham. These forthright conclusions are a restatement of a European humanism, made in the face of the most monstrous of all forms of inhumanity, formulated as an act of defiance after the most heinous of crimes that could be perpetrated on innocent humanity. Levi has no Rousseauist belief that man is naturally good, but neither would he give any succor to those who believed, and who in the postwar years, proclaimed the opposite. Sartre used self-vilifying terms such as "nausea" to depict his despairing vision of humankind, while Camus saw the metaphor for humankind in the mythical figure of Sisyphus, condemned for all eternity to the futility of rolling a boulder up a hill only to see it tumble down when he reached the top, and Samuel Beckett, a writer for whom Levi had the deepest antipathy, portrayed men and women as creatures enclosed in dustbins. Levi never succumbed to that vision, but his humanism survived the context of his own life, once again in keeping with notions trenchantly expressed by Todorov: "Modern humanism, far from ignoring Auschwitz and Kolyma, takes them as a starting point. It is neither proud nor naïve."[44]

The same humanist values underlie Levi's literary and aesthetic judgments. Levi was conscious of the fact that he delighted in looking at the twin worlds of literature and science "from unusual angles, inventing, so to speak, the instrumentation: examining matters of technique with the eyes of a literary man, and literature with the eye of a technician."[45] Nevertheless, the humanist perspective is present in his expression of his tastes and distastes. As he himself freely admitted, *The Search for Roots*, although an anthology of the writings by other authors, is the most revealing and personal of his works.[46] Marco Belpoliti puts the matter even more strongly when he refers to that book as "an intense human confession" and as "a key book for the comprehension of his complex personality as a writer."[47] The extracts are gathered under four, quasi-cabalistic headings, all tracing progressions of the human spirit from Job to Black Holes, and thereby straddling Levi's own "hybrid" or "centaur-like" identity as writer and man of science. The four routes towards wisdom are all expressions of a humanist frame of mind, not simply because one bears the significant title *The Stature of Man*. All four bear witness to a taste for wisdom writers over narrators or lyrical writers, to a disinterested quest for understanding and self-awareness, and to a questioning cult of the tortured dignity of *Homo sapiens*. I take that to be the sense of the puzzlement he himself felt over what the compilation of the anthology revealed to him about himself. In his introduction, he noted his own surprise that he had not selected any women or non-Westerners, and that there were no "*rogues*" in his choice. In an enigmatic phrase, he also noted that the *magicians* had pride of place over *moralists*, and that both categories had been subconsciously preferred to *logicians*.[48] He provides no explanation of these phrases, nor does he even advance any concrete examples. In the most revealing phrase of all, he recorded his bewilderment that in compiling the collection of writers that mattered to him was drawn up, his experiences in Auschwitz weighed less than he would rationally have predicted. His rational self was a construct of other influences.

However, if the book did not become another topos for the preservation of the memory of the offense that was Auschwitz, at the same time, he reveals himself to be, in another sense, an adherent of a wider humanist vision of Europe as, in George Steiner's phrase, *un lieu de la mémoire*:[49] the memory is of the vicissitudes of history, of the development science and of literary culture. Primo Levi's is not a mind marooned in the present.

His own deepest beliefs are revealed through his discussions of other writers. His unexpected fondness for Rabelais is based on the fact that Rabelais is "rich in all the virtues that today's man, sad, shackled, and weary lacks." Indeed Rabelais is "close to us as a model," precisely because of certain qualities displayed by the great French writer and which include "faith in tomorrow and in man."[50] It was a faith Levi shared, but after facing satanic forces unguessed by the great French writer. Levi prized clarity of language and of thought, so the obscurity of language in Paul Celan made Levi's view of him ambiguous. He believed that Celan was a poet to be "meditated upon and pitied rather than imitated," but that his was not "communication, not a language," or at best the dark language of a lonely man facing death. Levi's own belief, stated most unequivocally vis-à-vis Celan was that communication was a writer's duty, and that while a man facing death is necessarily alone, "we the living are not alone, (so) we must not write as if we were alone." He acknowledged that *Death Fugue*, the poem he included, had a "raw lucidity" but saw it as the opening point of a movement toward "the atrocious chaos without a glimmer of light of his last compositions."[51]

He uses a similar image of the progress from darkness to light to express his profound differences with Franz Kafka. Levi had translated Kafka's *The Trial*, but the experience, as is documented by his biographers, was traumatic.[52] Although it must have seemed to the publisher Giulio Einaudi, who commissioned the translation, that the two writers had deep affinities, there was a complete clash of sensibility and of worldview separating them. Perhaps Kafka became for Levi the supreme proponent of a modernist, irrationalist, posthumanist philosophy, embodying the view of "today's man" as "sad, shackled, and weary" that Levi rejected. The dethroning of reason, which is the core human attribute in the humanist tradition, the negation of understanding and of all rational schemes of justice, are central characteristics of Kafka's outlook and pivotal to the dilemmas facing Joseph K. "Nobody is innocent, nobody is absolved—this is the dreadful postulate on which Kafka has constructed his book," wrote Piero Citati in his biography of the Prague writer.[53] It is a view that Levi rejected:

> In my writing, for good or evil, knowingly or not, I have always striven to pass from the darkness into the light, as (I think Pirandello also said this, I don't remember where) a filtering pump might do, which sucks up turbid water and expels it decanted: possibly sterile. Kafka forges his path in the opposite direction: he endlessly unravels the hallucinations that he draws from incredibly profound layers, and he never filters them.[54]

The distinction Levi makes between himself and Kafka is analogous to that made by Camus on Sartre in a review Camus did of the novel *La Nausée*. Identifying certain similarities between Sartre and Kafka, Camus added: "It is the mistake of a certain kind of literature to believe that life is tragic because it is miserable."[55] Kafka found life tragic and senseless, but while Levi had every reason to conclude that life was miserable and even tragic, he never gave assent to the notion that it was senseless.

This deep reverence for humanity and for the value of life, even *in extremis*, remained intact. No extreme was more extreme than the extermination camp, but when writing about the monument that was planned for Auschwitz, he expressed the hope that it too would be a homage to humankind:

> It must be a warning dedicated by humanity to itself, which can bear
> witness and repeat a message not new to history, but all too often forgotten:
> that man is, and must be, sacred to man, everywhere and forever.[56]

The achievements of Primo Levi as man and writer can be seen as a literary monument to the same cause. Few modern writers, having faced the darkest depravity of European civilization, have achieved his synthesis of delicate poetics and robust humanism.

CHAPTER 7

Levi and the Two Cultures

Jonathan Druker

Primo Levi stresses and even exaggerates the importance of "hybridity" in his works and in his authorial persona.[1] He tells his readers more than once that he was both an Italian and a Jew, both a chemist and a man of letters who was formed intellectually by scientific texts and humanistic ones, too. Examples of both kinds of writing share the pages of *The Search for Roots*, his personal anthology of favorite passages by favorite authors.[2] Thinly veiled as the narrator of *The Monkey's Wrench*, Levi describes himself as a sort of Tiresias, the male seer who according to Greek mythology also lived many years as a female. Like Tiresias, Levi had experienced the world from opposite sides, as, in his case, both a chemist and a writer.[3] However, he thought the split between them was only provisional and not essential. In an effort that strikes me as more nostalgic than forward-thinking, Levi frequently hoped to reconnect the so-called two cultures, the sciences and the arts, to enable a return to a time when knowledge formed a homogenous whole, when words corresponded completely with the things that they named, and implicitly to a time before the Holocaust shattered our world.[4]

As a tool for bridging the "two cultures"—for Levi, the split between them was "an unnatural schism"—hybridity suggests a bringing together of opposites with the goal of forming a unity more fundamental than the differences between the parts.[5] Although this undertheorized concept has been much used to describe his hyphenated authorial position—Italian-Jew and chemist-writer—this essay is chiefly interested in how one of Levi's books problematizes hybridity, how it explores the unstable binaries that define the human condition, and how it stages the Holocaust as an encounter in which historical forces undermined hybrid forms of human identity and tore them apart.[6] I draw on the work of Michel Foucault to support my claim that *The Periodic Table*, Levi's memoir about his life as a chemist, dramatizes the violent separation of two aspects of the human hybrid that took place during the Holocaust: the human as subject and object, or, in other terms, as mind and body, as spirit and matter.[7]

Early in the book, Levi's autobiographical narrator recalls thinking, as a young man, that to master matter through chemistry is to make intellectual order out of natural chaos while gaining a deeper knowledge of our material essence. "The nobility of Man, acquired in a hundred centuries of trial and error, lay in making himself the conqueror of matter," he states. "Conquering matter is to understand it and understanding it is necessary to understanding the universe and ourselves" (*The Periodic Table*, 41). However, this youthful optimism is tempered as the memoir also describes how Levi was cruelly objectified as impure matter—that is, as an impure body—by scientific discourses promoting racial hierarchy and racial purity that were made to serve the political aims of both Nazism and Italian Fascism. While the Nazis concluded that Jews were not truly human, Italian Fascism formulated the milder but still harmful accusation that the Italian Jews were not truly Italian, and, indeed, were not Europeans at all.[8] These ideas, which had grave consequences for Levi, have a genealogy, and it is necessary to account for their origins in order to understand the crosscurrents running through *The Periodic Table*, whose contents I will briefly summarize.

Published in 1975, the volume is mostly made up of descriptions of school and university days studying chemistry, recollections of thorny problems that Levi confronted at various times in his professional career, and fictional pieces in which chemistry and the elements play an important role both concretely and metaphorically. Levi writes in an engaging style as his tone shifts from serious to wryly humorous to ironic. Despite its fragmentary quality—a number of the stories had been previously published in a variety of venues over a period of years—the coherent nucleus of *The Periodic Table* narrates Levi's personal Holocaust story in its "before," "during," and "after" phases. From the first chapter, "Argon," with its nostalgic view of Levi's Jewish-Piedmontese ancestors, the time frame shifts to the late 1930s and early 1940s, to the era of the Racial Laws that not only alienated Levi from his countrymen but also made it difficult for him to complete his university degree and to find employment (as recounted in the chapters "Zinc," "Iron," "Potassium," "Nickel," and "Phosphorus"); then, from Levi's capture by the Fascists in late 1943, when he was a hapless partisan, to an audacious and successful survival ploy in Auschwitz (in "Gold" and "Cerium"); and finally, from his difficulties adjusting to normal life following his return home, to an encounter some twenty years after the war with a German civilian chemist who had worked with Levi in a laboratory at Auschwitz (in "Chromium" and "Vanadium"). Excluding the five chapters of fiction integrated into this memoir, ten of the sixteen remaining chapters are Holocaust-related.

To unite the disparate material of his life into a coherent narrative, Levi combines two man-made organizing grids: a standard chronology of the major historical events of mid-twentieth century Europe and Mendeleev's periodic table. Just as Mendeleev's schema is an effort to organize and rationalize material reality, and is known to be imperfect even by novice students of chemistry, *The Periodic Table* is Levi's attempt to see himself clearly through the lens of his work. Beyond its autobiographical aspects, he would have the reader believe that the book's purpose is to show that chemistry has the capacity to bridge the gap between "the world of words and the world of things" (*The Periodic Table*, 42), and is therefore the link between mind and matter. However, in opposition to this harmonious meeting of the two cultures, there is also a counternarrative embedded in *The Periodic Table* that suggests that twentieth-century human beings were not truly liberated in the nexus of art and science, but instead trapped in the inherent fissure between mind and matter.[9] Moreover, this gap was never more evident than during the Holocaust, a traumatic event that profoundly interrupted the relationship between words and things, between language and experience. Auschwitz created an abyss remarked upon in nearly all Holocaust memoirs, including Levi's *Survival in Auschwitz*, in which he says, "Our language lacks the words to express this offence, the demolition of a man."[10]

My main claim here is that *The Periodic Table* testifies to the dialectic of separation and integration that not only characterizes the discourses of chemistry and science but also the history of modern Europe from the Enlightenment to the Holocaust. This fluctuation between multiplicity and unity, the different and the same, is the process that creates but also destabilizes the binaries that structure Levi's thought. He delights in Mendeleev's periodic table because it makes order out of chaos; however, as a

device for categorizing and normalizing material, it is also consonant with
the mentality exhibited by social engineers like the Nazis, who tried to
perfect and purify peoples through education, medicine, and psychology,
but also with biology, medicine, and eugenics.

The Order of Things

In *The Order of Things* (titled *Les mots et les choses*—"words and things"—in
French), Foucault describes the complex intellectual transition from the
preclassical age of science to modern science, that is, the shift from the
epistemologies of the late Renaissance to those of the Enlightenment and
on up to the twentieth-century.[11] In classical science, humankind and
nature were held to be completely separate. The Cartesian cogito ("I
think, therefore I am") epitomizes this attitude because it defines the mind
as our whole being without reference to our bodily existence. In the classical age, the scientific disciplines had not yet developed, so that the educated individual could still grasp the whole of human knowledge. There
was only one culture, not two, and there was no perceived gap between
our mental concepts of the material world, as rendered in language, and
the world itself. Then, according to Foucault, the rise of the human sciences, biology and psychology, but also linguistics and economics, affected
Man's view of himself: now, as both mind and body, as the possessor of
both transcendental qualities and empirical ones, he not only gazes reflec-
tively on nature but also understands himself to be a part of it, to be
embodied. For Foucault, "modernity begins when the human being begins
to exist within his organism." Now, man occupies "the ambiguous position as the object of knowledge and the subject that knows."[12] Modernity
constitutes, for the first time, an unstable hybrid of human subject and
human object, unstable because the two collapse into each other, because
the opposition of man to matter is no longer sustainable. As Foucault sees
it, humanism engages in a now impossible attempt "to recuperate the primacy and autonomy of the thinking subject and master all that is other to
it."[13] However, the mind is lodged within a body conditioned by preexist-
ing historical and biological forces that the mind cannot determine. Moreover, language has now lost its capacity to represent the world wholly and
transparently. No longer the privileged domain of the knowing subject, it
too becomes an object of study whose historical accretions and murky
imprecision are discovered by disciplines like philology.

The political implications of the modern perception that man is inescapably a product of nature and history are worked out in Foucault's essay, "Right of Death and Power Over Life."[14] In the past, the sovereign, by law, had the right to put any person to death for the purpose of protecting the state, but modern governments legitimate their power by means of scientific discourses like social Darwinism that give them the obligation to manage their populations: they have "power over life." "For the first time," Foucault asserts, "biological existence [is] reflected in political existence." The state legitimates violence by claiming to be engaged in a positive campaign to protect "the right of the social body to ensure, maintain, or develop its life." "Yet," Foucault writes, "wars were never as bloody as they have been since the nineteenth-century . . . never before did regimes visit such holocausts on their own populations. . . . It is as managers of life and survival, of bodies and the race, that so many regimes have been able to wage so many wars, causing so many men to be killed." Foucault enables us to see that science's claim on objective truth is precisely what gives it political power. Once biology, medicine and racial science gain acceptance as tools for improving the life and health of nations—what Foucault calls "bio-power" and "bio-politics"—the path is cleared for state-sponsored genocides aimed at protecting the national collective body from pollution by inferior races. As a humanist, Levi defends chemistry and physics as a source of truth, "clear and distinct and verifiable at every step," and as an "antidote" to Fascist lies (*The Periodic Table*, 42). He conceives of science as a "pure," truth-seeking practice that counters the impure stench of Italian Fascist ideology. Yet, after more than two centuries of scientific racism and scientific sexism, it was clear to Foucault that the discourses of science are inherently political and value-laden despite the indisputable truths revealed by legitimate research. Of course, it is a commonplace to say that "knowledge is power," but he goes further in that, for him, "the goals of power and the goals of knowledge cannot be separated: in knowing we control and in controlling we know."[15]

Although there is no space here for a coherent account of the work of Giorgio Agamben, nor to see what light it might shed on *The Periodic Table*, his ideas deserve a passing mention. Agamben's analysis of the concept of "bare life," a condition under ancient Roman law that left individuals completely outside of the polity and without rights, leans heavily on Foucault's account of "bio-politics." Moreover, Agamben carries Foucault's analysis to it logical conclusion when he calls the concentration camp "the fundamental bio-political paradigm of the West."[16]

Two Kinds of Scientific Knowledge

In effect, two kinds of scientific knowledge operate in *The Periodic Table*—the science of laws and the science of norms—and the conflict between them not only comprises the central drama of Levi's personal history, and that of his generation, but also sheds light on the troubling role played by science in the unfolding of the Holocaust. In the first instance, Levi's humanist subject constitutes itself by uncovering the universal scientific laws that matter must obey. By the time he was sixteen, as described in the "Hydrogen" chapter, Levi had endured years of the Italian Fascist school curriculum which, in its Crocean idealism, held that philosophy (the study of the spirit) was formative, while science (the study of matter) was merely informative. Enervated by "[school] lectures on the problem of being and knowing," Levi looked instead to chemistry as an alternative path to knowledge. Chemistry was verifiable and based on laws as eternal as the Ten Commandments, a testament like no other to the power of words. "Like Moses [on Sinai], from that [chemical] cloud, I expected my law, the principle of order in me, around me, and in the world . . . [the] key to the highest truths" (*The Periodic Table*, 23). However, the shadow looming over Levi's youthful idealism is the Fascist state, which eventually constituted itself on the basis of biological norms, as Nazism had done five years earlier. In 1938, the government sought to protect the "Italian Race" against "crosses and bastardizations" by prohibiting marriages between Italians and Jews (and non-Italian Jews, too).[17] This biological racism (not merely a form of xenophobia) drew on eugenics, a reputable science in the first half of the twentieth century that not only identified the degenerate genetic characteristics of individuals, but also developed a hierarchy of peoples that justified European imperialism and colonial expansion, including Italy's. In modernity's privileging of the norm over the law, the material over the abstract, science becomes implicated in the Holocaust.[18] The humanist's passion for laws that are always and everywhere true, in a Kantian fashion, has been overwhelmed by the state's clever application of the always-contingent norm. Levi tries to position science in a positive opposition to Italian Fascism, but, in the end, the regime, though less extreme than the Nazis, was invested more in the material body than in the spirit. No one had to prove that Italian Jews were not good Fascists in order to ostracize them; it was simply a biological question.

How do Foucault's ideas help us account for the "bio-politics" of Fascist Italy that loom so large in *The Periodic Table*? The fact that Italy had no history of significant anti-Semitism and no political party with an anti-Semitic platform underscores how the Racial Laws were shrewd policies created at the top of the government hierarchy. Recently, Giorgio Fabre has attempted to show that Mussolini was a deeply committed anti-Semite.[19] Perhaps—but this would not have been a condition necessary to the promulgation of anti-Jewish policies. It is sufficient to surmise that what Mussolini saw when he visited Berlin in 1937 was the mobilizing power of racist discourse. Or, as Foucault puts it in his collected lectures, *"Society Must Be Defended"* (a deliberately ironic title that contrasts productively with Levi's assertion, in *Survival in Auschwitz* and elsewhere, that the idea of the human must be defended in the wake of Holocaust), states do not obtain power so they can be racist; rather it is the frightening scenarios drawn from theories of racial degeneration and racial health that legitimate the exercise of power, even to the point of authorizing genocide.[20] "Racism justifies the death-function in the economy of bio-power," Foucault states, "by appealing to the principle that the death of others makes one biologically stronger insofar as one is a member of a race or a population, insofar as one is an element in a unitary living plurality."[21] And, of course, both Nazism and Italian Fascism conceived of the nation as a single body, and both represented the Jew as a dangerous pathogen within that body.

While its principles were contradictory, Italian Fascism's consistent program was national regeneration, a return to Roman greatness that would only be achieved after Italy rid itself of non-Latin elements. Levi lived through a time when Mussolini's government misused biology to contend that all true Italians were the descendants of the ancient Romans, and that the threat of miscegenation with Jews and the newly colonized Africans legitimated severe measures to protect that purity. Levi's experience of being categorized as a Jew capable of polluting the Italian race prompts him to remark, in the "Zinc" chapter, "Dissension, diversity . . . Fascism does not want them, forbids them, and that is why you are not a Fascist; it wants everyone to be the same and you are not" (*The Periodic Table*, 34). This is the autumn of 1938, when the hateful, anti-Semitic magazine *The Defense of the Race* began publication. Levi remarks that during this period, "there was much talk about purity." When he adds, with evident irony, "I had begun to proud of being impure," I do not believe that he actually accepts that the difference imposed on him by Fascism is a positive value. Indeed, he states that before the promulgation of the Racial Laws, "it had not meant much to me that I was a Jew" (*The Periodic Table*, 35). While it is an anti-Fascist position to be proud of one's "impure" status, this stance is largely rhetorical. The salient point is that Levi is forced to contend with a world governed by norms even though he places his own hope in the Kantian categorical imperative that would apply laws equally without respect to contingent definitions of normality.

Considered in this Kantian context, what "hybridity" comes to mean in Levi's texts, or "impurity" in this particular case, is that difference among people exists, but the deeper our understanding the less importance we give to it in the overall scheme of things. For example, in his Holocaust memoir, Levi fully acknowledges that he experienced the camp as an assimilated Jew, as an Italian, as a male, and as a scientist. However, the apparent lesson of Auschwitz offered by Levi to his readers is that all the differences among the victims, and even between the victims and the perpetrators, fall away to reveal a universal concept of the person that must be defended. Thus, the memoir's original title challenges the reader to consider "if this is a man" (*Se questo è un uomo*) in which, I would add, the word *uomo*, man, is a false universal that does not accommodate difference—it is meant to include woman as well. Levi's philosophical assumptions are humanist so his praise of impurity in "Zinc" is not a postmodern embrace of difference for its own sake as has been sometimes implied.[22]

It is at the chemistry lab at Auschwitz, as recounted in the "Vanadium" chapter, where the unstable hybrid of humankind as subject ennobled by science and man as the miserable object of science is most eloquently expressed. That a chemistry lab staffed by disposable slave laborers should exist near the death camp says a lot about the perils of using the principles of science to fight fascism. Of course, Levi's readers know that he worked in this very lab in late 1944. The occasion for recalling it twenty years after the Holocaust stems from a business dispute between Levi's employer, a varnish manufacturer, and a German resin manufacturer that had spun off from IG Farben, the same industrial conglomerate that exploited slave laborers like Levi during the war. By an implausible coincidence, the contact for the German company, a certain Müller, turns out to be same civilian chemist who worked at the Auschwitz lab. (Actually, the chapter does not read like authentic autobiography, and Levi admitted elsewhere to having faked much of it.[23] We might surmise that he has an urgent message to deliver about Auschwitz, never mind the details, and he wants his words to have the authenticity associated with lived experience.) Reflecting on that pitiable time, Levi confesses that his greatest desire is to have a face-to-face reckoning with "[those] who had disposed of us, who had not looked into our eyes, as though we didn't have eyes." Delving deeper into what the perpetrators might have thought about the dehumanized prisoners, Levi guesses that, in the lab, Müller saw him as a "strange hybrid of colleague and instrument" (*The Periodic Table*, 215), that is, as both a peer and a mere body subject to biological or medical classification. This description of Levi's troubled hybrid condition, the central concern of the book, is emblematic of modernity, of that time when man is understood to be both subject and object, when the opposition of man to matter is no longer sustainable.[24] The greatest point of tension in *The Periodic Table* is here: two notions of the human are in grave conflict, and the same may be said of the two notions of science that shaped Levi's life—science as truth and science as power, with the forces of modernity favoring the latter.

The vexed connection between words and things, between mind and matter, is a thread that runs all the way to the end of the book, and it reaches a tentative resolution there. The final chapter describes the "life" of a carbon atom as it passes through various animate and inanimate objects including, finally, the brain and the hand of the unspecified writer who tells the atom's story. To start, the narrator conceives of carbon as the universal signifier in that it says "everything to everyone" (*The Periodic Table*, 225). If any element can link the two cultures, literature and science, can unify our minds and our materiality, carbon, the very stuff of life, is the one. And yet, the narrator also insists on the inadequacy of language to this task, saying that "the trade of clothing facts in words is bound by its very nature to fail" (*The Periodic Table*, 232). Moreover, he repeatedly mentions, quite rightly, the arbitrary and capricious quality of the story. "Every verbal description [of photosynthesis] must be inadequate, and one will be as good as the next" (*The Periodic Table*, 227), he asserts. Surprisingly, this largely autobiographical book concludes with the most impersonal of all its chapters, such that the chemist's noble pursuit of battling and conquering matter gives way to what the narrator calls a "literary dream" (*The Periodic Table*, 225). Indeed, carbon, inky black, is the element most strongly associated with words and writing, and the literary craft in this story, especially at the end, is nearly sublime. Here, the subject is not formed by mastering all that is other to it; rather, this subject writes and is written, and this language, as Foucault says of modern literature, "is folded back upon the enigma of its own origin and exist[s] wholly in reference to the pure act of writing." In literature, language becomes "a silent, cautious deposition of the word upon the whiteness of a piece of paper, where it can possess neither sound nor interlocutor, where it has nothing to say but itself, nothing to do but shine in the brightness of its being."[25] Here are the final two luminous sentences of Levi's book, bright in their being.

The cell belongs to a brain, and it is my brain, the brain of *me* who is writing; and the cell in question, and within it the atom in question, is in charge of my writing, in a gigantic minuscule game which nobody has yet described. It is that which at this instant, issuing out of a labyrinthine tangle of yeses and nos, makes my hand run along a certain path on the paper, mark it with these volutes that are signs: a double snap, up and down, between two levels of energy, guides this hand of mine to impress on the paper this dot, here, this one. (233; emphasis in Rosenthal's translation but not in the original Italian)

By this time, the reader expects that book's final lines will bring together the knowledge of the chemist and the writer's conscious shaping of this knowledge on paper. Words and things will be joined again; the instability of modern man, who is both subject and object at once, will be overcome; the spirit will be manifested in material, in the paper and ink, in the shapes of letters and in the precise meanings of the words those letters form. On a second reading, however, what emerges is that this "literary dream" is less concerned with representing chemical knowledge, and thus in serving scientific discourses, whether malignant or benign, but in performing its own beautiful autonomy. This final chapter of *The Periodic Table* is not so much about carbon as it is about how the universality and impersonality of carbon serves as a metaphor for the self-sufficiency of literature. This "*me* who is writing" is not Levi, but a *me* that is just as arbitrary as the carbon atom of the story. By universalizing the narrating self, art and literature would seem to offer us our one chance to escape from history and the troubled binary of subject/object. In this sense, Levi's final chapter might be said to endorse the claim that, after Auschwitz, literature has more emancipatory potential than science, and that, of the two cultures, literature, if it wishes, can be even more disinterested than science and less subject to the effects of power.

The Discourses of Science

In describing minutely the development of the two discourses of science in modern European societies, knowledge as truth and knowledge as power, Foucault's analysis of modernity and the genealogy of the humanist subject point us toward a profounder, more historical reading of *The Periodic Table*. He argues persuasively that modernity is characterized by the transformation (completed by the late nineteenth century) of diverse scientific practices, each devoted to ascertaining particular, localized and competing truths, into a unitary, institutionalized scientific discourse that allows states to control their populations and individual human bodies.[26] In Foucault's terms, Levi's version of chemistry is a marginal, local discourse with little political power. Indeed, Levi describes his memoir as a "microhistory" of chemistry, one that focuses on the individual chemist in pursuit of scientific truth rather than the grand, triumphant chemistry of colossal institutions (*The Periodic Table*, 224). Moreover, in its alchemical roots, Levi's chemistry refers back to a time when human beings had not yet become the objects of scientific study, before the link between words and things broke apart.

In effect, *The Periodic Table* dramatizes the collision between the human subject and the human object that necessarily accompanies the technologically sophisticated genocides so characteristic of modernity. In describing the human condition as centaur-like but also unharmonious—that is, as "a tangle of flesh and mind, divine inspiration and dust" (*The Periodic Table*, 9)—Levi confirms, intentionally or not, Foucault's assertion that during the Enlightenment the discursive subject called Man was first conceived as a conflicted binary, as both the scientist/subject and also the specimen/object of modern scientific investigation. While Foucault's analysis of the social and political consequences of institutionalized science helps us to situate historically *The Periodic Table*, Levi's memoir, in turn, validates an idea rather new to Holocaust studies: that the Foucauldian genealogy of the humanist subject explains how state racism and the genocides that they foster are not antithetical to modernity but coherent parts of it.

CHAPTER 8

The Partisan and His Doppelganger: The Case of Primo Levi

Ilona Klein

Published in 1982, *Se non ora, quando?* (*If Not Now, When?*) is Primo Levi's first novel proper. Perhaps Primo Levi so regretted not fully living life as an Italian Jewish partisan that he re-created his lost dream through its pages, and had his partisan brigade not been captured, perhaps Levi's underground fighting might have continued until the end of the war. *If Not Now, When?* thus might reflect Levi's need to explore that sought-after life as a partisan, which he had been denied after only three months of activity.[1] Did Levi write *If Not Now, When?* as a mental antidote to his arrest? Was he trying to re-create for himself the underground world of freedom fighters, which he was not able to fulfill? Edoardo Bianchini points out that the main theme of the novel is to reclaim human dignity. During the time in which the fictional core of *If Not Now, When?* takes place, Primo Levi was a prisoner in Auschwitz. Since it is obvious that, while Levi was interned, he could not simultaneously also be a free man, I propose here that *If Not Now, When?* might be read and understood as the "other" story, the narrative of that partisan experience that Levi did not live in full, the story of his destroyed dream as an aspiring freedom fighter against the Nazi and Fascist tragedy. I submit, then, that the narrative of *If Not Now, When?* develops the theme of Levi's doppelganger through the discourse of a fictional, projected alter-ego protagonist. In the novel, Levi focuses on the vicissitudes of a group of Jewish partisan fighters of Eastern Europe, celebrating their courage and writing about their adventures perhaps as a way to counteract the misperception that Jews went to the gas chambers without trying to resist arrest and deportation.

The framework for this novel is not entirely fictional. Levi explained, in the author's note following the end of the book, that Emilio Vita Finzi "narrated to me the kernel of the story," for Vita Finzi had "worked as a volunteer at the assistance center [in Milan] described in the final chapter" (347–348). Moreover, Levi acknowledges that the resistance actions described in his novel are "invented but plausible. . . . Actions of harassment such as sabotaging railroads . . . are amply documented in the literature on partisan warfare in Eastern Europe" (348).

As Primo Levi wrote in the first chapter of *Se questo è un uomo* (*Survival in Auschwitz*), he was arrested by the Fascist militia on December 13, 1943. By then, he had spent about three months in the Italian regions of Val d'Aosta and Piedmont as part of a small Italian partisan brigade of young and inexperienced men.[2] During the interrogation following his arrest, Levi declared himself to be an "Italian citizen of the Jewish race." As his readers know, the long agony of Auschwitz and its aftermath were the consequences of such a statement.

A cursory glance at the table of contents of *If Not Now, When?* clearly shows that the fictional narrative time frame of this novel spans from July 1943 through August 1945. Comparing these dates to Levi's own life, parallels can be created: one finds a first temporal fragment spanning a seven-month block (July 1943–February 1944) that precedes Levi's internment in the concentration camp; a second and longer segment, which overlaps his year as a slave prisoner in Auschwitz (February 1944–January 1945); and a third part forming yet another seven-month block (January 1945–August 1945) whose vicissitudes are retold in his work *La tregua* (*The Reawakening*), the sequel to *Survival in Auschwitz*. In fact, Nicholas Patruno claims that *The Reawakening* "may be considered this work's [*If Not Now, When?*] direct antecedent since it too recounts the pilgrimage through central Europe of a group of prisoners."[3]

While in Auschwitz, like the majority of concentration-camp prisoners, Levi did not have a chance to participate in organized revolts against the Nazi machine (other than his own valiant struggle against death). Like most other Auschwitz inmates, he was kept unaware of any external partisan actions against the Nazis. Since the prisoner Levi could not fight against the Nazis nor against the civilians' general indifference, Levi lets the characters of *If Not Now, When?* do it for him instead.

Retelling, orally or in written form, a difficult part of one's life can be a constructive way of coping with past pains. Primo Levi recognized the value of this kind of logotherapy through the Yiddish proverb that he used as epigraph of *The Periodic Table* (*Il sistema periodico*, 1975): "*Ibergekumene tsores iz gut tsu dertseyln*" (It is good to talk about overcome troubles). He also inserts the proverb into the text of *If Not Now, When?* (300). Through the fictional re-creation of an alternate life story, one might learn to cope with past senseless losses and suffering, both of one's people and of the self. The narration of traumatic memory helps turn a forcibly passive experience into an act of logotherapy, which is validating, for the survivor exercises personal choices by controlling the perspective. Narrating becomes a moment of free will and of personal autonomy. In a well-thought-out and provocative study, Susan Brison analyzes the interconnections between trauma, memory, and personal identity. She asserts that "survivors of trauma frequently remark that they are not the same people they were before being traumatized." She differentiates between different types of traumatizing events in her study, focusing on those which are "of human origin and . . . intentionally inflicted."[4] The narrative self, argues Brison, aids the embodied self in dealing with the aftermath of the trauma. She points out that several Shoah survivors used pseudonyms for their postwar writings (Améry and Celan, to name two) in the attempt to construct a new authorial self, after their original self had been annihilated by the perpetrators.[5] Others yet wrote their autobiographies of survival in a new, adopted mother tongue (Elie Wiesel, for instance). "Not to be heard," argues Brison, "means that the self the survivor has become does not exist. Since the earlier self died, the surviving self needs to be known and acknowledged in order to exist."[6] Levi may have written *If Not Now, When?* in light of his need to be heard, then, and to validate his desire to have experienced life as a freedom fighter. Karin Lorenz-Lindemann clarifies, "The trauma transformed into language involves a process which binds self-determination to the constitution of self in mutual speech. Even more: the continuity of life realized through speech is self-assertion creating a future."[7]

The title of Levi's novel *Se non ora, quando?* stems from words found in the Talmud. Among *The Maxims of the Fathers* (1:13), Rabbi Hillel stated: "If I am not for myself, who will be for me? And even if I think of myself, what am I? And if not now, when?" From Rabbi Hillel, Levi extrapolates only the last question, leaving undeveloped those expressing concern for oneself. What Levi retains for the title, instead, is the temporal question,

"If not now, when?" This choice does not appear to be simply a coincidence, for temporality forms the almost obsessive backbone of the novel's
story line, in which Ashkenazi partisans take care of themselves in the
underworld of the resistance ("If I am not for myself, who will be for
me?") while defining their own lives and roles within their outlawed brigade ("And even if I think of myself, what am I?").

In the novel, the protagonist, Mendel Nachmanovich Dajcher, worked
as a watch repairman before joining the partisans. Temporality, thus, is
not only visible in the title of *If Not Now, When?* or in the almost too
precisely chronologically ordered chapters, but it is also embodied within
the plot's main character. Mendel is he who fixes watches, he who controls
time on a watch, he who is in control of time. Mendel the partisan is
"better at mending things than at blowing them up" (85). By contrast,
Levi the prisoner lived his days and nights in a slavery dictated by the
passing of sunrises and sunsets, by cyclical spasms of hunger, despair, and
survival subject to the passing of time over which prisoners had no control.
Thus here, Primo Levi the prisoner delegates to his doppelganger, Mendel the partisan, how to fix, manipulate, channel, and coordinate time:
allegorically, with the watches Mendel mends, more tangibly, by his
authority to decide the timing of partisan actions in his brigade. Mendel
has control over time. Or, at least, Levi would like his readers to believe
that he does.

Issues pertaining to the temporal perception of human beings (as well
as to the loss of a time line) are themes to which Levi often turns in his
works. Already as early as in his *Survival in Auschwitz*, Levi connects temporal awareness (in terms, for instance, of the passing of days, hours, minutes) to the sense of preservation of human dignity. In *If Not Now, When?*
time forms the underlying factor for each chapter, in contrast to the loss
of temporal perception in Auschwitz. Possibly, Levi intends to highlight
the concept of "time" as one of a human invention, and of "loss of time"
as a condition that deprives humans of some of their own parameters.
Patruno writes that there is a "feeling of sensory deprivation that comes
from not knowing what time it is." In the same light, Brison states that
"the ability to form a plan of life is lost when one loses a sense of one's
temporal being, as happened to Levi and other prisoners in Auschwitz."[8]

Mendel recounts that when he was young, the people in his village
judged the hour by the position of the sun and the moon, or by listening
to the time announced on the radio. Then, when personal watches became
somewhat more affordable and available, some villagers started wearing
them. Watches, explains Mendel, are like people, whom he sometimes sees

in terms of clockwork in need of repair. Early on in the novel, Mendel compares Leonid (another main character) to a dusty watch whose mechanism needs to be taken apart completely, cleaned with gasoline, and fixed (46). Patruno notes that "Leonid, who is nineteen years old, is a book-keeper by training. At sixteen, he was imprisoned in the Lubyanka Prison in Moscow for stealing a watch. This establishes the link between Leonid and Mendel."[9] When comparing human beings to watches, Mendel also points out how some clocks are brought in for repair when the damage done is already irreparable. Primo Levi is implying, then, that certain types of time cannot be corrected; in other words, that certain types of people cannot be mended, certain types of situations cannot be changed.

In *If Not Now, When?* "control" over time, however, does not mean that time passes in a regular and predictable flow. In fact, the general confusion of wartime (historical time, political time, personal time) is mir-rored structurally and stylistically in the novel. Some characters appear and disappear abruptly; often, factual information is fragmentary at best, while Levi carefully avoids long descriptive or narrative passages concern-ing only one character.

Within this narrative tension, a more canonical and developed form of confessional monologue would be inconceivable. In fact, through rigorous mathematical and statistical analyses of Levi's prose usage in *If Not Now, When?*, Jane Nystedt has demonstrated that the novel is overwhelmingly composed in dialogic form. She acutely observes that the characters' thoughts and the narratives of their brave assaults are included mostly within dialogic narrative patterns (100).[10] As in a puzzle taking shape, or as in a clock ticking out of sync with time, using dialogues among the novel's characters, Levi employs a quick narrative pace to describe partisan sabotages, combat techniques, moments of respite, friendships forming and dissolving by coincidence, while pondering upon life's contingencies and its needs.

In Levi's own months in Auschwitz, as well as in this novel, death is omnipresent, enormous in its irreversibility: it is irreparable, like a very badly broken watch. When the heroic partisans of Gedaleh's group are killed (and these are characters with whom the reader has become thor-oughly familiar), their lives are liquidated shockingly fast.[11] Levi presents death in its abruptness, as most of the time death does not allow for proper forewarning. In fact, the characters of Adam, Leonid, and Black Rokhele disappear from the plot as suddenly as they had appeared, hardly ever to be remembered again. In the narrative, the deaths of Vadim and Ber are of concern to Dov only because the perceived "Semitic physiognomy" of

Ber's abandoned corpse may reveal the presence of Jewish partisans to the Nazis patrolling the territory of Novoselki (94–95).

The psychological profiles of the characters in this book span the whole human gamut, from the meek and fearful to the impatient and bold. Correctly, Patruno points out how the characters "retain[ed] their dignity in the midst of upheaval."[12] Eamonn Callan writes that "our culturally dominant institutions about heroism revolve around the notions of the glorious and the great."[13] Levi never falls into this trap, and he is able to appreciate the microcosmic yet valiant forms of resistance of any human action. Callan recalls Levi's own words in describing the different types of courage exhibited by some of his characters in *If Not Now, When?*: "Ulybin's courage was stubborn and dull, a duty courage that seemed the fruit of study and discipline rather than a natural gift"; "Gedaleh's courage was extempore and varied"; "where Ulybin calculated, Gedaleh flung himself as into a game."[14] The continuous balancing and intertwining play between the attributes of "patience" and "courage," Callan claims, forges the moral and intellectual landscape of Levi's characters in *If Not Now, When?*

When time slows down, during quiet, nocturnal, introspective moments, the characters discover their inner selves. Their self-discovery leads to an attempt at understanding the historical times and spaces of Eastern European Ashkenazi Judaism, and specifically of the identity of Russian Jews. In Levi's narrative, this search for the tradition of the fathers is present in religious and agnostic partisans alike.[15]

Levi writes in *If Not Now, When?* about those Ashkenazim for whom their Jewish ancestry, culture, and religion played an important role. By contrast, Primo Levi's Jewish identity felt, as Levi himself clarified, almost imposed upon him by the racial laws of 1938 and by his subsequent internment in Auschwitz. Lorenz-Lindemann points out that, as in the case of Jean Améry, "before their deportation to Auschwitz, they both lived in a context where being Jewish was not an object of particular concern. They both were arrested as members of the resistance."[16] Levi dealt with the Jewish label, which the Nazis and Fascists had attached to him, but never in the sense of being a fervent Zionist or a religious man. For his whole life, Primo Levi remained an agnostic, secular Jew. His Jewish identity was something that Levi did not recognize in himself before his arrest, and he still struggled to define it fully after the war.

Primo Levi did not speak Yiddish (he only had a basic knowledge of the language, learned after the war), was not familiar with the culture of the *Ostjuden*, and was attracted to their history of resistance during World War II. The only extended exposure that Levi had with the world of the

Ostjuden was while in the Lager. In Auschwitz, Levi was surrounded by thousands of Ashkenazim, who spoke Yiddish as their lingua franca. For Levi, such a linguistic connection was an intriguing experience, because, overall, Italian Jews (Sephardim and Italkim) do not speak nor understand Yiddish; rather, they share different kinds of ties with one another and within their community. After the war, Levi wished to explore further the Jewish identity of Eastern Europe. In *If Not Now, When?* Levi reconstructed a world, a culture, a language, which, to a large extent, was unknown to him.[17] The novel can be regarded as Levi's attempt to introduce the culture and the traditions of the Ashkenazim and of the Yiddish-speaking Jews to the Italian readership.[18] It is in this light that one should read, toward the end of the novel, the lack of interaction between Gedaleh's group and the other guests at the reception by Signora Adele S. and her husband in Milano. This episode underlines the isolation and separation between the Ashkenazim Zionists and the Italian Jews. It further emphasizes how, to a certain extent, Italian secular Judaism was, and is, a somewhat indefinable state of being, based not solely upon a religious belief (or lack thereof), but also by the knowledge (or lack thereof) of a common language such as Yiddish. As one reads in *If Not Now, When?*, "*Redest keyn jiddisch, bist nit keyn jid*": If you do not speak Yiddish, you are not a Jew (201).

A declared agnostic, Primo Levi is valued by many readers as a humanist writer rather than as a "Jewish" author. However, his agnosticism notwithstanding, biblical themes penetrate his works. References to the Hebrew scriptures and to Judaism abound in *If Not Now, When?* As mentioned previously, the title itself is part of the Talmud, to which Levi added a contemporary twist.[19]

> Do you recognize us? We're the sheep of the ghetto,
> Shorn for a thousand years, resigned to outrage.
> We are the tailors, the scribes and the cantors,
> Withered in the shadow of the cross
> Now we have learned the paths of the forest,
> We have learned to shoot, and we aim straight.
> If I'm not for myself, who will be for me?
> If not this way, how? And if not now, when?
> Our brothers have gone to heaven
> Through the chimneys of Sobibor and Treblinka,
> They have dug themselves a grave in the air.
> Only we few have survived

For the honor of our submerged people,
For revenge and to bear witness.
If I'm not for myself, who will be for me?
If not this way, how? And if not now, when?
We are the sons of David, the hardheaded sons of Masada.
Each of us carries in his pocket the stone
That shattered the forehead of Goliath.
Brothers, away from this Europe of graves:
Let us climb together towards the land
Where we will be men among men.
If I'm not for myself, who will be for me?
If not this way, how? If not now, when? (168–169)

This poem is remarkable for several reasons. In it, Levi summarizes the highlights of the history of European Jewry, of its survival and the dignity of its culture. Once viewed by outsiders merely as the sheep of the ghetto, Jews instead claim for themselves a long tradition of active involvement in their communities. In the poem, Levi points out that Jews worked as tailors, clothing people in outfits that mirrored the many different positions Jews held within the larger society. They were scribes, both in the sense of the sacred profession that creates letter-perfect Torah scrolls, but also in the sense of those who wrote the history of the Jewish people, and the history of the holy books. They were cantors, *chazzanim*, who gave life, voice, and sound to the complex art of Jewish music. While for centuries they lived as minorities in the lands of Christians, being at times ostracized and at times tolerated "in the shadow of the cross," during the resistance in World War II, they left their established communities to take refuge in the forests nearby, claiming for themselves a small resemblance of freedom that they were being denied in the ghettos. As freedom fighters, Jews traded their former jobs as tailors, scribes, and cantors to become sharpshooters instead, ready to engage in violence when necessary to uphold their right to human dignity, making sure never to be mistaken again for sheep in the ghetto. The freedom fighters knew, Levi continues in the poem, what happened to the Jews who had been deported from their towns: they were burned in the crematoria and "gone to heaven through the chimneys." Thus, those who engaged in partisan combat did so in order to try to change the course of the genocide; to stay alive in order to write the history of a most courageous survival, and to bring both honor and revenge to a people whose civic and intellectual contributions to European history were inarguably seminal. The last strophe of the poem emphasizes the long history of courage of the Jewish people: their biblical ancestral lineage as children of King David who, still a youngster, slew the giant Goliath with just one perfect shot of his sling. Also, Levi brings forth Jews' legacy as defenders of freedom as he points the reader to the episode of the heroic resistance of 960 Jews on the isolated mountaintop of Masada. They committed suicide rather than give themselves up to be subjected to the Romans. Still today in Israel, Masada is the emblem of Jewish survival. All partisans, concludes the poem, are brothers, there to help each other, to take their own destiny into their own hands, for no one else will do it for them. The last lines of the third strophe leave the reader with an unmistakable call to Zionism, with the desire to leave behind "this Europe of graves."

As Patruno recognizes, Gedaleh's song is of "resurrection and triumph," as it also gives the title to the book. It is "the real turning point in the story. After this night, there is more purpose and direction."[20]

In his novel, based on much historical evidence of Jewish partisan action, Levi stressed how European Jews were not passively resigned to their destiny, and did not go to the slaughter like meek sheep without fighting. "Levi is inventive in devising and describing subversive actions, displaying a familiarity with the basics of guerrilla tactics that seems remarkable considering the short time he spent as a partisan in Italy."[21] For the millions killed in the genocide, there were thousands of organized Jews and Gentiles who attempted to resist the Nazi machine of annihilation.[22] The refrain of Gedaleh's song emphasizes the importance of personal contributions to political and ideological movements. Patruno states that "to those who have questioned the behavior of Jews during the Holocaust, this tale of collective and individual heroism and resistance is a powerful response." Moreover, Patruno observes that the novel is "Levi's answer to all those who have demeaned the Jews for not resisting."[23]

Usually not heavily and overtly politicized in his writings (and I propose that here the readers are witnessing yet another aspect of Primo Levi's alter ego), in *If Not Now, When?* the author stresses individual and political obligations toward society by placing the character of Mendel at the center of the narrative. While obviously not all Jews and Gentiles are mandated to play the biblical role of each other's keepers, nevertheless Levi stresses the moral responsibility of a shared civic duty in guaranteeing democracy for a free society. Primo Levi, in the true spirit of a secular Jew, offers no definite parameters for these considerations: rather, to each person his or her own solution, forged by the result of a long inquiry with one's conscience, exercising personal moral principles and ethics. Jews were forced to take care of their own protection during World War II; during the years of genocide, "no manna descended from the black sky, but only pitiless snow. Let each choose his own destiny," writes Levi (96). The degree to which one becomes the brother's keeper or the brother's killer (or the 'gray zoner' in between, for that matter) depends only on one's self, the author concludes.[24]

Toward the end of the novel, the Gedalists are taken to Glogau, a German mining center liberated by the Russians only a few weeks earlier. For the first time in the narration, the partisan unit finally freely engages in conversation with some ex-prisoners of the Nazi camps. A new character is introduced, the Auschwitz survivor and "assimilated" Jewess Francine. She fleetingly appears in the novel and then disappears, never to be mentioned again, for her fictional life spans just a few, short, but solidly built, paragraphs. Like Primo Levi, she too, at the moment of her arrest, had declared herself Jewish; she, too, did not speak nor understand Yiddish; she, too, had a well-proven scientific background, having practiced pediatric medicine professionally in Paris before her deportation. Her character is strong: no longer the woman with "eyes empty and womb cold / as a frog in winter" whom Levi had described in his poem "Shemà," the epigraph of *Survival in Auschwitz*. Francine therefore represents and behaves as a proud exception to the genocide. It is Francine who explains the overwhelming sense of guilt she bears for having survived the camp experience while many of her Jewish friends and relatives succumbed. Levi will wait until his *I sommersi e i salvati* (1986, *The Drowned and the Saved*) to address and discuss more directly and openly the topic of survivor's guilt in one of his chapters. It is apparent, however, that this subject already weighed on Levi while he wrote *If Not Now, When?* Francine represents all the prisoners who survived the Shoah and paid a hefty psychological price in terms of bearing the weight of their memories. Memories of the loved ones who did not survive, memories of those prisoners who followed—for better or for worse—their own instinct of survival, memories of the uncontrollable and arbitrary external factors that kept one person alive, while another one died. Francine then explains how the feeling of guilt for having survived the Shoah (vis-à-vis the next of kin who perished during the persecution) brought many survivors to commit suicide after the liberation. Like Levi, she had not been in contact with Eastern European Jews before her internment in Auschwitz; like him, she could not identify close spiritual affinities with those actively involved in Zionism. She considered herself first and foremost French and was not able to define clearly in what consisted her Jewishness, just as the secular Primo Levi thought of himself as an Italian citizen first and foremost, surrounded by many Italian Christian friends for whom his Jewishness was at best of little significance, since he had never been an observant Jew. The fictional Francine typifies the hundreds of courageous survivors who were able to identify and express their feelings of shame and guilt for a second chance at life, which they perceived as not having been earned.[25] "It's hard to explain," comments Levi's female alter ego (295). Within a different context, Douglas Kellner writes that "in pre-modern societies, identity was unproblematic and not subject to reflections of discussion. Individuals did not undergo identity crises, or radically modify their identity."[26] The characters in Levi's novel are fully modern in this sense, for most experience deeply moving or troubling moments of brutally honest soul searching.

The novel ends on Tuesday, August 7, 1945. Twenty-five months have passed since the first pages of *If Not Now, When?* As Giuseppe Tosi correctly observes, *If Not Now, When?* opens with one of Mendel's many flashbacks, indicating a general timelessness of events in the opening sentences, and ends with a specific temporal marker: Hiroshima, August 7, 1945. The whole novel is set in between these two temporal posts. By the end of *If Not Now, When?* time has passed for Mendel the watch repairman; time has passed for the reader. As the character named White Rokhele gives birth to Isidor's son at a hospital in Milano, doctors read headlines about the American atomic bomb's killing of tens of thousands at Hiroshima. At the moment of the atomic blast all the clocks in Hiroshima were destroyed, and time stopped in Japan. By contrast, for Mendel the watch repairman, the timekeeper, he who can fix the link between past and present, time continues to go by. Time ticks also for the newborn, and time goes on for Zionists on their way to Palestine. The tragic final tone of the novel certainly dampens the joy of a new birth: built around the suffering and deaths of World War II, the book ends with an image of death. The reader is led to ponder the juxtaposition between the pre-Shoah memories and the tragic turn of events during the war. Often in Levi's works, life and death are intertwined, their intrinsic connection hard to put in plain words. Tosi comments that this contrast is further exacerbated by a disintegrated and disintegrating past, leading to a future whose parameters need to be invented anew.[27] To paraphrase Primo Levi, "the drowned" and "the saved" are not necessarily two separate groups of people: sometimes one can survive a traumatic experience, while at the same time succumbing to it.

Perhaps Levi wrote this novel in an attempt to indicate the meaning of life to the next postwar generation. To quote Lorenz-Lindemann, "Jewish tradition has taught us that it belongs to the tasks of men to recreate the world: Levi has tried just this—through writing. That was his revolt." It could likewise be argued, as Callan does, that "yet the limits of our capacity to make the good we crave our own are often intractably narrow."[28]

At the end of *If Not Now, When?* time goes on, but only for those surviving characters who are now utterly aware of the death surrounding them. The atrocities of World War II have become the inherent legacy of the new postwar generation. It appears, then, that in his novel the author Primo Levi trades places with the character Mendel: when the first was prisoner in Auschwitz, the latter was on the forest trails fighting with the partisans. In fact, in a 1982 interview, Primo Levi stated, "I did identify with Mendel. What I mean is that he did what I would have done, or— better yet—what I should have done, had I been capable of doing it."[29]

Besides Levi trading places with Mendel, Mendel trades places within himself, too: after spending one erotic night with Line at the mill, a perturbed Mendel engages himself in a deep soul-searching moment (194).[30] Mendel the *factotum*, Mendel the watch repairman, perhaps the most rational character in the novel, is surrounded by ghosts, for the shadow of his deceased wife, Rivke, never abandons him. The character Francine's explanations of "shame" and "guilt" apply to Mendel, too.

If Mendel represents Levi's doppelganger, then Levi's ghosts are likely hidden through Mendel's. Mendel's stream-of-consciousness thoughts reveal the weight of the past during one of the most introspective moments of *If Not Now, When?*:

> He pressed, tried to draw her to him, but Sissl resisted, stony in sleep. On the vague screen of his dozing, names and faces pursued one another, present and distant. Sissl, blond and tired. Rivke with her sad black eyes, but Mendel dispelled her at once, he didn't want her, he couldn't think about her. Rivke, Strelka, the grave: go away, Rivke, please. Go back to where you came from, let me live. (192)

It is in this text, perhaps, that the seed was planted for Levi's later poem "The Survivor" (1984): "Stand back, leave me alone . . . / go away . . . / go back into your mist," pleads the survivor at bedtime, in need of sleep, but overwhelmed by the same sense of guilt that Francine tried to explain to others.

To conclude, I should point out that in *If Not Now, When?* one reads, "This story is not being told in order to describe massacres" (98). The problem with Weaver's translation of this sentence is that, *traduttore traditore*, it does not render the original, *"Non è per descrivere stragi che questa storia sta raccontando se stessa*" (64). "This story is narrating itself" is actually what Levi writes. As time passes, Levi suggests, life has a way of creating itself often independently of our control. Life narrates itself, the story narrates itself.

In significant ways, then, Levi *is* the watch repairman of this novel, which narrates itself while at the same time narrating the protagonists' fictional lives and mirroring the author's most inner thoughts. Levi's own search for identity is veiled and masked within the narrative, his own existentialist search remaining apparently dampened, apparently secondary only to Mendel's.[31]

An unsettled author hides within the lines of *If Not Now, When?* He searches for answers to many questions: questions about life and death, questions about choices not made, questions about the arbitrariness and necessities in life, questions about history created or history suffered, about control over one's life, about the guilt of survivorship, and, in general, about life's roads, the paths, and the forest trails, taken or not: Levi, the denied partisan; Levi, the Auschwitz survivor.

CHAPTER 9

Primo Levi in the Public Interest: Turin, Auschwitz, Israel

Risa Sodi

This essay focuses on three extraliterary facets of Primo Levi: his public associations with Auschwitz and Holocaust commemoration, his leadership role in the Jewish community of Turin, and his contribution to the intellectual debates over the Arab-Israeli conflict. Many of Levi's nonliterary pronouncements appeared in low-circulation publications, on Italian radio and television, in unexpected venues or were about subjects—like the crisis in the Middle East—with which Levi is not usually associated. A review of these facets sheds light on the man that was Primo Levi and also on the literary projects that occupied him at the same time.

In the late 1950s and 1960s, while he was working full-time as a chemist, Levi's political energy was largely directed toward undertakings related to Auschwitz. For one, in November 1957, Levi and Lello Perugia, otherwise known as "Cesare" from *The Reawakening*, joined a class-action suit brought by the Conference on Jewish Material Claims with over ten thousand claimants against IG Farbenindustrie.[1] The "Claims Conference," as it was known, collectively sued for indemnification of the slave labor provided to IG Farben during World War II by prisoners at Buna Monowitz. The suit was settled in 1960: IG Farben set aside three million Deutschemarks (or $720,000 in 1960 dollars) for political prisoners and twenty-seven million Deutschemarks, or $6.5 million, for "those persecuted because of their race." In October 1960, Levi received his personal settlement from this latter fund, 2,500 Deutschemarks (or $600).[2]

At roughly the same time, the Polish government announced plans to build a monument at Auschwitz. Levi commented on the announcement in a 1959 *La Stampa* article, "It doesn't matter if it's beautiful, it doesn't matter if it approaches the rhetorical, if it falls to pieces. It mustn't be used for partisan aims: it must be a monument-admonition that humanity dedicates to itself to bear witness, that repeats a message hardly new to history but too often forgotten: that man is, and must be, sacred to himself, everywhere and forever."[3] Nearly two decades passed, however, before the plans were actually implemented. At that time, in 1978, Levi was commissioned to help in the design of the museum at Auschwitz. He proposed that the walls of the Italian building be decorated with nonrepresentational artworks, the better to express the ineffability and indescribability of the Holocaust experience. Each abstract work, in his plan, would be accompanied by a plaque bearing a text he himself would write. Levi's full text survives: eight numbered paragraphs focusing on the history and interpretation of the Italian Holocaust, its victims and its perpetrators. The language, as ever, is direct, unflinching, and poetic—reminiscent of the imperatives and familiar *tu* of "Shemà," the epigraph to *Survival in Auschwitz*. The Polish government chose to erect only the last plaque, point 8, which states in part: "Visitor: observe the vestiges of this camp and meditate: Make sure your visit is not useless, so that our death will not be useless . . . make sure that the terrible fruit of hate, whose traces you have seen here, does not bear new seeds, not tomorrow, not ever."[4] Several years later, in 1982, Levi returned to Auschwitz with a team from *Sorgente di vita* (Springs of Life), a RAI TV program about Jewish life. Though he had been to Auschwitz before, in 1965, this second visit to Poland left him profoundly shaken. Perhaps it was the martial law crackdown imposed by General Jaruzelski in the wake of Solidarity agitation, or his renewed acquaintance with the sights and sounds of the Polish winter, but Levi is heard commenting on camera about a railyard, "Even now, the sight of those freight trains has a violent effect on me."[5]

A watershed event in the world perception of the Holocaust was the Adolf Eichmann trial and execution in 1961–62. Televised internationally from Jerusalem, the Eichmann trial galvanized world attention and, for the first time—for complex reasons explored by Sharon Roubach and Dina Wardi—put Holocaust survivors front and center in Israeli discourse.[6] Levi was among the hundreds called to testify, yet he refused to go. The reasons for his refusal are not clear, but may center on personal concerns or the then-current negative perception in Israel of Holocaust survivors: accused in some quarters of "Diaspora passivity," they were distinguished from the patently heroic efforts of Jewish ghetto combatants and partisan resisters. Levi, on the other hand, was an admittedly inept partisan during the war and, after, made his home in the Diaspora (not Israel), located the Holocaust in a European (not Zionist) context, illustrated it via Dante and the classics, and extolled Diaspora Jews as the creative force behind modern Jewish life. Indeed, during his 1968 trip to Israel, Levi sought an Israeli publisher for *Se questo è un uomo* with no success, and he would not live to see its publication in Hebrew, *Hazehu Adam* (Is This a Man) having been published only in November 1988, nineteen months after his death and more than forty years after its original publication in Italy.[7] Levi did enter the Eichmann debate, however tangentially (and on his own terms), with a stinging July 20, 1960, poem dedicated to "the son of death," "Per Adolf Eichmann" ("For Adolf Eichmann").

In the 1960s as well, Levi was repeatedly contacted by Austrian historian Hermann Langbein, founder of an international association of Holocaust survivors and author of the massive, authoritative *Menschen in Auschwitz* (*Humankind in Auschwitz*). Citing reasons of work and family, Levi regretfully declined Langbein's many invitations to address the association. On the twenty-fifth anniversary of the liberation of Auschwitz, January 25, 1970, the association released a declaration drafted by Langbein and signed, for the first time, by Levi, protesting the forced relocation and expatriation of Polish Jews by Polish Communist leader Wladyslaw Gomulka. At the same time, using his behind-the-scenes influence at Einaudi, Levi tried, over the course of a decade, to convince his new publisher to bring out an Italian translation of Langbein's work. His entreaties there failed, though in 1984 he succeeded with Mursia, and *Uomini ad Auschwitz* appeared with a preface by Levi himself.

With his appearance in 1959 at a Turin exhibition about deportation, Levi took his first step into what Robert Gordon terms "the sphere of cultural influence."[8] In the years that followed, Levi began to assume "many of the activities typical of an Italian intellectual of the day": writing op-ed pieces and newspaper columns, giving press interviews and public lectures, and attending conferences.[9]

Two things combined in the late 1960s to mid-1970s to induce Levi to assume a higher profile with regard to issues of foreign relations, and Israel in particular. One was the 1967 Six Day War. The other was Levi's retirement from his "day job" in a chemistry plant to dedicate himself to writing. The mid-1970s were also the years when Levi revisited a book idea he had contemplated several decades earlier: the story of Eastern European Jewish partisans in World War II and their eventual *aliyah* to Eretz Israel—the idea that was to become *Se non ora, quando?* (*If Not Now, When?*).

In Italy in the late 1960s Levi had already became known, variously applauded and excoriated, for his frank criticism of Israel in the context of the Arab-Israeli conflict. Levi himself had a prickly relationship with Judaism and Jewish causes. The religion of his fathers was, after all, the cause of much suffering in his own life, and he himself felt no true religious faith. Though wary of turning his back on Judaism, he nonetheless freely admitted: "I'm not a believer and I've never been; I'd like to be but I can't. . . . There was Auschwitz, so there can't be God. I don't find any solution to that dilemma. I look for it but I can't find it."[10] He was capable of admitting his ignorance of Jewish ritual one moment and yet writing a stirring tribute to the Turin synagogue and his coreligionists the next, of celebrating a bar mitzvah and wearing phylacteries for two years and yet remaining a stranger to synagogue services, of professing himself unmoved by religion and yet fighting for a Jewish day school, and of refusing the epithet of "Jewish writer" and yet applying himself to the study of Yiddish and Jewish holy texts.[11] This ambivalence in Levi largely remained below the surface yet also reached a flashpoint at many junctures in his life: we see it briefly in his scathing literary portrayals of some religious Jews (Kuhn in *Se questo è un uomo*, for example), in his often-bitter poetry (like "Shemà" and "Nel principio" [In The Beginning]), and in myriad interviews, especially during the period of his fullest fame, in the 1980s.

True to his forthright nature, statements proclaiming his estrangement from Jewish practice, expressed with the utmost sincerity, are also to be found in Italian Jewish bulletins, synagogue newsletters and Jewish community publications. He reiterated such statements for the mass-circulation *L'Espresso*, declaring, "I am Jewish for the record books, in other words, I'm enrolled in the Jewish Community of Turin, but I don't practice Judaism and I'm also not a believer."[12]

So at the same time as he declared his atheism, he proclaimed his identification with the Jewish community in Turin. His affection for his Turinese ancestors and their colorful Judeo-Piedmontese dialect suffuses the "Argon" chapter of *Il sistema periodico* (*The Periodic Table*), just as hope for "virtue and justice" underpins his April 9, 1984, poem "Pasqua" ("Passover"). Equally telling is his preface to the 1984 *Jews in Turin: Research for the Synagogue's Centennial (1884–1984)*, which opens with the phrase, "*noi ebrei torinesi*," "we Jews of Turin."[13] In a conversation with me in 1986,

Levi recalled with the gusto of a matador and the pique of a stakeholder the synagogue squabbles and internecine face-offs he and his rabbi were then engaged in.[14]

Levi thus occupied an anomalous position in Italian public life: a Holocaust survivor and—perhaps with the exception of Rabbi Elio Toaff—the best known of Italy's Jews at the time, yet a secular, non-believing Jew. Levi was aware of his unique and unusual position. Perhaps because of this awareness or perhaps because of his natural reticence, he stayed out of the limelight at length on questions of Zionism and Israeli politics. Only in the aftermath of the 1967 war, and sporadically until 1984, did Levi assume the mantle of political activist.

Levi's lifelong politics were leftist. He apparently never joined a political party, yet from his youthful adherence to the Justice and Liberty movement and participation in the Resistance with the Action Party, to the final pages of his last book, his sympathies were with democratic socialism.

He also professed a love of Israel: "My relationship with that land is out of the ordinary, for emotional and for personal reasons," he told Stefano Jesurum in 1986. "It is a State founded for those who were with me in the camps. A country of old companions, people who are dear to me. Statistically, they are only twenty, out of three million, but those twenty were in Auschwitz with me, and then they found their home, their language. I will say that for me it is an unacceptable thought, the idea that Israel might some day be destroyed."[15]

Levi made no public statements at the outset of the Six Day War. However, three days in, in a June 7, 1967, *La Stampa* photo feature, he was seen giving blood along with other Turin Jews for Israeli wounded. Three days later, on June 10, the Soviet Union announced it was cutting off diplomatic ties with Israel. The Italian Communist Party, with Enrico Berlinguer at its head, aligned itself with the Soviets. Jewish support of the Communist party and the left splintered, with one group supporting Brezhnev's pro-Arab stance and another organizing into cells aimed at encouraging Arab-Israeli dialogue and dissuading Diaspora Jews from endorsing right-wing Israeli positions. Levi, in this latter group, signed a manifesto to this effect, along with twenty-two other Turin Jews, published in the left-leaning journal *Il Ponte*.

In March 1968, Levi traveled to Israel with a group of Italian ex-partisans and intellectuals close to the Justice and Liberty movement. They eschewed the Jewish part of Jerusalem, choosing instead, significantly, a hotel in the Arab quarter of the city. While meeting with progressive members of the Israeli government, Levi also traveled under military escort through the Negev Desert to Gaza and the West Bank. He was disillusioned by Israel and returned to Italy overcome by a "sort of *general* tiredness."[16]

It soon became clear that the Turin cell, seat of one of the most progressive Italian Jewish communities, was moving well beyond the original goals of the so-called Jews of the Left. In early 1969, they circulated a manifesto supporting the Palestinian guerilla war, deeming it "resistance" and not "terrorism" and calling for the condemnation of the Israeli government. It was signed by some thirty Turin Jews, among them Primo Levi.[17] The reaction from Jewish quarters was swift and critical, including *Quaderni del Medio Oriente* (Middle East Notebooks) and *Hatikva*, the monthly publication of the Federation of Italian Jewish Youth. With the actual publication of the manifesto in *Unità* on January 28, 1969, the monthly *Shalom* wrote that the signers must either be wearing "blinders or are in contradiction to their own Jewishness."[18] This tempest, however heartfelt, largely remained in the teapot of low-circulation Italian-Jewish journals and Jewish communist circles. Not so the controversy of 1980.

Terrorism was the operative word in the opening years of the 1980s. The targets were the Jewish Diaspora communities of Europe, and the events included synagogue bombings in Milan and Rome, and the Achille Lauro highjacking. These were also the years of the war in Lebanon and the revolts in the Israeli-occupied territories. A grenade and machine-gun attack on the Rome synagogue on October 9, 1982, led by the Abu Nidal group, resulting in the death of a toddler and thirty-seven wounded, profoundly divided the Italian Jewish community. On one hand, there were those who denounced the Palestine Liberation Organization and its ties to the Red Brigades as evidence of an anti-Zionism that was just an exasperated version of anti-Semitism; on the other hand, there were those Jews of the Left, including Levi, who sought a progressive rapprochement with the PLO as the key to staunching further violence and as a reprimand to the repressive policies of the government of Israeli Prime Minister Menachem Begin.

The atmosphere of lacerating internecine polemics had been riven by previously by the Israeli Operation Peace in Galilee of June 6, 1982, in which, as a response to prior terrorist attacks, Israel invaded southern Lebanon up to the outskirts of Beirut. On June 16, 150 left-leaning Italian Jews, among them Natalia Ginzburg, Rita Levi Montalcini, Edith Bruck, Ugo Caffaz, and Primo Levi, published an appeal in *La Repubblica* calling for an Israeli pullout. Again, the reaction was swift from those in Jewish circles who accused the signers of being "self-hating Jews."[19] September

brought the events of Sabra and Chatilla, the massacre by the Phalang-
ists—perhaps with the complicity of the Israeli Defense Forces and
Defense Minister Ariel Sharon—of hundreds and perhaps thousands of
Palestinian refugees. The next week brought the almost contemporaneous
triumph of Yasser Arafat in Rome, where he was received by President
Sandro Pertini, Foreign Minister Emilio Colombo, and, on September 15,
Pope John Paul II—by all Rome, it seemed except for Prime Minister
Giovanni Spadolini. Some labeled Sabra and Chatilla pogroms and placed
the blame on Begin. Sharon was later held both "indirectly" and "personally" responsible by the Kahan Commission.[20] Levi was one of the signers
of a telegram—beginning, "Distressed by the infamy that stains the entire
country and anguished over its future"—informing the Israeli government
of plans for a protest rally in Italy against Israeli politics.[21] Soon after, still
in 1982, he granted an interview to Giampaolo Pansa of *La Repubblica*
entitled, "I, Primo Levi, call for Begin and Sharon to step down; Begin:
the Jews say 'Enough.'"[22] In it, Levi argues that it is more difficult than
ever to be a Jew, and that both Jews and Arabs are "victim peoples." Furthermore, he states that although Israel is a state founded on the ashes
of the Holocaust, this does not grant it any special dispensations. Other
editorials and interviews at the time were, "The Danger Comes from Mil-
itarism," "Who in Jerusalem Has Enough Courage?" and "Yes, Israel Has
Gone Too Far but It's Not Right to Speak of Nazism."[23] Privately, he told
Rita Levi Montalcini, "Sometimes I wonder if I belong to the Jewish people at all."[24] Thereafter, Levi strenuously rebuffed all attempts at eliciting
a comment from him on Israeli affairs.[25]

His silence was nearly complete—that is, until September 1984 when
Gad Lerner, a former *Lotta continua* journalist, published an interview in
L'Espresso titled "Se questo è uno stato" (If This Is a State), an obvious
and caustic reference to *Se questo è un uomo*.[26] The occasion for the Lerner
interview was the formation of the new Israeli "National Unity" government under Labor Party leader Shimon Peres, including Ariel Sharon in
a key position, combined with the ascendance in Israeli politics and the
national consciousness of right-wing agitator and Jewish Defense League
and *Kach* party founder Meir Kahane. In his interview, Levi recalls that he
had earlier called for Begin's and Sharon's resignation and now vehemently protests Sharon's nomination to head the Ministry of Industry and
Commerce. He condemns the degradation of Israeli politics and decries
the racism of Kahane and his followers. Lastly, he posits that the real
energy and soul of contemporary Jewry had shifted away from Israel to

the Diaspora. He goes on to say that were he "less tired," he would agitate for a pivotal role for the Italian Jewish community in world Jewish affairs.

"Tired" is a word many associated with Levi in these years; it was a stand-in for what we now know were bouts of depression. Indeed, one finds only two instances of public positions on current events by Levi after his 1984 *L'Espresso* interview.[27] The interviews he did grant to large-circulation magazines and small-circulation Jewish publications like *Rassegna Mensile d'Israele* (The Monthly Review of Israel), the *Bollettino della comunità ebraica di Milano* (The Bulletin of the Jewish Community of Milan), and *Shalom* from 1984 to 1987 instead focus on his literary writings and occasional pieces, not his polemics.

Through prefaces, editorial suggestions, and personal encouragement, Levi continued, as he had done throughout his life, to celebrate Italian Jewry and perpetuate memory of the Holocaust. This essay has aimed to examine a few lesser-known ways in which he also went about that goal—by means of legal recourse and proper commemoration. It also recalls here a facet of Levi that is little known abroad, namely his ties to organized religion in Turin, and one that was well known in Italy but perhaps obfuscated by the passage of time: his long and public involvement, as a progressive thinker, an intellectual, and a Jew, with the political direction and future of the State of Israel and, by extension with Jewry in Israel and beyond.

PART THREE

Literature

CHAPTER 10

Primo Levi's Struggle with the Spirit of Kafka

Massimo Giuliani

It has already been shown that Primo Levi's science-fiction stories are a kind of modern *midrashim*.[1] In the Jewish tradition, this term refers to an exercise of pedagogical hermeneutics that creates imaginary stories and dialogues about biblical figures and that intentionally forces the original texts or interprets the silence—the "not said"—of the tales with the goal of deducing a moral teaching, a psychological detail, a *davar acher* (that is, a new interpretation) of the text or figure to which the *midrash* refers. These stories use the science-fiction register to exorcise the fear generated by a technological world that appears as projected in the future only out of an excess of imagination, but that, in reality, is our present (to previous generations, this present would have appeared exactly as a science-fiction world). And every time something is said through an excess of imagination or a transgression, in this case of science and technology, the mechanism of irony is at work.

Irony is, by definition, ambivalent because it allows the listener or the reader to smile or to feel hurt. This is the reason why Primo Levi is a master in using irony; he is not a humorist (humor always forces us to smile), nor is he sarcastic (sarcasm always makes people suffer and feel hurt). Moreover, in order to write science fiction, it is not necessary at all to use technological material or language that is projected into the future.

As proved by Italo Calvino's hilarious *Cosmocomics*, and as shown by Levi himself, for example in the beautiful story "Quaestio de centauris," the material may be the prehistory or the classical mythology, or simply the "past tense" (*passato prossimo*) of the years of World War II or the postwar reconstruction, and the geographic context may be an imaginary country, such as Bitinia ("Censorship in Bitinia") or real cities such as Berlin ("Angelical Butterfly") or Turin ("Cladonia Rapida"). Once Levi has a moral message, which is the engine of the story, then characters and anecdotes develop and come out with the force of the paradox, of the unbelievable but possible, of the irrationality that generates surprise and admiration (hence the smile, and perhaps, at the same time, the hurt).

At the end of reading most of the stories of *The Sixth Day*—the stories originally included in *Storie naturali* (1966) and *Vizio di forma* (1971)—we, the readers, understand the message: *de te fabula narratur*. These stories, which are simultaneously natural and surreal, biological and technological, historical and fantastic, are the "new parables" of a humanistic gospel that Primo Levi has written, in different ways and out of his own experience in Auschwitz, aiming, first, at testifying to the complexity of human nature; second, at preventing the risks of a curiosity that pushes human beings into creating the most sophisticated instruments to better dominate matter (here is the essence of technology); and third, at making sense of a reality that, mixing rationality with chaos and logic with passion, seems to be completely meaningless. Good examples of this are the six tales, not consecutive, which have the tragicomic Mr. Simpson as the protagonist, the Italian representative of Natca, an American advanced-technology firm. Their conclusion (see the last story) is the defeat of Mr. Simpson, who is described by Levi with words taken from the Bible. Simpson has fought with the last technological invention—the Torec, or Toral Recorder, for living in a virtual reality—"like Jacob [has fought] with the angel, but his fight was lost from the very beginning," and now, in the rare pauses of losing himself in his virtual technological trips, Simpson finds consolation in reading *Qohelet*, the biblical book of *Ecclesiastes*, and in meditating on its famous sentence *nihil novi sub sole*, "there is nothing new under the sun," an ironic voluntary punishment for somebody who spent his life pursuing novelty. This reading, instead of atoning, serves the goal of allowing him to identify with the old king Solomon, the alleged author of *Qohelet*, described by Levi as "satiated with wisdom and days, who has seven hundreds wives and infinite wealth and the friendship of the black queen, who adored the true God and the fake gods. . . . But Solomon's wisdom was conquered through pain in a long life of works and errors; on the contrary,

Simpson's wisdom is the result of a complex electronic circuit and sophisticate tapes, and he knows it, and he feels shame about it, and to escape that shame he goes back into the Torec."[2]

These stories, of course, should be put in their historical context. It would be clear that they respond to a specific climate, the 1960s, when the Cold War had reached its peak and the fear of the atomic bomb, and in general of a technology that seemed unable to stop before the abyss, appeared like prophecies on the verge of becoming real. But, once read in a different context and without such historical conditions, the moral of the tale emerges with even greater clarity, and precisely their pseudo-naiveté makes them immune from the anachronism and literary irrelevance to which they could otherwise be destined.

With this premise, I would like to ponder the Italian title of the second book, *Vizio di forma*. This expression is found in the story "Head Hunters" (*"Procacciatori d'affari"*), and it is likely that the title of the book is a quote from here. This story is more midrashic than the others, insofar as it is an imaginary interview between three officers (who may be interpreted as angels) and a soul called to be "incarnated" and enter this world. Truly, according to an ancient Jewish legend, the souls wait in a kind of paradise or limbo before being called to enter the world. After having shown the soul all of the advantages of coming to Earth, in a more intimate dialogue the chief delegate (the angel G.) confidentially recognized that, to be honest, Earth is not the best of the possible worlds and that "there are many things that need to be fixed," because "somebody somewhere has made mistakes, and earthly plans show a fracture, a structural defect [*un vizio di forma*]."[3] Therefore, this *vizio di forma* is a mark of production, the fracture is in the structure, the error is inscribed in the DNA of the things of this world, and the task of the human beings—as elected souls, like the one to whom the three officers talk in the story, in a kind of a surreal icon of the encounter between Abraham with three men—is to fix and mend such a fracture and error. In Jewish theology this task is called *tikkun ha'olam*, repairing of the world. Primo Levi expresses this idea in an interview he gave to the Trent newspaper *L'Adige* (May 11, 1971) soon after this book was published. Questioned on the relation between science, technology, and politics, Levi—who always presented himself as a technician and not as a scientist—explained:

> In my opinion, the major guilt of the technicians (scientists deserve a
> different reflection) was not their giving in to power, but having underesti-
> mated their very force, and the measure of the transformations they were

able to produce: this is the *vizio di forma*, the structural defect. I do not think that this is irreversible, and I hope that all the technicians of the world would understand how the future depends on their return to the conscience.[4]

The *vizio di forma* is a defect of conscience, the fracture is a vacuum of consciousness and wisdom regarding the forces within the technological capability of the human being, and regarding the limits ("the measure") we need to pose to the technological transformations of which human intelligence has shown to be able to do. Transgressing that measure is precisely "original sin," a biological vice, and act of hubris that, in other works, Primo Levi has highlighted as the engine of Nazi ideology: the will to distill a "pure human being"—the *Übermensch*—in the same way the cursed plants of Buna (the Nazi concentration camp where Levi "worked" as a chemist) tried to distill and produce the synthetic rubber. Transgressing that measure is like taking "the dangerous trip beyond Hercules' pillars," the limits nature has established for humans. Transgressing that measure is the risk of every "learning sorcerer" who activates mechanisms that are bigger and more powerful than him and that are going out of his control. Hence the appeal, moralistic but nevertheless very urgent and concrete, to "return to conscience" and to the consciousness of human limits, to a sense of responsibility, to the measure established "*acciò che l'uom più oltre non si metta*" (so that humans would not go beyond), as we read in the Canto XXVI of Dante's *Inferno*, quoted by Levi in the chapter "Canto of Ulysses," in *If This Is a Man*. This quotation is, in my opinion, the highest hermeneutic cipher of Levi's entire experience in Auschwitz and perhaps Levi's conclusion of that "gigantic biological experiment" (other similar experiments are mentioned in the sad tales "Angelic Butterfly" and "Versamina").

The Jewish tradition knows very well the truth that a dangerous *vizio di forma* exists within human beings and that shows in its violent capability to destroy the world and other human beings. In light of this truth, the ancient rabbis have forged a *midrash* in which the creation of man happens while the angels/counselors were discussing the opportunity to insert (or not) this new creature among the others already created. Here is the version of this *midrash* given by Louis Ginzberg:

> The angels had different opinions: the angel of love was in favour of the creation of man, because the new creature would have leaned to affection and love; but the angel of truth was against it, because he would have been full of lies. And while the angel of justice was in favour, because he would

have pursued just causes, the angel of peace was against, because he would have been ready to fight. . . . And the objections of the angels would have been even stronger if they knew all the truth about man: indeed, God had told them only about the just people, and concealed the fact that, among the human beings, many are mean and evil.[5]

We have good reasons to suppose that Levi knew this *midrash*. In the story "Head Hunters" the angels/counselors behave like God and conceal from the soul who must incarnate the dark side of the world, the painful and unworthy side of humanity. But it is in the book *Storie naturali*, in particular, that Levi works in a midrashic way on this *midrash* by developing a significant dialogue under the title "The Sixth Day." This a tale full of irony, probably already written for the stage, and where the discussion is not limited to the judgment of opportunity for such a creation (the angel Ormuz expresses an "opposition by principle to the creation of the so-called Man . . . after having noted the dangers that are related to the insertion of the so-called Man into the current global equilibrium"). The discussion substantially covers the modality of the animal form of this new creature in homage to the complexity introduced by biology and in particular by Darwin's doctrine of evolution. But the discussion that will result is totally useless, because while the angelic council was still discussing, the Direction took the decision on its own and in the most heterodox way.

If it is necessary to go back to the origins in order to understand the *vizio di forma* that characterizes the human being and human destiny, the best thing is to go back to the moment of his or her appearance on Earth, the moment of creation about which we know through the biblical "myth" and the other *midrashim* in the first two chapters of Genesis, as read by the rabbinic imagination. This is the reason why this story is science-fictional: because it links, in a very unpredictable and ironic way, science and religious myth, and it connects them with the goal of showing such an impossible effort as well as their insufficiency for explaining the human enigma. The account of Genesis and the results of Darwin's studies are mixed here in a tale that wants to redescribe the old *midrash* in the bureaucratic language of the twentieth century and to revive the deepest meaning: the dramatic question if the appearance of the human being in the last minutes of the cosmic clock has been a good thing or a catastrophe for the planet Earth. Such a question may be perceived as totally meaningless, given that human existence is a fact; nonetheless, it remains significant, even fundamental, if the aim is to understand and be able to express an ethical judgment. Primo Levi, as a writer, is a moralist who uses his knowledge of biochemistry to discuss—beyond the fence that divides humanistic from scientific disciplines—the destiny and therefore the meaning of human life on earth. All of the so-called science-fictional stories pivot, with a plurality of themes, around this central topic, in which it is possible to detect the most profound connection with his books to the experience of the concentration camp: understanding who is the human being and what is a human society able to create that anti-Genesis and that anti-Sinai that we know with the name of Auschwitz.

Another example of midrashic rewriting of a *midrash* may be found in these stories collected under the title *Vizio di forma*. The tale "The Servant" ("Il servo") is the narration of a modern *midrash*, set in Prague between the sixteenth and the seventeenth centuries, even if the core legend is very ancient and goes back to the Talmudic era. It is the story of the creation of a golem.[6] As forged by the Prague's rabbi Arié, the golem is a creature similar to a man—that is, according to Levi himself, a centaur, half human and half beast, a mix of rationality and mere instinct. But, being created by a man, "the golem had no mind, only force and courage, and the capability to come alive when the box with the divine Name was inserted into its mouth." Here is its physical and spiritual description:

> It was a giant and had human semblance only from the waist up. Also for this there is a why: the waist is a frontier, only above the human being was created at the image of God, while below it, the human being is like a beast. For this reason the wise man does not forget to put on the belt. Beneath the waist the golem was just a golem, that is a fragment of chaos . . . a mixture of clay, metal, and glass. . . . Arié gave it the ire of Moses and the prophets, the obedience of Abraham, the stubbornness of Cain, the courage of Joshua, and also a little bit of the craziness of Ahab; but not the holy cunning of Jacob, nor the wisdom of Solomon, nor the illumination of Isaiah, because he did not want to transform him into a rival.[7]

The very figure of Arié, introduced with a mythic aura in the second paragraph of the story, is ironic and has a clear sign of Jewish pride, especially when we read that he "generated a huge number of children, one of them being the ancestor of Karl Marx, Franz Kafka, Sigmund Freud and Albert Einstein, and all those who, in the old heart of Europe, pursue the truth in a new and courageous way. . . . He lived until he was 105 years old, still vigorous in the body and the mind, and he was 90 when he began to build a golem."[8] This last part almost brings to mind the character of the patriarch Abraham, who sired Isaac when he was ninety.

As I have mentioned, this story brings Levi's mark in some details that are apparently minor. In fact, they constitute a creative new exegesis—and therefore a new *midrash*—of the more traditional version of this ancient legend. There is a passage that is very emblematic of Levi's creativity, and that also reveals the most important question a creature, both a golem and a human, should ask the Creator.

> [Arié] inserted the Name in its place, and the eyes of the monster shined and looked at him. He expected the golem to ask: "What do you want from me, Master?" Instead he heard another question, which was actually not new to him, and that was full of ire: "Why does evil prosper?" Then he understood that the golem was his son, and was happy, and at the same time he feared the Lord, because, as it is written, the joy of the Jew is tempered with a bit of fear.[9]

The biblical question "Why does evil prosper?" posed by Levi on the golem's lips at the first moment of its life—a question challenging every theodicy and all the religions of certainty, well known to the readers of the books of Job and Jeremiah—echoes Levi's experience in Auschwitz, and more generally the thousand forms of unjust suffering that accompanies life on earth (the life of the animals, not only the life of the humans). It is the cry of the just and of the innocent, who suffer without guilt and seem to atone an undeserved punishment or a punishment that is disproportionate to their errors (errors, by the way, made by a nature that is structurally defective, marked by a *vizio di forma*). It is the cry, often unexpressed, we perceive in Kafka's pages, and in particular in the book *The Trial*.

But there is another emblematic passage, when the golem refuses to obey the order to chop pieces of wood with an ax. Usually obedient, the refusing golem shocks its creator at first, and then leaves him "fascinated and frightened" when, instead of using the ax, the golem chops the pieces of wood with its hands. Ariè tries, in his rabbinical mind, to understand the behavior of his creature. And here is the discovery and the answer: "The golem was a servant who did not want to be a servant. For him, the ax was a slavish instrument, a symbol of slavery, as the bit is for the horse and the yoke is for the ox. It is not so for the hand, that part of oneself, and in whose palm is impressed your destiny."[10] Rabbi Arié was pleased with himself for this "acute-sharp, plausible, and joyful" answer. But this is Levi's answer. As a technician, Levi knows the heuristic value of the hand (and of the brain that guides the hand) for the construction of technological instruments and for the progress of science; moreover, he

appreciates the hand as an organ of human dignity, indispensable for
working, that is for the process of transformation of the unshaped matter
into a meaningful and useful creation. The creation of the golem by the
Prague's rabbi reproduces the very creation of man by God, and as such it
elevates "laboring the matter"—the vocation of the chemist—in a *maasè
bereshit*, in a "work of the beginning," in a creation similar to the divine
activity by definition.

The enthusiasm and the optimism are evident, because working/creat-
ing means giving shape to what is unshaped, ordering what is in chaos,
naming what is without a name. And making sense of what appears to be
senseless is always an exhilarating experience. But if the matter veers out
of control and if the creature disobeys his creator and also ruins the creator's house, then the exaltation becomes frustration, light becomes gray
or even dark, and a sense of claustrophobia—as in Kafka's castle—prevails.
The story of the golem is a modern *midrash* because it is already the story
of the "learning sorcerer" who plays with a technology that goes beyond
his control; because the humanlike creature undergoes—due to the transgression of the law of Shabbat—an involution in an antihuman force, leaving the humans in a world at risk of destruction, or better of self-
destruction. Such is the case of Mr. Simpson or other characters created
by the realistic imagination of Levi's science-fictional stories (see "Toward
West," which is also a reflection on the meaning and the plausibility of
suicide among animals and human beings).

Precisely this final option—the ever-present risk that the work of our
hands loses its positive force and becomes, against our will, a negative
force able to throw us down into the abyss of nothing (in an unnatural
death) or in the inferno of a "useless sufferance" (as in Auschwitz)—is the
bitter sentiment we feel after having read Kafka's work. Kafka is an author
admired but not loved by Levi, who translated *The Trial* from German
into Italian. "From this translation I came out like from a disease,"[11] he
confesses, because "once we've read *The Trial*, we feel in a siege by banal,
unjust, and often deathful processes."[12] Only with time does Levi's repul-
sion for Kafka soften. He recognizes that, after many years from *If This Is
a Man*, but also from *The Sixth Day*, his "stupid optimism" left the place to
a more pessimistic and probably more tragic vision toward life and human
destiny. "At that time," he says in a 1983 interview, "I did an illogical
transfer of my own 'happy end' to all human tragedies. . . . Then [soon
after my return from Auschwitz], it seemed absurd to think that out of
that bottom, of that pit, of the Lager, a better world should not have been
born. Today I have an opposite opinion. I think that out of the Lager only

another Lager can come, out of that experience only evil can come. . . . [Kafka] had guessed and predicted the signals of what would have been the destiny of Europe twenty years later, after his death. In *The Trial* there is an early intuition that violence comes with bureaucracy, an increasing and irresistible power that is the result of this our century."[13] In Kafka's *The Trial*, in its labyrinths of anonym bureaucracy, of gratuitous violence, and banal evil, Levi perceives a negative prophecy, the same prophecy he saw come true in Auschwitz but also in the degeneration of a technology no longer guided by conscience and the sense of human limits, that is, by ethics.

For these reasons, I believe that in Levi's science-bio-fictional stories there is more spirit of Kafka than Levi himself is ready to admit; and there is a deep link between the "testimony" of Auschwitz, written by Levi, and his midrashic/parabolic stories of imagination, that work on extreme technological hypotheses and almost absurd projections of our scientific and technical knowledge. Beyond the limits of Hercules' pillars, once the ethical prohibitions are transgressed, there is only a tragic destiny, a mass suicide, a self-destruction—in Kafka's words, a death sentence that will be carried out like a banal bureaucratic task. Here is the cipher of Auschwitz; and in a world where Auschwitz happens, shame is the only thing that remains. Attention: it is not a divine court that issues that death sentence, but only a human court, made of human beings. Therefore, Primo Levi concludes, after identifying himself more with the protagonist of *The Trial* than with its author, "Joseph, with the knife already near the heart, feels shame—the shame of being human."[14] In the short text "Translating Kafka," Levi says again: "The famous and strongly commented sentence that closes the book like a tombstone ['and it was as if shame would have survived him'] does not appear enigmatic to me."[15] About this shame Levi has already spoken on *The Truce/The Reawakening*, when he describes the entrance of the Russian soldiers into the camp of Auschwitz to free the prisoners; and he has extensively written about it in a chapter of *The Drowned and the Saved*. Perhaps in this sentiment we may find the last, residual trace of humanity, a trace that no bureaucratic power, no totalitarian system, and no violent technology can annihilate. This shame is one with *pudore* (modesty) before death, a feeling that Kafka—according to Levi—did not know, as the Germans did not know the "shame of the just" before the mere existence of evil. On the contrary, Levi knew and knows these feelings, *pudore* and shame, and therefore chose to speak about and to write on the *vizio di forma* within human nature by using irony, always suspended between hope and desperation, between (relative) optimism and (never radical) pessimism, between enthusiasm and resignation. In his irony, the salvation/*salv-action* through understanding and the salvation/*salv-action* through laughter come together and become one.[16] For this reason, even after many years and in different cultural settings, his stories remain valid parables and make us think.

CHAPTER 11

Ethics and Literary Strategies

Sara Vandewaetere

Any reader of Primo Levi's work will be struck by its degree of sensory detail: the reader is provided with precise information about the appearance, sound, scent, taste, and feel of people and objects. The most obvious explanation for Levi's attention to such sensorial aspects has been cited by many a critic: Levi, it would seem, was blessed with a special—scientific, even—"observer's eye."

Today, the distance in time since the work was first published and the effect Levi's writing continues to have on his readers twenty years after his death can offer new insights into the functioning of the sensory detail in Levi's work. Indeed, in recent years, readers, critics, and experts from various fields (historians, anthropologists, psychologists, and so forth) have emphasized the powerful ethical system underlying Levi's work. Given the overwhelming importance of this ethical component, it seems worthwhile reconsidering the author's sensory descriptions in this light. Here, I first take a philosophical approach to the significance and purpose of the senses in Levi's ethics. Subsequently, I consider to what extent this purpose is attained, at a practical as well as a rhetorical level.

An interesting starting point is provided by Robert Gordon's book *Primo Levi's Ordinary Virtues: From Testimony to Ethics*, one of the most comprehensive studies of the ethical aspects of Levi's body of work.[1] Strikingly, in his moral catalogue of Primo Levi's virtues, the first that Gordon mentions relates to one of the five traditional senses, namely "looking."[2] Gordon begins by analyzing Levi's experience with the refusal of the Nazi guards to acknowledge visually the prisoners at the Auschwitz labor camp. As Levi testifies in *If This is a Man*, neglecting or disregarding looks were rife, the most memorable example undoubtedly being Doktor Pannwitz's frozen gaze: "That look was not one between two men; and if I had fully understood the nature of that look, which seemed to come through the glass of an aquarium between two beings living in different worlds, I could also have explained the essence of the great insanity of the Third Reich."[3]

How, we may wonder, would French philosopher Emmanuel Levinas have answered Levi's implicit question regarding the nature of this gaze, given the former's continuous reflection on "encounters" between individuals, especially in his ethics of the "face-to-face," which he primarily explores in his early work *Totality and Infinity*.[4] It seems to me that the image of the "aquarium glass" that separates Doktor Pannwitz from Levi may be seen as an extreme, poetical expression of the typical "gaze" of the Western intellectual tradition, so vigorously criticized by Levinas for turning the Other into an object of visual knowledge or aesthetic contemplation, rather than seeing him as an evolving subject whom one has to take care of.[5] In Levinas's philosophy, looking at the Other serves as a reminder that one must respect that Other. In fact, the act of "looking" is to be interpreted metaphorically, as pointed out by Martin Jay, and it stands for a manner of "being" and for a respectful approach of the Other.[6]

It would appear that from Levi's work emerges a similar ethical idea on the significance of encounters, but also that in Levi's view the role of the sensory experiences is taken rather literally, whereas Levinas tends towards symbolic interpretations. In Levi's view, the very act of "perceiving" the Other through the senses—rather than Levinas's general face-to-face encounter—should lead automatically to a respectful treatment of that Other. In an essay published in *Other People's Trades* entitled "Against Pain," it becomes clear that, to Levi, pain is indeed the founding "sense." From this perspective, the existence of suffering eliminates all doubt regarding the existence of all other "minor" senses.[7] Given the fact that we experience pain, it becomes futile to question the reality of any of our senses. Levi goes on to call pain the only certainty of the layperson. On the basis of his writings, one can see that, to him, the argument remained valid the other way around (even if he never explicitly said so): "sensing" the Other ought to suffice for us to remember that man is a suffering being and that we should not inflict pain. So by being aware of the presence of the Other through our own senses, we are—in a way—automatically moved away from creating pain and toward a respectful treatment of the Other.

This line of reasoning is very apparent in Levi's position vis-à-vis "ordinary" Germans during the Nazi era. According to Levi, there was only one explanation for the fact that the majority of Germans did not come to the assistance of the suffering Jews: they deliberately refused to see or hear what was going on. Had they "seen" in an ethical sense, they would have helped. Levi repeatedly uses the expressions "voluntary blindness" and "voluntary deafness" to describe the attitude of the German population during the Nazi regime.

Even after the war, such voluntary blindness, deafness, and even muteness persisted in some ordinary Germans, according to the author. In *The Reawakening*, Levi tells of how, toward the end of his long journey back home from Auschwitz, he observed the Germans in their own country:

> Did "they" know about Auschwitz, about the silent daily massacre, a step away from their doors? If they did, then how were they able to walk around, return home and look at their children, cross the threshold of a church? If they did not, they ought, as a sacred duty, to listen, to learn, everything and immediately, from us, from me: I felt the number that had been tattooed on my arm burning like a sore. . . .
>
> It seemed to me that everyone should interrogate us, read from our faces who we were, and listen to our tale with humility. But no-one looked us in the eyes, no-one accepted the challenge: they were deaf, blind and dumb, imprisoned in their ruins, as in a fortress of willful ignorance, still strong, still capable of hatred and contempt, still prisoners of their old tangle of pride and guilt.[8]

Levi did not stand up to talk to these Germans, as he had done to people in the other countries he passed through on his way home, and as he intended to do back in Italy, on trains, in the streets, and so on. In Germany, it seemed, there was no willingness to listen at all.

"Reaching" the Germans who "looked away" must have become a kind of obsession after his return from Auschwitz to Italy. In the *Drowned and the Saved*, Levi writes how he had already wanted to "tie down German readers upon the mirror,"[9] to oblige them to look at what had happened and to respond to it when writing *If This Is a Man*. In the preface to the German translation, Levi even explicitly invited his German readers to write to him in order to help him understand what had happened to their people. So it would seem that Levi's primary goal in writing *If This Is a Man* was not so much to tell his own story, but to "make people talk."

With this premise, Levi's writing may be seen as an attempt to reconstruct on a literary level the Levinasian dialogue. It is as if Levi wanted the books themselves to serve as a type of "Other" who by their presence—especially their sensorial presence—induce the reader, be that reader German or not, to assume responsibility. This is indeed what typically should happen in the ethical encounter between two individuals as described by Levinas: the "face" of the Other induces him to do justice.[10] To Levinas, "looking" is, however, not the most important sensory aspect of the "face-to-face" encounter. He attributes a more important role to hearing and touching. Levi, for his part, enacted all of the senses in his writing in an attempt to reach his readers and compel them to respond.

Before we consider how Levi achieves this ethical purpose from a more practical, rhetorical, point of view, let us first take a look at a less philosophical transposition of Levi's ideal of what we might refer to as the "communicating senses" in one of his science-fiction stories in *The Sixth Day and Other Tales*. In this story, Levi describes a newly invented machine called Torec, which is able to induce a series of sensations in its users through signals that access their brain directly through a headphone. According to the narrator, *Torec* causes a "total experience":

> The result is a total experience. The spectator relives the event of the tape, he feels like participating or even as if he were the actor of the experience: this sensation has nothing in common with hallucinating or dreaming, because, as long as it lasts, it cannot be distinguished from reality.[11]

It seems to us that the effect of Torec approximates the impact that a novel should ideally have on its readers in the eyes of Levi.

Literary Strategies

But how to "reach" the reader in a way that will make him or her respond? Which literary strategies may be deployed in order to stimulate the internal senses of the reader? As we shall see, the manner in which the author employs such techniques are revealing about his poetics. We consider three types of literary strategy Levi uses to present the text to the reader as if it were the Other, namely the strategies of (de)familiarization, of metaphoric writing, and of metafictional writing.

Shoah Memories and Visuality: The Search for Familiarization

Trauma psychologists generally distinguish between two possible effects on traumatized subjects: they either tend to erase the experience from their memories, or they seem to remember events with excessive precision.[12] Levi obviously belonged to the second group. In fact, he himself often expressed surprise at just how well he seemed to remember certain details of the deportation, referring to this ability as a "pathological precision."[13] This "second" type of memory is usually marked by the fact that, while the victims are able to remember everything, they are unable to make sense of what they remember. They are unable to incorporate it into their normal "narrative" memories. They are haunted by the kind of "flashbacks" that typically present themselves in their minds in the shape of "frozen" or "petrified" images.

In the case of Levi, however, it has been pointed out that apparently he had no difficulty whatsoever integrating those traumatic memories into his "narrative memory." His extremely controlled and balanced style is considered as proof of this. The critic Ezrahi Dekoven, for instance, compared Levi's testimony in *If This Is a Man* to those of other *Shoah* writers and concluded that Levi's writing bore no traces of traumatic memory.[14] Unlike in the work of Levi, the narration in texts by other survivor-writers, such as Charlotte Delbo or Tadeusz Borowski, is often interrupted by seemingly out-of-place descriptions.

Nevertheless, we would argue that certain scenes in Levi's *If This Is a Man* do rather stand out from the rest of the text in that they appear to be typical manifestations of such petrified images. Sometimes these passages are recognizable even at a purely linguistic level, for instance by a sudden switch from past to present tense. In one of the first chapters of *If This Is a Man*, Levi describes events as if they were unfolding before his eyes:

> The outside door opens, a freezing wind enters and we are naked and cover ourselves up with our arms. The wind blows and slams the door shut; the German opens it again and stands there watching with interest as we writhe to hide from the wind, one behind the other. Then he leaves and closes it.[15]

Interestingly, this passage has also been quoted as an example of Dantesque intertextuality in Levi's texts. The prisoners in this scene are reminiscent of the sinners in Dante's Hell, as represented, for example, in Gustave Doré's infernal landscapes, which were so particularly loved by Levi.[16]

Hence, they remind us of a characteristic literary style known as *ekphrasis*, whereby a visual work of art—in this case Dante's iconography—is integrated into the written text. So even if Levi was not able to fully integrate the supposedly frozen images of his traumatic memory into his "narrative" memory, he certainly integrated them successfully into the text by means of a rhetorical device that allowed him to express quite explicitly the visual nature of the traumatic memory. Levi thus succeeded in finding a collective visual frame of reference whereby the reader could identify particularly closely with the events described.

DEFAMILIARIZATION

Immersing the reader in "familiar" surroundings in the context of the Shoah holds the risk that he will feel so much at "home" with the text that he fails to realize what he is reading is not akin to anything he knows. It is therefore necessary to once again rip the reader out of this familiar-looking world, his *"tiepida casa"* or "sweet house," to which Levi refers in the introductory poem to *If This Is a Man*.[18] One way of achieving this is by exploiting the contradistinction between the "physical" character in the "black-on-white" text and the reality it stands for. Levi efficiently reminds the reader of the fact that what he is reading *about* is quite different from the reassuring text *itself* by constantly inserting foreign language words into the narration, so that the normal reading process is "disrupted." In this manner, Levi conveys to the reader the sensation of extreme alienation experienced by the deportees as they heard the Lager jargon. As Levi explains in *The Drowned and the Saved*, to many prisoners the linguistic barrier was like a death sentence.

Let us consider some examples. Even before the prisoners' deportation to Auschwitz, in the Italian transit camp of Fossoli, a visiting German officer enquires about the number of prisoners in the camp. *"Wieviel Stück?"* he asks, as if he were talking about articles.[17] And at Auschwitz itself, there is the recurrent Polish order *"Wstawac,"* "Get up," which Levi would later also use in the poem that precedes the *Reawakening*, and which is a clear trace of his traumatic memory.[18] Other examples are the words *Häftlinge* for prisoner, *Lager* for concentration camp, and *Block* for building. Every one of these foreign expressions can be seen as an acoustic signal by which the reader is suddenly reminded of the horror of the concentration camp.

This kind of plurilinguism is a characteristic feature of Levi's writing, and not only as a representation of the oppressor. Already in *If This Is a*

Man, he occasionally uses foreign language terms or sentences to evoke a sense of "cultural" richness through the variety of nationalities among the detainees at Auschwitz. The sentence uttered by a French prisoner, "*Si j'avey une chien, je ne le chasse pas dehors*," in which Levi combines French spelling with phonetic transcription, may, for example, be regarded as a foreshadowing of the dialectal speech of Cesare in the *Reawakening* or the idiosyncratic language of Faussone in *The Monkey's Wrench*.

The Principles of Metaphor

The techniques of familiarization and defamiliarization rely on a systematic replacement of the unknown with the known and vice versa. A similar principle is often at work in metaphors and comparisons, where, in the cognitive interpretation of George Lakoff and Mark Johnson, one conceptual domain becomes understood in terms of another.[19] Such rhetorical devices often enhance the reader's level of comprehension by making the unknown approximate more closely to what he does know. It is about replacing an abstract notion with a concrete one.

This is exactly what Levi does in many of the metaphors and comparisons he uses. In cognitivist terms, one might say he replaces abstract "target" terms (the terms that need to be "metaphorized") with concrete "source" terms. In a sense, then, Levi was concerned with how he could use his experience as a chemist in the writing process:

> There is an immense resource of metaphor in the field of today's and yesterday's chemistry from which the writer may borrow, and which those who have never frequented a laboratory or factory know only approximately. Even the layman knows the meaning of to filter, to crystallize and to distil, but he has it at second hand: he is unaware of the indelible passion, he is ignorant about the emotions involved, he has not perceived its symbolic shadow.[20]

In fact, though, it would seem that such chemistry metaphors in the work of Levi, which have been studied at length, occur less frequently than those relating to the field of medicine and, more generally, to the realm of the body. Medicine, in other words, in the broadest sense—not as a specialist field, but as people encounter it in their everyday lives. We would argue that precisely the fact that most "common" readers are not familiar with chemistry, as Levi himself points out, inspired him to rely more on images borrowed from the field of medicine, with which people are more familiar. Faussone, the main character in *The Monkey's Wrench*, for instance, looks after a separation column he has constructed, and that subsequently seemed to "move," as if it were a patient of his:

> It happened to me as to a doctor, who—when someone is in pain—first of all puts his ear onto the patient's back, and then taps him all over and takes his temperature, and the project leader and I were doing just that.[21]

Similarly, Levi repeatedly refers to the experience of Auschwitz as a wound, infection, plague, and the like that afflict Holocaust victims.

SENSES AND METAFICTION

Another means of making the physical more directly present to the reader is to remind him through a metafictional comment of the fact that what he is reading has been written by a person of flesh and blood. An example that comes to mind is the passage in *If This Is a Man* where Levi describes himself behind his desk while he is reflecting on what he is writing: "Today, sitting at my table writing, I myself am not convinced that those things really happened."[22]

In other instances, Levi draws attention specifically to his hands. The most obvious example of this is to be found toward the end of *The Periodic Table*, in the chapter entitled *Carbon*. We actually "see"—or rather "feel"—the author's writing hand extruding from the text:

> It is that which at this instant, issuing out of a labyrinthine tangle of yeses and nos, makes my hand run along a certain path on the paper, mark it with these volutes that are signs: a double snap, up and down, between two levels of energy, guides this hand of mine to impress on the paper this dot, here, this one.[23]

We encounter the same motif in one of Levi's poems, "L'Opera" (The Work of Art), written in 1983:

Ecco, è finita: non si tocca più
Quanto mi pesa la penna in mano!
Era così leggera poco prima,
Viva come l'argento vivo:
Non aveva che da seguirla,
Lei mi guidava la mano[24]

Look it is done: it can no longer be touched
It weighs heavily in my hand
It was so light before

Like living silver
I only had to follow it
while it was leading my hand.

The notion of Levi's hands becoming part of the text is, of course, significant in the context of a combination of an ethical approach with literary strategies. Many philosophers have reflected on the fact that touch is both active and passive. Touching an object implies being touched by it. The presence of Levi's hands in his work may also be seen as the clearest manifestation of what we would like to call an "ethics of proximity," whereby the author tries to approach the reader as closely as possible and, vice versa, whereby he tries to draw in the reader as closely as possible to himself, to the point of almost touching one another.

To Remember or "Recorporalize"

The strategies adopted by Levi stem not just from a scientific approach. They are also strongly connected with the author's wish literally to touch his readers. Levi's strong attention for the senses means that his work is not completely alien to the returning attention for the body, a much-debated topic in the 1990s. However, in Levi's work, the "return to the body" is primarily a return to the senses as a means of addressing the reader in a most personal way. Consider, if you will, the introductory poem to *If This Is a Man*, "Shemà." In this poem, Levi implores his readers to remember what he writes, or rather to "impress it on their heart" (*scolpitelo nel vostro cuore*).[25] Levi likes to compare the human memory to a "stone" on which events are inscribed, rather than a wax tablet, another traditional metaphor of memory that, however, suggests that the memories could as yet be erased. As Massimo Giuliani has pointed out, with this verse from "Shemà," Levi goes back to the etymological sense of the word *ricordare* (to remember), namely, "to replace it in the heart," right at the center of the body.

In conclusion, it could be useful to remember that Levi, even though he strove deliberately to enhance the concrete quality and the mimetic force of his novels through the senses, never overestimated the power of literature. He was convinced that novels can never have the same impact as actions. Yet he wanted his own books to come alive and be as tangible as possible. Therefore, "writing the senses" was an essential literary strategy. Only in this way could his books transform the act of reading into an encounter between the text and the reader.

CHAPTER 12

Literary Encounters and Storytelling Techniques

Elizabeth Scheiber

At first glance, Primo Levi's *Lilìt* appears to be a loosely connected collection of stories divided into three unequal parts. The first section contains autobiographical material from Auschwitz and descriptions of other Shoah victims that Levi discovered in literature. The next two sections are a hodgepodge of fictional stories that range from fantasy tales and science fiction to musings on literature and stories about apparently everyday people. The tendency to view these stories as merely a heterogeneous assembly of material is reinforced by the fact that the tales themselves were written at different times and often published in newspapers such as *La Stampa*. English translations of the work have broken the collection up as well: the tales about the Holocaust have been published under the title of *Moments of Reprieve*, while other stories have been placed with stories from other collections to form *A Tranquil Star*. As such, the stories in *Lilìt* are usually read in the register of memoir to elucidate Levi's experiences at Auschwitz.[1] Such readings tend to regard the collection as a miscellany and seek out reflections of Levi's biography and philosophy in the stories he tells.[2] *Lilìt* is, however, a more unified collection than it appears to be, and, as I will argue in this essay, the work deserves to be examined as a cohesive work. The three section titles frame their content, orienting an encounter of some kind toward a crisis or catastrophe. Taken as a whole, the collection makes an interconnected statement on the nature of writing and communication.

The organizational structure centers on Levi's intriguing section titles and borrow from the realm of grammar, using verb tenses as an orientation. At first glance, however, these titles may appear whimsical, since they do not always reflect the time frame of the stories. While the first section, "Passato prossimo" ("Recent Past") clearly deals with a past time, since its stories focus on the Holocaust, "Futuro anteriore" ("Future Perfect") and "Presente indicativo" ("Present Indicative") only sometimes pertain to the content. The second section, "Disfilassi" ("Disphylaxis," an invented word in both Italian and English), which recounts a future time when a vaccine allows different species to interbreed, could appropriately be housed in "Future Perfect," but others take place in a past or are set in our present. One story, "Cara Mamma" (Dear Mom), an epistolary story about a Roman soldier in Britain, most obviously belongs to a more remote past. Similarly, in "Present Indicative," some stories occur in the past, among them "Ospiti" (Guests) and "Finesettimana" (Weekend), both of which are set during the Second World War. Andrea Rondini argues that Levi's section titles are "temporal hybrids" (*ibridi temporali*) that "indicate not only the circularity of time . . . or indeed the prison of time and of the past that does not pass but also, maybe, a way to announce a new beginning, the spark that is born from the union of what is different, from vital chaos" (268).

Rondini has touched on a central aspect of Levi's literary universe. Circularity is certainly present in *Lilìt*, as it is in other works by Levi. In addition, the section titles indicate a compression of time, in which all times seem to constrict or constrain the present. The tenses chosen to describe each section indicate a nearness or relationship to the present time. It is not the "passato remoto" (remote past) of historical experience but the "passato prossimo" (near or recent past), with its connection to the present, that Levi chooses for the Holocaust encounters. Also, it is not the simple future, but the "futuro anteriore," the "near" future, so to speak, that gives voice to the second section. Finally, the "Presente indicativo" stands in sharp contrast to a subjunctive present. Levi points to a present of fact, not one of opinion, emotion, or necessity.

A paratextual analysis of the titles in the collection elucidates the literary drive behind these tales and Levi's organizational scheme. Rather than being plot-driven, the narrative impulse throughout the collection stems from an encounter, one that reveals something about human beings in general or a single character in particular. Each encounter is the result of or produces some catastrophe or crisis, either personal or collective. Although it contains only a portion of the stories in *Lilìt*, the English title of the collection, *Moments of Reprieve*, is equally appropriate for the whole collection. Levi provides this title in the preface as an overview of the Holocaust stories: "They [the stories] are bizarre, marginal moments of reprieve, in which the compressed identity can reacquire for a moment its lineaments" (viii). Although he is referring only to the Holocaust tales grouped under the title, the moment of reprieve nonetheless is an important element of the entire Italian collection as well because it also determines the placement of the story within the subsections. Each tale centers on an encounter with another and unfolds during a "moment of reprieve" when the character's personality emerges. The section titles take on the narrative role of designating the relationship between the encounter at the center of the story with an extratextual event, generally some catastrophe or disaster.

In "Recent Past," the disaster precedes the encounter. The tales share a common catastrophe: Levi's own deportation and incarceration. Inspired by real people, the characters originate in his experiences at Auschwitz or in the literature of the ghettos. Many of their personalities take shape during a brief moment of calm, when the "real self" could express itself because of a break in horror and backbreaking work. Levi is both narrator and character, describing his encounter as a direct participant, lending his voice directly or indirectly to another who can no longer speak for himself. Most of the characters described here are ambiguous characters whose ethics are dubious; nonetheless, they impress Levi, and through him, the reader, with the weight of their personalities. In fact, Levi writes in his preface to *Moments of Reprieve*, "The protagonists of these stories are 'men' beyond any doubt, even if the virtue that allows them to survive and makes them unique is not always one approved of by common morality" (viii). "Rappoport's Testament," the tale of the epicurean Rappoport, is the first of these stories. As we marvel at his arrogance, his defiance of fate, his ability to remain human despite the horror, we read structurally Levi's own defiance of Hitler and time. Through literature and Rappoport, Levi raises his own fist, demanding that this past event remain as a literary relic.

"Rappoport's Testament" ("Capaneo," in the Italian original) also creates a birthplace for Levi's writing. In this tale, Levi listens to fellow inmate Rappoport's life philosophy of Epicureanism, even hedonism: he has enjoyed life, eaten and drunk well, made love, traveled without wasting any time. As he launches into his philosophy, he positions himself as an author: "If I were free, I'd like to write a book with my philosophy in it. But for now, all I can do is tell it to you two wretches. If you can use it, fine. If not, and you get out of here alive and I don't, which would be rather strange, you can spread it about and maybe it would be of use to somebody" (*Moments of Reprieve*, 7). Levi surmises that Rappoport died on the death marches, so, as an *envoi*, he finishes the tale by claiming to fulfill Rappoport's wish (378). By placing the impetus for writing with the Holocaust material, in the section called "Recent Past," Levi is placing the inception of his own writing at a key moment of his life. It is the Holocaust that set him on this task, a catastrophe that caused him to reflect on other forms of crises that he will narrate in later sections.

Another means of understanding the collection occurs through the insertion of what Ross Chambers calls "narrational embedding," that is, the placement of a narrative act within a narrative act as means of designating a text's mode of functioning.[3] This "story-within-a-story," as one might call it, also justifies the inclusion of biographical material with fictional stories. "Lilìt" ("Lilith") describes how tales are born and hints at Levi's intentions as author. In the midst of the myths concerning the "*diavolessa*" (she-devil) Lilith, the narrator Tischler brushes aside Levi's laughter and claims that he himself does not believe all of the details of the stories, but *belief* in them is not the point of narration. Rather, *pleasure* is the reason to recount these stories: the pleasure of listening, imagining, telling: "Why are you laughing? Of course I don't believe this, but I like to tell these stories. I liked it when they were told to me, and it would be a shame if they were lost" (*Moments of Reprieve*, 22). He even warns Levi that the joke may be on the listener since he may have added details to the stories for his own pleasure and that perhaps all those who have told these tales have embellished them: "In any case, I won't guarantee that I myself didn't add something, and perhaps all who tell them has add something: and that's how stories are born" (ibid.). In giving the title of this story to the entire collection (the Italian edition, that is), Levi appears to be making a statement about the contents of the work: that he has written these stories not from a sense of duty, but from a quest for pleasure and a desire not to let these tales die. In the 1986 preface to the *Moments of Reprieve*, Levi echoes Tischler's desire to see these stories survive: "a host of details continued to surface in my memory and the idea of letting them fade away distressed me" (vii–viii). Furthermore, through Tischler, Levi seems to be adding a disclaimer to these tales and to literature in general. Even those that are inspired by true events may contain embroidered details. In

"Recent Past," Levi is the audience for another's narration, and he relates that person's story to a new reader.

Certainly, the pleasure of recounting the tales from the Lager is not that of remembering atrocity and Auschwitz, but the bittersweet pleasure of recalling companions from the camp and performing this *mitzvah* of lending his own voice to those who cannot speak. The backdrop of the Holocaust gives the encounters a poignancy and the full weight of their meaning. In "The Cantor and the Barracks Chief," Levi expresses amaze-ment that a pious Jew, Ezra, dare ask the block leader, a camp veteran named Otto who has been incarcerated for almost a decade, to set aside his soup ration so that he may fast on Yom Kippur. Amazing, too, is that Otto acquiesces after engaging in a detailed theological and moral discus-sion about religion and atonement. Otto's reaction stuns in the violent world of the Lager, where prisoners can be beaten for any sign of inso-lence. The tale of Ezra and Otto is very different from usual tales of horror and atrocity. During this reprieve, Levi sees in Ezra the personification of a millennial tradition of commentary on the Judaic Law.

The pleasure of writing these stories may not be obvious when the subject matter is tragic. However, some tales are a way for Levi to pay homage to friends who helped him. For example, "Lorenzo's Return" recounts the slow, painful demise of the Italian worker at Auschwitz, a non-Jew, who showed signs of posttraumatic stress syndrome upon his return to Italy. As in all of the portraits of "Recent Past," Lorenzo demon-strates some admirable characteristic that puzzles and amazes. Because of Lorenzo's altruism in Auschwitz, Levi feels that he owes his life in part to this companion: "In the violent and degraded environment of Auschwitz, a man helping other men out of pure altruism was incomprehensible, alien, like a savior who's come from heaven" (*Moments of Reprieve*, 113). However, the portrait is not wholly idealized; Levi also describes a man who spoke little and with whom it was difficult to have a relationship. After the war, Levi reestablished contact with Lorenzo and encountered a depressed and suffering person: "I found a tired man; not tired from the walk, mortally tired, a weariness without remedy" (117). Falling into alco-holism and unable to emerge from a depression, Lorenzo commits slow suicide: "He, who was not a survivor, had died of the survivors' disease" (118). For Levi, "Lorenzo's Return" is a way to pay tribute to his complex and generous friend.

In each of the stories of "Recent Past," two very different characters come together during some break in the horror, and something of their humanity and their mystery emerges. We understand an essential feature of the characters, but we cannot fully explain what motivates them. Clear examples of this are "The Juggler" and "The Gypsy." "The Juggler" places Levi in the company of a "*Grüne Spitze*," a common criminal, Eddy. Levi explicitly expresses his curiosity about these ambiguous inmates: "I have often asked myself what kind of humanity was massed behind their symbol" (*Moments of Reprieve*, 15). He describes Eddy as unpredictable, indifferent to everything around him, and yet, when he catches Levi in the act of writing a letter, his response is mild in the violent atmosphere of the camp: he slaps Levi and checks on the translation of Levi's letter, chiding Levi for a stupid act that could have cost both of their lives. Within the context of Auschwitz, Eddy's act surprises, and we do not fully understand his motivations. In "The Gypsy," Levi ponders the paradoxical wisdom and naïveté of Grigo, an illiterate Roma-Sinti, who asks Levi to write a letter for him since he does not know how. Although Levi at first feels superior to Grigo, his reaction changes to one of amazement since the young man shows that he was clever enough to hide a picture and a knife upon arrival. Grigo is a mystery to Levi, a sign of a different kind of world and a different life from his own. Grigo's past seems to have prepared him for life in the Lager, and the ways of Auschwitz do not surprise him as they do Levi.

Many of the tales in "Recent Past" serve the purpose of posing ethical questions. In each story, Levi describes an encounter with someone very different from himself and appears to ask what is the right way to be in the world of the Holocaust. The section title, with its emphasis on a recent past (as compared to the remote past, the *passato remoto*) and a past that is seen as complete in the past (compared to the imperfect tense), Levi appears to insist on the connection of history to the present. Although these events are completed in the past, their lesson is valid still for today. In "Story of a Coin, which closes the first section and serves as a transition to "Future Perfect," Levi attempts to understand the mayor of the Lodz ghetto. Rumkowski sent many fellow Jews to their deaths thinking that by collaborating he could save his own life. As he describes this figure that he places in the "Gray Zone," Levi concludes that the National Socialist system corrupted its victims. Rumkowski was arrogant and probably thought of himself as a *signore*, a "lord" (*Moments of Reprieve*, 123), but he was liquidated along with the rest of the Lodz ghetto. In ways that are reflected in some of the fictional tales of the collection, especially those of the following section, Rumkowski is blind to the inevitable catastrophe. In this way, Levi is able to turn this unique historical figure into an everyman

despite the unusual circumstances: "Like Rumkowski, we too are so daz-
zled by power and money as to forget our essential fragility, forget that all
of us are in the ghetto, that the ghetto is fenced in, that beyond the fence
stand the lords of death, and not far away the train is waiting" (128).

"Story of a Coin" serves as a transition piece, making of Rumkowski an
everyman that we should ponder as it sends us into the fictional material
of the second section, "Future Perfect." Here, the crisis lies in the future
of the encounter at the heart of the tale, as an extratextual event that the
reader knows or can predict but does not actually witness. As in "Recent
Past," we meet the characters in a lull, a reprieve, but in these stories, the
encounter occurs *before* the catastrophe and we understand their personalities. "A tempo debito"[4] depicts Giuseppe, a dissatisfied cloth salesman
who meets his future assassin. We do not know the outcome of this
encounter, since the tale ends with the end of their meeting, and nothing
in the tale provides follow-up information. In the beginning, we learn that
Giuseppe is tired of his life: "Tired of standing on his feet, tired in his
feet, tired of saying 'Yes, Madam', tired of selling cloth, tired of being
Giuseppe, tired of being tired." Despite his fatigue, it is quite clear that
he does not want to die, as the omniscient narrator informs us: "It is not
certain that he who is tired of life, or says he is, always wishes to die: in
general, he only wishes to live better." When he asks to know *when* he is
going to die, the assassin bristles and refuses to tell him, giving him the
advice "to live day by day, hoping that it is not the last." The tale ends
with the assassin leaving in a taxi, and we receive no information about
Giuseppe's future, whether he will try to live better or just be happy with
the life he has. As he did with Rumkowski, Levi makes Giuseppe into an
everyman. None of us knows the hour of our demise, and we can only live
each day. Will we live being tired of our existences, or will we try to make
our lives better?

Many of the characters in the middle section are well intentioned, and
their stories are poignant due to the future they face. In "The Bridge
Builders," for example, the gentle giants Danuta and Brokne are vegetarians, living in peace in an idyllic setting. One day, Danuta captures a human
with the intention of keeping him as one would a pet. It is clear that the
man does not understand Danuta's tenderness toward him. He is afraid
and tries to escape. Eventually, Brokne convinces Danuta to let the man
go, albeit reluctantly and tearfully. Through the narrator, the reader
understands her good intentions, but the humans think otherwise. The
title reveals itself as ironic, since the humans are not *communicative* bridge
builders. They set fire to the forest, and, with no exit from the forest, the

two giants sit peacefully as it burns, showing no violence. One can only presume that their lives are about to come to an end. From the outset of "Dear Mom," the reader learns in an incipit that the events narrated involve a garrison of Romans who were killed by the local population. The archaeological find on which the story turns includes a package with a pair of woolen stockings. The tale then is the imagined response that a Roman soldier would have written, or rather would have dictated to a scribe, to his mother, thanking her for the gift. The naive letter-writer seems to believe that all will be well, and he will return to his beloved Italy to introduce his British wife to his mother. Despite the soldier's optimism, there are hints of problems. For instance, he criticizes the local sport of "tree trunk throwing," and the scribe feels the need to interject his own opinion on what he considers a noble sport. Also, the British wife has cheated at dice with the soldier. Finally, the Roman also alludes to unrest, but tells his mother not to believe all the news that she hears. Like Rumkowski, the soldier shows how an individual can be blind to happenings around him and not foresee his own future.

In this section, the catastrophe foreshadowed may not be of a personal nature but rather a community crisis. For example, "Una stella tranquilla" ("A Tranquil Star"), about the birth of a supernova, anticipates our own star's future explosion and the death of our planet. "Disfilassi" ("Disphylaxis") depicts a world in which species can interbreed, and through the protagonist, who wants to become pregnant through insemination from tree pollen, it foreshadows the demise of humans and indeed the notion of species as we know it. "La bestia nel tempio" ("The Beast in the Temple") tells of beast trapped in a cave. The locals await its exit from the cave in order to kill it in a purification sacrifice so that "*il mondo sarà risanato*" (the world will be healed). The narrator, who has witnessed the beast, depicts an animal that is systematically closing all exits, ensuring its own demise within walls of its own creation. There is no entirely satisfactory outcome for the tale: either the beast dies of starvation within the temple and forbids a purification, or it emerges and loses its life for the betterment of the world.

In "Future Perfect," the foreshadowed catastrophe seems unavoidable. The very name (in Italian, *futuro anteriore* means "preceding" or "earlier future") indicates a proximity to the present. It is the future-before-the-future. Although it is ostensibly not too late to change the future, the seeds for those events have been planted through actions today, and outcomes do not always depend on the protagonist's actions. Danuta and Brokne can no longer control the fire. The beast in the temple will be killed by the people waiting for him or die in seclusion. The man meeting his future assassin cannot change what will happen and he does not even understand why he must die. The notion that we do not have complete control over our lives can be found in all of these stories, and symbolically in "La fuggitiva" ("The Fugitive") an entertaining tale about a would-be poet, Pasquale, who thinks he has penned the most beautiful verses. Unfortunately for him, the poem is so full of life that it literally runs away from him. He finds the paper on the ceiling, in the out file, in a desk drawer. Eventually, even the words run from the page. In addition to symbolizing the work of art that leaves the author's control once it has been written, the tale warns readers that they do not control as much of their lives as they think.

In the final section of *Lilìt*, "Presente indicativo," the crisis is in progress and often resolved by the story's end. In "Gli stregoni" ("The Sorcerers"), two anthropologists are prisoners of a tribe whose language they are trying to record. The crises in this story are rich and varied. First there is the narrative crisis of the two anthropologists, whose camp burns and who must ask for help from the tribe they are studying. Unfortunately, these two men appear "useless" to the tribe because they cannot create the goods of their technology. If help does not come in time, they fear for their lives. Then there is the crisis of the tribe itself. They used to possess the knowledge of how to make fire but have lost it. Now, old women maintain the fire, like primitive vestal virgins, says Levi. Finally, because of the lost technology, the author concludes a crisis on a larger scale: humans do not necessarily progress.

Another tale in "Presente Indicative," "Ospiti" (Guests), may seem to belong to the past because it relates events from World War II. However, it finds its place in the final section because it recounts a personal ethical struggle in progress as the war comes to a close. In the tradition of *"italiani brava gente"* ("good Italians"), it gives the account of the noble actions of Italian citizens, here represented by the protagonist Sante, who captures two hungry German soldiers toward the end of the war. On his way home from the local *osteria*, Sante encounters the soldiers. They do not seem to pose a threat. He takes them back to his home with the intention of making them his prisoners and stealing their goods. However, as Sante and his brother Ettore begin to go through the Germans' backpacks, their father arrives and forbids them: "Others might be thieves, but we are decent people." Since the Germans have eaten in the house, they are *ospiti*, guests, and will be treated as such, even if they are prisoners. Sante does as his father instructs, and more than that, he ensures that the two Germans will not be shot in prison, "not that he considered them his friends, but for starters it didn't seem honest to shoot people whose hands were in the air, even if they had done it." As the story comes to an end, the war is over, and Sante sees the fruit of his actions: the Germans are still alive and look well. In an act of purification, Sante jumps into the clear water of the Brenta River, "and he felt happy to have ended the war in that way." The Italians of this story show themselves to be more ethical, not treating Germans the way they had been treated.

The pleasure involved in telling the stories of the "Future Perfect" and "Present Indicative" stems from the rehabilitation of characters who have been misunderstood. Levi depicts noble, naive, well-meaning characters struggling against unbearable circumstances. Danuta and Brokne are gentle giants. Since they are vegetarians, they do not even hurt other animals to survive. Yet, the human Danuta captures as a pet does not comprehend. In "The Sorcerers," the anthropologists really are technologically advanced, not "useless" as the Siriono feel, but there is no way to communicate this. In "Guests," Sante is tempted to exact revenge, but in the end, in part thanks to his father, he acts in a noble manner. He represents right-thinking Italians, a theme which appears in an earlier story from "Recent Past," "La storia di Avrom" ("The Story of Avrom"). Literature seems to be a potential locus of bringing about understanding of people who otherwise might appear ambiguous, their motivations unclear. As a matter of fact, even the encounter with others might not bring about understanding. As with the giants, Brokne and Danuta, there is no way for them to communicate their harmless intentions to the human they have captured. They are too imposing and do not speak his language.

The centrality of *encounter* focuses attention on the act of communication. As with the story "Lilith," which provides a key to understanding Levi's narratives, the encounter often serves as a *mise en abyme* to decipher *literary* communication. In this way, Levi the author attempts through Levi the narrator to control the reception of the text. In particular, Levi depicts the inability of people to communicate. A prevalent theme throughout the collection, incommunicability is the main message in "Decodificazione" ("Decoding"), a tale about an eleven-year-old boy fed up with others, life, and the world. Placed in the third section, "Present Indicative," the reader witnesses the helplessness of the narrator to understand the young boy. Borrowing from the genre of the detective novel, the story follows the narrator on the path to find the person who has spray-painted fascist symbols on signs around town. The "solution" to the mystery, however, only deepens the real mystery of human nature as the protagonist attempts to discuss the symbols with the young culprit. The young boy expresses his anger and dissatisfaction with life as he tosses a number of objects into the river. Despite the "explanation," it is not quite clear what motivated the boy to adopt fascist symbols; this must be decoded. The narrator watches the young boy and ponders the fact that as humans we do not always communicate well:

> I thought too about the essential ambiguity of the messages that each of us leaves behind, from birth to death, and about our profound inability to reconstruct another person through these, man who lives starting with the man who writes, he who writes, even if only on walls, writes in a code that is his alone, and the others do not know it; he who speaks also. To transmit clearly, express, express oneself and make oneself clear, is [the gift] of the few: some could and do not want to, other would like to but do not know how, most people neither want to nor know how to.

The young boy, emblematic of the human condition, demonstrates the importance of literature. The author occupies a privileged position and has the ability and desire to interpret the ambiguous messages of others and translate them into a language that others can understand. Even in an ambiguous encounter, as described earlier, the author still maintains the privileged position by understanding a situation of *noncommunication* and, more important, demonstrating the ability to express it.

At times Levi questions the ethics of *creating* literary portraits, thus pointing to the subjective nature of writing about others. In "Lorenzo's Return," Levi begins the sad tale of his friend from Auschwitz with his literary thoughts on portraits while explaining the reason he delayed penning a description of a friend. Writing about a living person is challenging, he writes, because it "verges on the violation of privacy" (*Moments of Reprieve*, 107), because individuals have an internal view of themselves that is often in contradiction with the version others see. In a Pirandellian moment, Levi shows his awareness of the chasm that separates the subject of literary works from the real-life person described: "Finding oneself portrayed in a book with features that are not those we attribute to ourselves is often traumatic, as if the mirror of a sudden returned to us the image of somebody else. . . . What the 'true' image of each of us may be in the end is a meaningless question" (107–108). This same dilemma is mirrored in the final tale of the collection, "Brief Dream." Here the protagonist, Riccardo, imagines the life of an unknown woman traveling in the same train car. Intertextual references to tales about train encounters in stories by Tolstoy, Maupassant, and Calvino send the reader outside the story to contemplate the literary project of portraits in general. But the main literary reference, through the tale's title and a book the young woman is reading, alludes to Petrarch and the *Canzoniere*. Riccardo finds himself in the position of embarking on a romantic adventure (romantic because of the potential love interest but also because idealized) with the young woman. However, he hesitates, struggles with how to begin such an adventure. As he invents the details of her personality, he ponders the ethics of creating an imaginary woman based on his own dreams and desires:

> Was it legal, was it decent for a good person, to invent a woman, distilling her from his own dreams with the purpose of loving her image for his whole life and using this love with the purpose of becoming a famous poet and becoming a poet with the purpose of not completely dying, and at the same time seeing that other woman on Gioberti Street? Was it not hypocritical?

With such comments, Levi asks the reader to ponder literature in general and the portraits he has created in particular.

"The Girl in the Book," which provides a woman's perspective on the portrait another person has created, restates the concerns stated in "Lorenzo's Return" and anticipates Riccardo's concern in "Brief Dream." In this tale, Umberto becomes intrigued by a reclusive woman he observes at a beach resort where he goes to convalesce. By coincidence, he comes across a memoir written by an English soldier in which the woman's name appears. In it, she is described in romantic terms from an earlier period of her life: "A memorable portrait of the Lithuanian emerged: tireless and indestructible, a good shot when necessary, extraordinarily vital: a Diana-Minerva grafted onto the opulent body (described in detail by the Englishman) of a Juno" (*A Tranquil Star*, 132). Umberto reads on voraciously and decides to use the book as an excuse to approach the woman. Ultimately, he realizes too that he wants to savor the pleasure of the woman reading about herself. However, his excitement and pleasure is dampened by the woman's reaction. Neither flattered nor angry, she seems weary and refuses to recognize herself in the portrait drawn of her: "More than thirty years have passed, and I am different. Memory, too, is different. It's not true that memories stay fixed in the mind, frozen: they, too, go astray, like the body. Yes, I remember a time when I was different. I would like to be the girl in the book: I would be happy also just to have been her, but I never was" (135). She doesn't know which of the memories (hers or those of the book) are prettier; she leaves it up to the reader (Umberto) to choose.

Although Levi chose to focalize "The Girl in the Book" through an observer and reader, it speaks to his own autobiographical project in which he has described people he encountered in many of his works. In fact, it would be easy to imagine the story told in the first person, inspired by Levi's own experience. Would the real-life people who inspired the stories in "Recent Past" recognize themselves in the portraits Levi has drawn?

Reminding the reader that the truth that literature purports to communicate cannot be confused with facts, the story underscores literature's intrinsic artifice. As Umberto and Riccardo's situations, and whatever dilemma the men face, resolve, seemingly on their own, the reader is asked to question literature's relationship with reality. The Lithuanian woman dismisses Umberto abruptly, claiming that her memories for her are like dried faded flowers, but that through the book they have become "shiny and bright like plastic toys" (135). She then rejects the book and him in one phrase: "Come, take your book and go back to Milan" (ibid.). Her gesture is a declaration that literature fails to portray faithfully lived experience. Whatever spell the young train traveler had over Riccardo is dispelled when she quotes Petrarch's famous line *"la vita è breve sogno"* (life is a brief dream) and mispronounces the final word as *"sogh-no."* Here it is the poetry of words that need to be spoken correctly for the charm to hold. After correcting her, Riccardo is able to walk away, and the story (and indeed the volume) ends, the spell of literature broken for the reader, too.

The organizational elements of the collection seem to be attempts at avoiding the failures of communication (in literature especially) apparent in the content of the stories. The content of the stories taken as a whole, with an emphasis on encounters with Otherness where the other is misunderstood or not wholly understood, have an entropic force that risks leaving meaning aside, whereas the structural elements, such as *mise en abyme* and intertextual references, and the paratextual elements, such as the titles, are a negentropic move to rein the text in and point back to itself. Paradoxically, both content and structure are means that Levi uses to control his text and avoid the problems that aspiring poet Pasquale from "The Fugitive," whose text runs away and fades.

CHAPTER 13

Primo Levi and the History of Reception

William McClellan

Today, it is imperative that reception history be put in the context of a reception ethics.[1] The old historicist regimen regulating our relation to the past no longer is adequate to guide us in comprehending our historical situation and moral universe. In a previous paper, "Primo Levi, Giorgio Agamben, and the New Ethics of Reading," presented at the first Hofstra Conference on Levi and published in *The Legacy of Primo Levi*, I concluded that we need to develop a new reading model to account for the way the unprecedented event called the Holocaust has changed our relation not only to our present and future but also to our past, and, consequently, to traditional texts from our past.[2] In that article, I draw upon the political philosophy of Giorgio Agamben, who in several works—most notably, *Remnants of Auschwitz: The Witness and the Archive* and *Homo Sacer: Sovereign Power and Bare Life*—comes to grips with the destructive effects of power on the human subject, a fundamental political and moral problem laid bare in the Nazi death camps.[3] Agamben argues that Auschwitz, as a metonym for the Holocaust or the extermination of the European Jews, is the site where power absolutely degraded and destroyed human beings before exterminating them.

Agamben, in turn, draws heavily on the memoirs of Primo Levi, including *Survival in Auschwitz*, and *The Drowned and the Saved*, calling Levi the cartographer of our new moral universe.[4] There have been some critics who call Agamben's engagement with Levi's work an "appropriation." Dominick LaCapra, for one, takes issue with what he characterizes as Agamben's hyperbolic statements and his "projective identification" with Levi. LaCapra asserts that Agamben "ventriloquizes" Levi in order to speak for the "ultimate victim and instance of abjection," the Musselman.[5] While I think that Agamben is more respectful of Levi's "subject position" than LaCapra acknowledges, my main concern here is that we not lose sight of the fundamental issue regarding Agamben's insistence on the necessity of a sustained inquiry of the Musselman. This project, Agamben says, was inspired by the focus of Levi's writing on Auschwitz, and it is one that LaCapra himself agrees is important. The other crucial issue that Agamben engages is the moral and political dilemma that Levi raises in reference to the Musselman. Attentive to Levi's focus on the issue of human dignity—or rather, loss of dignity—Agamben concentrates his analysis on the figure of the Musselman, who Levi says, "touched bottom"; that is, lost conscious awareness of himself and his environment. Levi further testifies that the Musselmänner constituted the "anonymous mass of the camp."[6] Yet the Musselman, who has lost his dignity, his self-consciousness, and his ability to see and evaluate what is going on around him, Levi insists, paradoxically, is the "complete witness" of Auschwitz. Agamben, in thinking through what he calls "Levi's paradox," draws a number of inferences.

One is that the Musselman is a limit figure that marks the threshold not only between life and death, but also between the human and nonhuman. Agamben states: "The Musselman is the non-human who obstinately appears as human; he is the human that cannot be told apart from the inhuman."[7] A second conclusion he reaches is that this conflation of the human and nonhuman in the figure of the Musselman presents a profound challenge to an ethics based on human dignity. However, if the extreme figure of the Musselman ruins an ethics based on dignity, Agamben insists that it is not acceptable merely to write off the Musselman as beyond the pale, as some have done. Instead, he argues that it is necessary to develop a new ethics based on the knowledge the survivors brought back from the experience of Auschwitz.

Levi's insistence that the Musselman is the complete witness then challenges our ideas both of what it is to be human and what constitutes an ethics. And, as Agamben argues, the testimony Levi gives us of the camps demands an ethical response from us, one we cannot evade without forgoing our human condition as moral beings. The new moral terrain that

Levi's testimony begins to define poses a challenge to us most immediately in reading his work. But, as Agamben insists, it places an injunction on us to use it "as a touchstone by which to measure all morality and dignity,"[8] especially in extreme situations where sovereign power degrades human dignity and destroys human beings.

I argue that we must extend Agamben's moral imperative to use Levi's meditations on the Holocaust as a touchstone to read the writing and literature from our past, precisely because the Holocaust has profoundly transformed our relation not only to the present and the future but also to our past. In this sense, the Holocaust has changed the ethics of reception. The Holocaust demands an ethical response from us that those real and imagined figures from our past that have been dehumanized by sovereign power not be ignored, condemned out of hand, or dismissed as pathological. We should use the knowledge that the survivors bring back from Auschwitz to read narratives from the past, especially those that deal with the issue of power and the human subject.

The moral imperative announced by Agamben and Levi demands a new paradigm of reception history that takes into consideration the change the Holocaust has wrought. I argue that a fundamental effect of that transformation in our relation to traditional texts includes how we think about history itself. In order to accommodate the moral shift made imperative by the Nazi extermination of European Jews, and the consequent need to place texts and images from different historical periods in greater proximity to each other, we have to bend our traditional concept of history. We have to modify and complicate the historicist idea that construes history as a simple linear continuum and employs the concept of discrete periodicity.

There has been much controversy regarding the Holocaust and the question of history. Berel Lang, for example, who argues for understanding the Holocaust *within* history, suggests a paradigm that has dual filiations regarding the same historical evidence; one linkage would be a causal material history, with the second tracking a moral history.[9] I agree with Lang that the Holocaust has to be understood within the domain of human history, but I think there are risks to construing the moral filiation separate from the material causal one.

I argue that Levi's and Agamben's deliberations demand that we construct a new paradigm of reception history that recognizes the profound interconnection between the historical and moral domains. To that end, I think Walter Benjamin's reflections on the philosophy of history provide us with some key concepts that are immeasurably useful in this project, especially his concept of image and the corollary idea of constellation:

"Image is that wherein what has been comes together in a flash with the now to form a constellation."[10]

Agamben associates Benjamin's concept of constellation and the method of reading it entails with an earlier mode of typological interpretation that was practiced in the Middle Ages.[11] The two hermeneutical frameworks are similar in important ways. Both are grounded by a historical facticity; that is, the relationships they discover are not made merely through an abstract system of ideas but connect historical figures and events. This gives both modes a historical specificity and concreteness. Yet neither asserts a causal relation between the figures or events they connect; nor does one cause or determine other. Only when the connection is discovered or recognized is the real pertinence between them realized.

Yet there are significant differences between the two hermeneutical systems. In the medieval practice of typological exegesis the focus is strictly on figures. The second figure fulfills the first figuration (or prefiguration), which is incomplete until then. And the act of interpretation relating the two figures and events is a "spiritual act," one that derives its authorization from a divine source which is not of this world, and thus outside of history.[12] However, in Benjamin's framework, figure is construed as image, and past and present images form a constellation, but whose relations are not predetermined. Most important, for Benjamin, the act of interpretation of the images in the constellation is a political act, one that is *within* the bounds of human history.

As Agamben argues, Benjamin redefines the key term of figure to the more amplified concept of image: "Bild [image] thus encompasses, for Benjamin, all things (meaning all objects, works of art, texts, records, or documents)."[13] Benjamin's concept of *Bild* [image] includes not only figures from texts and history as in the earlier hermeneutical framework but is expanded to include all cultural productions and records of historical events, thus greatly enhancing the value and flexibility of the concept as an interpretative instrument.

Furthermore, Benjamin's corollary concept of constellation provides us with a way of juxtaposing past and present images in conjunction with one another and a set of principles to guide our reading them in relation to one another: "It is not that what is past casts it light on what is present, or what is present its light on what is past; rather, image is that wherein what has been comes together in a flash with the now to form a constellation."[14] This is a two-way street, so to speak. In the constellation the image from what-has-been becomes a part of the present image. The past and present constitute an image; they are fused in a constellation. It is not that the past informs the events of the present or the present gives meaning to the past. But both past and present illuminate each other. We read the images in the constellation together.

As Agamben points out, Benjamin's concept of constellation is enigmatic, and contains at least two senses of history: one is the linear continuum by which we relate the present to the past, usually within some kind of continuous narrative; the second sense of historical time is that in which an event or image from the past constitutes an immediate relation to the present. In a sense it seems to come out of the blue to form a constellation.

Benjamin defines the nature of the relationship: "For while the relation of the present to the past is purely temporal (continuous), the relation of what-has-been to the now is dialectical, in leaps and bounds."[15] By dialectical Benjamin means that it is not an archaic image from the past. An archaic image is that of the past fully understood as the past; that is, there is a well-defined relation between past and present and a clear demarcation between present and past. But in the constellation that demarcation is abridged, transformed so that the image of past becomes fused with an image of the present. Yet, they are still distinct and they interact. However, such an interaction depends, in large measure, on our being able to read them. The legibility of the constellation depends on the beholder, whose comprehending its significance is a moral and political act. The relation formed between the reader and the constellation is a historiographical and ethical relation.

Furthermore, these images from the past are not eternal essences according to Benjamin, but are linked to a "historical index": "For the historical index of the images not only says that they belong to a particular time; it says above all, that they attain to a legibility only at a particular time."[16]

The time of the "now" is when the image from the past and that of the present attains a legibility, where the present recognizes the image of the past as having a pertinence and meaning for the present. I argue that the particular time constituted by the event of the Holocaust is the "historical index" that makes the images of degraded and destroyed human subjects from our past especially visible and understandable in a way never before possible. The historical reality of the Musselman, a figure of the most extreme degradation, throws new light on those real and imagined figurations of the human who in the past have been deformed by power and are, in some way, beyond the "normal."

Furthermore, Benjamin regards the time of legibility for specific images as not for all time, but as having a particular historical instantiation. Agamben infers from Benjamin's "now of legibility" a distinctive and original hermeneutic principle which he says is "the absolute opposite of the current principle according to which each work may become the object of infinite interpretation."[17] This introduces a sense of contingency in reading past and present and emphasizes the changing relations of past and present to one another. Benjamin argues that it is possible to misread the past if we fail to see the pertinence of images. In fact it is even more fraught and dangerous than that, he asserts, because if we do not grasp the opportunity to read the image, there is no second chance. If we do not see what shows up on our radar screen, the image from the past threatens to disappear: "for every image of the past that is not recognized by the present as one of its own concerns threatens to disappear irretrievably."[18] The image of the past runs the risk of completely vanishing if the present fails to recognize it. I would add that unless we can grasp or read the images from the present in relation to the past, we run the risk of failing to comprehend fully the enormous gravity of those images from the Holocaust, and subsequently fail to grasp the monumental consequences the event holds for us. This introduces a sense of crisis in the project of reading the images constituting the constellations from present and past. It also intensifies the sense of moral urgency in the project of reading.

Levi himself records such a "now " moment in his memoir, *Survival in Auschwitz*, and it contains the features theorized by Benjamin and Agamben of such an experience, including a strong sense of moral urgency. In "The Canto of Ulysses" chapter, Levi goes beyond his usual way of citing, echoing, and incorporating Dante's *Inferno* and presents us with a constellation of images from past and his present.[19] In that chapter he describes the spontaneous recollection he has of lines from Dante's Canto as he is trying to teach Italian to Pikolo while they are on the way to the kitchen to fetch the work crew's daily ration of soup. The lines Levi recalls contain the image of "a wavering flame" of Ulysses, who begins to speak to Dante. But Levi's faulty memory threatens to disrupt the transmission of the images from the past. His struggle to recuperate the canto dramatizes his sense of urgency because he feels that this opening up to an image of the past will be foreclosed once they reach the soup kitchen. And then Levi remembers the lines:

> Think of your breed; for brutish ignorance
> Your mettle was not made; you were made men,
> To follow after knowledge and excellence.

These lines Levi remembers are from Ulysses' speech to his men when urging them to go beyond the Pillars of Hercules into the unknown. And Levi exclaims, "As if I also was hearing it for the first time: like the blast of a trumpet, like the voice of God. For a moment I forget who I am and where I am."[20] Levi describes a constellation of images from the past and his present. He reads the image from the past in a new way as if it were in the present, and he records the effect it has on him as a moment of transcendence; it takes him out of the present, the "inferno" of Auschwitz, if only for a moment.

Levi evinces the same sense of urgency that Benjamin had theorized, and he experiences in the constellation of images from the past and present an epiphanic "now," a moment that he says is an "unexpected anachronism, but still more, something gigantic and I myself have only just seen, in a flash of intuition, perhaps the reason for our fate, for our being here today." Exactly what it is that Levi sees remains an enigma because he does not tell us. His attempt at interpretation breaks off as they arrive at the soup kitchen and he ends the chapter with the concluding line of Dante's canto, "And over our heads the hollow seas closed up." The moment of the "now" stands as metonymy of Levi's experience of the "indecipherable inferno" that is Auschwitz. While Levi does not give us an explicit interpretation of this moment, he does provide us with a set of images from Dante's canto and his own situation in Auschwitz. Just as Dante presents himself as an interlocutor of Ulysses and his putative reader, so Levi presents Pikolo as an interlocutor of Levi and us as readers. Reading Levi's memoir, we construct a constellation of images from Dante and from Levi. There is a moral imperative for us to know, 'to follow after knowledge," to interpret the constellation of images that Levi presents to us. And there is a moral necessity that we try to understand what he so urgently tries to impart to us.

To conclude, Benjamin's concept of the constellation helps us to place images from the present and past in immediate and intimate relation, allowing us to discover what was previously occluded, thereby adding depth and breadth to our understanding. This aids in the monumental project of what an increasing number of scholars and historians (for example, Enzo Traverso in *The Origins of Nazi Violence*) are now engaged: embedding the Holocaust more explicitly in European history.[21] Such is the project that Levi began with his meditations: thinking the historical, social, and moral consequences of the event. The effort to think about the historical context of the Holocaust helps us comprehend the unprecedentedness of the event with even greater clarity. It also contributes to the more recent task of the third generation, where contextual memory and textual survivors are increasingly important. The image that flashes up before us registers a sense of crisis, giving a sense of moral urgency to the project of trying to understand what the Holocaust, our immediate past, holds for us in all of its manifold implications.

CHAPTER 14

Autobiography and the Narrator

Nancy Harrowitz

In the last chapter of *The Periodic Table*, entitled "Carbon," Primo Levi traces the itinerary of an atom of carbon as it moves from limestone to air to leaf. The energy of the carbon eventually emerges in the hand of the writer as he places the last dot of the essay upon the piece of paper, thus concluding the text:

> This cell belongs to a brain, and it is my brain, the brain of the *me* that is writing; and the cell in question, and within it the atom in question, is in charge of my writing, in a gigantic minuscule game which nobody has yet described. It is that which at this instant, issuing out of a labyrinthine tangle of yeses and nos, makes my hand run along a certain path on the paper, mark it with these volutes that are signs: a double snap, up and down, between two levels of energy, guides this hand of mine to impress on the paper this dot, here, this one.[1]

Proposing a radical erasure of self, the text ends by giving the atom of carbon the last word, or rather the last dot. Levi the writer becomes the cipher; the carbon, the agent as Levi tells us that the cell is "in charge of my writing." Aside from its figural appeal, Levi's gesture of the grand conclusion based on a speck of carbon becomes particularly relevant when

177

examined in relation to two interrelated questions. The first is Levi's self-portrayal as a writer, and the second is the concept of autobiography within his work.

The critical reception of Levi as an author most approvingly points to his objectivity, his "dispassionate" witnessing, and his ability to universalize, to delineate, and to explore a broad humanistic context within which to examine the moral and ethical questions that arise from a study of the Holocaust. His scientific training is often cited as what permits him to take a long view, to write in a style which Irving Howe called "unadorned and chaste,"[2] and that Cynthia Ozick described as "lucid and calm," demonstrating "magisterial equanimity."[3] Levi himself advanced this view of his writing and his philosophy, even directly connecting his process of writing to scientific method and to chemical reaction in interviews and essays.

Even among scholars who have looked less hagiographically and more critically at Levi's work, there are still facile assumptions made about Levi that range from taking him at his word to a presumed authorial omniscience. In an essay on Levi entitled "Figural Realism and Witness Literature," Hayden White argues that Levi deliberately fosters a representation of himself as a writer based on a scientific objectivity. At the same time, White demonstrates that Levi's writing is highly figural and that Levi sees these two as incompatible:

> Levi's own writing practices run directly counter to his stated aim as a stylist. His writing is consistently and brilliantly figurative throughout and, far from being void of rhetorical flourishes and adornments, constitutes a model of how a specifically literary mode of writing can heighten both the referential and the semantic valences of a discourse of fact.[4]

White points out that Levi rejects notions of modern literature that do not deliver their message in a straightforward manner: for example, his essay entitled "Communication" in *The Drowned and the Saved*.[5] And yet, Levi's writing is anything but straightforward exposition, as White ably demonstrates by looking at the complex figural language that Levi employs in *Survival in Auschwitz*.

White claims that Levi gives himself authorial credibility through his connecting scientific method with the ability to give accurate and meaningful testimony. But oddly enough, White concludes, "Levi believed that his was a style more scientific than artistic." It appears that White misses the implicit point of his own argument: after making a strong case for the sheer artistry of Levi's writings, he is now claiming that Levi did not understand his own craft and was not a good reader of himself. He takes Levi at his word when he says, "Levi's own writing practices run directly counter to his stated aim as a stylist," as if this statement leads incontrovertibly to the conclusion that Levi actually believed that his style was not particularly artistic.

In an article about what he terms Levi's "ethical uncertainty," Bryan Cheyette also argues against a simplistic view of Levi as a "dispassionate" detached narrator, but he ends up in a similar position to that of White, a stance that severely undervalues and undermines Levi's abilities as a writer in his choices of style and genre.[6] Cheyette looks at what he calls the "painful ambiguity of Levi's task," namely that Levi needed to balance the exigencies of commemorative remembrance against the demands of storytelling. He concludes that Levi had an "inability to settle on any one way of telling his story" rather than understanding Levi as a writer with a multiplicity of voices for whom that multiplicity was a way of exploring his skill.

Another critical approach, in many ways as limiting as the first, is to presume that Levi had complete control over his texts. Elizabeth Scheiber, for example, in her analysis of *The Periodic Table*, asserts that Levi is able in that book to "unite his different selves, using chemistry as a link between his identity before, during and after his experiences at Auschwitz."[7] Scheiber's insightful exposition betrays an expectation of unity in Levi's works, as if Levi, who has indeed created so many moments of absolute clarity and comprehension in his works, would always as a matter of course invariably produce unity, that contradictions and complications cannot exist in Levi's works except insofar as they constitute controlled moments of his arguments.[8]

These critics implicitly raise an important question even through their presumptions and contradictory conclusions. Why did Levi find it necessary to hide his writing persona behind the screen of objectivity? The concept of Levi as a writer who is driven not by questions of style and aesthetics but by "scientific objectivity" has made it close to impossible to arrive at any profound knowledge of his texts or to appreciate the depth of his narrative voices. It has, however, made it possible for the reader or the critic to accept complex figurative exposition on Levi's part as "scientific" or "detached" without performing the close reading that would make the interest in his self-expression apparent. They are also driven by a strong desire to find order and unity in a text that represents the Holocaust and the Holocaust survivor: the fragmented self that Levi displays in his writings is as chaotic and frightening as his subject matter.

There is no question that Levi represents himself as a chemist and survivor first and as a writer second. Yet if the contradictions found between what Levi says he is doing—namely, writing that is straightforward, chemical—and the actual writing are examined, another scenario becomes equally obvious but generally unrecognized. The usual path we think of for Levi, a story told by Levi himself, is that he was trained as a chemist in Fascist Italy, was deported as an Italian Jew, became a Holocaust survivor, then became a writer because of a moral imperative to write after his experiences in the Holocaust. If, however, we look at Levi as a writer first and a chemist or survivor second or third, then both his texts and the way we need to read them acquire more clarity. His changing of factual details in some of the other chapters of *The Periodic Table* points precisely in this direction, that Levi was much more interested in being a writer's writer than he acknowledged. The exigencies of narrative, of telling a powerful story, were more important that the exigencies of fact, with the exception of his testimony, *Se questo è un uomo* (*If This Is a Man*, published in the United States under the title *Survival in Auschwitz*). It is in the particulars and subtleties of his texts that we see his writer's vocation as dominant, not an accident of circumstance as it is so often described. His shifting and displacing authorial self, expressed through an autobiographical crisis in *The Periodic Table*, are indications not only of his complexity as a writer but also what that writer's identity meant to him.

The Periodic Table is a text in which many of the tensions and conflicts regarding Levi's self-conception and self-presentation as an author come to light, partially due to the hybrid nature of the text itself. Generic considerations are confounded from the start by this text. It is in part a testimony, if we consider the episode in the transit camp and the one that takes place in Auschwitz. It has the flavor of a bildungsroman in the early chapters, in which Levi explores his scientific vocation in school, and it contains wildly imaginative stories that Levi wrote before and after deportation. There are episodes that follow the simultaneous events of the war and Levi's marginalization from the Italian mainstream, post-Holocaust chapters that engage themes of Holocaust denial and of the role of Levi's chemistry in the war, and tales that focus upon his life at work. Levi sternly disavows the notion that *The Periodic Table* also belongs to the genre of autobiography, but nonetheless tensions abound regarding the presence of an autobiographical mode in the work.

The two chapters that most powerfully explore these tensions in Levi's work are the first and the last, the framing texts: "Argon" and "Carbon."

The conflicts within them go far beyond the parameters of generic hybridism and diversity of topic. These two tales work in conjunction to illustrate the dominance of the narrator over the dominance of the authorial self.

Levi makes some intriguing pronouncements about autobiography in the introduction to "Carbon," as he discusses the textual status of *The Periodic Table* as a whole. He states what this book is not, as if he needed, at the very end of the text, some disclaimers: "This is not a chemical treatise, my presumption does not extend that far—*ma voix est faible, et même un peu profane*. Nor is it an autobiography, save in the partial and symbolic limits in which every piece of writing is autobiographical." Perhaps trying to avoid the danger, asserted by Paul de Man, that autobiography "always looks slightly disreputable and self-indulgent in a way that may be symptomatic of its incompatibility with the monumental dignity of aesthetic values,"[9] Levi continues by situating his text in a much broader perspective. Breaking the text out of the realm of the individual self, which he perhaps sees as constricting, self-indulgent, or worse, he universalizes it not only for other chemists but also for "everyone": "But it is in some fashion a history . . . a micro-history, the history of a trade and its defeats, victories and miseries, such as everyone wants to tell when he feels close to concluding the arc of his career, and art ceases to be long [*l'arte cessa d'essere lunga*]."[10] "Carbon" is framed so as to dodge autobiography by reducing it to a matter-of-fact condition to which "any piece of writing" is subject. The framing is finished at the end by reducing the author to a biological condition that appears to exclude conscious thought or control in the culmination of the text.

The question of autobiography, however, is not so easily dispatched. The majority of the chapters in *The Periodic Table* recount specific events that happened to Levi in his life as a chemist. The poetic and metaphoric shaping of each tale, the philosophical and ethical musings in which Levi engages, and finally the obvious autobiographical foundation of the text can only underscore the presence of self, not lead to the erasure of same that Levi posits as a *fait accompli* at the end of "Carbon." His tales only complicate what we might call his reluctant and unwilling autobiographical project.

The first chapter of *The Periodic Table*, "Argon," also has a lot to say about autobiography. At a glance the chapter might seem to be an anomaly, an odd way of opening *The Periodic Table*: the tale is, after all, mostly about his idiosyncratic ancestors, and the tone as well as the topic is quite different from the chapters that follow. "Argon" recounts the complicated lives of Levi's ancestors, many generations back: in fact, he informs us that they settled in Piedmont beginning around 1500. But are they in fact his ancestors? Levi, after generically calling them *antenati*, refers to specific ones as "aunt" or "uncle":

> As for this term "uncle," it is appropriate here to warn the reader immediately that it must be understood in a very broad sense. It is the custom among us to call any old relation uncle, even if he is a distant relation, and since all or almost all of the old persons in the community are in the long run relations, the result is that the number of uncles is very large.[11]

If we follow the inferred logic of this sentence, it would end, "which then implies that the number of actual uncles is very small." Levi is climbing a genealogical slippery slope, as he claims as an ancestor almost any old Jewish person in the area, thus disclaiming the need for an actual blood relation for his ancestry. Levi's genea-logic moves from "all or almost all" to "in the long run," *alla lunga*. We have to wonder, however, for just how long we are expected to go: after all, the period he is describing is more than four hundred years. Does an uncle remain an uncle within that time frame, given all the possible genealogical permutations, or is the use of the term "uncle," and by association this fantastical genealogy, a rhetorical strategy whose meaning needs to be looked at closely?

The imaginary genealogy melds into his actual genealogy as the chapter ends with an anecdote about his paternal grandmother, an episode in which Levi as a child appears. Levi's entertaining narration provides the space in which this long jump from specific relatives to the history of a community can appear to take place seamlessly, according to the rhetorical terms of his narration, but there is much imbedded behind that purported seamlessness that needs to be examined. A fictive, rather than historical, mode is the bedrock upon which this story is built, underscored by the oral tradition which Levi tells us has handed down the tales of these ancestors from generation to generation. At one point Levi separates the first group of characters from the second by using the words "mythical characters" to refer to the first group. The second group is distinguished by the fact that they are only one or two generations removed from his own, so even if he had never met them (with the exception of his paternal grandmother), a stronger claim for truth is made for them.

Alberto Cavaglion has gone so far as to call Levi's narrative strategy in this chapter "dissimulation" as a way of underscoring the fact that the details given, as precise as they may seem on the surface, simply cannot be trusted as a source of truth or certainty, as much as the reader or biographer may try. "In Argon imagination reigns over truth," Cavaglion argues,

"The biographers have ransacked the story, and the articles connected with the story, wrongly believing them to be a precious source through which to 'read' Levi's life. Nothing is more mistaken."[12]

If Levi's "relatives" are not ancestors, are they in the end more literary "characters," in the Italian sense of *personaggi*, than anything else? The Italian word *personaggio* demonstrates the connection between the character, the mask that promotes the existence of the character, and the larger world that the character inhabits, whether within the world of the text or the visual world of the stage. The origins of the word *persona* (person) from the *Vocabolario Etimologico della Lingua Italiana di Ottorino Pianigiani*, reveals this more expansive meaning and also allows us to better understand Levi's use of *personaggi* in *Argon*:

> The Latins said person (from *per-sonar*, to resound through) the wooden mask always worn by actors in the theaters of ancient Greece and in Italy. In these the facial features were exaggerated so that they could be better seen by the spectators and the mouth was made in such a way as to reinforce the sound of the voice (*ut personaret*): this was necessary because of the usual vastness of ancient theaters. This word then became used to mean the individual represented in the scene that now we call *personaggio*: then (the definition that persists today) any man, and subsequently his physique or the whole of his qualities.[13]

The wooden mask creates the character and allows for its public exposition. The word for mask, interestingly enough, is a description of its function rather than a physical description: it "resounds through." The word performs through a series of displacements and metonymical associations: the word for mask is the function of the mask, which in turn becomes the character that the mask represents. The mask is specifically designed to promote and disseminate the character through its mouth being specially cut so to make the voice louder and more easily heard in a large public space. The word always hearkens back to theatricality, to the function of resounding. A persona (person), therefore, can only be a public self, antithetical to any notion of a private self.

The character in its masking, exaggeration, and staging thus becomes larger than life, just as anecdotes over time can take on larger dimensions and a theatrical quality. Levi's characters in *Argon* demonstrate these features, for they are represented through outrageous and obviously embellished anecdotes about their behavior and in some cases vivid descriptions of what they looked like or the Piedmontese/Hebrew jargon that they spoke. Thinking about Levi's relatives/characters as *personaggi* not only sheds light on the nature of his fictive constructions in this chapter, and the staging that he creates for them, but it also makes us think about his self-presentation as a narrator rather than an autobiographer, as the public function of narrative masks the private self that lies behind it. The lines are blurred between *person* conceived as a historical individual and *personaggio* as a fictive creation. *Person* as mask thus becomes the trope for fiction: both for the characters Levi creates and for the narrator himself.

What lies behind both sets of masks, however, is more unsettling than entertaining: Levi's rendition of "family" history is fictive in omission as well as in detail. It is all very well for Levi to make up stories about far-fetched "relatives" that constitute the community of Jews in Piedmont over a period of several hundred years, but what is screened about his closer family history that strikes much nearer to home for a Holocaust survivor? His disturbing family history contradicts his heavily homogenized version of the community described in *Argon* in times of persecution; as he says about them, "stories of unusual persecutions have not been handed down."[14] Here Levi really is talking about his own family: he mentions stories from his father, Giuseppe, and his paternal grandparents. The closer we get to Levi's actual family, however, the more intense the narrative masking becomes. The following is Levi's version of how his grandmother became a widow:

> In her youth she was known as "the heartbreaker"; she was left a widow very early and the rumor spread that my grandfather had killed himself in desperation over her infidelities. She raised alone three boys in a Spartan manner and made them study; but at an advanced age she gave in and married an old Christian doctor, a majestic, taciturn, bearded man, and from then on was inclined to stinginess and oddity.[15]

The rest of the episode not mentioned in this chapter (nor anywhere else in Levi's work) is the actual context of his grandmother's widowhood. Levi's paternal grandfather Michele and his great-grandfather Giuseppe had owned a family bank in Bene Vagienna in the latter part of the nineteenth century. In July 1888, as the bank was recovering from economic downturn along with the rest of the region, a Dominican friar forced the family out of business. The friar spread a rumor that the bank was failing, a self-fulfilling prophecy that resulted in a catastrophic run on the bank, indeed causing it to fail. Using anti-Semitic rhetoric, the friar incited mobs, ruined the bank, and ran the Jewish family out of town. His true motives became clear when he subsequently opened his own bank in the same town. Levi's great-grandfather came close to being lynched by an angry mob, and his son, Levi's grandfather Michele, committed suicide. The family then moved to Turin. The precise relationship of Michele Levi's suicide to his wife's rumored infidelities and the loss of the family business (and subsequent need to leave the town altogether) is not completely clear, but it appears that the anti-Semitism and subsequent bank failure was the immediate catalyst for this tragedy. These disquieting and alarming facts regarding the Levis' "integration" into the town of Bene Vagienna stand in sharp contrast to the benign picture of Jewish life in the Piedmont countryside that Levi draws for us.

Some compelling questions are raised by Levi's assertion that "stories of unusual persecutions have not been handed down." Did Levi view this vicious persecution as "usual" rather than unusual, or is he stating that it was not handed down—in other words, did the oral tradition in Levi's family exclude this painful true story? What could the relationship of autobiography and the self of the narrator be to an imaginary familial past, narrated to the exclusion of the real past? The relationship of autobiography to genealogy is, in some rather misleading ways, transparent: the self begins, is thus grounded, in family history. If Levi can slip family into community as he does for most of "Argon," then with the same sleight of hand the author as subject can also disappear into his topic, which is precisely Levi's move in the last sentence of "Carbon." "Argon" and "Carbon" thus share a strategy of containment through displacement.

We find a useful way of looking at Levi's shift from family to community and what is at stake in this transformation in the critical distinctions drawn by Pierre Nora between history and memory. Nora writes that the two can be distinguished by their differing roles: the first, history, creates *lieux de mémoire*, sites of memory; the second, memory, *milieux de mémoire*, environs of memory. Memory is defined as that which takes place within a community or a group, a living tradition that needs no historical documentation for future generations' memory; in fact, the presence of institutionalized history is antithetical to memory conceived in this way:

Memory and history, far from being synonymous, appear now to be in fundamental opposition . . . [memory] remains in permanent evolution, open to the dialectic of remembering and forgetting, unconscious of its successive deformations, vulnerable to manipulation and appropriation. . . . Memory is a perpetually active phenomenon, a bond tying us to the eternal present; history is a representation of the past. Memory . . . only accommodates those facts that suit it; it nourishes recollections that may be out of focus or telescopic.[16]

Nora's distinctions are useful here to the extent that they elucidate Levi's shift from what he calls "history" to a more accurate description of his text, namely Nora's concept of "memory." Levi's anecdotes, insofar as they shun both historical and genealogical accuracy, take on the qualities of a mythic oral tradition. In the light of Levi's actual family history, the anecdotes recounted in "Argon" follow closely Nora's predictions of how memory functions, since they "accommodate only those facts that suit it."

Shunning autobiography in favor of what he claims is "microhistory," Levi's rendition of "family" history turns out to be ahistorical, mythical, and grounded in transmitted memory rather than in fact. The memory environment that he creates in "Argon" is antithetical to both factually based history and personal autobiography. The narrative milieu that Levi creates does far more than denying autobiography or teasing it out from between the lines. The very constructions that he depends on to avoid autobiography—fictive genealogy, denial of actual family history in favor of "cognates" that really are false in the end—create the fiction that, *alla lunga*, reveals the most.

Paul de Man analyzes what he calls the "series of questions and approaches" that restrict any understanding of autobiography, including how generic considerations are applied to texts that appear to contain autobiographical discourse. De Man's arguments are quite useful for our understanding of Levi's rhetorical strategies, as de Man discusses concerns regarding autobiography's claim to authority:

> We assume that life *produces* the autobiography as an act produces its conse-
> quences, but can we not suggest, with equal justice, that the autobio-
> graphical project may itself produce and determine the life and that
> whatever the writer *does* is in fact governed by the technical demands of
> self-portraiture and thus determined, in all its aspects, by the resources of
> his medium? . . . Does the referent determine the figure, or is it the other
> way around?[17]

Offering critical arguments regarding the ability of every text to be autobiographical, at the same time de Man points out that autobiography is inherently unstable and based on linguistic and not empirical structures. Autobiography claims authority for empirical truths where there can be no empirical certainty.

The question of authority in the text and that of the text is directly relevant to central questions of witnessing and of the role of Holocaust commemoration in Levi's writing. Is the position of the narrating self that I have outlined in "Argon" and in "Carbon" conditioned or even dictated by the demands of commemoration? Is Levi's stance on autobiography related to his other writing imperatives, namely testimony and witnessing? Massimo Lollini argues convincingly,

Levi's autobiographical perspective is focused on a subject inextricably open to the presence of another, the shame and guilt of being alive in the place of another. . . . Levi's works help us appreciate the subject's position in autobiographical text which is different than that conceived by traditional notions of autobiography. Levi forces us to discover a subject whose memory is driven not by personal remembrance but by the death of the other.[18]

Lollini cites the chapter entitled "Iron" and its story of Sandro Delmastro, whom Levi commemorates at the end, as an example of the conflation of the goals of autobiography and commemoration. Levi ends the chapter on his friend Sandro, murdered by the Fascists, with these words:

Today I know that it is a hopeless task to try to dress a man in words, make him live again on the printed page, especially a man like Sandro. He was not the sort of person you can tell stories about, nor to whom one erects monuments—he who laughed at all monuments: he lived completely in his deeds, and when they were over nothing of him remains—nothing but words, precisely.[19]

It is here that Levi most openly expresses his frustration with written words as his only commemorative tool. Levi conveys the same frustration at the end of his description of Hurbinek, a child he met in Auschwitz during his last days there; as he comments, "Nothing remains of him: he bears witness through these words of mine."[20]

Lollini's points regarding the motivations of Levi's writing are well taken: If we think of Levi's text as being imbued with the need to commemorate, his self-erasure becomes a strategy to highlight commemoration. But Levi attributes part of the failure of commemorative language in Sandro's case—"especially a man like Sandro"—to the fact that Sandro was a man of action who laughed at monuments. The attitude of the commemorated one toward commemoration itself is quite beside the point: commemoration, like funereal rites, is meant for the survivors, not for the dead.

In this seemingly endless circular epistemology of shifts and displacements, an intertextual moment occurs that focuses on the role of the poetic voice in both establishing and abolishing narrative authority. A very writerly moment appears in Levi's text, when he cites Voltaire in the first paragraph of "Carbon": "This is not a chemical treatise, my presumption does not extend that far—*ma voix est faible, et même un peu profane*."

The citation is taken from the second line of Voltaire's satirical epic poem on Joan of Arc, entitled "La Pucelle D'Orleans," the Serving Girl of Orleans, of 1750–1762. The first three lines of the poem are:

Vous m'ordonnez de célébrer des saints
Ma voix est faible, et même un peu profane.
Il faut pourtant vous chanter cette Jeanne

You command me to celebrate the saints,
but my voice is weak and also a little profane.
Yet it is necessary to sing to you of this Joan.

Voltaire's introduction to his poem mocks the conventional disclaimer regarding the unworthiness of the poet, a voice that Levi adopts as his own through this citation. Usually, however, the convention stops with the poet's modesty and is not extended to the profane. Yet if we think about Voltaire's poem to follow, the profane makes sense: secular, satirical, viciously mocking the notion of Joan of Arc's purity, the poem reduces the debate about Joan's saintliness to a debate about her virginity, a question that is definitively settled when she has an affair within the narrative. The profane moves from the initial disclaimer to becoming the expression of the poetic voice. Levi's citation of Voltaire introduces "Carbon" in a highly enigmatic fashion, and it works retroactively, along with the rest of his disclaimers that I have already discussed, to define and condition the text we have just read.

Levi is simultaneously disavowing the poetic nature of his text by casting his own poetic voice as weak and profane while at the same time embracing the literariness of the text through this citation from a well-known eighteenth-century author. He continues to frame the end of his text within the parameters of high culture through a transformative partial citation of Horace: "*ars longa vita brevis*" becomes "*l'arte cessa di essere lunga*," art ceases to be long-lasting.

The Horace citation is invoked in "Carbon" just as Levi makes his move of denying *The Periodic Table* as autobiography through the dislocation onto the notion of "everyone" reaching the end of his or her career. As this end approaches, the logical assumption is that it is *vita* that is even more *brevis*, but instead Levi displaces the brevity of life unto art. In Horace, art stands in temporal opposition to life: art is long-lasting while life is fleeting. To render art as ceasing to be long-lasting is a reversal of Horace's terms. Even more, it strongly suggests that the art dies with the poet, that it has, in the end, no lasting effect.

This reversal functions as a double reflection on the nature of art and autobiography and their relation for Levi. First, Levi's reversal comments on the quality of the art of the poet, substantiating the citation from Voltaire. Second, it speaks to what we might call Levi's theory of autobiography. For Levi, autobiography must take place through a displaced poetic voice: it can never be direct, it must pass through a series of filters and displacements. Its claim to authority comes from this very displacement. As Levi rejects the text as autobiography, he embraces the role of the poet—but he also ironically undermines it. We hear an echo of de Man on autobiography: always trapped within its own specularity, attempting to claim authority while at the same time embracing the impossibility of authority. As de Man says, "As soon as we understand the rhetorical function of prosopopeia as positing a voice or face by means of language, we also understand that what we are deprived of is not life but the shape and the sense of a world accessible only in the privative way of understanding."[21]

De Man's conclusions regarding autobiography, "the restoration of mortality by autobiography (the prosopopeia of the voice and the name) deprives and disfigures to the precise extent that it restores,"[22] are, ironically enough, also those of Levi. Levi's rhetorical tropes for himself give and take away as his language restores the self of his poetic voice and masks it at the same time.

The issues that de Man explicates are quite different, however, in the context of Holocaust commemoration, to which Levi's text is inextricably tied. Levi's conflation of autobiography into commemoration speaks to the grave burden that post-Holocaust commemorative language must bear. De Man claims that prosopopeia, the conferring of a voice and then face to the absent dead, is the trope of autobiography. This trope is integrally attached to burial rituals and to sites of memory, tombs and cemeteries.[23] For the Nazi victims, however, there are no individual physical sites of memory, except for memorials designed to represent the masses: no graves, no cemeteries. Brutality toward the victims was extended to their death: the corpses were treated as material traces that had to be obliterated rather than remembered. As Elie Wiesel comments, "the sky became a common grave" for the victims "whose death numbs the mind."[24]

There is a miserable irony in that if millions of victims had not been murdered in the Holocaust, the very commemoration essential to their memory that must depend on figural language would not be necessary. Their collective commemoration would not impose this impossible burden onto figural language in the way it has in the post-Holocaust era. From this point of view, de Man's essay can be read as a nostalgic evocation of a bygone world where commemoration had only the paradox of prosopopeia to contemplate, where the biggest challenge to understanding commemoration was to analyze a poem of Wordsworth. The "absent dead" of whom he speaks and to whom prosopopeia can give a voice and then a face, are, in the case of Holocaust victims, doubly absent: absent through death, and materially absent as well, deprived of even de Man's "privative understanding."

Levi leaves us with a set of paradoxes at the end of *The Periodic Table*, just as he demonstrates precisely how long his art is and will continue to be. He openly reduces and then rejects autobiography, only to reclaim it in the form of a displaced poetic voice that he celebrates and simultaneously undermines. His attempted removal of self from the text only leads to a stronger poetic voice, which he cannot successfully shake off onto a fictive and nostalgic notion of history. The attempted displacement onto "microhistory" in the end results in underlining the creativity of his voice.

Levi's own words, found in *La ricerca delle radici* (*A Search for Roots*), in the chapter on the influence that Conrad's "Youth" had upon him, perhaps illustrate best of all his relationship to the self and to telling the story of the self:

> Marlow appears here for the first time, his alter ego, and the narration is attributed to him. The reasons for this doubling are deep; I believe that the principle reason is Conrad's reserve: Marlow, so similar to him, frees him from the anguish of saying "I."[25]

PART FOUR

Reflections on Writing

CHAPTER 15

Writing Against the Fascist Sword

Fred Misurella

Pro Archia, Cicero's important speech urging Roman citizenship for a Greek poet, famously defends poetry because it is one of the arts that "civilize and humanize men." He argues that literature provides important models of virtue for men of action, exemplary language for speeches by lawyers and politicians, and, perhaps most important, spiritual "food" for youth, "delight" for old age, comfort in adversity, and "companionship by night and in travel." When, in 1333, Francesco Petrarca, known to readers in English as Petrarch, discovered the speech among a group of manuscripts in Liege, his translation and publication of it reinvigorated the argument over the value of literature in life for his time. "Theology is actually poetry," Petrarch wrote to his brother, Gherardo, a monk. It is, Petrarch added, "poetry concerning God."

That humanistic concern for the value of poetry—and all artistic writing, for that matter—became one of the foundations of Renaissance thought. It would promote character in an individual, increase human understanding, expand knowledge of the world, and make possible the passing from one generation to the next of more than land and possessions. Dare I say that it became a particularly Mediterranean, perhaps Italian, tradition—begun by the Greeks, debated by the Romans of Cicero's time, and encoded fully by Renaissance Tuscan and Italian scholars and writers.

Encoded or not, the perception evolved through the centuries, became eighteenth- and nineteenth-century Europe's most important received idea, paving the way for increased literacy as well as artistic realism, ultimately situating itself mid-battle between the authoritarianism and democratization that rocked twentieth-century Europe, north and south. In Italy, the dispute drew lines between those who saw literature and art as a means of political control and those who regarded all art as a means of destroying taboos. With Gabriele D'Annunzio as a historical and literary model, Mussolini's Fascism promoted romantic individualism, but always within the context of larger social needs: Aeneas, the national hero, abandons his foreign love, Dido, in order to perform his patriotic duty and found a state. Similarly, Fascist heroes were urged to subsume private affections and concerns to the larger needs of the party. In *The Conformist*, for example, Alberto Moravia portrays a decidedly unheroic twentieth-century Aeneas, Marcello Clerici, who mistakenly believes that as a young boy he killed a man who tried to seduce him and spends the rest of his life hiding the act by chasing normality. Married, working for Mussolini's government, he paves the way for the murder of his admired former professor, Quadri, now a leader of the antifascist opposition, only to find that Lino, the man he thought he killed so long ago, still lives. "When I met you I was innocent!" he tells Lino. "And afterward, I wasn't, not ever again." The anguish he has felt separate him from the world is now groundless, and so instead he carries Lino's reply to his death: "We all lose our innocence, one way or another," Lino says. "That's normality."[1]

Such a worldly evaluation replaces clear-cut moral standards of church and Fascist ideology with psychological realism (for an earlier example, see Moravia's *The Time of Indifference*, from 1929). It is an analysis that demonstrates, I believe, the hallmark twentieth-century Italian writer's response to complex political issues. Frequently, though not always, leftist, the psychological, humanistic response bridges centuries of literary movements, enduring at least since Boccaccio collected classical Greek and Roman texts, championed *The Divine Comedy*, and instituted Italian realism with the publication of his *Decameron*. The artistic stance that followed, at times emphasizing Darwinian science like Zola, has led to realistic Italian novels such as Moravia's, memoirs about historical events such as Primo Levi's and Carlo Levi's accounts of wartime experience, as well as *verismo* in nineteenth-century operas and contemporary films. The roots of that realism go deep: After Homer and Virgil, Dante's clear, calculated depiction of Florentine history and personalities in the *Commedia* reveals a social, political leaning far beyond church dogma. In addition, his *De Vulgari Eloquentia* represents a landmark in the history of Western poetics, essentially laying the groundwork for the progressive democratization of European literary language, content, and form. It is a liberalization promoted by Boccaccio and Petrarch in Italy and continuing in the works, for example, of Flaubert, Whitman, Joyce, Ginsberg, and, much as we may hesitate to admit them in such company, twentieth- and twenty-first century rap lyricists. Like Dante's, their work challenges established values, questions moral authority, and promotes new, sometimes dangerous ambiguities about humans and their use of power.

Italian narratives about the Fascist period, from Primo Levi's *Survival in Auschwitz* in 1947 through Alberto Moravia's *The Conformist* (1951) and *Two Women* (1957) and Giorgio Bassani's *The Garden of the Finzi-Continis* (1962), along with Levi's *The Awakening* in 1963, remain clear, objective demonstrations of this literary trend, particularly as critiques of a certain innocence on the part of their principal characters. Moravia makes Clerici's innocence manifest in the scene I quoted earlier, and he continues with Cesira, the narrator of *Two Women* who, earthy and apolitical, manages to express much of Moravia's antifascist and antiwar attitudes during her time in exile in the hills south of Rome.

Married to a shopkeeper in the working class section of Trastevere, Cesira is widowed at a young age but finds herself in the early 1940s, despite the war, having the best years of her life. She knows nothing of political issues, has no desire for love from a husband, and finds herself— with shop, apartment, and a daughter, Rosetta—perfectly content. But with the Nazis controlling Rome and northern Italy, she experiences food shortages. Those shortages, plus the likelihood of Rome coming under attack as the Allied armies march north, makes her rent her store to an old friend and leave with Rosetta for the hills around the village where she was born. There she and Rosetta meet Michele, a young farmer's son in hiding to avoid military service who is philosophically opposed to the Fascists. Curiously, while he and Rosetta are young and attracted to each other, the real camaraderie among them seems to grow between Cesira and Michele. Her practical, country-bred earthiness appeals to Michele's own family background, while his intelligence, youthful idealism, and obvious gentleness appeal to Cesira. The three wander the hills enjoying natural beauty as they search for food and general provisions, but the war invades their unworldly idyll, first in the form of artillery shells, then of actual foot soldiers. Finally, when Allied armies break through German lines and drive the Nazi army northward so that Cesira feels they may soon return to Rome, several separated German soldiers take Michele away at gunpoint so he can lead them back to the German lines. Cesira's reaction to the event surprises her: "We did not realize," she says, "that the disappearance of Michele . . . was a more important thing than the liberation and at least should have had the effect of embittering and saddening it for us."[2] But her happiness over her prospective return home overwhelms her grief, which she sees in retrospect as a flaw. When they witness a friend's murder while he tries to drive them back to Rome, Cesira cringes when she realizes that her main concern is getting the dead man's money: "I had now come to fear that this war would continue to survive in our souls long after the real war was over."[3] But then, as they approach Rome, Rosetta starts to sing again, although with tears in her eyes now, and Cesira considers it a sign that war has not changed her daughter for the worse. She thinks of Michele again, of a day he had read them the story of Lazarus from the Bible, and she thinks that she and Rosetta have risen from the dead inside themselves: "We had emerged from the war that had enclosed us in its tomb of indifference and wickedness, and had started to walk again along the path of our own life."[4]

In that way, Moravia shows, the human spirit survives, preserving, despite the violence of war, joy in living and the realization that although death always lurks, the breath of life is more immediate—and, perhaps, sustainable. Also, note the importance of art in Rosetta's joyful singing and the fact that Cesira's realization comes along with her narration. Giorgio Bassani presses a similar idea in *The Garden of the Finzi-Continis*, when the narrator, a student of literature, tells of his long infatuation with the beautiful Micol Finzi-Contini and the cloistered, privileged life her wealthy family has built. The family grounds and garden take on a bastionlike quality, a twentieth-century Troy walling out the realities and stigmas of life, including the debilitating illness of Micol's brother as well as the growing anti-Semitism in 1930s Italy that places the Finzi-Continis under siege. In a story of frustrated love played out against the background of the gathering Holocaust, the narrator grows to understand that the privileged Micol and his best friend, the idealistic political dreamer, Giampiero Malnate, have deceived him with their own secret affair. When he revisits the Finzi-Contini grounds many years later, after the family has perished in Nazi concentration camps, he realizes that Micol's affair with Malnate revealed something important: In her own way Micol rejected her family's denial of Italy's restrictive racial laws, as well as the narrator's romantic innocence. "The future, in itself, was something she detested," he says, because she preferred the blank, the lively, and the beautiful present. Then the narrator adds, "even more, the past, the dear, sweet, *sainted* past,"[5] which, of course, because of the italicized "sainted" points to a passionate, imaginative interaction with history.

Such an intellectual and emotional retreat from the future as Micol's carries a challenge to the writer of fiction and nonfiction, essentially calling into question the reason for narratives in the first place. If we are not concerned with the next epoch, we cannot effectively influence it, and so remembering the past becomes an exercise in nostalgia and studying the present a useless excuse for romantic adventure. Yet narrative, fiction or nonfiction, grips us, pulling us from the present, carrying us somewhere else, to some other time, and for some unknown purpose as it changes our lives and thinking. Primo Levi affirmed that mysterious pull in his own writing career. Although he frequently wrote speculative fables and science fiction and translated Kafka into Italian, he consistently examined the past through literary allusions or his own experience with Fascism and its aftermath.

In *The Reawakening*, a picaresque tale of his drawn-out return to Turin, Levi uses lived experience, his own and others, to ground an examination of human character, seeing it as profoundly gregarious, profoundly in need of social structures. As a result, communication and human interaction form the basis of Levi's social vision. In his work, people in the most stressful circumstances trade, huddle, and eat, all the while creating human communities. But his vision of those communities is stark, concerned about their fragility, the ease with which they collapse or become oppressive, primarily because the needs of individuals forming the community frequently compete. Violence, selfishness, and chicanery always loom, and individuals as well as communities inevitably suffer from Darwinian pressures. The stories of Mordo Nahum, also called "The Greek" in *The Reawakening*, and Chaim Rumkowski in "The Gray Zone" chapter of *The Drowned and the Saved*, prove exemplary and show Levi's simple hope that telling their stories can prevent a return to the conditions that made them the men they were.

In strict Darwinian terms, both Nahum and Rumkowski, though victimized by Germans, possess strength as leaders: each communicates well, understands politics, drives a hard bargain, and has little conscience against using other people, whether victims like them or not. Nahum is a comic figure, a parody of human interaction of sorts, who uses Levi as his lackey, making him carry all the goods they use in trade but at the same time teaching some very practical ideas: "A man who has no shoes is a fool," he says.[6] Levi acknowledges the truth of that and follows the statement with lines of praise: "He was a great Greek. Few times in my life, before or after, have I felt such concrete wisdom weigh upon me."[7] He also portrays Nahum as "a rogue, a merchant, expert in deceit and lacking in scruples, selfish and cold," but among warm, sympathetic people, he also shows the man as having "an unsuspected humanity, singular but genuine, rich with promise,"[8] a man who, along with discussions of money and material needs, can debate the great questions at the end of the day: "What is . . . 'knowledge,' 'spirit,' . . . 'truth'. . . . What is liberty, and how can one reconcile the conflict between the liberty of the spirit and fate."[9] As a philosophic Greek, as a merchant, even as a rogue, Nahum represents for Levi, I believe, the quintessence of Western humanity, the small, flawed, average man whose strength lies in a combination of ruthless survival skills and sensual bonhomie. They meet again toward the end of Levi's homeward journey, and although Nahum now pimps for women who service Russian soldiers, his fraternal good nature shows through when he sees Levi again: "He asked how I was, did I need anything? Food? Clothes? . . . . 'It will be seen to' . . . here I count for something,'" Nahum says.[10]

In *The Drowned and the Saved*, on the other hand, Levi portrays Chaim Rumkowski as a tragic figure, a negative image of that same ordinary Western man. Where Nahum is humble, materialistic, and, in the right circumstances, good-natured, making for a comic interlude, Rumkowski's story holds tainted glory and a pathetic irony that can only convey a sense of tragic despair. The president of the Lodz ghetto, he acted like a dictator, lending himself princely airs, developing a court of flatterers and poets who sang his praises, a guard of some six hundred men armed with clubs; he also printed stamps and coins that bore his image and exercised a dictator's control of the material taught in Lodz classrooms. Still, he subjugated himself to the Germans, turned thousands of his "subjects" over to them for shipment to Auschwitz and Treblinka, and then died among them himself when in September 1944 the Gestapo liquidated the last of the Lodz ghetto survivors by shipping them off to the gas chambers.

Levi tells Rumkowski's story as part of his meditation on the moral "gray zone" that forms so much of human history, especially in the ghettos and *lagers* of World War II. "We are all mirrored in Rumkowski," he writes, "his ambiguity is ours, it is our second nature, we hybrids molded of clay and spirit."[11] Oppressive, totalitarian regimes take advantage of and encourage that ambiguity, promoting bogus hopes, big lies, increased violence. And, as Levi writes in his chapter on communication in *The Drowned and the Saved*, "where violence is inflicted on man it is also inflicted on language."[12] In response to that idea, he, Moravia, Bassani, and other Italian writers, seek to restore the language, shine brighter light on the gray zone, and, perhaps, increase human understanding. It affirms the importance of narrative art to the human condition and explains their inability to find a more powerful subject than Italy's years under Fascism and their generation's experience fighting an evil idea. Levi's epigraph for *The Drowned and the Saved* underscores it. From Coleridge's Ancient Mariner, it sums up the passion of an ordinary man who has gone through hell:

Since then, at an uncertain hour,
That agony returns,
And till my ghastly tale is told
This heart within me burns.

It is a moral, passionate, political need. As a result, Italian writing of the Fascist period presents a collection of narratives and spiritual witnessing that preserve history, but more important, as Cicero argued, provide models of virtue, exemplary language, spiritual food, and comfort in adversity while attempting to "humanize men" in the face of evil.

CHAPTER 16

"*Singoli Stimoli*": Primo Levi's Poetry

Nicholas Patruno

For Primo Levi, to communicate was of the utmost importance. In Auschwitz he quickly learned that to communicate increased one's slim chances of survival, and as a man of science, whose inclination it was to observe with patience, to analyze, and to understand, he was able to absorb and then to communicate the Shoah as a didactic as well as a personal experience.

In both his full-length books and his essays, both related and not related to the camp experience, Levi's style is consistently sober, lean, and reflective of a mind guided by reason and civility. He is clear, dispassionate, and accurate in his observations, all of which speaks to his scientific training. His need to be clear and detached in his presentation of the facts emerged also from his awareness that he was speaking for the millions of other victims whose lives had been brutally taken away.

There were times, however, when Levi was unable to contain an urgent need to express his emotions and frustration. Often he did so by turning to poetry. Today, at a distance of more than twenty years from his death, his poetry—although an essential component of his literary persona—has yet to receive the full recognition it deserves. For this, Levi himself must bear a good share of the blame. In the 1984 preface to *Ad ora incerta* (*At an Uncertain Hour*), the title he gives to his complete collection of poems,

Levi appears to place little importance on his poems, claiming that anyone who puts a poem down on paper every now and then, as he does, cannot truly be called a poet.[1] He maintains that his verses are not "*eccellenti*" (excellent), and he tells the reader, in a tone between the apologetic and the ironic, that they are but "*singoli stimoli*" (single stimuli) that "in rare moments (on average not more than once a year) have taken *naturaliter* a certain form that my rational half continues to consider unnatural."[2]

Levi is no kinder to his own verses in the little volume *Dialogo*, a 1984 dialogue between himself and the physicist Tullio Regge, where he claims that he places little faith in their quality. And in a letter (dated July 28, 1984) to his friend and fellow writer Mario Rigoni Stern, he treats lightly the art of writing poetry: "I know very well that to write poetry is not such a serious trade." Glimpses of the lack of seriousness he attributes to poetry go even farther back. In the chapter "Oro" (Gold) in his book *Il sistema periodico* (*The Periodic Table*), Levi reveals that he and the group of friends with whom he lived in Milan immediately prior to his joining the partisan movement wrote poetry as a way of ignoring what was taking place all around them. He writes: "We wrote sad, crepuscular poems, and not all that beautiful, while the world was in flames, it did not seem to us either strange or shameful."[3]

Although there can be no denial that his poems are not all "*eccellenti*," (and what poet can honestly make such a claim?) it would be shortsighted on our part to disregard them simply because he disparages his efforts. In the already mentioned Italian edition of *Ad ora incerta*, regarded today as Levi's most complete collection of poems, there are no fewer than eighty-one poems, in addition to at least ten of his translations into Italian of other poets. Most of these poems have been translated into English by Ruth Feldman and Brian Swann in *Primo Levi: Collected Poems*. In this collection, which is neither vast nor very slim, as he does with his prose, Levi touches on a variety of topics and subjects, thus showing the same "encyclopedic vein"—to use Calvino's term in reference to Levi—that is evident in his prose.

Some of these poems have been composed for particular occasions, and they reveal an unusually tender and more open emotional side of Levi, one rarely seen in his writings. This is the case, for instance, of two poems with calendrical titles: "11 February 1946" and "12 July 1980." In "11 February 1946" the reader does see, if only for a fleeting moment, Primo Levi the fighter and victor, the one who, when face to face with death, shouted "no" from "every fiber" of his being as he refused to bend to the will of his persecutors, for he knew that, in the future, there would have been the woman to whom he addresses this poem—his wife, Lucia, to whom the entire collection of poems is dedicated—with whom to share the rest of his life, as confirmed by the last verse: "I returned because there was you." And in "12 July 1980," a poem he writes in occasion of his wife's sixtieth birthday, he tells her, "I wouldn't be in this world without you."

There are other instances in which unusual creatures emerge as the subject of his poems. For instance, such is the case with a cluster of poems, close to fifteen, related to animals. Most of them carry animal titles and are written in the first person. Given their number, which constitutes roughly one-sixth of the entire collection, it would be fair to surmise that Levi places on them a considerable degree of importance, an interest in animals that he seems to share with the Triestine poet Umberto Saba. In one of the rare interviews in which Levi speaks about his poems, Giovanni Tesio asks, "In your poems you often give voice to plants and animals. Is this something that derives from your scientific training?" Levi's response is the following:

> It is the result of an unfulfilled curiosity. . . . For me there exists this one sided love, satisfied only in part. Love for nature as a whole and especially for the "*fruschi*," as Carlo Levi would say using a term of the dialect of Lucania, to refer to poor beasts. In animals there is the huge and the miniscule, wisdom and folly, generosity and cowardice. Each of them is a metaphor, a hypostasis of all of man's vices and virtues.[4]

Thus, in the midst of these zoological poems, many of which not included in the English edition, consisting of large and miniscule animals, the reader finds "Il dromedario" (The Dromedary) as well as "La mosca" (The Fly); "La vecchia talpa" (The Old Mole), "Aracne" (Arachne), and "La chiocciola" (The Snail) as well as "L'elefante" (The Elephant).

In these poems, the poet's sentiments find an outlet by way of the anthropomorphic process of giving human voice to these animals. Among these of notable interest are "Il canto del corvo" (The Crow's Song, poems I and II), "L'elefante" and "Pio" (Pious). In "Il canto del corvo," written, significantly enough, on January 9, 1946, the day before Levi wrote his famous "Shemà," the epigraphic poem in *If This Is a Man*, the crow, the bird of ill omen, gives a strong sense of unmitigating doom with its promise to make miserable the life of the person he addresses, which can very well be Levi himself. The anaphoric lines

That rob you of sleep's joy,
That taint your bread and wine
Lodge every evening in your heart

make the point clear. And, with the words "As he fell silent, he looked about, malign" in the third from the last line, the crow, with his silence and evil glance, puts a seal on his sinister message, further confirmed by the two final lines,

Marked a cross on the ground with his beak,
And opened his black wings wide.

With these last lines the crow makes it clear he has the power to put any one he wishes on the cross. All this echoes closely the experience of the Lager itself, the evil experience that, just like the crow, will never abandon Levi. The crow (as the Lager will), marking the sign of the cross, will remind him that his life will be a constant Via Crucis and to remind him once again that the suffering will never end.

The crow's disturbing image will appear again seven years later, on August 22, 1953, in "Il canto del corvo II," to renew the hounding, as promised in the earlier encounter. The sense of predestination and the forced suffering continues, with no way to escape one's fate. The crow's promise to persist with the torment will not end and it will be "*vano, vano fuggire*" (vain, vain to flee). The poet is reminded that his days are counted and that they will continue to be filled with "*affanni*" (troubles) up to the day he will lose all strength and end his life, "Not with a clash but silently." Here the reference to T. S. Eliot's closing line of the "Hollow Men," ("not with a bang, but with a whimper") is quite fitting and gloom-ily powerful.[5]

In the poem "L'elefante" (77–78), as the elephant reminisces about crossing the Alps as part of, presumably, Hannibal's army, and dies in that region, there is a kind of digging back into history, on a global as well as on a personal level, to find what is left of one's self. The poem raises the issue of displacement and how the removal from the familiar diminishes the value of life. That "I was tired of marching and heavy loads," it being the camp experience, has exhausted the elephant. It sees the absurdity (and "*assurdo*" is the keyword, appearing several times throughout the poem) of how one ends up in a place so inconceivable to one's preordained life road and the sense that whatever he started with (in his youth) has been shattered. Equally absurd is the expectation of having to do that for which he was not born and for which he did not have the real capacity to endure even if forced.

An elephant in snow and ice is an unfamiliar sight, and for our elephant, "Forced here among these enemy mountains" that are so hostile and unnatural to its native surroundings, there is no salvation. Once it has slipped on ice, this "invulnerable, gentle and terrible" creature is doomed. The suggestion that one encounters an unfamiliar situation with a foreseeable dark outcome is very pertinent, for Levi, to the camp experience. And the elephant's final "useless dying trumpeting" of "*Assurdo, assurdo*" echoes Levi's own sentiments that his writing can never achieve a parity of description with the actual events. Also, in consideration of the proximity of this poem's date (March 23, 1984) to his death, Levi may have also been conveying his deep disappointment in the absurdity of the revisionist movement questioning the occurrence of the Shoah.

In "Pio," a rather humorous but at the same time a sad poem, Levi gives voice to the ox's real sentiments in response to Giusoè Carducci's poem "Il bove," a sonnet that most schoolchildren had to learn by heart and that begins, "T'amo, o pio bove" (I love you, pious ox). Levi's ox responds,

> Pio bove like hell. Pio because of constriction
> Pio against will, pio against nature,
> Pio as in Arcadia, pio as euphemism.

With the repetition of the word "pio," the ox demolishes the meaning of that word. The Nobel laureate Carducci says how impressed and moved he is by the meekness of this animal,

> bending happily to the yoke
> you gratify man's heavy work

He adds that it responds to the prodding and pricking of its human master with "*occhi pazienti*" (patient eyes), which demonstrates, to the ox's way of seeing, a deep insensitivity to the suffering to which he is being subjected. The poet, as part of humankind, fails to realize that the ox is being rendered "pio" by way of forced submission. Powerful and painful at the same time are Levi's last two lines of this poem:

> Oy gevalt!
> Unheard of violence
> the violence of making me nonviolent.

It would seem that there is little difference between this act and what was taking place in the death camps. There, too, was not the violence—both physical and mental—of the perpetrator carried out for the sake of rendering the inmates nonviolent?

And then there are poems with a more personal reverberation, in which Levi responds, often in the "we" form, to social issues that have touched him deeply. In the poem "Dateci" (Give Us), for example, he raises an angry voice against humanity's propensity toward violence and destruction, with the hammering repetition of the word *dateci* appearing at set intervals throughout the poem:

> Give us something to destroy . . .
> Give us something to rape . . .
> Give us something that burns, offends, cuts, smashes, fouls,
> Give us a club or a Nagant,
> Give us a syringe or a Suzuki.[6]

Levi's ironic tone pounds on a society that, in its arrogance, is blind to the decline of its moral values. The two closing words of the poem, "Pity us," is his sad reply for the human condition. His accusing finger, from which he does not spare himself, is even more evident in the poems "Almanacco" (Almanac) and "Delega" (Proxy), neither of which has been translated into English.

In "Almanac," written in 1987, just months before his death, Levi lashes out at humankind's senselessness:

> We, a rebel lot, with much talent and little wisdom
> will destroy and corrupt
> always with an increasing hurry.

And in "Proxy" composed in June 1986, Levi admits to his pessimism as he cautions an imaginary reader who looks to the past for guidance to be careful and not overestimate humankind's achievements. Levi warns him that humanity, in spite of its achievements, still leaves much to be desired. Can we, then, be called teachers?

> We have
> Combed the tail of the comets,
> Deciphered the secrets of our beginnings,
> Have tread on the sand of the moon,
> Have built Auschwitz and destroyed Hiroshima.
> You see: we have not remained immobile.
> Go on, get moving, albeit unsure;
> Do not call us teachers.

Levi's desperate cry reaches new heights in the poem, not included in the English edition, "Canto dei morti invano" (The Song of the Dead in Vain). Here, he unites his voice to those he calls the "army of the dead in vain." These are the "invincible" ones because they have already been vanquished. They compel those in power to talk and negotiate, rather than settling matters by resorting to violence. The order is plain, direct and unwavering:

> Sit and negotiate
> Until your tongue is parched:
> If injury and shame endure
> We (the army of those who died in vain) will drown you in our decay.

This is a ubiquitous wish of the disenfranchised victims of atrocities and tragedies of the last sixty years or so. This is the wish of the dead of Monte Cassino, Treblinka, and Hiroshima; of the *desaparecidos* of Argentina; of the victims in Cambodia; of those who died as a result of the terrorist attack in the Bologna train station in August 1980.

Seen collectively, these poems convey a pervasive sense of pain and sadness for the human condition. With his cry, at times loud and at other times subdued, he exhorts humanity to look at itself with more humility for, on the scale of achievements, its destructive tendencies considerably outnumber its triumphs.

As one would expect, however, the most painful poems are those through which Levi relives and responds to the agonizing experience of the Lager. In "Shemà," Levi paraphrases the prayer (see Deuteronomy 6:4, 6:5–9, 11:13–21; Numbers 15:37–41) that Herman Wouk has called the "Creed" of the Jew. In the poem, which opens his memoir *Survival in Auschwitz*, he places a curse on those who are living in the comfort and warmth of their homes and neglect to meditate on the suffering inflicted on their fellow human beings in the concentration camps. In the poem "For Adolf Eichmann," Levi's punishing wish for the son of death, Adolf Eichmann, is not for his own death, but for a very long, sleepless life—a night for each of the five million he sent to their death. "Annunciation" reveals Levi's pungent irony. With no disrespect intended for Catholicism, he gives voice to an angel, different from the one who at another time descended to earth to announce the coming of another Lord, to reveal to the expectant mother the coming of a Hitler-like, evil, self-declared savior. In "Alzarsi" (Reveille), which is also the opening poem of his book *The Reawakening*, Levi, now living in relative comfort and serenity, continues to be haunted by the expression "Wstawac." This word, Polish for "get up," is the feared and painfully awaited wake-up call of the Lager that no one could disobey, and that is a constant irritant as it keeps on reminding him of the anguish and despair it brought, to him and to the other prisoners, in anticipation of the abuse, suffering, and hardships that the day ahead had in store for them.

In "Ostjuden" (Eastern Jews, the official term attributed to the Polish and Russian Jews), Levi pays tribute to the Eastern European brothers and sisters who, despite their suffering and continuous persecutions, have remained a steadfast and tenacious ("stiff-necked") people. The sight of the body of a young girl imprisoned in a wall of petrified ashes as described in "The Girl-Child of Pompeii" recalls Anne Frank, also imprisoned by four walls and then turned into ashes and scattered in the wind. In this poem, as in "The Song of The Dead In Vain," his anguish and anger confront those who have the power and the means to be ruthless and destructive, begging them to stop, for nature, without anybody else's help can spew out enough punishment on her own, as evidenced by the eruption of Mount Vesuvius. In "Schiera bruna" (Dark Band), a title he takes from line 34 of Canto XXVI of Dante's *Purgatorio*, the observation of an almost insignificant but laborious and struggling anthill close by the trolley tracks in one of Turin's streets reanimates for Levi the disconsolate scene of prisoners in the concentration camps, slave laborers deemed no more important than ants by their oppressors. The image is so painfully overwhelming that it becomes impossible for him to continue writing the poem:

> I don't want to write it,
> I don't want to write about this band,
> Don't want to write about any dark band.

A nagging and lingering "guilt of survival," is reflected in the powerful poem "Il superstite" (The Survivor), which opens with the verse from Coleridge's "Rime of the Ancient Mariner": "Since then, at an uncertain hour," and from which the entire collection of poems takes its Italian title. Levi touches the nadir of his despair and alludes to the state of affliction of the detainees—and of his own—in the concentration camp, and to their eventual death. Overcome by a sense of inexplicable guilt at his survival, he feels the need to justify his fate by shouting, but with little self-assurance, that his survival, unlike that of other prisoners, did not come at anyone else's expense. The Coleridge verses, which at other times he found so fitting to his own circumstances and fortified him and that will continue to stimulate in him the need to tell what he had witnessed, appear to plague and haunt him in this poem. His "agony" endures because of his survivor's guilt, as it becomes increasingly difficult for him to justify to himself his task to bear witness on behalf of those who could not speak themselves. After all, how could he, a survivor, know what it meant to touch bottom and, that being the case, how trustworthy could his "ghastly tale" be? Of noticeable interest, in this poem, is the closing line, "*E mangio, e bevo e dormo e vesto panni*" (I eat, drink, sleep, and put on clothes), taken almost verbatim from Dante's *Inferno* (XXXIII, l. 141). In the *Commedia*, Dante, surprised to see Branca d'Oria in Hell, with these words insists that he has seen him alive and well in Florence. He learns, though, that there are instances when the soul leaves the body even before a person has physically died. In this poem, by using these same words, could Levi be implying that, even though the survivor pretends to go on living, the guilt that he feels has already had, internally, a dooming effect from which there is no escape?

A close reading of Levi's poems will reveal that, on the whole and contrary to his claim, they are far from not being "*eccellenti.*" Considering that Levi never stopped writing poetry, a case can be made that his seemingly dismissive comments regarding his poems might have been motivated in good part by his modesty and a sense of caution. Hiding behind his claim of being ignorant of theories on poetry, in a somewhat self-effacing way he appears to beg the readers' indulgence not to expect too much from him. More important, however, except for a few small glimpses, Levi appears to be genuinely uncomfortable in disclosing his more intimate and "emotional" side. "Scrivere è denudarsi" (To write is to get naked), he writes in a letter addressed to a fictional reader in the essay "A un giovane lettore" (To a Young Reader).[7] It seems that for him, to lay bare to the reader his intellectual and rational capacities is one thing; quite another is to bare himself in an emotional and deeply personal way. His modesty and privacy make him feel embarrassingly awkward and naked, this the result, perhaps, of the scar Auschwitz must have left on him, being forced to physically strip in the presence of others, an act which marked the beginning of the process of dehumanization and the elimination of dignity. Subconsciously, Levi's insistence on having—to use his own words—"an acute need for clarity and rationality"[8] may be a way to compensate for the memory of that outrageous act and of other irrational ones. Levi will, in fact, never distance himself completely from his "rationalistic" style. It is, for him, a kind of safety device with which he feels protected. Thus, whether writing prose or poetry, although the need to express himself in one genre or in the other may change with circumstances and mood, Levi will remain constant in his lucid style.

Levi's reservations about his poetry, I submit, may have to do primarily with his style, whose clarity and proselike quality contrasts sharply with the dark and emblematic language of the predominant poetic currents of his time. Levi will not accept the unclear, and he states so in his essay "Dello scrivere oscuro" (On Obscure Writing), where he denounces writers such as Ezra Pound who obscure their messages for the expressed purpose of not wanting to be understood.[9] He reiterates this same point in another essay in *La ricerca delle radici* (*The Search for Roots*) where, in reference to Paul Celan's poetry, he states, "I am diffident toward those who are poets for the few, or only for themselves."[10] The responsibility he places on writers, and on himself, to make certain that the message is understood by the average reader "of good will" leads him to reject any writing that falls short of this objective, and he is especially resentful of those writers who do so on purpose.

Since the "obscure" style he disapproved of was often met with critical acclaim, Levi may have questioned whether his own discursive, explicit style, albeit praised in his prose, was the appropriate vehicle with which to write poetry. His answer is provided by the poems themselves. Levi continued to write them until his death, and with increasing frequency. In the thirty-eight-year span from 1943 to 1981, he released forty-three poems, and in the period between 1982 and 1986 he wrote, in addition to translations of other poets, no fewer than thirty-six poems. Thus, over time, his poems, those "single stimuli"—as he called them—become more recurrent. Regardless of how "unnatural" they are regarded by his rational "half," their presence cannot be ignored. In fact, during his last years, as the rise in revisionism gave him cause—impelled him, even—to question how effective he had been in his insistence on the rational, Levi turned more frequently to his poetry as a means to express his disappointment and anger. "A giudizio" (Judgment) is an example of this disillusionment. In this powerful poem, Alex Zink, a weaver from Nuremburg who has just died, appears for judgment before the poet who, assuming a godlike role, finds Zink guilty and sentences him to hell. Even though Zink had not taken active part in the atrocities of the Holocaust, he, not unlike the majority of the Germans, found it more convenient to remain blind to what was taking place and preferred not to question the provenance of "Black, brown, tawny, and blond wool; More often gray or white."

It would appear, in the final analysis, that Levi approaches his poetry with the same intensity that moves him to write his prose. Once he accepts his own statement that "one ought never impose limits or rules to creative writing,"[11] Levi can proceed on his way, largely unconcerned about following any one poetic current and seemingly unmindful of being considered an "outsider" in terms of literary trends. In fact, as an "outsider," he

can write with a greater degree of stylistic freedom and with less reverence
for established literary norms. To him, it is more important to stay faithful
to the literariness of the word, to its precision in placement and meaning
than to twist the language for the sake of satisfying any particular meter
or rhyme scheme. Furthermore, in his poetry Levi cannot comply with his
own observation, "Since poetry is an intrinsic violence done to everyday
language, it is understandable how every true poet feels the urge to
become a violator, that is, an innovator in his own right."[12] To become an
innovator by doing violence to language is something that he finds troubling. Auschwitz had shown him the harm that can come from doing violence to language. And, if this is what it takes to be a "true" poet, then
Levi cannot see himself as one.

Levi will continue to write poems on his own terms and in his own way.
Why? His response lies in the preface to *Ad ora incerta*. "I am a man," he
writes. He goes on to say, "In some moments poetry has seemed to me
more suited than prose to transmit an idea or an image." Poetry, therefore,
fulfills the same need that prose has at other times. The intensity remains
the same, as is clearly implied by the title he gives to his complete and
final collection of poems. Even though "Ad ora incerta" can and does
imply, on a more superficial level, "every now and then" (in reference to
the "occasional" occurrence of his poems), the deeper significance of these
words lies in the already cited verses of Coleridge's "Rime of the Ancient
Mariner:"

> Since then, at an uncertain hour,
> That agony returns:
> And till my ghastly tale is told
> This heart within me burns.

To Levi, the profound importance of these verses is reflected in their
appearance in the opening page of his last book, *The Drowned and the
Saved*, and in the opening lines of "Il superstite," one of this collection's
most memorable and powerful poems. Thus, as Levi has relied on these
words as inspiration to write much of his prose, he turns again to them to
validate that the agony is an enduring one and that, in his poetry too, the
need to tell the "ghastly tale" continues to engage his creative qualities.

As with his prose, his "acute need for clarity and rationality" will stay
with him in his poetry and continue to define "the personality of the one
who writes."[13] Since the motivating force that moves Levi to write his
poems emerges from a deep sense of morality he feels the need to convey,

it makes sense that he would want to clothe these with a language reflective of reason. Levi's position is quite unique. As opposed to other poets who, often, with their elliptical and allusive verses close to the verge of obscurity, expect the reader to rise to their level, Levi brings his poetry to the level of the average reader. This might help explain why Levi published many of his poems in newspapers and journals before gathering them in book form. The critic Giovanni Raboni is correct in noting that, subconsciously, Levi's wish may have been to invite the reader "to read the poems as if one were reading a newspaper."[14]

At one other level, however, Levi's poetry may have also been responding to another need. The philosopher Theodor Adorno stated that, after the Holocaust, "to write a poem is barbaric." Without dwelling on all its ramifications, this disturbing statement does have validity. It would indeed be cruel to extract aesthetic pleasure out of an artistic representation after having witnessed the atrocities of the death camps. For a time Levi agreed with this statement, but with the slight modification that it would be "barbaric" to write poetry except for that dealing with Auschwitz. However, Adorno and Levi both modified their opinion with time, to the reader's benefit, because, with silence as an alternative, we would not hear the voices of those who need to be heard. Levi perhaps may be suggesting a different poetical approach that does not offend the sacredness of the memory. After such a horrifying event, poetry should invite reassessment of the substance that provides it with aesthetic gratification and that responds with more sensitivity to human suffering and needs. One way to achieve this, as Levi has always tried to do in his prose as well as in his poems, is through clear and concise communication.

CHAPTER 17

Primo Levi's Correspondence
with Hety Schmitt-Maas

Ian Thomson

On April 11, 1987, more than forty years after his rescue from Auschwitz, Primo Levi fell to his death in the block of flats where he lived in Turin. The authorities pronounced a verdict of suicide. Levi had pitched himself three flights down the stairwell. Not since Pasolini was found murdered on the outskirts of Rome had there been such clamorous coverage in Italy of a writer's death. "Italy Mourns the Maestro," ran a representative front-page headline.

Twenty years on, it remains hard for friends and admirers of Levi to reconcile the calm reasonableness of his literary intention—to furnish "documentation for a quiet study of the human mind"—with so violent a death. Levi's chronicle of Auschwitz, *If This Is a Man* (1948), remains a marvel of luminous precision and poise. Yet there are collective condemnations, colored by the author's rage, of the German people. At one point the Germans are addressed aggressively in the vocative—"You, Germans, you have succeeded." Any German who had shown Levi a scintilla of humanity in the camp—and there were several—is pointedly omitted. It was only in later life that Levi would investigate the exceptions that defied the stereotype: the good German, the kind *kapo*.

A complicated, difficult man, Levi was noted for his determination to keep secret what he wished to keep secret. He wrote almost nothing of his immediate family, and other real-life people are often alluded to in his books by their initials only. His late essay collection *The Drowned and the Saved* (1986) typically contains many elisions and concealments. In one chapter Levi refers to a German admirer of his as "Mrs. Hety S"; in the course of her life she wrote a total of fifty-seven letters to Levi, to match his forty-nine to her. She was interested in the moral and material ruins of post-Nazi Europe, and her letters to Levi were typed with great speed and gusto.

A number of other survivors and even ex-Nazis were in correspondence with "Mrs. Hety S"; her letters were treasured (and carefully collected) by all who received them, including Albert Speer. Who was "Mrs. Hety S"? Her former husband had been a chemist for IG Farben, the German chemical giant that operated out of Auschwitz and other camps; but more than that, Levi does not say. In the hope of identifying the mystery correspondent I placed advertisements in a number of European journals and newspapers, asking for information. The response was good. A filmmaker in Holland telephoned to say that Mrs. Hety S's daughter had given her a copy of the entire correspondence; this was more than I could have hoped for.

Hety Schmitt-Maas, the real-life "Mrs. Hety S," had corresponded with Levi for almost twenty years and was vitally important to him as a writer. Sections of Levi's books could not have been written without her. From her home in Wiesbaden she put Levi in touch with writer friends and other contacts in Germany, creating an ever-expanding network of correspondence among them. In this way she hoped to counteract Himmler's cynical pledge that the destruction of European Jewry would be an "unwritten page of glory." Hety's great ambition, she told Levi, was to "understand" the Nazi past.

Running to a total of three hundred typewritten pages, and written in both German and Italian, the Primo Levi-Hety Schmitt-Maas correspondence was gold dust to me. Levi's other biographers had not seen it. I contacted Hety's daughter, Marianne Felsche, for permission to use the material. To my surprise, she spoke to me of a "very difficult and obsessive woman," who would bring books on Treblinka and Auschwitz to children's tea parties in case she got bored. "Some things were too important for my mother to dance attendance on a nursery tea," she told me crossly. I was welcome to the correspondence; Felsche even offered to send me a copy of her mother's unpublished diary, which chronicled Levi's depressions and domestic unhappiness.

Hety sent her first letter to Primo Levi on October 18, 1966, twenty years after Germany's defeat. It radiated a terrific candor and intelligence: "You will never really be able to understand the Germans, we Germans do not understand ourselves." Hety had written to Levi care of his publishers in Turin; *If This Is a Man*, she told him, was *Pflichtlektüre*—compulsory reading—and she was prepared to move mountains to have it read in German schools.

Levi understood at once that his unseen correspondent was a decent, ordinary German with moral struggles of her own. Many Germans, in an excessive self-flagellation, had turned national guilt into a virtue. But Hety was not like that. Over the coming months she was able to provide Levi with an epistolary lifeline out of his difficult home life, and became his soul mate. So her opening letter marked a new epoch for Levi, the start of an extraordinary seventeen-year correspondence, though he little suspected it when he replied a month later, on November 5, 1966:

> Yes, even today I find it hard to understand the Germans. *If This Is a Man* did have the response in Germany I had hoped for, but I do believe it came from the very Germans who least needed to read the book. The innocent, not the guilty, repent: it's absurd—it's so human.

Levi's attitude to postwar Germany, until now mistrustful, changed as he learned of Hety's extraordinary background. A Catholic divorcee, she was born in 1918 to an exemplary anti-Nazi family: when Hitler came to power, her liberal-minded father lost his teaching post. Following his stern example, Hety refused to join the Nazi BDM (Association of German Girls) and was expelled from school. Her family's Jewish doctor had committed suicide in despair at the Nazi persecution; Hety could never forget that day. When, in 1959, she settled in Wiesbaden to work for the local Ministry of Culture, she began to investigate what she called the entire "*Komplex*" of Nazism.

Hety's second letter to Primo began "*Sehr geehrter*"—most honored, a very formal greeting—"Herr Dr. Levi," and she seemed to want to unburden herself of guilt. "The only consolation for those of us who were on the other side of the barbed-wire fence is to know that people like you were able to start new lives after all." Hety's restless mission to understand Germany had been provoked, she said, by her husband's tacit compliance with IG Farben and the Hitler government; in his impotent silence, Hety thought she could detect many of postwar Germany's problems.

With Hety's help, Levi was now able to track down his former IG Farben overseer at Auschwitz, Dr. Ferdinand Meyer, an inadequate rather than infamous man who had issued Levi with leather shoes and shown him other kindnesses in the camp. Levi could hardly see Meyer as representative of the Auschwitz butchers; yet in his memoir *The Periodic Table* (1975) he portrayed Meyer as the slyly mendacious ex-Nazi "Dr. Lothar Müller," who apparently felt no shame for his past. Hety, shocked by the "unkind" transformation of Meyer, suspected literary untruthfulness in Levi. (There was always a special risk, Levi knew, with putting real-life people into books.)

As the years passed, Hety's letters to Levi became five, six, sometimes ten pages long, and contained personal disclosures about personal and family life. Furious rows had erupted between Hety and her daughter, who did not want to listen to her talk of Nazism. Undeterred, Hety sent Levi German books and newspaper clippings on the subject; as the material began to pile up unread at his end, Levi resolved to make his letters more skimpy ("Don't be cross"); but still this did not abate Hety's postal onslaught. It was time they met.

In September 1968, while touring Germany, Levi called on Hety at her home in Wiesbaden. They had not exchanged photographs during their correspondence, and Levi had expected Hety to look rather intense. Instead he found an unprepossessing, pale-faced woman in glasses; the real surprise was Primo Levi. From his photograph on the German edition of *If This Is a Man*, Hety was sure he would look "tormented" or "worn down"; in reality, he was "relaxed" and even "blooming." More, he seemed to emanate "*Strahlkraft*"—a kind of charisma.

Three years later, however, when they met again, Hety found Primo Levi quite transformed. The Levi she encountered in Turin in 1971 was a fear-ridden and nervous man, whose German revealingly dried up as soon as his wife, Lucia, came into the room. Levi's "*Sprachprobleme*" (speech problems), as Hety referred to them in her diary, may have been connected to the guilt he felt at betraying his marital problems to her in the correspondence. Not for the first time, Levi was depressed—and his depressive inarticulacy was striking. Afterward, Hety watched in embarrassment as Levi's wife shrank from view across the restaurant table until she was "quite absent": Lucia spoke no German, and Levi soon gave up on his attempts to include her in the conversation.

On November 12, 1975, hoping to fathom a darker side of post-Hitler Germany, Hety visited the repentant former Nazi Albert Speer in his home at Heidelberg. Though she was under no illusions about this Faustian figure, she wanted to commend Primo Levi's books to him. Afterward she wrote excitedly to Levi that she had left a copy of *If This Is a Man* with the ex-Nazi. "I said he absolutely *must* read it!" Levi was bewildered: as Hitler's arms minister, Speer had been the principal Nazi exploiter of slave and Jewish labor. To Hety he wrote: "It looks to me like an odd dream that this book of mine, born in the mud of Auschwitz, is going to sail upstream—to one of the very Almighties of that time!" Nevertheless he was unsettled by Hety's cozy audience with the enemy. "Explain to me: what moved you to interview Speer? Curiosity? Sense of duty? Mission?" This was the only time that Levi sounded at all annoyed with Hety.

Did Speer read *If This Is a Man*? On New Year's Day 1976 Speer wrote to Hety that he had "skimmed" part of the book. Two weeks later, on January 16, Speer added that he did not wish to "disturb" Levi by reading his Auschwitz testimony. Meaning? To this puzzling utterance, Hety, sounding more weary than annoyed, replied a full six months later: "I find it a great pity that you have not yet read *If This Is a Man*; if you did, the insanity and diabolicism of the Nazi system would finally be made clear to you." Speer never replied: Hety's last letter to him, dated May 5, 1981, went unanswered. Four months later, Speer died of a cerebral hemorrhage in a London hospital. As for Levi, he was relieved not to have to correspond with Hitler's faithful former paladin (as Hety surely wanted him to do). "I would have had some problems with writing to this ambiguous fellow," Levi told me when I interviewed him in 1986.

In 1983, suddenly and unexpectedly, Hety Schmitt-Maas died. She was sixty-five. Her admiration for Levi (not always reciprocated) had been extraordinary, and Levi was always fond of her; she had helped to fill a void in Levi's life and gave him access to the intellectual ferment of post-war Germany. Now she was dead, and her death precipitated another depressive episode for Levi. Part of his moral support had gone: everything about the friends' mutual solicitude, affection, and trust stemmed from their shared hatred of Nazism and their need to understand Hitler's war against the Jews. For as long as he was in contact with Germans like Hety Schmitt-Maas, Primo Levi could believe that a Fourth Reich would be impossible; she had become his idea of the Good German.

CHAPTER 18

A Note on the Problem of Translation

Ann Goldstein

Although Primo Levi is known for his writings about the Holocaust and for the autobiographical book *The Periodic Table*, he also wrote poems, stories, essays, and reviews. He began writing poems and stories when he returned from Auschwitz, even as he was writing about his experiences there, and he continued to write throughout his life. Of his stories, Levi once said in a letter to his publisher, "I wrote them mostly straight off, trying to give narrative form to a pointlike intuition." The stories convey that "point" or intuition—an emotion, a moment, a thought—in a few concise pages.

Many of the stories feature animal or nonhuman protagonists, made-up machines or devices, magical events, otherworldly landscapes. Some are overtly satirical, or allegorical; most are conversational in tone and have a lightly humorous quality. They are usually grounded in reality, with just one element or aspect that may remove them into another realm. For example, the story "Buffet Dinner" has all the elements of a fancy evening party, but the observer-guest is a kangaroo. And in "Gladiators" the details of going to a sporting event are completely realistic and matter-of-fact, including the halftime show; it is just that the gladiator-athlete's antagonist is driving a car. (In fact, this story was first published in the magazine *L'Automobile*.) These shifts are not wry or whimsical; in the case

of gladiators we are, among other things, being led, gently, to think about
our own barbarous instincts.

"The Fugitive," like many of Levi's stories, starts off in an ordinary
office; the details are utterly familiar to the reader—the broken copier, the
annoying boss, the piles of papers in the desk drawers—but the poem that
the protagonist writes turns out to have a life of its own. Similarly, in
"Bureau of Vital Statistics," the office is familiar (here we have the
crowded, slow elevator and the coffee machine as well) but the office
worker is assigned to think up ways for people to die.

Levi was a working scientist, of course, and the language of his stories
reflects that: it is one of the particular difficulties of translating them. The
language can be literally scientific, with specialized technical terms, such
as *osservatori adiabatici* (adiabatic observatories) or *polimerizzazione precoce*
(premature polymerization)—the translator has to be sure of the correct
English term (and also has to decide whether to use it). The opposite
problem is where Levi describes a technical or scientific process, such as
how to make a compass or how molecules bond, in nonscientific language;
the translator has to make sure that not only the language but also the
process are correct. His animals, whether real or invented, are described
in terms of both physical and behavioral characteristics. In a mixture of
the scientific and the fantastic, the heroines of the story "TV Fans from
Delta Cep" tell us, "We have ten armpits: we are all built according to
decadal symmetries, so that our length is the golden section of our radius"
and, "Our men are ten or twelve centimeters long and look like your
asparagus, and when we want to be inseminated we put them under our
armpits for two or three minutes." Even when the subject is not explicitly
scientific, there is a precision, an exactness of description, that we associate
with science. The invented device called the knall is "a small, smooth cyl-
inder, as long and thick as a Tuscan cigar, and not much heavier: it is sold
loose or in boxes of twenty. . . . It shatters stone and cement and in general
all solid materials—the harder the material the more easily. It pierces
wood and paper, and sometimes sets them on fire; it melts metals; in water
it creates a tiny steaming whirlpool." When the creaturelike poem of
"The Fugitive" is examined by the protagonist under a microscope, the
language, though not describing a strictly scientific procedure, has a scientific precision that can be hard to get right: "Tiny hairs were sticking out
from the page, corresponding to attributes of the letters on the other side.
In particular the extremities stuck out, the legs of the 'd's and 'p's, the
little legs of the 'n's."

Levi's combination of exactness, or true-to-lifeness, and invention is a way of urging us to look at our world and the world around us, and our own actions in it, with a different intention, and from a different angle. Landscapes, too, are carefully described, whether the real mountains, or the imaginary park. Of the trees in the story "In the Park" we are told, "Flowers hung from the branches, yellow and flesh-colored—some even seemed made of flesh—and trailed in garlands to the ground."

Levi said, "I hope that each story properly fulfills its task, which is only that of condensing into a few pages, and conveying to the reader, a particular memory, a state of mind, or even just a thought. Some are happy and some sad, because our days are happy and sad."[1]

CHAPTER 19

Primo Levi: A Bibliography of English and Italian Scholarly Writings, 2003–2010

James Tasato Mellone

The heuristic value of Primo Levi's approach to living and writing is evident by the different ways scholars in various disciplines are using his writings. Increasingly, the study of Primo Levi is not only the purview of literary critics and historians. Through an exploration of Levi's work, some psychologists, philosophers, and chemists are starting to gain new insights in their own fields of study. The ready availability of Levi's works in English, and the enormous scholarly attention given to his life and work by English language scholars contributes to what appears to be a worldwide "Levi phenomenon" whereby Levi speaks to many people, about many things, on many levels. Perhaps a sign of the growing international recognition of Levi as a major writer and thinker of the twentieth century is his inclusion in the *Cambridge Companion* series, in Robert S. C. Gordon's important volume (2007). The appearance of an authoritative English edition of Levi's complete works, scheduled to be published by Norton in 2012, will only solidify his global reputation as not only an eminent Italian-Jewish writer and Holocaust survivor and witness, but also as a first-rate European intellectual and moral philosopher.

The bibliography that follows is an update to my "Bibliography of English and Italian Scholarly Writings on Primo Levi, 1985–2002," published in *The Legacy of Primo Levi*, edited by Stanislao G. Pugliese. Both bibliographies are part of a larger project upon which I am working, whose goal is an annotated bibliography on the scholarly writings about Primo Levi from the past twenty-five years. The citations here are to scholarly writings whose main focus is on Levi, or that analyze Levi in a substantial way within a comparative framework. Some studies have not been included because they only touch upon Levi, deriving inspiration from his work but placing the main focus elsewhere. The bibliography includes listings of material published through the summer of 2010.

The bibliography is organized into five thematic sections. The last three are closely related because the interconnectedness of Levi's life and work, fiction and nonfiction, makes the placing of a citation in one section as opposed to another, at times, an arbitrary exercise. Nevertheless, the intent is to group studies together with others of a similar subject matter whenever possible. "Works by Primo Levi" lists newly published or translated books written by Levi, as well as important new editions of previously published work. "Edited Collections of Essays" provides complete citations for important conferences or books of essays devoted to Levi. "Biographical Studies" lists entries that are mostly about the events in Levi's life, or that are of a general or summary nature. "Studies on Memory, Testimony, and the Holocaust" includes scholarship on the important historical role that Levi plays as a witness to, and chronicler of, the Holocaust. "Critical Studies" groups the rest of the Levi scholarship together, most of which analyzes his literary contributions and reputation, or compares him to other writers. Also included are studies of a more eclectic nature.

Notes that have been taken from the publication being cited are indicated in angle brackets, while my own notes are in curly braces.

Works by Primo Levi

Levi, Primo. *Ad ora incerta*. Milan: Garzanti, 2004. [Includes three essays by Cesare Segre, Franco Fortini, and Giovanni Raboni.]

———. *The Black Hole of Auschwitz*. Edited by Marco Belpoliti. Translated by Sharon Wood. Malden, Mass.: Polity Press, 2005. Originally published in Italian as *L'Asimmetria e la vita. Articoli e saggi, 1955–1987*. Edited by Marco Belpoliti. Turin: Einaudi, 2002.

———. *Iron, Potassium, Nickel*. Translated by Raymond Rosenthal. London: Penguin, 2005. {Selections from the *Periodic Table*.}

———. *I sommersi e i salvati*. Introduction by David Bidussa. Turin: Einaudi, 2003.

————. *I sommersi e i salvati*. Preface by Tzvetan Todorov. Afterword by
    Walter Barberis. Turin: Einaudi, 2007.

————. *La chiave a stella*. Preface by Ernesto Ferrero. Turin: UTET, 2007.

————. *Le parole di un uomo: Incontro con Primo Levi*. Edited by Milvia Spadi.
    Rome: Di Renzo, 2003.

————. "Map of Reading." In *Hell in Contemporary Literature: Western Descent
    Narratives Since 1945*, edited by Rachel Falconer, 232. Edinburgh: Edin-
    burgh University Press, 2005.

————. *Se questo è un uomo*. Afterword by Cesare Segre. Turin: Einaudi, 2005.

————. "Shemà." In *Poet's Choice*, edited by Edward Hirsch, 116–118.
    Orlando, Fla.: Harcourt, 2006.

————. *A Tranquil Star: Unpublished Stories*. Translated by Ann Goldstein and
    Alessandra Bastagli. London: Penguin, 2007; New York: Norton, 2007.
    {Stories previously unpublished in English, but readily available in Italian.}

————. *The Truce: A Survivor's Return from Auschwitz*. Translated by Stuart
    Woolf. Introduction by David Mendel. Etchings by Jane Joseph. London:
    Folio Society, 2002.

————. *Tutti i racconti*. Edited by Marco Belpoliti. Turin: Einaudi, 2005.
    [Complete short stories, comprising the collections *I racconti* (1996), made
    up of the collections *Storie naturali* (1966), *Vizio di forma* (1987 ed.), and
    Lilít (1981); *Il sistema periodico* (1975); and *L'ultimo Natale di guerra* (2000);
    plus two additional stories, "Fine del Marinese" and "La carne dell'orso."]

Levi, Primo, and Alberto De Benedetti. *The Auschwitz Report*. Edited by
    Robert S. C. Gordon. Translated by Judith Woolf. New York: Verso, 2006.

Edited Collections of Essays

Dei, Luigi, ed. *Voci dal mondo per Primo Levi: In memoria, per la memoria*. Flor-
    ence: Firenze University Press, 2007. {See citations herein for the essays by
    Angier, Anissimov, Cambi, Cerruti, Cicioni, Dei, Fiano, Gordon, Luciano,
    Mattioda, Neiger, Nezri-Dufour, Roubach, Speelman, and Suh.}

Farrell, Joseph, ed. *Primo Levi: The Austere Humanist*. New York: Peter Lang,
    2004. {See citations herein for the essays by Cicioni, Farrell, Frassica,
    Gordon, Harrowitz, Lollini, Puppa, Tesio, Thomson, and Usher.}

Gordon, Robert S. C., ed. *The Cambridge Companion to Primo Levi*. New York:
    Cambridge University Press, 2007. {See citations herein for the essays by
    Alexander, Antonello, Belpoliti and Gordon, Cheyette, Cicioni, Harrowitz,
    Lepschy and Lepschy, Ross, Usher, Ward, and Woolf.}

Meghnagi, David, ed. *Primo Levi: Scrittura e testimonianza*. Proceedings of the
    Conference "Scrittura e testimonianza" (Rome, 2004). Florence: Libri
    liberi, 2006. {See citations herein for the essays by Bidussa, Bravo, Bruck,
    Cavaglion, Della Terza, Levi Della Torre, Meghnagi, and Mengaldo.}

Neiger, Ada, ed. *Mémoire oblige: Riflessioni sull'opera di Primo Levi.* Proceedings
of an International Conference, Trent, 19 April 2007. Trent: Università
degli Studi di Trento, Dipartimento di Studi Letterari, Linguistici e Filo-
logici, 2009. {See citations herein for the essays by Beschin, Cacciola,
Cavaglion, Cossu, De Angelis, Fichera, Giuliani, Guagnini, Guiso, Linari,
Marfè, Neiger, Nezri-Dufour, Pellizzi, Speelman, and Tenuta.}

Pugliese, Stanislao G., ed. *The Legacy of Primo Levi.* New York: Palgrave Mac-
millan. {See citations herein for the essays by Baird, Bertoletti, Campbell,
Druker, Leshem, Losey, McClellan, Mendel, Misurella, Parussa, Patruno,
Philippe, Pugliese, Pytell, Speelman, Stille, Stone, Sungolowsky,
Thomson, and Warmund.}

Tesio, Giovanni, ed. *Diffusione e conoscenza di Primo Levi nei paesi europei: La
manutenzione della memoria—Atti del convegno, Torino 9–10–11 ottobre 2003.*
Turin: Centro studi piemontesi, Regione Piemonte, 2005. {Since each essay
is similar in addressing Levi's reputation in a country or region of Europe,
the citations are listed together to facilitate browsing: Daniela Amsalem,
"Primo Levi in Francia," 33–44; Francesco Ardolino, "Primo Levi in
Spagna e Catalogna," 311–356; Monica Bandella and Luisa Ricaldone,
"Primo Levi in Austria," 201–228; Ghiorgos Bramos, "Primo Levi a
Salonico e in Grecia," 87–94; Doina Condrea Derer, "Primo Levi in
Romania," 149–156; Giuseppe Dell'Agata, "Primo Levi in Bulgaria,"
177–184; Elena Dmitrieva and Evgenij Solonovich, "Primo Levi in
Russia," 299–310; Pietro U. Dini, "Primo Levi nel Baltico orientale,"
95–106; Joseph Farrell, "Primo Levi in Great Britain," 107–138; Ernesto
Ferrero, "Primo Levi in Italia," 23–32; Pietro Frassica, "Primo Levi negli
Stati Uniti," 45–64; Lone Klem, "Primo Levi in Norvegia," 267–278;
Suzanna Kokkonen, "Primo Levi in Finlandia," 243–250; Rita Marnoto,
"Primo Levi in Portogallo," 75–86; Anna Moc, "Primo Levi in Polonia,"
139–148; Anne Neuschäfer, "Primo Levi in Germania," 185–200; Jane
Nystedt, "Primo Levi in Svezia," 251–266; Nevin Özkan, "Primo Levi in
Turchia," 357–368; Jiří Pelán, "Primo Levi nella Repubblica Ceca,"
165–176; Lene Waage Petersen, "Primo Levi in Danimarca," 229–242;
Giorgio Pressburger, "Primo Levi in Ungheria," 157–164; Sharon Rou-
bach and Dina Wardi, "Primo Levi in Israel," 279–298; Raniero Speelman,
"Primo Levi nei Paesi Bassi," 65–74.}

Biographical Studies

Acocella, Joan. "A Hard Case: Primo Levi." In *Twenty-eight Artists and Two
Saints: Essays,* 99–114. New York: Pantheon, 2007. Originally published as
"A Hard Case: The Life and Death of Primo Levi." *New Yorker* 78, no. 16
(17–24 June 2002): 162–170. {Review essay on Angier's *The Double Bond.*}

Anissimov, Myriam. "Vent'anni dopo." In Dei, *Voci dal mondo per Primo Levi*, 21–32.

Berenbaum, Michael. "Levi, Primo (1919–1987)." In *Encyclopedia Judaica*, 2nd ed., edited by Fred Skolnik and Michael Berenbaum, 2:691–692. New York: Thomson Gale, 2007.

Cavaglion, Alberto. "Primo Levi, il 1938, il fascismo e la storia d'Italia." *Belfagor: Rassegna di Varia Umanità* 63, no. 6 [378] (November 2008): 719–723.

Druker, Jonathan. "On the Danger of Reading Suicide into the Works of Primo Levi." In Pugliese, *The Legacy of Primo Levi*, 221–231.

Ferrero, Ernesto. *Primo Levi: La vita, le opere.* Turin: Einaudi, 2007.

Geerts, Walter. "Primo Levi (1919–1987)." In *Encyclopedia of Italian Literary Studies*, edited by Gaetana Marrone, 2:1039–1042. New York: Routledge, 2007.

Harrowitz, Nancy. "Primo Levi's Jewish Identity." In Gordon, *The Cambridge Companion to Primo Levi*, 17–31.

James, Clive. "Primo Levi and the Painted Veil." In *As of This Writing: The Essential Essays, 1968–2002*, 274–283. New York: Norton, 2003. Also published in *The Meaning of Recognition: New Essays, 2001–2005*, 174–183. London: Picador, 2005.

———. "Primo Levi's Last Will and Testament." In *As of This Writing: The Essential Essays, 1968–2002*, 259–273. New York: Norton, 2003.

Judt, Tony. "The Elementary Truths of Primo Levi." In *Reappraisals: Reflections on the Forgotten Twentieth Century*, 44–62. New York: Penguin Press, 2008. Originally published as "The Courage of the Elementary," *New York Review of Books* 46, no. 9 (20 May 1999): 31–38. {Review essay on Anissimov's *Primo Levi: Tragedy of an Optimist*.}

Lucrezi, Francesco. *La parola di Hurbinek: Morte di Primo Levi.* Preface by Daniel Vogelmann. Florence: Giuntina, 2005.

Mesnard, Philippe. *Primo Levi: Una vita per immagini.* Venice: Marsilio, 2008.

Perez, Rolando. "Primo Levi (1919–1987)." In *Multicultural Writers Since 1945: An A-to-Z Guide*, edited by Alba Amoia, 329–334. New York: Greenwood, 2004.

Simpson, Richard B. "Introduction: Jean-Jacques Blévis' 'Remains to Be Transmitted: Primo Levi's Traumatic Dream.'" *Psychoanalytic Quarterly* 73, no. 3 (July 2004): 737–750.

Sodi, Risa. "Primo Levi." In *Holocaust Novelists*, edited by Efraim Sicher, 201–213. Detroit: Gale, 2004.

Stajano, Corrado. "Primo Levi: Il sogno ossessivo del Auschwitz." In *Maestri e infedeli: Ritratti del novecento*, 145–149. Milan: Garzanti, 2008.

Stille, Alexander. "The Biographical Fallacy." In Pugliese, *The Legacy of Primo Levi*, 209–220.

Thomson, Ian. "My Race Not to Be the Second Primo." In *Lives for Sale: Biographers' Tales*, edited by Mark Bostridge, 134–138. London: Continuum, 2004.

Titelman, David. "Primo Levi's Loneliness: Psychoanalytic Perspectives on Suicide-Nearness." *Psychoanalytic Quarterly* 75, no. 3 (July 2006): 835–858.

Ward, David. "Primo Levi's Turin." In Gordon, *The Cambridge Companion to Primo Levi*, 3–16.

Studies on Memory, Testimony, and the Holocaust

Alford, C. Fred. "Sisyphus, Levi, and Job after Auschwitz." In *After the Holocaust: The Book of Job, Primo Levi, and the Path to Affliction*, 94–128. New York: Cambridge University Press, 2009.

Al-Zubi, Hasan. "Coming to an End: The Narrative of Holocaust Autobiographies and Memoirs." *Interactions: Ege University Journal of British and American Studies* 18, no. 1 (2009): 31–42. {Comparative study of Levi's *If This Is a Man*, Wiesel's *Night*, Wolf's *Patterns of Childhood*, and Améry's *At the Mind's Limits*.}

Anidjar, Gil. "Reluctant Memory." *Tikkun* 21, no. 1 (January–February 2006): 71–73.

Baird, Marie L. " 'The Gray Zone' as a Complex of Tensions: Primo Levi on Holocaust Survival." In Pugliese, *The Legacy of Primo Levi*, 193–206.

Baxter, Jeannette Anne. "Writing as a Means of Survival in the Testimonies of Primo Levi." In *The Camp: Narratives of Internment and Exclusion*, edited by Colman Hogan and Marta Marín Dòmine, 384–402. Newcastle upon Tyne: Cambridge Scholars, 2007.

Belpoliti, Marco, and Robert S. C. Gordon. "Primo Levi's Holocaust vocabularies." In Gordon, *The Cambridge Companion to Primo Levi*, 51–65.

Benchouiha, Lucie. *Primo Levi: Rewriting the Holocaust*. Leicester: Troubador, 2006.

Bernstein, J. M. "Bare Life, Bearing Witness: Auschwitz and the Pornography of Horror." *Parallax* 10, no. 1 [30] (January–March 2004): 2–16.

Bertoletti, Isabella. "Primo Levi's Odyssey: *The Drowned and the Saved*." In Pugliese, *The Legacy of Primo Levi*, 105–118.

Beschin, Giuseppe. "Le riflessioni di J. Moltmann su Auschwitz." In Neiger, *Mémoire oblige*, 11–32. {Context for interpreting Levi's Holocaust thought by examining the post-Auschwitz Christian "theology of hope" of Moltmann and his attempt at Christian-Jewish reconciliation through belief in one suffering God.}

Bidussa, David. "Memoria e testimonianza." In Meghnagi, *Primo Levi: Scrittura e testimonianza*, 70–85.

Bigsby, C. W. E. "Primo Levi: From the Darkness to the Light." In *Remembering and Imagining the Holocaust: The Chain of Memory*, 285–317. New York: Cambridge University Press, 2006.

Blévis, Jean-Jacques. "Remains to Be Transmitted: Primo Levi's Traumatic Dream." *Psychoanalytic Quarterly* 73, no. 3 (July 2004): 751–770.

Bravo, Anna. "Il corpo e la memoria (prigioniere e prigionieri)." In Meghnagi, *Primo Levi: Scrittura e testimonianza*, 56–69.

Butler, Judith. "Primo Levi for the Present." In *Re-figuring Hayden White*, edited by F. R. Ankersmit, Ewa Domanska, and Hans Kellner, 282–303. Stanford: Stanford University Press, 2009.

Cacciola, Giuliana. "Kein starker, eine starke frau: Primo Levi e Ruth Klüger—La *Memoria offesa* di un uomo e di una donna." In Neiger, *Mémoire oblige*, 33–46.

Cambi, Franco. "La trilogia della Shoah di Primo Levi: Una 'lectio' pedagogica." In Dei, *Voci dal mondo per Primo Levi*, 33–40.

Campbell, Timothy C. "The Object(s) of Memory: Models of Remembering in Primo Levi's *Se questo è un uomo*." In Pugliese, *The Legacy of Primo Levi*, 97–104.

Carrera, Alessandro. "'Se tutti i mari fossero d'inchiostro': Aporie della testimonianza da Primo Levi a Derrida." *Intersezioni: Rivista di Storia delle Idee* 23, no. 1 (April 2003): 51–65.

Carmagnani, Paola. "La luce della memoria: Figure e funzioni della memoria involontaria in *Se questo è un uomo*." *Levia Gravia: Quaderno Annuale di Letteratura Italiana* 7 (2005): 141–150.

Cavaglion, Alberto. "Attualità (e inattualità) della zona grigia." In Meghnagi, *Primo Levi: Scrittura e testimonianza*, 44–55. Also published in *La memoria del male. Percorsi tra gli stermini del Novecento e il loro ricordo*, edited by Paolo Bernardini, Diego Lucci, and Gadi Luzzatto Voghera, 135–146. Proceedings of the conference organized by the Center for Italian and European Studies, Boston University (Padua, 14–15 February 2004). Padua: Cleup, 2006.

———. "Per un Levi mal noto." *Archivi del Nuovo: Notizie di Casa Moretti* 16–17 (2005): 163–166. {Contains a preface written by Levi for a 1987 photographic exhibition in Trieste, "Rivisitando i lager."}

———. "Una grammatica del ordinarie virtù." In *Pensare e insegnare Auschwitz. Memorie storie apprendimenti*, edited by Gadi Luzzatto Voghera and Ernesto Perillo, 41–58. Milan: FrancoAngeli, 2004.

Cheyette, Bryan. "Appropriating Primo Levi." In Gordon, *The Cambridge Companion to Primo Levi*, 67–85.

Chiampi, James T. "Rewriting Race Law: Primo Levi's *La tregua*." *MLN* 122, no. 1 (January 2007): 80–100.

Cinelli, Gianluca. "Il paradosso della testimonianza: *I sommersi e i salvati* di Primo Levi." In *Ermeneutica e scrittura autobiografica: Primo Levi, Nuto Revelli, Rosetta Loy, Mario Rigoni Stern*, 63–88. Milan: UNICOPLI, 2008.

Ciuffi, Fausto. "Questo è un uomo: Parole e immagini di Primo Levi—per un uso didattico della testimonianza." In *Pensare e insegnare Auschwitz: Memorie storie apprendimenti*, edited by Gadi Luzzatto Voghera and Ernesto Perillo, 177–187. Milan: FrancoAngeli, 2004.

Consonni, Manuela. "Primo Levi, Robert Antelme, and the Body of the Muselmann." *Partial Answers: Journal of Literature and the History of Ideas* 7, no. 2 (June 2009): 243–259.

Cristiani, Paolo. "Memoria e iniziazone in *Se questo è un uomo* di Primo Levi." *Riscontri* 27, no. 1 (January–March 2005): 49–57.

Davidson, Arnold I. *La vacanza morale del fascismo: Intorno a Primo Levi*. Pisa: ETS, 2009.

De Angelis, Luca. "Nell'oscurità le parole pesano il doppio: Note a Primo Levi." In Neiger, *Mémoire oblige*, 73–107.

Dell'Asta, Adriano. "Gulag, l'Europa sapeva: Le sviste dell'intellighenzia." *Vita e Pensiero: Rivista Culturale dell'Università Cattolica del Sacro Cuore* 87, no. 5 (September–October 2004): 96–104.

Di Giorgi, Franco. "Note sull'esperienza concentrazionaria di Primo Levi." *Rassegna Mensile di Israel* 72, no. 2 (2006): 97–114.

Dorland, Michael. " 'Crimes and Words': The Language of the Nazi Concentration Camps and the Banality of Modern Language." *Phrasis: Studies in Language and Literature* 47, no. 1 (2006): 69–87.

Druker, Jonathan. "Ethics and Ontology in Primo Levi's *Survival in Auschwitz*: A Levinasian Reading." *Italica* 83, nos. 3–4 (Fall–Winter 2006): 529–542.

———. *Primo Levi and Humanism After Auschwitz: Posthumanist Reflections*. New York: Palgrave Macmillan, 2009.

———. "A Rational Humanist Confronts the Holocaust: Teaching Primo Levi's Survival in Auschwitz." In *Teaching the Representation of the Holocaust*, edited by Marianne Hirsch and Irene Kacandes, 337–347. New York: Modern Language Association of America, 2004.

———. "Strategies for Teaching Wiesel's *Night* with Levi's *Survival in Auschwitz*." In *Approaches to Teaching Wiesel's Night*, edited by Alan Rosen, 91–98. New York: Modern Language Association of America, 2007.

Eaglestone, Robert. "Not Read and Consumed in the Same Way as Other Books: The Experience of Reading Holocaust Testimony." *Critical Quarterly* 45, no. 3 (October 2003): 32–41. Also published as "Not Read and Consumed in the Same Way as Other Books: Identification and the Genre of Testimony." In *The Holocaust and the Postmodern*, 15–41. New York: Oxford University Press, 2004.

Fadini, Matteo. "Su un avantesto di *Se questo è un uomo* (con una nuova edizione del 'Rapporto' sul lager di Monowitz del 1946)." *Filologia Italiana* 5 (2008): 209–240.

Feinstein, Wiley. "Dante at Auschwitz: Primo Levi, God's Revenge on Ulysses, and the Supreme Pleasure of the Jews, God, and Hitler." In *The Civilization of the Holocaust in Italy: Poets, Artists, Saints, Anti-Semites*, 336–367. Madison, N.J.: Fairleigh Dickinson University Press, 2003.

Frunză, Sandu. "The Memory of the Holocaust in Primo Levi's *If This Is a Man.*" *Shofar* 27, no. 1 (Fall 2008): 36–57.

Geerts, Walter. "*La tregua*, 1963, Novel/Memoir by Primo Levi." In *Encyclopedia of Italian Literary Studies*, edited by Gaetana Marrone, 2:1043–1044. New York: Routledge, 2007.

———. "*Se questo è un uomo*, 1947, Novel/Memoir by Primo Levi." In ibid., 1044–1045.

Giuliani, Massimo. "Il 'Canto di Ulisse' e i paradossi della memoria in Primo Levi." In Neiger, *Mémoire oblige*, 125–136.

———. "La stella della salvazione nella selva di Auschwitz: L'approccio di Primo Levi." In *La memoria del male: Percorsi tra gli stermini del Novecento e il loro ricordo*, edited by Paolo Bernardini, Diego Lucci, and Gadi Luzzatto Voghera, 123–134. Proceedings of the conference organized by the Center for Italian and European Studies, Boston University (Padua, 14–15 February 2004). Padua: Cleup, 2006.

Gordon, Robert S. C. "Per una 'storia naturale della distruzione'. Levi e De Benedetti tra medicina e 'memoria concreta.'" In Dei, *Voci dal mondo per Primo Levi*, 101–112.

———. "Which Holocaust? Primo Levi and the Field of Holocaust Memory in Postwar Italy." *Italian Studies* 61, no. 1 (Spring 2006): 85–113.

Harrowitz, Nancy. "The Gray Zone of Scientific Invention: Primo Levi and the Omissions of Memory." In *Obliged by Memory: Literature, Religion, Ethics—A Collection of Essays Honoring Elie Wiesel's Seventieth Birthday*, edited by Steven T. Katz and Alan Rosen, 83–103. Syracuse, N.Y.: Syracuse University Press, 2006.

———. "Primo Levi and Holocaust Tourism." In Farrell, *Primo Levi*, 203–214.

Henry, Patrick. "The Gray Zone." *Philosophy and Literature* 33, no. 1 (April 2009): 150–166.

Howes, Dustin Ells. "'Consider If This Is a Person': Primo Levi, Hannah Arendt, and the Political Significance of Auschwitz." *Holocaust and Genocide Studies* 22, no. 2 (Fall 2008): 266–292.

Innocenti, Orsetta. "La metropoli infernale del Lager: Primo Levi tra testimonianza, narrazione, identità." *Nuova Antologia* 139, no. 2232 (2004): 311–332.

————."L'ipertesto del Lager: Su alcuni racconti di Primo Levi." *Bollettino '900: Electronic Newsletter of '900 Italian Literature* 1–2 (June–December 2005). Accessed online at: http://www3.unibo.it/boll900/numeri/2005-i/Innocenti.html.

Insana, Lina N. *Arduous Tasks: Primo Levi, Translation, and the Transmission of Holocaust Testimony.* Toronto: University of Toronto Press, 2009.

Kuon, Peter. "'Chi potrebbe dire che cosa sono?' Questioning Humanism in Concentration Camp Survivor Texts and the Category of the 'Muselmann.'" *Annali d'Italianistica* 26 (2008): 203–221.

Lucamante, Stefania. "The 'Indispensable' Legacy of Primo Levi: From Eraldo Affinati to Rosetta Loy, Between History and Fiction." *Quaderni d'Italianistica* 24, no. 2 (2003): 87–104.

Luciano, Bernadette. "Primo Levi: Interpretazioni cinematografiche—Da *La tregua* di Francesco Rosi a *La strada* di Davide Ferrario." In Dei, *Voci dal mondo per Primo Levi*, 113–124.

Magavern, Sam. *Primo Levi's Universe: A Writer's Journey.* New York: Palgrave Macmillan, 2009.

Magni, Stefano. "Le parole di felicità e la coscienza della tragedia nell'opera di Primo Levi." In *Scrittori italiani di origine ebrea ieri e oggi: Un approccio generazionale [Atti di un convegno Utrecht-Amsterdam, 5–7 ottobre 2006]*, edited by Raniero Speelman, Monica Jansen, and Silvia Gaiga, 47–55. Utrecht: Igitur, 2007.

Mauro, Roberto. *Primo Levi. Il dialogo è interminabile.* Florence: Giuntina, 2009.

Meghnagi, David. "Scrittura e testimonianza." In Meghnagi, *Primo Levi*, 1–31.

Mendel, David. "Primo Levi and the Jews." In Pugliese, *The Legacy of Primo Levi*, 61–73.

Mengaldo, Pier Vincenzo. "*Se questo è un uomo* e *La tregua*: Due strutture narrative." In Meghnagi, *Primo Levi: Scrittura e testimonianza*, 32–43.

Neiger, Ada. "In difesa di Kuhn: Considerazioni intorno a un personaggio minore di *Se questo è un uomo*." In Neiger, *Mémoire oblige*, 183–190.

Nezri-Dufour, Sophie. "Lo scontro di due testimonianze: Henri il salvato risponde a Primo Levi." *Studi Piemontesi* 37, no. 2 (December 2008): 351–376.

————. "Primo Levi, poeta ebreo della memoria." In Dei, *Voci dal mondo per Primo Levi*, 143–152.

Nissenson, Hugh. "By the Light of Darkness: Six Major European Writers Who Experienced the Holocaust." In *Jewish American and Holocaust Literature: Representation in the Postmodern World*, edited by Alan L. Berger and Gloria L. Cronin, 57–75. Albany: State University of New York Press, 2004. {Compares Borowski, Frank, Hillesum, Levi, Presser, and Ringelblum.}

Parussa, Sergio. "The Shame of the Survivor." *Journal of Modern Jewish Studies* 7, no. 1 (March 2008): 91–106.

Porcelli, Bruno. "Cerniere onomastiche nei racconti del lager di Primo Levi." *Giornale Storico della Letteratura Italiana* 180, no. 591 (2003): 408–413.

———. "'Il canto di Ulisse' in *Se questo è un uomo* di Primo Levi." *Rassegna Europea di Letteratura Italiana* 21 (2003): 91–95.

Portnoff, Sharon. "Levi's Auschwitz and Dante's Hell." *Society* 46, no. 1 (January 2009): 76–84.

Possenti, Ilaria. "Stranieri della memoria: Hannah Arendt, Primo Levi e la narrazione come forma cognitiva." *Critica Sociologica* 154–155 (Summer 2005): 83–94.

Pugliese, Stanislao G. "Trauma/Transgression/Testimony." In Pugliese, *The Legacy of Primo Levi*, 3–14.

Pytell, Timothy E. "A Typology of Gray Flowers: Primo Levi and Viktor Frankl on Auschwitz." In Pugliese, *The Legacy of Primo Levi*, 177–192.

Rastier, François. *Ulisse a Auschwitz: Primo Levi, il superstite*. Translated by Rossella Saetta Cottone and Daria Francobandiera. Naples: Liguori, 2009. Originally published as *Ulysse à Auschwitz: Primo Levi, le survivant*. Paris: Cerf, 2005. {Argues for the importance of Levi's poetry as testimonial literature.}

Renda, Maria Elena. "Il rovescio del diritto: Il racconto della violenza in Primo Levi." *Bollettino '900: Electronic Newsletter of '900 Literature* 1–2 (June–December 2005). Accessed online at: http://www3.unibo.it/boll900/numeri/2005-i/Renda.html.

Richardson, Anna. "Mapping the Lines of Fact and Fiction in Holocaust Testimonial Novels." In *Comparative Central European Holocaust Studies*, edited by Louise O. Vasvári and Steven Tötösy de Zepetnek, 53–66. West Lafayette, Ind.: Purdue University Press, 2009. {Comparative study of Levi's *If Not Now, When?*, Jerzy Kosinski's *The Painted Bird*, Jorge Semprún's *The Long Voyage*, and Georges Perec's *W, or, the Memory of Childhood*.}

Roth, John K. "Deliver Us from Evil? Kuhn's Prayer and the Masters of Death." In *Fire in the Ashes: God, Evil, and the Holocaust*, edited by David Patterson and John K. Roth, 243–258. Seattle: University of Washington Press, 2005.

Rothberg, Michael, and Jonathan Druker. "A Secular Alternative: Primo Levi's Place in American Holocaust Discourse." *Shofar* 28, no. 1 (Fall 2009): 104–126.

Roubach, Sharon. "Se questo è un uomo all ricerca del senso: Viktor Frankl e Primo Levi in Israele." In Dei, *Voci dal mondo per Primo Levi*, 153–164.

Rowland, Antony. "Poetry as Testimony: Primo Levi's Collected Poems." *Textual Practice* 22, no. 3 (September 2008): 487–505.

Sanders, Mark. "Reparation and Translation: Primo Levi's 'Letters from Germans.'" In *Literary Responses to Mass Violence*, Brandeis University Symposium, 16–18 September 2003, 75–83. Waltham, Mass.: Brandeis University, 2004.

Scheiber, Elizabeth S. "Demeter at Auschwitz: The Use of Mythology in Primo Levi's *Il sistema periodico.*" *Forum Italicum* 41, no. 1 (Spring 2007): 43–58.

Signorini, Alberto G. "Writing as Anthropology." *Studia Judaica* 13 (2005): 100–124. {On *Se questo è un uomo* and *I sommersi e i salvati.*}

Smith, Nancy A. "'To Return, to Eat, to Tell the Story': Primo Levi's Lessons on Living and Dying in the Aftermath of Trauma." *International Forum of Psychoanalysis* 13, nos. 1–2 (May 2004): 66–70.

Sodi, Risa B. "Primo Levi's Holocaust Lexicon." In *Narrative and Imperative: The First Fifty Years of Italian Holocaust Writing (1944–1994)*, 39–85. New York: Peter Lang, 2007.

———. "*Survival in Auschwitz* by Primo Levi." In *Italian Literature and Its Times*, edited by Joyce Moss, 439–449. Detroit: Thomson Gale, 2005.

Soltes, Ori Z. "Words, God and Memory: Elie Wiesel, Nelly Sachs, and Primo Levi Engage the Ineffable." In *The Ashen Rainbow: Essays on the Arts and the Holocaust*, 13–32. Washington, D.C.: Eshel Books, 2007.

Stone, Marla. "Primo Levi, Roberto Benigni, and the Politics of Holocaust Representation." In Pugliese, *The Legacy of Primo Levi*, 135–146.

Sungolowsky, Joseph. "The Jewishness of Primo Levi." In Pugliese, *The Legacy of Primo Levi*, 75–86.

Tager, Michael. "Primo Levi and the Language of Witness." In *Literature of the Holocaust*, edited by Harold Bloom, 129–151. Philadelphia: Chelsea House, 2004. Originally published in *Criticism: A Quarterly for Literature and the Arts* 35, no. 2 (Spring 1993): 265–288.

Thomson, Ian. "The Genesis of *If This Is a Man.*" In Pugliese, *The Legacy of Primo Levi*, 41–58.

———. "Writing *If This Is a Man.*" In Farrell, *Primo Levi*, 141–160.

Tosi, Giuseppe. "Cura del sé nello stato di eccezione: *La tregua* di Primo Levi." *Rivista di Studi Italiani* 22, no. 2 (December 2004): 121–140.

Valabrega, Paola. "Che cosa fanno gli uomini quando sanno di dover morire. La lezione di Tucidide in *Se questo è un uomo.*" *Cartevive* 18, no. 2 (December 2007): 146–153.

Vetlesen, Arne. "A Case for Resentment: Jean Améry Versus Primo Levi." *Journal of Human Rights* 5, no. 1 (January–March 2006): 27–44.

Warmund, Joram. "The Gray Zone Expanded." In Pugliese, *The Legacy of Primo Levi*, 163–176.

White, Hayden. "Figural Realism in Witness Literature." *Parallax* 10, no. 1 [30] (January–March 2004): 113–124.

————. "Historical Discourse and Literary Writing." In *Tropes for the Past: Hayden White and the History/Literature Debate*, edited by Kuisma Korhonen, 25–33. Amsterdam: Rodopi, 2006.

Woolf, Judith. "From *If This Is a Man* to *The Drowned and the Saved*." In Gordon, *The Cambridge Companion to Primo Levi*, 35–39.

————. "The Starving of Auschwitz and the Gluttons of Purgatory." *PN Review* 33, no. 4 (March–April 2007): 49–53.

Yacobi, Tamar. "Fiction and Silence as Testimony: The Rhetoric of Holocaust in Dan Pagis." *Poetics Today* 26, no. 2 (Summer 2005): 209–255. {Comparison with *I sommersi e i salvati*.}

Yudkin, Leon I. "Telling It as It Is: Primo Levi." In *Literature in the Wake of the Holocaust*, 144–165. London: European Jewish Publication Society (EJPS), 2003.

Critical Studies

Acocella, Silvia. "Dal filtro della scrittura all'ingorgio dei versi: La poesia decantata di Primo Levi." *Critica Letteraria* 37, no. 2 [143] (2009): 302–315.

Åhr, Johan. "On Primo Levi, Richard Serra, and the Concept of History." *Journal of the Historical Society* 9, no. 2 (June 2009): 161–189.

Angier, Carole. "Le storie di Primo Levi: Messaggi in bottiglia." In Dei, *Voci dal mondo per Primo Levi*, 1–20.

Antonello, Pierpaolo. "La materia, la mano, l'esperimento: Il centauro Primo Levi." In *Il ménage a quattro: Scienza, filosofia, tecnica nella letteratura italiana del Novecento*, 79–123. Grassina, Florence: Le Monnier, 2005.

————. "Primo Levi and 'Man as Maker.'" In Gordon, *The Cambridge Companion to Primo Levi*, 89–103.

Alexander, Zaia. "Primo Levi and Translation." In Gordon, *The Cambridge Companion to Primo Levi*, 155–169.

Balakian, Peter. "Poetry in Hell: Primo Levi and Dante at Auschwitz." *American Poetry Review* 37, no. 1 (January–February 2008): 3–5.

Baldasso, Franco. "Figure dell'incomunicabilità nell'opera di Primo Levi." *Poetiche* 9, no. 1 (2007): 35–75.0

————. *Il cerchio di gesso: Primo Levi narratore e testimone*. Bologna: Pendragon, 2007.

————. "*Stanco di finzioni*: Primo Levi, the Narrator and his Literary Disguises." In *About Face: Depicting the Self in the Written and Visual Arts*, edited by Lindsay Eufusia, Elena Bellina, and Paola Ugolini, 85–95. Newcastle upon Tyne: Cambridge Scholars, 2009.

Baldini, Anna. "Commento ad un racconto di Primo Levi: 'Ferro.'" *Per Leggere* 8 (Spring 2005): 87–107.

———. "Intertestualità biblica nell'opera di Primo Levi." *Allegoria* 45 (September–December 2003): 43–64.

———. "Primo Levi's Imaginary Encounters: 'Lavoro creativo' and 'Nel parco.'" *Arcadia: Internationale Zeitschrift für Literaturwissenschaft* 41, no. 1 (2006): 65–73.

Baldwin, Debra Romanick. "The Horror and the Human: The Politics of Dehumanization in *Heart of Darkness* and Primo Levi's *Se questo è un uomo*." *Conradiana: A Journal of Joseph Conrad Studies* 37, no. 3 (Fall 2005): 185–204.

———. "The Voice of Comedy in Conrad's *Typhoon* and Primo Levi's *The Monkey's Wrench*." *Conradiana: A Journal of Joseph Conrad Studies* 39, no. 1 (Spring 2007): 17–28.

Band, Arnold J. "Two Travelogues: Bialik's *In the City of Slaughter* and Levi's *If This Is a Man*." *Prooftexts: A Journal of Jewish Literary History* 25, nos. 1–2 (Winter–Spring 2005): 121–127.

Belpoliti, Marco. *La prova*. Turin: Einaudi, 2007. {About visiting the places of Levi's journey in *La tregua*, with director Davide Ferrario, for his film *La strada di Levi*.}

Benchouiha, Lucie. "The Perversion of a Fairy Tale: Primo Levi's 'La bella addormentata nel frigo.'" *Modern Language Review* 100, no. 2 (April 2005): 356–366.

Bignami, Marialuisa. "La presenza di Conrad nell'opera di Primo Levi." *Acme: Annali della Facoltà di Lettere e Filosofia dell'Università degli Studi di Milano* 60, no. 2 (May–August 2007): 273–279.

Bruck, Edith. "Levi lo scrittore e Primo l'amico." In Meghnagi, *Primo Levi: Scrittura e testimonianza*, 112–114.

Cannon, JoAnn. "Memory and Testimony in Primo Levi and Giorgio Bassani." In *The Cambridge Companion to the Italian Novel*, edited by Peter Bondanella and Andrea Ciccarelli, 125–135. New York: Cambridge University Press, 2003.

Carasso, Françoise. *Primo Levi: La scelta della chiarezza*. Turin: Einaudi, 2009.

Castronuovo, Antonio. "Primo Levi e le macchine celibi." *Belfagor: Rassegna di Varia Umanità* 59, no. 5 [353] (September 2004): 513–528.

Cavaglion, Alberto. *Notizie su argon: Gli antenati di Primo Levi da Francesco Petrarca a Cesare Lombroso*. Turin: Instar Libri, 2007.

———. "'Ultime notizie da Argon.'" In Neiger, *Mémoire oblige*, 47–55.

Cerruti, Luigi. "Una vita concreta: Materia, materiali e lavoro umano." In Dei, *Voci dal mondo per Primo Levi*, 41–62.

Chang, Natasha V. "Chemical Contaminations: Allegory and Alterity in Primo Levi's *Il sistema periodico*." *Italica* 83, nos. 3–4 (Fall–Winter 2006): 543–562.

Cicioni, Mirna. "'Do Not Call Us Teachers': Primo Levi and the Next Generations." In Farrell, *Primo Levi*, 19–35.

———. "'Familiarity with Proteus': Primo Levi's Sons and Daughters." *A/B: Auto/Biography Studies* 19, nos. 1–2 (Summer–Winter 2004): 33–45.

———. "Primo Levi fra 'autos,' 'bios' e 'graphos.'" *Intersezioni* 27, no. 3 (December 2007): 391–403.

———. "Primo Levi's Humour." In Gordon, *The Cambridge Companion to Primo Levi*, 137–153.

———. "Un'amicizia asimmetrica e feconda: Levi e Manzoni." In Dei, *Voci dal mondo per Primo Levi*, 63–70.

Cossu, Maria Grazia. "*La ricerca delle radici*: Viaggio nell'immaginario letterario di Primo Levi." In Neiger, *Mémoire oblige*, 57–72.

Cortellessa, Andrea, Davide Ferrario, and Marco Belpoliti. *La strada di Levi: Immagini e parole dal film di Davide Ferrario e Marco Belpoliti*. Venice: Marsilio, 2007.

Daley, Chris. "The 'Atrocious Privilege': Bearing Witness to War and Atrocity in O'Brien, Levi, and Remarque." In *Arms and the Self: War, the Military, and Autobiographical Writing*, edited by Alex Vernon, 182–201. Kent, Ohio: Kent State University Press, 2005.

Dei, Luigi. "L'arte letteraria di un chimico." In Dei, *Voci dal mondo per Primo Levi*, 71–90.

Della Terza, Dante. "I racconti di Primo Levi: Memorie, tecnologia, invenzione." In Meghnagi, *Primo Levi: Scrittura e testimonianza*, 96–111.

Dogà, Ulisse. "Dello scrivere oscuro: Paul Celan e Primo Levi." *Derekh Judaica Urbinatensia* 3 (2005): 47–57.

Druker, Jonathan. "The Shadowed Violence of Culture: Fascism and the Figure of Ulysses in Primo Levi's Survival in Auschwitz." *Clio: A Journal of Literature, History, and the Philosophy of History* 33, no. 2 (Winter 2004): 143–161.

Dusinberre, Juliet. "Rival Poets in the Forest of Arden." *Shakespeare-Jahrbuch* 139 (2003): 71–83. {Compares Levi, Shakespeare, and Seamus Heaney.}

Falconer, Rachel. "Selfhood in Descent: Primo Levi's *The Search for Roots* and *If This Is a Man*." *Immigrants and Minorities* 21, nos. 1–2 (2002): 203–230. Also published in *Representing the Holocaust: In Honour of Bryan Burns*, edited by Sue Vice, 203–230. Portland, Ore.: Vallentine Mitchell, 2003.

———. "Teaching Primo Levi." In *Teaching Holocaust Literature and Film*, edited by Robert Eaglestone and Barry Langford, 114–125. Basingstoke: Palgrave Macmillan, 2008.

Farneti, Roberto. "Of Humans and Other Portentous Beings: On Primo Levi's *Storie Naturali*." *Critical Inquiry* 32, no. 4 (Summer 2006): 724–740.

Farrell, Joseph. "From Darkness to Light: Primo Levi, Man of Letters." In Farrell, *Primo Levi*, 117–140.

Fiano, Andrea. "I motive del tardivo successo di Primo Levi negli Stati Uniti." In Dei, *Voci dal mondo per Primo Levi*, 91–100.

Fichera, Vittorio. "Primo Levi e George Orwell." In Neiger, *Mémoire oblige*, 109–123.

Frassica, Pietro. "Changing and Unchanging Truths: Primo Levi versus Francesco Rosi." In Farrell, *Primo Levi*, 171–182.

Geerts, Walter. "Le nozze feconde: Sui racconti fanta-biologici di Primo Levi." In *Lingua e letteratura italiana dentro e fuori la penisola: Atti del III convegno degli italianisti europei, Cracovia, 11–13 ottobre 2001*, edited by Stanislaw Widlak, 109–115. Krakow: Jagiellonian University, 2003.

Gioanola, Elio. "Primo Levi: Diversità della letteratura, letteratura della diversità." In *Psicanalisi e interpretazione letteraria: Leopardi, Pacoli, D'Annunzio, Saba, Montale, Penna, Quasimodo, Caproni, Sanguineti, Mussapi, Viviani, Morante, Primo Levi, Soldati, Biamonti*, 371–392. Milan: Jaca Book, 2005.

Giuliani, Massimo. *A Centaur in Auschwitz: Reflections on Primo Levi's Thinking*. Lanham, Md.: Lexington Books, 2003.

———. "La complessità di Primo Levi: Conoscere Primo Levi attraverso le sue interviste, gli articoli di giornali e altri testi brevi." *Humanitas: Rivista Bimestrale di Cultura* 62, nos. 5–6 (2007): 1123–1139.

Goldman, Anne. "Questions of Transport: Reading Primo Levi Reading Dante." *Georgia Review* 64, no. 1 (Spring 2010): 69–88.

Gordon, Robert S. C. " 'How Much Home Does a Person Need?' Primo Levi and the Ethics of Home." In Farrell, *Primo Levi*, 37–65.

———. *Primo Levi: Le virtù dell'uomo normale*. Translated by Dora Bertucci and Bruna Soravia. Rome: Carocci, 2004. Translation of *Primo Levi's Ordinary Virtues: From Testimony to Ethics*. Oxford: Oxford University Press, 2001.

———. *"Sfacciata fortuna": La Shoa e il caso / "Sfacciata fortuna": Luck and the Holocaust*. Translated by Chiara Stangalino. Turin: Einaudi, 2010. {In Italian and English; based on a lecture delivered at the Centro Internazionale di Studi Primo Levi, Turin, 10 November 2009.}

Gregson, Nicky. "Material, Literary Narrative and Cultural Economy." *Journal of Cultural Economy* 2, no. 3 (2009): 285–300. {Critique of the industrial short stories in *The Periodic Table*, *The Monkey's Wrench*, and *A Tranquil Star*.}

Guagnini, Elvio. "Letteratura, scienza e tecnica in Primo Levi." In Neiger, *Mémoire oblige*, 137–148.

Guiso, Angela. "Tra mimesi e inverosimiglianza: Memoria e invenzione nella narrativadi Primo Levi." In Neiger, *Mémoire oblige*, 149–161.

HaKarmi, Batnadiv. "Hubris, Language, and Oppression: Recreating Babel in Primo Levi's *If This Is a Man* and the Midrash." *Partial Answers: Journal of Literature and the History of Ideas* 7, no. 1 (January 2009): 31–43.

Hoveyda, Amir H. "Primo Levi's *The Periodic Table*: A Search for Patterns in Times Past." *Angewandte Chemie* (International Edition) 43, no. 48 (2004): 6592–6594.

Howland, Jacob. "Primo Levi's Nostalgia." *Society* 45, no. 6 (December 2008): 540–543.

Jochnowitz, George. "Judeo-Italian, Primo Levi's Grandmother Tongue." *Midstream* 52, no. 4 (July–August 2006): 30–32.

Lakatos Osorio, Viktoria Klara, Peter Wilhelm Tiedemann, and Paulo Alves Porto. "Primo Levi and *The Periodic Table*: Teaching Chemistry Using a Literary Text." *Journal of Chemical Education* 84, no. 5 (May 2007): 775–778.

Lazzarin, Stefano. "Il racconto inascoltato: Eduardo De Filippo, Dino Buzzati, Primo Levi." *Narrativa* no. 24 (January 2003): 227–243.

Lepschy, Anna Laura, and Giulio Lepschy. "Primo Levi's Languages." In Gordon, *The Cambridge Companion to Primo Levi*, 121–136.

Leshem, Dan. "The Question of Ethical Discourse: Emmanuel Levinas, Primo Levi, and Giorgio Agamben." In Pugliese, *The Legacy of Primo Levi*, 153–160.

Levi Della Torre, Stefano. "Primo Levi: Una stella tranquilla." In *Italienische Erzählungen des 20. Jahrhunderts in Einzelinterpretationen*, edited by Manfred Lentzen. Berlin: Schmidt, 2003. Also published in *Zone di turbolenza: Intrecci, somiglianze, conflitti*, 2nd ed., 131–139. Milan: Feltrinelli, 2004.

———. "Primo Levi etnologo." In *Zone di turbolenza: Intrecci, somiglianze, conflitti*, 142–151. Milan: Feltrinelli, 2004. Also published in Meghnagi, *Primo Levi: Scrittura e testimonianza*, 86–95.

Linari, Franca. "La ripresa di alcune figure del mito classico nella narrativa di Primo Levi." In Neiger, *Mémoire oblige*, 163–171.

Lockard, Joe. "Facing the Wiindigoo: Gerald Vizenor and Primo Levi." In *Survivance: Narratives of Native Presence*, edited by Gerald Vizenor, 209–220. Lincoln: University of Nebraska Press, 2008.

Lollini, Massimo. "Primo Levi and the Idea of Autobiography." In Farrell, *Primo Levi*, 67–89.

———. "Primo Levi's Testimony, or Philosophy Between Poetry and Science." In *Engaging Europe: Rethinking a Changing Continent*, edited by Evelyn Gould and George J. Sheridan, 131–152. Lanham, Md.: Rowman & Littlefield, 2005.

Losey, Jay. "'The Pain of Remembering': Primo Levi's Poetry and the Function of Memory." In Pugliese, *The Legacy of Primo Levi*, 119–131.

Luzi, Alfredo. "L'altro mondo di Levi: Scienza e fantascienza ne *Le storie naturali*." In *Scrittori italiani di origine ebrea ieri e oggi: Un approccio generazionale* [*Atti di un convegno Utrecht-Amsterdam, 5–7 ottobre 2006*], edited by Raniero Speelman, Monica Jansen, and Silvia Gaiga, 67–76. Utrecht: Igitur, 2007.

Marfè, Luigi. "Vous n'êtes pas à la maison: Il tema del viaggio tra Primo Levi e Jorge Semprún." In Neiger, *Mémoire oblige*, 173–182.

Massariello Merzagora, Giovanna. "Repertorio linguistico, regionalità e traduzione." *Plurilinguismo: Contatti di Lingue e Culture* 10 [Supplement] (2003): 253–277. {Critique of *La chiave a stella.*}

Mattioda, Enrico. "Primo Levi fra scienza e letteratura." In Dei, *Voci dal mondo per Primo Levi*, 125–134.

———. "Teorie scientifiche e sapere poetico in Primo Levi." *Giornale Storico della Letteratura Italiana* 186, no. 613 (2009): 17–50.

Mazzotta, Giuseppe. "Letterature e verità, la lezione di Primo Levi." *Vita e Pensiero: Rivista culturale dell' Università Cattolica del Sacro Cuore* 91, no. 3 (May–June 2008): 116–122.

McClellan, William. "Primo Levi, Giorgio Agamben, and the New Ethics of Reading." In Pugliese, *The Legacy of Primo Levi*, 147–152.

Misurella, Fred. "A Clear Eye on Life: Renaissance Style in Primo Levi's Writing." In Pugliese, *The Legacy of Primo Levi*, 17–31.

Neiger, Ada. "Itinerario d'uno scrittore ebreo: Una lettera dei saggi di Primo Levi di argomento ebraico (1981–1987)." In Dei, *Voci dal mondo per Primo Levi*, 135–142.

Neppi, Enzo. "Bibbia e modernità nell'opera di Levinas e di Primo Levi." In *Emmanuel Levinas: Prophetic Inspiration and Philosophy*, atti del convegno internazionale per il centenario della nascita, Roma, 24–27 maggio 2006, ed. Irene Kajon, 197–210. Florence: Giuntina, 2008.

Nezri-Dufour, Sophie. "Primo Levi: L'università dell'ebreo diasporico." In Neiger, *Mémoire oblige*, 191–201.

Norridge, Zoë. "After Such Knowledge? Holocaust Legacies in Two Southern African Novels." In *The Camp: Narratives of Internment and Exclusion*, edited by Colman Hogan and Martin Marín Dòmine, 225–245. Newcastle upon Tyne: Cambridge Scholars, 2007.

Paolin, Demetrio. "La memoria e l'oltraggio: Primo Levi interprete di Dante." *Levia Gravia: Quaderno Annuale di Letteratura Italiana* 5 (2003): 225–249.

Parussa, Sergio. "A Hybridism of Sounds: Primo Levi Between Judaism and Literature." In Pugliese, *The Legacy of Primo Levi*, 87–94.

———. "The Modesty of Starbuck: On Hybrids, Judaism, and Ethics in Primo Levi." In *Writing as Freedom, Writing as Testimony: Four Italian Writers and Judaism*, 132–166. Syracuse, N.Y.: Syracuse University Press, 2008.

Parvikko, Tuija. "To This Side of Good and Evil: Primo Levi as a Truth-Teller." In *Terror and the Arts: Artistic, Literary, and Political Interpretations of Violence from Dostoyevsky to Abu Ghraib*, edited by Matti Hyvärinen and Lisa Muszynski, 97–112. New York: Palgrave Macmillan, 2008.

Patruno, Nicholas. "Primo Levi, Dante, and the 'Canto of Ulysses.'" In Pugliese, *The Legacy of Primo Levi*, 33–40.

Pell, Gregory M. "From Document to Fable: The Simulacrum of History in Mihaileanu, Benigni, and Primo Levi." *Forum Italicum* 38, no. 1 (Spring 2004): 91–114.

Pellizzi, Federico. "Asimmetria e preclusione." In Neiger, *Mémoire oblige*, 203–218.

Porro, Mario. "La cultura ibrida di Primo Levi." In *La letteratura come filosofia naturale*, 87–140. Milan: Medusa Edizioni, 2009.

———. "Un etologo del Lager." In ibid., 141–158.

Portelli, Sandro. "Who Ain't a Slave? On the University of Frederick Douglass." *GRAAT: Publication des Groupes de Recherches Anglo-Américaines de l'Université François Rabelais de Tours* 27 (2003): 59–73.

Puppa, Paolo. "The Hidden Theatre of Primo Levi." In Farrell, *Primo Levi*, 183–201.

Regazzoni, Luisa. *Selezione e catalogo: La costruzione narrativa del passato in Omero, Dante e Primo Levi*. Translated by Loretta Monti. Bologna: CLUEB, 2010. Originally published as *Selektion und Katalog: Zur narrativen Konstruktion der Vergangenheit bei Homer, Dante und Primo Levi*. Munich: Wilhelm Fink, 2008.

Rondini, Andrea. "Bello e falso: Il cinema secondo Primo Levi." *Studi Novecenteschi* 34, no. 73 (January–June 2007): 57–100.

———. "Da Umberto Saba a Primo Levi." *Rivista di Letteratura Italiana* 26, nos. 2–3 (2008): 45–53.

———. "Parini, Primo Levi e la comunicazione." *Studi sul Settecento e l'Ottocento* 1 (2006): 19–29.

———. "'Ve lo giuro': Primo Levi tra Konrad, Lorenz e Marco Polo." *Rivista di Letteratura Italiana* 25, no. 3 (2007): 131–140.

Ross, Charlotte. *Primo Levi's Narratives of Embodiment: Containing the Human*. London: Routledge, 2010.

———. "Primo Levi's Science-Fiction." In Gordon, *The Cambridge Companion to Primo Levi*, 105–118.

Rubinacci, Domenico. "L'attualità di Primo Levi per un rinnovato umanesimo nel mondo." *Affari Sociali Internazionali* 31, no. 2 (2003): 135–146.

Santagostino, Giuseppina. *Primo Levi: Metamorfosi letterarie del corpo*. Moncalieri, Turin: Centro Interuniversitario di Ricerche sul Viaggio in Italia, 2004.

Scarpa, Domenico. "Calvino, Levi e la scoperta letteraria dei buchi neri." *Sinestesie* 6 (2006): 297–308.

Scheiber, Elizabeth S. "The Failure of Memory and Literature in Primo Levi's *Il sistema periodico*." *MLN* 121, no. 1 (January 2006): 225–239.

Shankman, Steven. "The Promise of Language in the Depths of Hell: Primo Levi's 'Canto of Ulysses' and *Inferno* 26." In *Other Others: Levinas, Literature, Transcultural Studies*, 23–36. Albany: State University of New York Press, 2010.

Sher, Antony. *Primo Time*. London: Nick Hern, 2005.

Simborowski, Nicoletta. "'Il ritegno': Writing and Restraint in Primo Levi." In *Secrets and Puzzles: Silence and the Unsaid in Contemporary Italian Writing*, 22–49. Oxford: Legenda, European Humanities Research Centre, 2003.

Smith, Dominic. "Deleuze's Ethics of Reading: Deleuze, Badiou, and Primo Levi." *Angelaki: Journal of the Theoretical Humanities* 12, no. 3 (December 2007): 35–55.

Soltes, Ori Z. "Words, God, and Memory: Elie Wiesel, Nelly Sachs, and Primo Levi Engage the Ineffable." In *The Ashen Rainbow: Essays on the Arts and the Holocaust*, 13–32. Washington, D.C.: Eshel Books, 2007.

Sparti, Davide. "Let Us Be Human: Primo Levi and Ludwig Wittgenstein." *Philosophy and Literature* 29, no. 2 (October 2005): 444–459.

Speelman, Raniero M. "I libri gemelli di Primo Levi." In Neiger, *Mémoire oblige*, 219–227.

———. "I numeri di Primo Levi." In Dei, *Voci dal mondo per Primo Levi*, 165–176.

———. 'Primo Levi's Short Stories: A Modern Midrashim." In Pugliese, *The Legacy of Primo Levi*, 23–31.

Stoddard, Roger Eliot. "Primo Levi: Some Uncollected Authors LIX." *Book Collector* 55, no. 4 (Winter 2006): 525–554.

Suh, Kyungsik. "Leggere Primo Levi a Seoul e a Tokyo: 'Battaglia per la memoria' in Estremo Oriente." In Dei, *Voci dal mondo per Primo Levi*, 177–196.

Tenuta, Carlo. "Ambiguità: Tra argilla e spirito—per un'ipotesi di rapporte tra Primo Levi e sabbatianesimo." In Neiger, *Mémoire oblige*, 229–241.

Tesio, Giovanni. "At an Uncertain Hour: Preliminary Observations on the Poetry of Primo Levi." In Farrell, *Primo Levi*, 161–170. Published originally in Italian as "Excursus marginale sulla poesia *Ad ora incerta* di Primo Levi." In *Al di qua del bene e del male: La visione del mondo di Primo Levi—Atti del convegno internazionale, Torino, 15–16 dicembre 1999*, edited by Enrico Mattioda, 175–181. Milan: FrancoAngeli, 2000.

Traversi, Valeria M. M. "Per dire l'orrore. Primo Levi e Dante." *Dante: Rivista Internazionale di Studi su Dante Alighieri* [Pisa] 5 (2008): 109–125.

Ujcich, Veronica. "Primo Levi, 'A Strange Power of Speech.'" *L'intervista tra giornalismo e letteratura: Alberto Moravia, Pier Paolo Pasolini, Primo Levi*, 185–206. Rome: Aracne, 2008.

Usher, Jonathan. "'Libertinage': Programmatic and Promiscuous Quotation in Primo Levi." In Farrell, *Primo Levi*, 91–116.

———. "Primo Levi, the Canon and Italian Literature." In Gordon, *The Cambridge Companion to Primo Levi*, 171–188.

Vandewaetere, Sara. "L'esperienza sensoriale nella narrative di Primo Levi: Una rivisitazione." In *I cinque sensi (per tacer del sesto): Atti della Scuola europea di studi comparati, Bertinoro, 28 agosto–4 settembre 2005*, edited by Francesco Ghelli, 311–319. Florence: Le Monnier, 2007.

———. "La forza dell'immagine nella letteratura di testimonianza: 'Ekphrasis' dantesche in *Se questo è un uomo* di Primo Levi." *Studi Piemontesi* 34, no. 1 (June 2005): 89–96.

———. "La narrativa italiana degli anni Sessanta e Settanta: Primo Levi, un caso atipico?" In *La narrativa italiana degli anni Sessanta e Settanta*, edited by Gillian Ania and John Butcher, 139–150. Selected papers presented at a conference held at the University of Salford, England, March 2006. Naples: Dante & Descartes, 2007.

———. "Primo Levi e il mondo statunitense: A proposito di un film di Woody Allen." *Lettere Italiane* 56, no. 1 (January–March 2004): 122–129.

———. "Primo Levi e le future generazioni: L'etica del dialogo." In *Scrittori italiani di origine ebrea ieri e oggi: Un approccio generazionale [Atti di un convegno Utrecht-Amsterdam, 5–7 ottobre 2006]*, edited by Raniero Speelman, Monica Jansen, and Silvia Gaiga, 57–66. Utrecht: Igitur, 2007.

Veronese, Cosetta M. "Paying the Price of Perpetuating Memory: Francesco Rosi's Interpretation of Primo Levi's *The Truce*." *Studies in European Cinema* 5, no. 1 (2008): 55–66.

Vianello, Marco. "Madre è di parto e di voler matrigna: Primo Levi lettore di Leopardi." *Critica Letteraria* 32, no. 3 (2004): 419–433.

Woolf, Stuart. "Tradurre Primo Levi." *Belfagor: Rassegna di varia umanità* 64, no. 6 (November 2009): 699–705.

Zaccaro, Giovanna. "La 'tregua' di Primo Levi." *La Nuova Ricerca* 12 (2003): 335–352.

Zaccaro, Vanna. "I racconti fantastici di Primo Levi." *Rivista di Letteratura Italiana* 24, no. 3 (2006): 131–141.

Zinato, Andrea. "27 gennaio giorno della memoria: La voce dei sefarditi di Salonicco—Mordo Nahum, il Greco." *Rassegna Iberistica* 78 (September 2003): 97–100.

Zublena, Paolo. "Un sistema quasi periodico: Il linguaggio chimico del *Sistema periodico* di Primo Levi." In *L'inquietante simmetria della lingua*, 65–92. Alexandria: Edizioni dell'Orso, 2003.

Primo Levi's Gray Zone:
A Sequence of Drawings

Terri Bowman

"Such Will Be Our Life"

"It Was Better Not to Think"

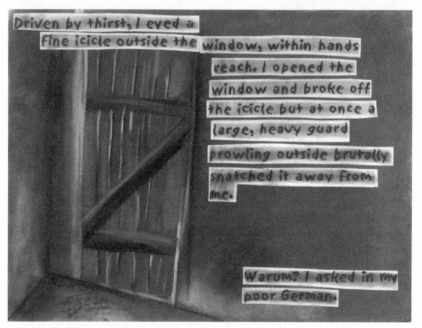

"Warum/Why?"

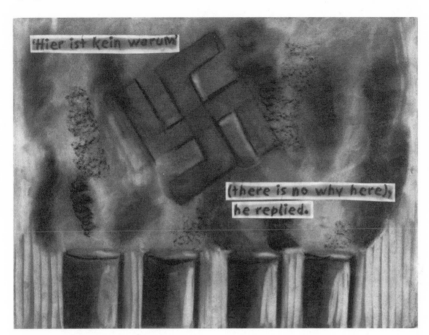

"There Is No Why Here"

"174517"

"THIS IS HELL"

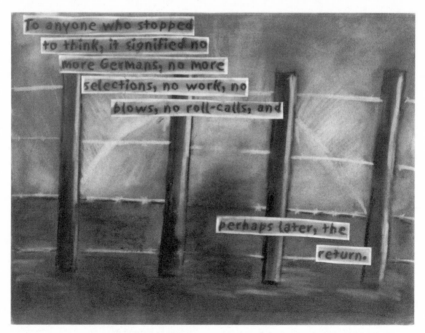

"PERHAPS LATER, THE RETURN"

"WSTAVAC"

"Shemà"

PROLOGUE. ANSWERING AUSCHWITZ:
LEVI'S SCIENCE AND HUMANISM AS ANTIFASCISM
Stanislao G. Pugliese

1. Theodor Adorno, from his 1949 essay "Cultural Criticism and Society," reprinted in *Prisms*, trans. Samuel and Shierry Weber (Cambridge, Mass.: MIT Press, 1981 [1967]), 17–34.

2. Theodore Adorno, *Negative Dialectics*, trans. E. B. Ashton (New York: Seabury Press, 1973), 361.

3. Primo Levi, *Survival in Auschwitz*, trans. Stuart Woolf (New York: Collier, 1961), 59.

4. Ibid., 22.

5. The reader should know of a recent work by one of this volume's contributors, Jonathan Druker, *Primo Levi and the Fate of Humanism After Auschwitz* (New York: Palgrave Macmillan, 2009), that offers a radically different interpretation than the one presented here.

6. From "Vanadium," in *The Periodic Table*, 223.

7. "Trauma/Transgression/Testimony," in *The Legacy of Primo Levi*, ed. Stanislao G. Pugliese (New York: Palgrave Macmillan, 2005), 3–15, and in a paper "Primo Levi's Politics" at a conference at Yale University in April 2008, published in *New Reflections on Primo Levi: Before and After Auschwitz*, ed. Millicent Marcus and Risa Sodi (New York: Palgrave Macmillan, 2010).

8. "Why Auschwitz?" in *Shema: Collected Poems of Primo Levi*, trans. Ruth Feldman and Brian Swann (London: Menard Press, 1976), 45–46.

9. Ibid., 51.

10. Primo Levi in *Corriere della Sera*, May 8, 1974; reprinted in *L'asimmetria e la vita*, ed. Marco Belpoliti (Turin: Einaudi, 2002); translated as "The Past We Thought Would Never Return," in *The Black Hole of Auschwitz*, trans. Sharon Wood (New York: Polity Press, 2005), 34.

11. "Itinerary of a Jewish Writer," in *The Black Hole of Auschwitz*, 164.

12. Elie Wiesel, *Legends of Our Time*, trans. Stephen Donadio (New York: Avon, 1970), 230.

13. Eva Hoffman, *After Such Knowledge: Memory, History and the Legacy of the Holocaust* (New York: Public Affairs, 2004).

14. Emil L. Fackenheim, *To Mend the World: Foundations of Post-Holocaust Jewish Thought* (Bloomington: Indiana University Press, 1994), 303.

15. Dustin Kidd, "The Aesthetics of Truth, The Aesthetics of Time: George Steiner and the Retreat from the World," December 1998, http://xroads.virginia.edu/~ma99/kidd/resume/steiner.html.

16. Harold Kaplan, *Conscience & Memory: Meditation in a Museum of the Holocaust* (Chicago: University of Chicago Press, 1994), 150.

17. For the only biography of Rosselli in English, see Stanislao G. Pugliese, *Carlo Rosselli: Socialist Heretic and Antifascist Exile* (Cambridge, Mass.: Harvard University Press, 1999).

18. The best study of Nello's religious beliefs is Bruno Di Porto's essay "Il problema ebraico in Nello Rosselli," in *Giustizia e Libertà nella lotta antifascista*, ed. Carlo Francovich (Florence: La Nuova Italia, 1978), 491–499. Nello's speech is quoted in Renzo De Felice, *Storia degli ebrei italiani sotto il fascismo*, 89–90; English translation in Susan Zuccotti, *The Italians and the Holocaust* (New York: Basic Books, 1987), 246.

19. See especially Robert S. C. Gordon, *Primo Levi's Ordinary Virtues: From Testimony to Ethics* (Oxford: Oxford University Press, 2001).

20. Stanislao G. Pugliese, "The Antidote to Fascism," in Carla Pekelis, *My Version of the Facts* (Evanston, Ill.: Marlboro Press/Northwestern University Press, 2004), vii.

21. Isaiah Berlin, "Notes on Prejudice," in *New York Review of Books*, October 18, 2001, 12.

22. Carlo Levi, *Paura della libertà* (Turin: Einaudi, 1946); reprinted in *Scritti politici*, edited by David Bidussa (Turin: Einaudi, 2001), 132–204; for a recent English translation, see *Fear of Freedom*, trans. Adophe Gourevitch, ed. Stanislao G. Pugliese (New York: Columbia University Press, 2008).

23. Carlo Levi, *Christ Stopped at Eboli*, trans. Frances Frenaye (New York: Farrar, Straus and Giroux, 2006), 252.

24. See, for example, the interview with Frank Bruni that appeared on the front page of the *New York Times*, May 10, 2003.

25. "Lascerei volontieri ad altri l'amaro calice." See Federico Garimberti, "È Fini il mio successore," in *America Oggi*, January 27, 2007, 5.

26. See the interview with Boris Johnson and Nicholas Farrell, *The Spectator*, September 11, 2003.

27. Bruce Cutler, "Final Examination," in *Seeing the Darkness* (Kansas City, Mo.: BkMk Press, 1998), 13–14.

28. Umberto Eco, "Ur-Fascism," *New York Review of Books*, 22 June 1995, 12–15.

29. Ibid.

30. Miklos Nyiszli, *Auschwitz: A Doctor's Eyewitness Account* (New York: Arcade, 1993), 57–58.

31. Primo Levi, *The Drowned and the Saved*, trans. Raymond Rosenthal (New York: Summit, 1988), 55.

32. Levi, *Survival*, 36.

33. Pelagia Lewinska, *Twenty Months at Auschwitz* (New York: Lyle Stuart, 1989), 141, 150; quoted in Rubenstein, *After Auschwitz*, 186–187.

34. Levi, *Survival*, 79.

35. Tzvetan Todorov, *Imperfect Garden: The Legacy of Humanism* (Princeton: Princeton University Press, 2002).

36. "Argon," in *The Periodic Table*, 9.

37. "A Conversation with Philip Roth," in *Survival in Auschwitz* (New York: Touchstone, 1996), 185.

38. Ibid., 94, 111.

39. "Itinerary of a Jewish Writer," in *The Black Hole of Auschwitz*, 164.

40. "Afterword," trans. Ruth Feldman, in *The Reawakening*, trans. Stuart Woolf (New York: Collier, 1986), 217.

41. Ferdinando Camon, *Conversations with Primo Levi*, trans. John Shepley (Marlboro, Vt.: Marlboro Press, 1989), 68.

1. *"WARUM?"*
Joram Warmund

1. Alexander Donat, *The Holocaust Kingdom* (Washington, D.C.: U.S. Holocaust Memorial Museum, 1999).

2. Abraham J. Edelheit and Herschel Edelheit, *History of the Holocaust: A Handbook and Dictionary* (Boulder: Westview Press, 1994), 188.

3. Primo Levi, *Survival in Auschwitz*, trans. Stuart Woolf (New York: Collier Books, 1993), 29.

4. Raul Hilberg, *Perpetrators, Victims, Bystanders: The Jewish Catastrophe, 1993–1945* (New York: HarperCollins, 1992).

5. Levi, *Survival in Auschwitz*. See also, Primo Levi, *The Drowned and the Saved*, trans. Raymond Rosenthal (New York: Vintage International, 1989).

6. Robert Jay Lifton, *The Nazi Doctors: Medical Killing and the Psychology of Genocide* (New York: Basic Books, 1986), 418–429.

7. Hilberg, *Perpetrators, Victims, Bystanders*, ix.

8. Ibid.

9. Ibid., x.

10. Ibid., 3–102.

11. See Christopher R. Browning, *Nazi Policy, Jewish Workers, German Killers* (New York: Cambridge University Press, 2000), for his treatment of

the "spectrum of response" of members of the Order Police who participated in the incremental steps of the Holocaust, from deportations to ghetto clearings to hands-on killings; see as well his *Ordinary Men, Reserve Police Battalion 101 and the Final Solution in Poland* (New York: Harper Perennial, 1998).

12. Browning, *Nazi Policy*, 156.

13. Ibid., 175.

14. Ibid.

15. Ibid., 144.

16. See Eric A. Zillmer, Molly Harrower, Barry A. Ritzler, and Robert P. Archer, *The Quest for the Nazi Personality: A Psychological Investigation of Nazi War Criminals* (Mahwah, N.J.: Lawrence Erlbaum Associates, 1995).

17. Ibid. See Jochen von Lang with Claus Sibyll, *Eichmann Interrogated: Transcripts from the Archives of the Israeli Police* (New York: Da Capo Press, 1999), 107, 150–151; Gitta Sereny, *Into That Darkness: An Examination of Conscience* (New York: Vintage Books, 1983); Rudolf Höss, *Death Dealer: The Memoirs of the SS Kommandant at Auschwitz* (Buffalo, N.Y.: Prometheus Books, 1992); and the opening narration on Greise in film documentary *The Nazis: A Warning From History* (New York: Video Group, BBC Documentary).

18. Browning, *Ordinary Men*, 184.

19. Ibid.

20. Daniel J. Goldhagen, *Hitler's Willing Executioners: Ordinary Germans and the Holocaust* (New York: Knopf, 1996), 417–455.

21. Yehuda Bauer, *Rethinking the Holocaust* (New Haven: Yale University Press, 2001).

22. Ibid., 86.

23. Ibid., 92.

24. Ibid., 99.

25. Ibid., 106–107.

26. Ibid.,108.

27. Browning, *Nazi Policy*, 175.

28. Browning, *Ordinary Men*, 165–176, for the degrees of relevance of the Adorno, Asch, Zimbardo, and Milgram experiments for explaining perpetrator behavior; see also Zillmer et al., *Quest*, 5–6.

29. Richard Rhodes, *Masters of Death: The SS-Einsatzgruppen and the Invention of the Holocaust* (New York: Vintage Books, 2003), 22.

30. Ibid., xii, 26–27, for the references to Omer Bartov; see also, Goldhagen, *Hitler's Willing Executioners*, 206–207, where he profiles the members of Police Battalion 101 as virtually interchangeable with any random sample of ordinary Germans; see also Omer Bartov, *Germany's War and the Holocaust: Disputed Histories* (Ithaca, N.Y.: Cornell University Press, 2003), where the

Wehrmacht shot thousands of commissars, conducted a "uniquely savage war," and was thoroughly implicated in the Holocaust, 8, 13, 14–15.

31. Hilberg, *Perpetrators*, 93–102; see also Rhodes, *Masters of Death*, 119, where the Baltic volunteers were used by the Einsatzgruppen to do the "dirty work" of face-to-face killings.

32. See Rhodes, *Masters of Death*, 39–43, for early examples of brutal public murders by Lithuanian civilians.

33. See Jan T. Gross, *Neighbors: The Destruction of the Jewish Community in Jedwabne, Poland* (New York: Penguin Books, 2002); see also Martin Dean, *Collaboration in the Holocaust: Crimes of the Local Police in Belorussia and Ukraine, 1941–44* (New York: St. Martin's Press, 2000), which concludes: "In Belorussia and Ukraine it was not only Germans who became "willing executioners" (167).

34. See James M. Glass, *"Life Unworthy of Life"* (New York: Basic Books, 1997).

35. See Edward B. Westermann, *Hitler's Police Battalions: Enforcing Racial War in the East* (Lawrence: University Press of Kansas, 2005).

36. Heribert Schwann and Helgard Heindrichs, *Der SS-Mann: Josef Blösche—Leben und Sterben eines Mörders* (Munich: Droemersche Verlagsanstalt, 2003), especially 66–72, 349–359.

37. Zilmer et al., *Quest*, 104–107.

38. Ibid., 116. Ritzler discovered that the Danish rank-and-file, especially the ones most involved with genocidal activities, exhibited a high incidence of low esteem; that contrary to the stereotypically aggressive Nazi image so often presented, these subjects possessed negative self-images, which is consistent with those who would perceive themselves as victims of circumstances. They would also be strongly attached to the Nazi ideology and organizational structure. Ibid, 111.

39. See Westermann, *Hitler's Police Battalions*, 231–239, where he reviews the various interpretive schools and concludes with the existence of an "organizational culture" and ideology that facilitated the annihilation process; see also Christopher R. Browning with contributions by Jürgen Matthäus, *The Origins of the Final Solution, The Evolution of Nazi Jewish Policy, September 1939–March 1942* (Lincoln: University of Nebraska Press, 2004), which recapitulates his earlier modified situational interpretation and includes instances where the killers express self-delusional rationalizations to explain their killing of babies as a protective measure for their own children, even though the brutal manner of executions clearly belies their testimony (294–300).

40. Wendy Lower, *Nazi Empire Building and the Holocaust in Ukraine* (Chapel Hill: University of North Carolina Press, 2005), where she also argues that the anti-Jewish violence was applied incrementally from one stage to another, pushing the limits of what one "could get away with" (71).

41. Martin Gilbert, *The Righteous: The Unsung Heroes of the Holocaust* (New York: Henry Holt, 2003); see also Samuel P. Oliner and Pearl M. Oliner, *The Altruistic Personality* (New York: Free Press, 1992).

2. GUILT OR SHAME?
Amy Simon

1. Ruth Leys, *From Guilt to Shame: Auschwitz and After* (Princeton: Princeton University Press, 2009), 11.

2. Ibid., 10.

3. Primo Levi, *The Drowned and the Saved*, trans. Raymond Rosenthal (New York: Vintage Books, 1988), 73.

4. As cited in Leys, *From Guilt to Shame*, 132.

5. Levi, *The Drowned and the Saved*, 77–78.

6. Ibid., 81.

7. Ibid., 75.

8. Ibid., 78.

9. Ibid., 85.

10. Ibid., 86.

11. Anthony Rudolf, *At an Uncertain Hour: Primo Levi's War Against Oblivion* (London: Menard Press, 1990), 9.

12. As cited in Leys, *From Guilt to Shame*, 171.

13. Levi, *The Drowned and the Saved*, 75

14. Primo Levi, *If This Is a Man*, trans. Stuart Woolf (London: Abacus, 1987), 28–43.

15. Ibid., 26, 60.

16. Ibid., 148.

17. Primo Levi, *The Truce*, trans. Stuart Woolf (London: Abacus, 1987), 237.

18. Levi, *The Drowned and the Saved*, 77.

19. Levi, *If This Is a Man*, 156.

20. Levi, *The Drowned and the Saved*, 77.

21. Ibid., 78.

22. Levi, *If This Is a Man*, 94.

23. Gian Paolo Biasin, "Our Daily Bread," in *Primo Levi as Witness*, ed. Pietro Frassica (Fiesole: Casalini, 1990), 18.

24. Levi, *The Drowned and the Saved*, 80.

25. Ibid., 79.

26. Ibid., 85.

27. Levi, *The Truce*, 188.

28. Shoshana Felman and Dori Laub, eds., *Testimony: Crises of Witnessing in Literature, Psychoanalysis, and History* (New York: Routledge, 1992), 80.

29. Nicholas Patruno, *Understanding Primo Levi* (Columbia: University of South Carolina Press, 1995), 120.

3. PRIMO LEVI AND THE CONCEPT OF HISTORY
Johan Åhr

For advice on this essay, I thank Alec Marsh, Stanislao Pugliese, and Mary Anne Trasciatti. A version of it appeared as "On Primo Levi, Richard Serra, and the Concept of History" in *Journal of the Historical Society* 9 (2009): 161–189, copyright The Historical Society and Wiley Periodicals, Inc.

1. Arthur Koestler et al., *The God That Failed: Six Studies in Communism* [1949], ed. Richard H. Crossman (New York: Columbia University Press, 2001). In this essay, "historicism" refers to mechanistic or messianistic determinism, the idea of a unified human history—as criticized in Karl R. Popper, "The Poverty of Historicism, I," *Economica* 11 (1944): 86–103; "The Poverty of Historicism, II," *Economica* 11 (1944): and "The Poverty of Historicism, III," *Economica* 12 (1945): 69–89. See also Georg G. Iggers, "Historicism," in *Dictionary of the History of Ideas: Studies of Selected Pivotal Ideas*, ed. Philip P. Wiener (New York: Charles Scribner's Sons, 1973–74), 456–464.

2. François Furet, *The Passing of an Illusion: The Idea of Communism in the Twentieth Century* [1995], trans. Deborah Furet (Chicago: University of Chicago Press, 1999); Neil Jumonville, *Critical Crossings: The New York Intellectuals in Postwar America* (Berkeley: University of California Press, 1991); Jerry Z. Muller, *The Other God That Failed: Hans Freyer and the Deradicalization of German Conservatism* (Princeton: Princeton University Press, 1987). Offers of power and money, however, did make for bargains with capitalism, as with the American Congress for Cultural Freedom. See Volker R. Berghahn, *America and the Intellectual Cold Wars in Europe: Shepard Stone between Philanthropy, Academy, and Diplomacy* (Princeton: Princeton University Press, 2001).

3. Elisabeth Young-Bruehl, *Hannah Arendt: For Love of the World* (New Haven: Yale University Press, 1982), 113–188.

4. Hannah Arendt, "History and Immortality," *Partisan Review* 24 (Winter 1957): 11.

5. Hannah Arendt, "The Concept of History: Ancient and Modern," in *Between Past and Future: Six Exercises in Political Thought* (New York: Viking Press, 1961), 41–90.

6. "The future is not the ineluctable result of a given historical evolution." Michael Löwy, *Fire Alarm: Reading Walter Benjamin's "On the Concept of History"* [2001], trans. Chris Turner (New York: Verso, 2005), 109; Dimitris Vardoulakis, "The Subject of History: The Temporality of Parataxis in Walter Benjamin's Historiography," in *Walter Benjamin and History*, ed. Andrew Benjamin (New York: Continuum International, 2005), 118–136.

7. David Frisby, *Fragments of Modernity: Theories of Modernity in the Work of Georg Simmel, Siegfried Kracauer, and Walter Benjamin* (Cambridge, Mass.: MIT Press, 1986), 187–265; Irving Wohlfarth, "Et cetera? De l'historien comme chiffonnier," in *Walter Benjamin et Paris (Ecoles des hautes études en sciences sociales, colloque international, 27–29 juin 1983)*, ed. Heinz Wismann (Paris: Editions du Cerf, 1986), 559–609; Margaret Cohen, "Walter Benjamin's Phantasmagoria: The Arcades Project," in *The Cambridge Companion to Walter Benjamin*, ed. David S. Ferris (Cambridge: Cambridge University Press, 2004), 199–220; Graeme Gilloch, *Myth and Metropolis: Walter Benjamin and the City* (Cambridge: Polity Press, 1996); Susan Buck-Morss, *The Dialectics of Seeing: Walter Benjamin and the Arcades Project* (Cambridge, Mass.: MIT Press, 1989).

8. Gershom Scholem, "Walter Benjamin," *Leo Baeck Memorial Lecture* 8 (New York: Leo Baeck Institute, 1965), 8; Hannah Arendt, "Walter Benjamin," trans. Harry Zohn, New Yorker, October 19, 1968, 80; Walter Benjamin, *The Arcades Project* [1982], ed. Rolf Tiedemann, trans. Howard Eiland and Kevin McLaughlin (Cambridge, Mass.: Harvard University Press, 1999), 461.

9. Bram Mertens, *Dark Images, Secret Hints: Walter Benjamin, Gershom Scholem, Franz Joseph Molitor and the Jewish Tradition* (New York: Peter Lang, 2007), 23–65.

10. Primo Levi, *The Periodic Table*, trans. Raymond Rosenthal (New York: Schocken Books, 1984).

11. Robert D'Amico, *Historicism and Knowledge* (New York: Routledge, 1989), xi.

12. See *History and Theory* 40 (2001), theme issue on "Agency After Postmodernism," ed. David Gary Shaw.

13. Primo Levi, *The Drowned and the Saved*, trans. Raymond Rosenthal (New York: Simon and Schuster, 1988). Parenthetical page and chapter citations herein are to this edition.

14. Stuart Woolf, "Primo Levi's Sense of History," *Journal of Modern Italian Studies* 3 (1998): 273–292.

15. Jonathan Wilson, "Primo Levi's Hybrid Texts," *Judaism* 48 (1999): 67–72; Adam Epstein, "Primo Levi and the Language of Atrocity," *Bulletin of the Society for Italian Studies* 20 (1987): 31–38.

16. Woolf, "Levi's Sense of History," 275.

17. Anthony Rudolf, *At an Uncertain Hour: Primo Levi's War Against Oblivion* (Berkeley: Menard Press, 1990), 5.

18. Nicholas Patruno, *Understanding Primo Levi* (Columbia: University of South Carolina Press, 1995), 5.

19. See, for example, Stanislao G. Pugliese, ed., *The Legacy of Primo Levi* (New York: Palgrave Macmillan, 2005).

20. Lawrence L. Langer, *Holocaust Testimonies: The Ruins of Memory* (New Haven: Yale University Press, 1991).

21. See Fernand Braudel, "Histoire et sciences sociales: La longue durée," *Annales ESC* 13 (1958): 725–753 ("History and the Social Sciences: The *Longue Durée*," in *On History* [1969], trans. Sarah Matthews [Chicago: University of Chicago Press, 1980], 25–54); Georg G. Iggers, *Historiography in the Twentieth Century: From Scientific Objectivity to the Postmodern Challenge* [1993] (Middletown, Conn.: Wesleyan University Press, 2005), 51–64; Bertolt Brecht, "Questions from a Worker Who Reads" [1935], in *Bertolt Brecht: Poems, 1913–1956*, trans. Michael Hamburger et al. (New York: Methuen, 1987), 252–253.

22. Carlo Ginzburg, "Microhistory: Two or Three Things That I Know About It," trans. John and Anne C. Tedeschi, *Critical Inquiry* 20 (1993): 10–35; Giovanni Levi, "On Microhistory," in *New Perspectives on Historical Writing*, ed. Peter Burke (Cambridge: Polity Press, 1991), 93–113; see also Iggers, *Historiography in the Twentieth Century*, 101–117; David A. Bell, "Total History and Microhistory: The French and Italian Paradigms," in *A Companion to Western Historical Thought*, ed. Lloyd Kramer and Sarah Maza (Oxford: Blackwell, 2002), 262–276.

23. Primo Levi, "The Invisible World," in *Other People's Trades* [*L'altrui mestiere*, 1985], trans Raymond Rosenthal (New York: Simon & Schuster, 1989), 58–62; John Henry, *Knowledge Is Power: Francis Bacon and the Method of Science* (Cambridge: Icon Books, 2002).

24. Ian Thomson, *Primo Levi: A Life* (New York: Henry Holt, 2002), 497–505.

25. Primo Levi, *Survival in Auschwitz: The Nazi Assault on Humanity*, trans. Stuart Woolf (New York: Simon & Schuster, 1961), 9.

26. "We felt in our veins the poison of Auschwitz . . . where should we find the strength to begin our lives again, to break down the barriers, the brushwood which grows up spontaneously in all absences?" Primo Levi, *The Reawakening*, trans. Stuart Woolf (New York: Simon & Schuster, 1965), 206. Art Spiegelman, a son of survivors, one of them a suicide, starkly illustrates in his cartoons this ordeal of misery's endurance: *Maus: A Survivor's Tale/My Father Bleeds History* (New York: Pantheon Books, 1986); *Maus II: A Survivor's Tale/And Here My Troubles Began* (New York: Pantheon Books, 1991).

27. Marco Belpoliti and Robert S. C. Gordon, eds., *The Voice of Memory: Primo Levi, Interviews, 1961–87* (New York: New Press, 2001).

28. Thomson, *Primo Levi*, 121–137.

29. Primo Levi (with Leonardo de Benedetti), *Auschwitz Report* [*Rapporto sulla organizzazione igienico-sanitaria del campo di concentramento per ebrei di Monowitz (Auschwitz)*, 1946], ed. Robert S. C. Gordon, trans. Judith Woolf (New York: Verso, 2006), 35–36.

30. Jean Améry, *At the Mind's Limits: Contemplations by a Survivor on Auschwitz and Its Realities*, trans. Sidney Rosenfeld and Stella P. Rosenfeld (Bloomington: Indiana University Press, 1980), 2–4.

31. Ibid., 19.

32. Ibid., 6.

33. Levi, *Survival in Auschwitz*, 88–90.

34. Primo Levi, "Preface to *People in Auschwitz*" [1984], in *The Black Hole of Auschwitz* [*L'asimmetria e la vita*, 2002], ed. Marco Belpoliti, trans. Sharon Wood (Cambridge: Polity Press, 2005), 78–81.

35. Giorgio Agamben, *Remnants of Auschwitz: The Witness and the Archive* [1998], trans. Daniel Heller-Roazen (New York: Zone Books, 1999), 41–86.

36. Hermann Langbein, *People in Auschwitz* [1972], trans. Harry Zohn (Chapel Hill: University of North Carolina Press, 2004), 89–105; Eugen Kogon, *The Theory and Practice of Hell: The German Concentration Camps and the System Behind Them* [1950], trans. Heinz Norden (New York: Farrar, Straus and Giroux, 2006), 116; Hans Marsálek, *Die Geschichte des Konzentrationslagers Mauthausen: Dokumentation* (Vienna: Österreichischen Lagergemeinschaft, 1974).

37. Ferdinando Camon, *Conversations with Primo Levi* [1987], trans. John Shepley (Marlboro, Vt.: Marlboro Press, 1989), 13.

38. Levi, *Periodic Table*, 50–60.

39. Primo Levi, *The Monkey's Wrench*, trans. William Weaver (New York: Penguin Books, 1986), 78.

40. Primo Levi, *A Tranquil Star: Unpublished Stories* [1949–1986], trans. Ann Goldstein and Alessandra Bastagli (New York: Norton, 2007), 153.

41. Primo Levi, "The Spider's Secret," in *The Mirror Maker: Stories and Essays* [*Racconti e saggi*, 1986], trans. Raymond Rosenthal (New York: Schocken Books, 1989), 158.

42. Patricia Sayre and Linnea Vacca, "On Language and Personhood: A Linguistic Odyssey," in *Memory and Mastery: Primo Levi as Writer and Witness*, ed. Roberta S. Kremer (Albany: State University of New York Press, 2001), 128.

43. Primo Levi, *Moments of Reprieve*, trans. Ruth Feldman (New York: Penguin Books, 1986).

44. Nancy Harrowitz, "Primo Levi's Jewish Identity," in *The Cambridge Companion to Primo Levi*, ed. Robert S. C. Gordon (Cambridge: Cambridge University Press, 2007), 17–31. See James T. Chiampi, "Testifying to His Text: Primo Levi and the Concentrationary Sublime," *Romanic Review* 92 (2001): 491–511; and Bryan Cheyette, "The Ethical Uncertainty of Primo Levi," in *Modernity, Culture, and "the Jew,"* ed. Laura Marcus (Cambridge: Polity Press, 1998), 268–281.

45. Thomson, *Primo Levi*, 42–43.

46. Carole Angier, *The Double Bond: Primo Levi, a Biography* (New York: Farrar, Straus and Giroux, 2002), 14.

47. Myriam Anissimov, *Primo Levi: Tragedy of an Optimist* [1996], trans. Steve Cox (Woodstock, N.Y.: Overlook Press, 1998), 2–4.

48. Robert S. C. Gordon, *Primo Levi's Ordinary Virtues: From Testimony to Ethics* (New York: Oxford University Press, 2001), 113–132, 149–172.

49. Levi, *The Search for Roots*, 4, 31.

50. Thomson, *Primo Levi*, 473–496.

51. Cynthia Ozick, "The Suicide Note," *New Republic*, March 21, 1988, 32–36.

52. "Almanac," in Primo Levi, *Collected Poems* [1984; 1991], trans. Ruth Feldman and Brian Swann (London: Faber and Faber, 1992), 98.

53. Primo Levi, "Asymmetry and Life" [1984], in *Black Hole of Auschwitz*, 143.

54. Gabriel Piterberg, "Zion's Rebel Daughter: Hannah Arendt on Palestine and Jewish Politics," *New Left Review* 48 (2007): 48–53. The quotation continues, "I indeed love only my friends . . . persons." Hannah Arendt, "A Letter to Gershom Scholem, New York City, July 24, 1963," in *The Jewish Writings*, ed. Jerome Kohn and Ron H. Feldman (New York: Schocken Books, 2007), 466–467.

55. Woolf, "Levi's Sense of History," 274.

56. William Taussig Scott and Martin X. Moleski, *Michael Polanyi: Scientist and Philosopher* (New York: Oxford University Press, 2005).

57. Michael Polanyi, *Science, Faith, and Society* (Chicago: University of Chicago Press, 1946), 21–41. The quotation is from Michael Polanyi, *Personal Knowledge: Towards a Post-Critical Philosophy* (Chicago: University of Chicago Press, 1958), 64.

58. Mark T. Mitchell, *Michael Polanyi: The Art of Knowing* (Wilmington, Del.: Intercollegiate Studies Institute [ISI], 2006), 59–103; Drusilla Scott, *Everyman Revived: The Common Sense of Michael Polanyi* (Lewes, UK: Book Guild, 1985), 45–61.

59. Michael Polanyi, *The Tacit Dimension* (London: Routledge and Kegan Paul, 1967), 17.

60. Karl R. Popper, *The Poverty of Historicism* (London: Routledge and Kegan Paul, 1957), vii.

61. Malachi Haim Hacohen, *Karl Popper, The Formative Years, 1902–1945: Politics and Philosophy in Interwar Vienna* (Cambridge: Cambridge University Press, 2000); Karl R. Popper, *Unended Quest: An Intellectual Autobiography*, new ed. (London: Routledge, 1992); Roberta Corvi, *An Introduction to the Thought of Karl Popper* [1993], trans. Patrick Camiller (London: Routledge, 1997),

51–78; T. E. Burke, *The Philosophy of Karl Popper* (Manchester: Manchester University Press, 1983), 132–173.

62. Popper, *Poverty of Historicism*, v.

63. Michael Polanyi, *The Logic of Liberty: Reflections and Rejoinders* (London: Routledge and Kegan Paul, 1951); Karl R. Popper, *The Open Society and Its Enemies* (London: George Routledge and Sons, 1945).

4. *KENOSIS*, SATURATED PHENOMENOLOGY, AND BEARING WITNESS
Marie L. Baird

1. Primo Levi, *The Reawakening*, trans. Stuart Woolf (New York: Simon & Schuster, 1965), 207. All further references to this text will be made parenthetically.

2. See Marion, *Being Given: Toward a Phenomenology of Givenness*, trans. Jeffrey L. Kosky (Stanford: Stanford University Press, 2002), 227, for his analyses of saturated phenomena's unforeseeability, unbearability, absoluteness, and anamorphic quality.

3. Jean-Luc Marion, *In Excess: Studies in Saturated Phenomena*, trans. Robyn Horner and Vincent Berraud (New York: Fordham University Press, 2002), 112.

4. See Marion, *Being Given*, 248–249, 262–269; *In Excess*, 34–38.

5. Marion characterizes certain phenomena as "saturated" "in that [conceptual] constitution encounters there an intuitive givenness that cannot be granted a univocal sense in return. It must be allowed, then, to overflow with many meanings, or an infinity of meanings, each equally legitimate and rigorous, without managing either to unify them or to organize them." Marion, *In Excess*, 112. See also Marion, *Being Given*, 227.

6. This assertion is in no way intended to relativize Levi's extraordinary genius as the "writer-witness" of Auschwitz.

7. Marion notes that "the saturated phenomenon in the end establishes the truth of all phenomenality because it marks, more than any other phenomenon, the givenness from which it comes." *Being Given*, 227.

8. Marion's analyses demonstrate this conclusively; see *In Excess*, chapters 2–5. In addition, to provide another example, saturated phenomenality can be used to analyze experiences of ecstatic mystical encounter.

9. William James, *The Principles of Psychology* (Cambridge, Mass.: Harvard University Press, 1981), 1:462.

10. Marion, *In Excess*, 30.

11. Marion notes that givenness "is equivalent in fact to the phenomenon itself, the two sides of which, the appearing (from the side of consciousness) and that which appears (from the side of the thing), are articulated according to the principle of an "admirable correlation" only because the first is taken

as a given, given by and according to the second, givenness itself." *In Excess*, 21.

12. This fact of the saturated phenomenon giving *itself* and showing *itself* is highly significant, a point to which I will return. See note 5.

13. Marion, *Being Given*, 228.

14. Ibid., 200.

15. Ibid., 229.

16. Marion, *In Excess*, 36.

17. I would imagine the same is true concerning the events of September 11, 2001.

18. Marion, *Being Given*, 200.

19. Ibid., 201.

20. Primo Levi, *Survival in Auschwitz*, trans. Stuart Woolf (New York: Macmillan, 1960), 20–21. Emphasis added.

21. Marion, *Being Given*, 227.

22. Ibid., 203.

23. This statement by General Dwight D. Eisenhower of April 15, 1945, is inscribed on a wall at the United States Holocaust Memorial Museum, Washington, D.C.

24. Marion, *Being Given*, 203–206.

25. Ibid., 202–203.

26. Ibid., 202.

27. There may be some degree of convergence between Marion's categories of unforeseeability and unbearability. He justifies the distinction between the two as being based on Kant's distinction between the categories of quantity and quality. Ibid., 199.

28. Ibid., 227.

29. Ibid., 207–209. This particular claim of "uniqueness" is limited to a phenomenological analysis of a "pure event" of which I consider Auschwitz to be an example. To the best of my knowledge, this claim of Auschwitz as a "pure event" has not figured in the analysis (and debate) surrounding the claims made about the Holocaust's "uniqueness."

30. Terrence Des Pres, *The Survivor: An Anatomy of Life in the Death Camps* (Oxford: Oxford University Press, 1976), 153.

31. Levi, *Survival in Auschwitz*, 88.

32. Ibid., 90.

33. These are two instances of testimony given, respectively, by survivors Karol Talik and Bronislaw Goscinki, and cited by Giorgio Agamben in *Remnants of Auschwitz: The Witness and the Archive*, trans. Daniel Heller-Roazen (New York: Zone Books, 1999), 167, 171. Goscinki's testimony cites the lyrics of a song sung in the camp where he was incarcerated.

34. Primo Levi, *The Drowned and The Saved*, trans. Raymond Rosenthal (New York: Random House, 1989), 83–84.

35. Agamben, *Remnants of Auschwitz*, 51.

36. Marion, *Being Given*, 209. There are three ways in which saturated phenomena exceed their horizon: the intuition of such a phenomenon fills the horizon entirely, leading to "bedazzlement;" such intuition "pass[es] beyond all horizonal delimitation," opening up an "infinite hermeneutic;" or saturation "redoubles the first two cases by lumping them together," 209–211.

37. Ibid., 211.

38. Ibid., 218.

39. Ibid., 214, 227.

40. Ibid., 227; emphasis added.

41. For a critique of Marion's analysis of saturated phenomenality, see Dominique Janicaud, "The Theological Turn of French Phenomenology," trans. Bernard G. Prusak, in *Phenomenology and the "Theological Turn": The French Debate*, trans. Bernard G. Prusak, Jeffrey L. Kosky, and Thomas A. Carlson (New York: Fordham University Press, 2000), 16–103.

42. Marion, *Being Given*, 248–249.

43. Ibid., 249.

44. Although the most common understanding of *kenosis* is Pauline (Philippians 2:7), I am using the term to denote the overthrow of the transcendental "I" as inspired by the work of Italian philosopher Gianni Vattimo. See *Belief*, trans. Luca D'Isanto and David Webb (Stanford: Stanford University Press, 1999), 38–43; see also *After Christianity*, trans. Luca D'Isanto (New York: Columbia University Press, 2002), 23–24, 68. Although Vattimo's use of the term highlights the Incarnation of Christ as inaugurating the movement that has led to secularization and the overthrow of metaphysics as first philosophy, my use of the terms focuses on the (transcendental) self-emptying of the witness-recipient who has been cast as such precisely in light of the "self" of the saturated phenomenon that gives "itself."

45. We recall Levi's own claim, "if I had not lived the Auschwitz experience, I probably would never have written anything." *The Reawakening*, 230.

46. Marion, *In Excess*, 45.

47. Primo Levi, *Moments of Reprieve: A Memoir of Auschwitz*, trans. Ruth Feldman (New York: Penguin Books, 1986), viii–ix. Emphasis added.

48. Primo Levi, *The Periodic Table*, trans. Raymond Rosenthal (New York: Schocken Books, 1984), 153.

49. Ibid.

50. Primo Levi, "A Tranquil Star," trans. Ann Goldstein, 72–74. This issue of *The New Yorker* includes the following note: "Primo Levi (Fiction, 72), who died in 1987, wrote fiction, poetry, and memoirs, including 'Survival

in Auschwitz.' A book of previously untranslated stories, 'A Tranquil Star,' will be published in April. This story originally appeared in Italian in 1978."

5. AFTER AUSCHWITZ: WHAT IS A GOOD DEATH?
Timothy Pytell

1. A number of literary scholars have weighed in on the issue of Levi, Améry, and suicide. Perhaps most notable is Cynthia Ozick's "Primo Levi's Suicide Note" (in *Metaphor and Memory* [New York: Knopf, 1989], 34–48). In Ozick's interpretation, the aggressive tone of Levi's *The Drowned and the Saved* is unlike the very measured tenor of his earlier work, and therefore it reads as essentially a suicide note. Central to her argument is Levi's interpretation that Améry's suicide stems from his willingness to trade punches. *The Drowned and the Saved* thus becomes Levi's punch by a "pen of fire" and also deciphers for us Levi's suicide (47). Although her overarching thesis is somewhat convincing, in my opinion (as we shall see) Levi, and subsequently Ozick, is misreading Améry's suicide. Eugene Goodheart (in "The Passion of Reason: Reflections on Primo Levi and Jean Améry," *Dissent* [Fall 1994], 518–527) disagrees with Ozick's reading of *The Drowned and the Saved*. Although the central concern of Goodheart's essay is the capacity of reason to render and withstand extreme experience, he chides Ozick for not recognizing that Levi is actually rebuking Améry for "his self-destructive retaliatory impulses as the sign of someone preoccupied with death . . . in contrast [to] his own devotion to the aims of life" (526). Similar to Ozick, Goodheart follows Levi's misinterpretation of Améry's death. However, Goodheart does accurately, in my opinion, distinguish between the temperaments of Levi and Améry (525). I believe my historical analysis provides the background on why in Goodheart's words, "Améry is the man of reason" while "Levi is the reasonable man" (525). Finally, there is the work of Michael Bernstein and Alvin Rosenfeld. Bernstein's "Victims-in-Waiting: Backshadowing and Representation of European Jewry" (*New Literary History* 29, no. 4 [1998]: 625–651) touches only lightly on Améry and Levi; it is concerned with how the Holocaust impacts our understanding of Jewish identity, and the role of culture in the construction of that identity. Bernstein suggests that Levi, almost despite himself, and unlike Améry, is successful in relying on culture to sustain his identity, and quotes Levi's famous passages on Dante's *Inferno* to make his point (638). Rosenfeld's "Primo Levi: The Survivor as Victim" (in *Perspectives on the Holocaust: Essays in Honor of Raul Hilberg*, ed. James S. Pacy and Alan P. Wertheimer [Boulder: Westview, 1995], 123–144), is in contrast to Bernstein, and in a way replicates Ozick's reading of Levi's last work, by suggesting Levi's reliance on his writing to sustain himself came to a bitter end. I believe my historical analysis provides some corrective and adds much needed depth to these literary interpretations.

2. Diego Gambetta, "Primo Levi's Last Moments," *Boston Review* (Summer 1999).

3. Jonathan Druker, "On the Dangers of Reading Suicide Into the Works of Primo Levi," in *The Legacy of Primo Levi*, ed. Stanislao G. Pugliese (New York: Palgrave Macmillan, 2004), 229.

4. Ibid., 225.

5. J. Améry, "Mein Tod soll meine Sache sein" (interview), *Der Spiegel* 44 (October 30, 1978), 236.

6. See Irene Heidelberger-Leonard, *Jean Améry: Revolte in der Resignation* (Stuttgart: Klett-Cotta, 2004), 291.

7. J. Améry, *On Suicide: A Discourse on Voluntary Death*, trans. John D. Barlow (Bloomington: Indiana University Press, 1999), 52.

8. See H. Kesting, "Der Tod des Geistes als Person: Leben und Werk des Jean Améry," *Frankfurter Hefte: Zeitschrift für Kultur und Politik*, June 6, 1979, 51.

9. See W. G. Sebald, "Heimat und Exil: Bermerkungen zu Jean Améry," *Die Presse*, August 31, 1986.

10. Heidelberger-Leonard, *Jean Améry*, 349.

11. J. Améry, *At the Mind's Limits: Contemplations by a Survivor on Auschwitz and Its Realities*, trans. Sidney and Stella P. Rosenfeld (Bloomington: Indiana University Press, 1980), 70. Originally published as *Jenseits von Schuld und Sühne* in 1966.

12. Kesting, "Der Tod des Geistes als Person," 57.

13. Heidelberger-Leonard, *Jean Améry*, 348.

14. Ibid., 350.

15. Ibid., 351–352.

16. A reference to Charles Bovary. Améry's last book was a novel titled *Charles Bovary: Landartz*.

17. Heidelberger-Leonard, *Jean Améry*, 354.

18. J. Améry, *Radical Humanism: Selected Essays*, trans. Sidney and Stella P. Rosenfeld (Bloomington: Indiana University Press, 1984), 11.

19. Ibid., 12.

20. Ibid., 15.

21. Ibid., 16.

22. See Heidelberger-Leonard, *Jean Améry*, 67.

23. Améry, *Radical Humanism*, 15–16.

24. Ibid., 5. See also the preface to J. Améry, *Unmeisterlich Wanderjahre* (Stuttgart: Klett, 1971).

25. Heidelberger-Leonard, *Jean Améry*, 89.

26. See the afterword to Améry, *At the Mind's Limits*, 106. Levi also held this opinion. See Primo Levi, *The Drowned and the Saved* (New York: Vintage Books, 1988), 128.

27. Heidelberger-Leonard, *Jean Améry*, 30–31.

28. Ibid., 37–38.

29. Ibid., 73–74.

30. Ibid., 77.

31. Améry, *Radical Humanism*, 17.

32. Heidelberger-Leonard, *Jean Améry*, 81.

33. Améry, *Radical Humanism*, 17.

34. Heidelberger-Leonard, *Jean Améry*, 89.

35. Ibid., 91.

36. Myriam Anissimov, *The Tragedy of an Optimist*, trans. Steve Cox (New York: Overlook Press, 1999), 38.

37. Ibid., 56.

38. Ibid., 95.

39. Primo Levi, *Survival in Auschwitz*, trans. Stuart Woolf (New York: Touchstone, 1996), 9.

40. Anissimov, *The Tragedy of an Optimist*, 177.

41. Améry, *At the Mind's Limits*, 6.

42. Heidelberger-Leonard, *Jean Améry*, 113.

43. Améry, *Radical Humanism*, 72.

44. Heidelberger-Leonard, *Jean Améry*, 115.

45. Améry, J. *At the Mind's Limits*, x, viii.

46. Levi, *The Drowned and the Saved*, 130.

47. Thomson, *Primo Levi*, 308–309.

48. Ibid., 39.

49. Primo Levi, *The Black Hole of Auschwitz*, ed. Marco Belpoliti, trans. Sharon Wood (Cambridge: Polity Press, 2005), 12.

50. Thomson, *Primo Levi*, 39.

51. Levi, *The Drowned and the Saved*, 127.

52. Ibid., 136.

53. Ibid., 138.

54. Améry, *At the Mind's Limits*, 42.

55. Ibid., 60.

56. Levi, *The Drowned and the Saved*, 144.

57. Primo Levi, *The Voice of Memory: Interviews, 1961–1987*, ed. Marco Belpoliti and Robert Gordon (New York: Polity Press, 2001), 206.

58. Améry, *At the Mind's Limits*, 20.

59. Levi, *The Drowned and the Saved*, 148.

60. Ibid., 137.

61. Levi, *The Black Hole of Auschwitz*, 49.

62. Thomson, *Primo Levi*, 369.

63. Ibid., 495.

64. Primo Levi, *The Search for Roots: A Personal Anthology*, trans. Peter Forbes (Chicago: Ivan R. Dee, 2003), viii.

6. THE HUMANITY AND HUMANISM OF PRIMO LEVI
Joseph Farrell

1. Primo Levi, "Racial Intolerance," in *The Black Hole of Auschwitz*, trans. Sharon Wood, ed. Marco Belpoliti (Cambridge: Polity Press, 2005), 107.

2. Ibid., 109.

3. Primo Levi, *If This Is a Man* and *The Truce*, trans. Stuart Woolf (London: Penguin Books, 1979). All references are to this edition.

4. Levi, "Racial Intolerance," 119.

5. Ibid.

6. Primo Levi, *Other People's Trades*, trans. Raymond Rosenthal (London: Michael Joseph, 1989), 76.

7. George Steiner, "The Idea of Europe," *The Liberal* 8 (July–August 2006): 9.

8. Terry Eagleton, *The Meaning of Life* (Oxford: Oxford University Press, 2007), 72.

9. Primo Levi, "On Obscure Writing," in *Other People's Trades*, trans. Raymond Rosenthal (London: Michael Joseph, 1989), 157–163.

10. Levi, *If This Is a Man*, 15.

11. Ibid., 33.

12. Giorgio Agamben, *Remnants of Auschwitz: The Witness and the Archive*, trans. Daniel Heller-Roazen (New York: Zone Books, 1999).

13. Primo Levi, *The Drowned and the Saved*, trans. Raymond Rosenthal (London: Abacus, 1989), 114.

14. Levi, *If This Is a Man*, 94–95.

15. Ibid., 96.

16. Agamben, *Remnants of Auschwitz*, 82.

17. This point is debated by William McClellan, "Primo Levi, Giorgio Agamben and the New Ethics of Reading," in *The Legacy of Primo Levi*, ed. Stanislao G. Pugliese (New York: Palgrave Macmillan, 2005), 148.

18. Levi, *If This Is a Man*, 47.

19. Ibid.,114.

20. Ibid., 119.

21. Levi, "Racial Intolerance," 116.

22. Christopher Bigsby, *Remembering and Imagining the Holocaust: The Chain of Memory* (Cambridge: Cambridge University Press, 2006).

23. Agamben, *Remnants of Auschwitz*, 11.

24. Ibid., 88.

25. Levi, *The Drowned and the Saved*, 114.

26. George Steiner, interview, in Eleanor Wachtel, *Original Minds* (Toronto: Harper Flamingo, 2003), 120.

27. Harry Mulisch, *Siegfried*, trans. Paul Vincent (London: Allen Lane, 2003); Norman Mailer, *The Castle in the Forest* (New York, Random House, 2007). See also the epic novel by Harry Mulisch, *The Discovery of Heaven*, trans. Paul Vincent (London: Penguin, 1996).

28. Arthur Miller, "The Nazi Trials and the German Heart," in *Echoes Down the Corridor: Collected Essays 1944–2000*, ed. Steven R. Centola (London: Methuen, 2000), 62–68.

29. Hugh Trevor-Roper, *Hitler's Table Talk* (London: Allen Lane, 1953).

30. Levi, *The Drowned and the Saved*, 32.

31. Primo Levi, "Preface to L. Poliakov's Auschwitz," in *The Black Hole*, 28.

32. Levi, "Preface to L. Poliakov's Auschwitz," 27.

33. Tzvetan Todorov, *Facing the Extreme* (London: Weidenfeld and Nicolson, 1999), 16, 17, 32–33.

34. Tzvetan Todorov, *Imperfect Garden: The Legacy of Humanism* (Princeton: Princeton University Press, 2002), 233.

35. Myriam Anissimov, *Primo Levi: Tragedy of an Optimist*, trans. Steve Cox (London: Aurum, 1998).

36. Levi, "Preface to L. Poliakov's Auschwitz," 28.

37. Ibid.

38. Levi, *If This Is a Man*, 93.

39. Levi, *The Drowned and the Saved*, 114

40. Ibid., 54.

41. Primo Levi, "The Language of Odors," is a chapter in the Italian version of *Other People's Trades*, omitted from the English translation. See Primo Levi, *Opere II* (Turin: Einaudi, 1997), 840.

42. Levi, *The Drowned and the Saved*, 115.

43. Wachtel, *Original Minds*, 117.

44. Todorov, *Imperfect Garden*, 233.

45. Levi, *Other People's Trades*, vii.

46. Primo Levi, *The Search for Roots*, trans. Peter Forbes (London: Allen Lane, 2001).

47. Marco Belpoliti, "Animali e fantasmi," postface to Primo Levi, *L'ultimo natale di guerra*, (Turin: Einaudi, 2002), 135. Translation mine.

48. Levi, *The Search for Roots*, 5.

49. Steiner, "The Idea of Europe," 8.

50. Primo Levi, "Francois Rabelais," in *Other People's Trades*, 124.

51. Levi, "On Obscure Writing," 161.

52. Ian Thomson, *Primo Levi* (London: Hutchinson, 2002), 427.

53. Piero Citati, *Kafka*, trans. Raymond Rosenthal (London: Minerva, 1991), 139.

54. Primo Levi, "Translating Kafka," in *The Mirror Maker*, trans. Raymond Rosenthal (London: Methuen, 1990), 106–107.

55. Albert Camus, "La Nausée de Jean-Paul Sartre," in *Essais d'Albert Camus* (Paris: Gallimard, 1965), 1417.

56. Primo Levi, "The Monument at Auschwitz," in *The Black Hole of Auschwitz*, 7.

7. LEVI AND THE TWO CULTURES
Jonathan Druker

1. Of a short story of Levi's published in the early 1960s, "Quaestio de Centauris," Ian Thomson writes, "This equine whimsy marks the beginning of an enduring, even obsessive attempt on Levi's part to present himself as two halves or twin poles. Levi was not the only Italian literary figure engaged in two careers, but he alone tried to create a grand personal mythology out of this cloven state." Ian Thomson, *Primo Levi: A Life* (New York: Metropolitan Books, 2002), 298.

2. Primo Levi, *The Search for Roots*, trans. Peter Forbes (Chicago: Ivan R. Dee, 2002).

3. "I really did feel a bit like Tiresias . . . being a chemist in the world's eyes, and feeling, on the contrary, a writer's blood in my veins, I felt as if I had two souls in my body, and that is too many." Primo Levi, *The Monkey's Wrench*, trans. William Weaver (New York: Summit Books, 1986), 52.

4. In the late 1950s, C. P. Snow's influential essay "The Two Cultures" pointed out the growing cultural gap between the arts and sciences, expressed great concern at the consequences, but offered no solutions. The idea that scientific and literary cultures are inherently different and distinct began to be discussed in earnest around the turn of the twentieth century, especially in England. In polemic with T. H. Huxley, Matthew Arnold maintained the superiority of the humane letters while asserting that science provides us with knowledge that has no relation to beauty or morality. Arnold's ideas are in harmony with the Crocean idealism that informed Italian Fascism and the educational system in place in Levi's youth. Knowledge and goodness are attained through the spirit, Croce argued, while scientific concepts derived from the properties of base material are unable to point the way to genuine knowledge.

5. Primo Levi, *Other People's Trades*, trans. Raymond Rosenthal (New York: Summit Books, 1989), 10.

6. As an example of scholarship claiming that hybridity is a key aspect of Levi's oeuvre, see Jonathan Wilson, "Primo Levi's Hybrid Texts," *Judaism: A*

Quarterly Journal of Jewish Life and Thought 48 (Winter 1999): 67–72; see also Natasha V. Chang, "Chemical Contaminations: Allegory and Alterity in Primo Levi's *Il sistema periodico*," *Italica* 83, nos. 3–4 (Fall–Winter 2006): 543–562.

7. Primo Levi, *The Periodic Table*, trans. Raymond Rosenthal (New York: Schocken Books, 1984).

8. See, for example, the 1938 "Manifesto of the Racial Scientists," a document produced by a group of young scientists serving as the government's mouthpiece. "The Jews represent the only population that has never assimilated in Italy because they are constituted from non-European social elements, absolutely different from the elements from which Italians originated." Cited in Susan Zuccotti, *Under His Very Windows: The Vatican and the Holocaust in Italy* (New Haven: Yale University Press, 2000), 28.

9. Without employing the theoretical framework I adopt here, other scholarship has discussed how Levi's texts navigate, often unwittingly, the gap between the ideals of science and its actual history as a tool for oppression. See, for example, Nancy Harrowitz, "From Mt. Sinai to the Holocaust: Primo Levi and the Crisis of Science in *The Periodic Table*," in *Celebrating Elie Wiesel: Stories, Essays, Reflections*, ed. Alan Rosen (Notre Dame, Ind.: University of Notre Dame Press, 1998), 19–39.

10. Primo Levi, *Survival in Auschwitz: The Nazi Assault on Humanity*, trans. Stuart Woolf (New York: Simon & Schuster, 1996), 26.

11. Michel Foucault, *The Order of Things: An Archaeology of the Human Sciences* (New York: Pantheon Books, 1971).

12. Ibid. The two quotations are respectively at pages 318 and 312.

13. Steven Best and Douglas Kellner, *Postmodern Theory: Critical Interrogations* (New York: Guilford Press, 1991), 42. Best and Kellner admirably clarify the three principle binaries that fracture Man, as discussed in chapter 9 of *The Order of Things*, and how humanism tries to paper them over. "Foucault describes how modern philosophy constructs 'Man'—both object and subject of knowledge—within a series of unstable 'doublets': the cogito/unthought doublet whereby Man is determined by external forces yet aware of this determination and able to free himself from it; the retreat-and-return-of-the-origin doublet whereby history precedes Man but is the phenomenological source from which history unfolds; and the transcendental/empirical doublet whereby Man constitutes and is constituted by the external world, finding secure foundations for knowledge through a priori categories (Kant). . . . In each of these doublets, humanist thought attempts to recuperate the primacy and autonomy of the thinking subject and master all that is other to it" (42).

14. Michel Foucault, "Right of Death and Power Over Life," *The History of Sexuality, Volume I: An Introduction*, trans. Robert Hurley (New York: Vintage Books, 1990), 133–159.

15. Gary Gutting, "Michel Foucault," *Stanford Encyclopedia of Philosophy*, first published April 2, 2003; substantive revision September 17, 2008, http://plato.stanford.edu/entries/foucault/#3.3, January 15, 2009. The quotations from Foucault in this paragraph are from *Words and Things* at pages 142, 136, and 136–137, respectively.

16. Giorgio Agamben, *Homo Sacer: Sovereign Power and Bare Life*, trans. Daniel Heller-Roazen (Stanford: Stanford University Press, 1998), 181.

17. Michele Sarfatti, *La Shoah in Italia: La persecuzione degli ebrei sotto il fascismo* (Turin: Einaudi, 2005), 134.

18. For Foucault, "the entry of medicine, psychiatry, and some social sciences into legal deliberations in the nineteenth century led . . . [to] an increasing appeal to statistical measures and judgments about what is normal and what it not in a given population rather than adherence to absolute measures of right and wrong [i.e., the Law]." *The Foucault Reader*, ed. Paul Rabinow (Pantheon: New York, 1984), 21.

19. Giorgio Fabre, *Mussolini razzista: Dal socialismo al fascismo—La formazione di un antisemita* (Milan: Garzanti 2005).

20. Michel Foucault, *"Society Must Be Defended": Lectures at the Collège de France, 1975–1976*, ed. Mauro Bertani and Alessandro Fontana, trans. David Macey (New York: Picador, 2003), 256.

21. Ibid., 258.

22. See, for example, Wilson, "Primo Levi's Hybrid Texts," 67–72; and Chang, "Chemical Contaminations," 548–551.

23. Primo Levi, *Dialogo* (Princeton: Princeton University Press, 1989), xv.

24. Elizabeth Scheiber reads this chapter, and *The Periodic Table* as a whole, differently. She takes a remark of Levi's in "Vanadium" about the instability of varnish to refer by analogy to the instability of memory, and especially to his traumatic memories of Holocaust. Elizabeth Scheiber, "The Failure of Memory and Literature in Primo Levi's *Il sistema periodico*," *MLN* 121 (2006): 225–239.

25. Foucault, *The Order of Things*, 300. Furthermore, just when language became an object of knowledge it was also remaking itself in "the pure act of writing." By the twentieth century, literature "becomes merely a manifestation of a language which has no other law than that of affirming . . . its own precipitous existence. . . . It addresses itself to itself as a writing subjectivity, or seeks to re-apprehend the essence of all literature in the movement that brought it into being; and thus all its threads converge upon the finest of points—singular, instantaneous, and yet absolutely universal—upon the simple act of writing."

26. Foucault, *"Society Must Be Defended,"* 179–185.

8. THE PARTISAN AND HIS DOPPELGANGER: THE CASE OF PRIMO LEVI
Ilona Klein

1. Translated by William Weaver, *If Not Now, When?* was published in English in 1985. In Italy it reaped immediate success, praised by both critics and readership alike, and Levi was awarded the Premio Viareggio and the Premio Campiello in 1982. This was his second Campiello, having also won it nine years earlier with *La tregua* (*The Truce*).

2. See also the chapter "Gold" in Levi's *The Periodic Table*.

3. Nicholas Patruno, *Understanding Primo Levi* (Columbia: University of South Carolina Press, 1995), 90.

4. Susan J. Brison, "Outliving Oneself: Trauma, Memory, and Personal Identity," in *Feminists Rethink the Self*, edited by Diana T. Meyers (Boulder: Westview, 1997), 12, 14.

5. One might certainly add Damiano Malabaila (Primo Levi's *nom de plume* for *Storie naturali*) to this list, too.

6. Brison, "Outliving Oneself," 29.

7. Karin Lorenz-Lindemann, "Wieviel Heimat braucht der Mensch? Aspects of Jewish Self-Determination in the Works of Jean Améry and Primo Levi," in *The Jewish Self-Portrait in European and American Literature*, ed. Hans-Jürgen Schrader, Elliott M. Simon, et al. (Tübingen: Niemeyer, 1996), 228.

8. Patruno, *Understanding Primo Levi*, 93; Brison, "Outliving Oneself," 22.

9. Patruno, *Understanding Primo Levi*, 93.

10. Jane Nystedt, "Lunghezza della frase e interpunzione: Mezzi stilistici in Primo Levi," *Studi Italiani di Linguistica Teorica e Applicata* 21, nos. 1–3 (1992): 100.

11. As examples, one can look at Leonid, the introvert young Jew from Moscow, paratrooper and bookkeeper; and at Black Rokhele, a twenty-year-old veteran who was as strong as any of the men in the unit. Both perish from sudden bullet wounds. Their names are hardly mentioned again in the novel after their deaths.

12. Patruno, *Understanding Primo Levi*, 91.

13. Eamonn Callan, "Patience and Courage," *Philosophy* 68, no. 266 (1983): 528.

14. Ibid., 536.

15. Personalities and beliefs range from those of White Rokhele, the widow of a rabbi, not too religious herself, to Mendel, who is continuously searching his soul to find the meaning of God, the meaning of war, the meaning of his ancestral traditions.

16. Lorenz-Lindemann, "Wieviel Heimat braucht der Mensch?" 224.

17. One of the characters in the novel is the Christian Russian Piotr Fomich, who believes in Jewish and anti-Nazi resistance to the point of putting his own life on the line more than once for Gedaleh's comrades. This character represents he who must be initiated gradually into the fundamental principles of Judaism. He does not know about, nor has he ever read, the Talmud. The other partisans compare the Talmud for him to a soup with several different and sometimes contrasting edible ingredients among which each Jew may subjectively choose.

18. Tosi points out that the Italian editions of both *The Truce* and *If Not Now, When?* include sketched maps to aid the reader in negotiating the geographic areas of the narrative.

19. Located in the center of the novel in the chapter entitled "May 1944," the lyrics celebrate Gedaleh's camp. The group sings and dances around the campfire, in one of the few moments of respite experienced by the partisans throughout the story. Late that night, after most members are sleeping off the fumes of alcohol, Gedaleh takes his violin and plays a brisk tune learned at the Kossovo ghetto. Character Martin Fontasch (a peaceful carpenter) was the author of the words he had composed half an hour before dying at the hands of a Nazi.

20. Patruno, *Understanding Primo Levi*, 103.

21. Ibid., 101.

22. The film *Defiance*, directed by Edward Zwick, was released in the United States in 2008.

23. Patruno, *Understanding Primo Levi*, 92, 106.

24. See Primo Levi's own definition of a moral gray zone, in the chapter by that name in his *The Drowned and The Saved*.

25. Claude Lanzmann's documentary film *Shoah* (1985) is filled with interviews in which such anguish is present in each person discussing his or her survival. These Jews perceive their being alive as a privilege not earned. The overwhelming pain of memories, together with the observation that the events of the Shoah find no logical explanation, led some survivors to suicide.

26. Douglas Kellner, "Popular Culture and the Construction of Postmodern Identities," in *Modernity and Identity*, ed. Scott Lash and Jonathan Freidman (Cambridge, Mass.: Basil Blackwell, 1992), 141.

27. "*Al passato distrutto si associa il dissolvimento del futuro . . . non disponendo di modelli di riferimento che affondano le loro radici nel passato.*" Giuseppe Tosi, "Dall'attesa alla storia-esilio: La memoria e l'identità in *Se non ora, quando?* di Primo Levi," *Annali d'Italianistica* 20 (2002): 287.

28. Lorenz-Lindemann, "Wieviel Heimat braucht der Mensch?" 230; Callan, "Patience and Courage," 539.

29. "*Mi sono effettivamente indentificato con Mendel: Voglio dire che lui fa quello che avrei fatto io, o meglio quello che avrei dovuto fare io, se ne fossi stato capace.*"

Interview with Rossellina Balbi *La Repubblica*, April 14, 1982. Quoted from Marco Belpoliti, *Primo Levi: Conversazioni e interviste: 1963–1987* (Turin: Einaudi, 1997), 132.

30. On one hand, the character Mendel needs to be free of all romantic ties so as to reinstate trust and sincerity in his camaraderie with Leonid. On the other hand, Mendel needs the support of a woman in his life, after the tragic death of his wife Rivke, killed by the Nazis in Strelka.

31. When Mottel askes about Italy, this answer comes:

> Italy is an odd country. . . . The Italians don't like laws: in fact, they like disobeying them: it's their game, like the Russians' game is chess. . . . The Italians have proved to be friends of all foreigners. . . . They helped us not in spite of the fact we're Jews, but *because* of it. They also helped their own Jews; when the Germans occupied Italy, they made every effort they could to capture the Italian Jews, but they caught and killed only a fifth. . . . Even as Christians, the Italians are odd. They go to Mass, but they curse. . . . They know the Ten Commandments by heart, but at most they observe two or three. I believe they help those in need because they're good people, who have suffered a lot, and who know that those who suffer should be helped. . . . Italian Jews are as odd as the Catholics. They don't speak Yiddish, in fact they don't even know what Yiddish is. They only speak Italian; or rather, the Jews of Rome speak Roman, the Jews of Venice speak Venetian, and so on. They dress like everybody else; they have the same faces as everybody else. . . . The Christians don't give them any thought, and they themselves don't think much about being Jews. . . . There, this is the country you're entering: a country of good people, who don't much like war, who like confusing issues. . . . This is really the ideal place. (323–325)

9. PRIMO LEVI IN THE PUBLIC INTEREST: TURIN, AUSCHWITZ, ISRAEL
Risa Sodi

1. Myriam Anissimov, *Primo Levi: Tragedy of an Optimist* (London: Aurum Press, 1998), 273–275.

2. Anissimov writes, "Before [Levi and Perugia] received their rightful compensation of DM 2,500, they had to pay DM 122.70 to Henry Ormond, lawyer of Frankfurt am Main" (ibid.). Ian Thomson, in *Primo Levi* (New York: Metropolitan Books, 2002), reports instead, "the German courts awarded [Levi] damages of 122.70 deutschmarks (which at today's exchange rate amounts to £6,000)" (269). In late 1960s, through his job at the SIVA paint factory, Levi unexpectedly came into contact and exchanged letters with Dr. Ferdinand Meyer, his erstwhile supervisor at IG Farben. The episode is recounted in the "Vanadium" chapter of *The Periodic Table*. Meyer, whom Levi called "Lothar Müller" in his book, died in 1967 before the two could meet.

3. Primo Levi, "Monumento ad Auschwitz," *La Stampa* 19 July 1959, cited in Gabriella Poli and Giorgio Calcagno, *Echi di una voce perduta* (Milan: Mursia, 1992), 173.

4. My translation. The original text reads,

> Visitatore, osserva le vestigia di questo campo e medita: da qualunque paese tu venga, tu non sei un estraneo. Fa' che il tuo viaggio non sia stato inutile, che non sia inutile la nostra morte. Per te e per I tuoi figli, le ceneri di Auschwitz valgano di ammonimento: fa' che il frutto orrendo dell'odio di cui hai visto qui le trace, non dia nuovo seme, né domani né mai (Poli and Calcagno, 175).

Levi sent a copy of his draft of the full text, dated November 8, 1978, and entitled "Bozza di testo per l'interno del Block italiano ad Auschwitz." He also delivered the typescript reproduced below to his friend Bruno Vasari, a founding member of ANED (Associazione Nazionale Ex Deportati Politici nei Campi di Sterminio Nazisti) and the person to whom Levi's poem "Il superstite" is dedicated:

Al visitatore

La storia della Deportazione e dei campi di sterminio, la storia di questo luogo, non può essere separata dalla storia delle tirannidi fasciste in Europa: dai primi incendi delle Camere di Lavoro nell'Italia del 1921, ai roghi di libri sulle piazze della Germania del 1933, alla fiamma nefanda dei crematori di Birkenau, corre un nesso non interrotto. È vecchia sapienza, e già così aveva ammonito Enrico Heine, ebreo e tedesco: chi brucia libri finisce col bruciare uomini, la violenza è un seme che non si estingue.

È triste ma doveroso rammentarlo, agli altri ed a noi stessi: il primo esperimento europeo di soffocazione del movimento operaio e di sabotaggio della democrazia è nato in Italia. È il fascismo, scatenato dalla crisi del primo dopoguerra, dal mito della «vittoria mutilata», ed alimentato da antiche miserie e colpe; e dal fascismo nasce un delirio che si estenderà, il culto dell'uomo provvidenziale, l'entusiasmo organizzato ed imposto, ogni decisione affidata all'arbitrio di un solo.

Ma non tutti gli italiani sono stati fascisti: lo testimoniamo noi, gli italiani che siamo morti qui. Accanto al fascismo, altro filo mai interrotto, è nato in Italia, prima che altrove, l'antifascismo. Insieme con noi testimoniano tutti coloro che contro il fascismo hanno combattuto e che a causa del fascismo hanno sofferto, i martiri operai di Torino del 1923, i carcerati, i confinati, gli esuli, ed i nostri fratelli di tutte le fedi politiche che sono morti per resistere al fascismo restaurato dall'invasore nazionalsocialista. E testimoniano insieme a noi altri italiani ancora, quelli che sono caduti su tutti i fronti della II Guerra Mondiale, combattendo malvolentieri e disperatamente contro un nemico che non era il loro nemico, ed accorgendosi troppo tardi dell'inganno. Sono anche loro vittime del fascismo: vittime inconsapevoli.

Noi non siamo stati inconsapevoli. Alcuni fra noi erano partigiani e combattenti politici; sono stati catturati e deportati negli ultimi mesi di guerra, e sono morti qui, mentre il Terzo Reich crollava, straziati dal pensiero della liberazione così vicina. La maggior parte fra noi erano ebrei: ebrei provenienti da tutte le città italiane, ed anche ebrei stranieri, polacchi, ungheresi, jugoslavi, cechi, tedeschi, che nell'Italia fascista, costretta all'antisemitismo dalle leggi di Mussolini, avevano incontrato la benevolenza e la civile ospitalità del popolo italiano. Erano ricchi e poveri, uomini e donne, sani e malati. C'erano bambini fra noi, molti, e c'erano vecchi alle soglie della morte, ma tutti siamo stati caricati come merci sui vagoni, e la nostra sorte, la sorte di chi varcava i cancelli di Auschwitz, è stata la stessa per tutti. Non era mai successo, neppure nei secoli più oscuri, che si sterminassero esseri umani a milioni, come insetti dannosi: che si mandassero a morte i bambini e I moribondi. Noi, figli cristiani ed ebrei (ma non amiamo queste distinzioni) di un paese che è stato civile, e che civile è ritornato dopo la notte del fascismo, qui lo testimoniamo. In questo luogo, dove noi innocenti siamo stati uccisi, si è toccato il fondo delle barbarie.

Visitatore, osserva le vestigia di questo campo e medita: da qualunque paese tu venga, tu non sei un estraneo. Fa che il tuo viaggio non sia stato inutile, che non sia stata inutile la nostra morte. Per te e per i tuoi figli, le ceneri di Auschwitz valgano di ammonimento: fa che il frutto orrendo dell'odio, di cui hai visto qui le tracce, non dia nuovo seme, né domani né mai.

5. Thomson, *Primo Levi*, 401.
6. Sharon Roubach and Dina Wardi, "Primo Levi in Israel," in Giovanni Tesio, ed., *La Manutenzione della Memoria: Diffusione e conoscenza di Primo Levi nei paesi europei—Atti del convegno, Torino 9–10–11 ottobre 2003* (Turin: Centro Studi Piemontesi, 2005), 279–299.
7. Ibid., 279.
8. Robert S. C. Gordon, "Which Holocaust? Primo Levi and the Field of Holocaust Memory in Post-War Italy," *Italian Studies* 61, no. 1 (Spring 2006): 93.
9. Ibid., 93–94.
10. "Non sono credente, non lo sono mai stato; vorrei esserlo, ma non riesco. . . . C'è Auschwitz, quindi non può esserci Dio. Non trovo soluzione al dilemma. La cerco ma non la trovo." Poli and Calcagno, *Echi di una voce perduta*, 281.
11. See Levi's "Preface" (x–xvi) to *Ebrei a Torino: Ricerche per il centenario della sinagoga 1884–1994* (Turin: Allemandi, 1984).
12. "Io sono ebreo come anagrafe, vale a dire che sono iscritto alla Comunità israelitica di Torino, ma non sono praticante, e neppure sono credente." Poli and Calcagno, *Echi di una voce perduta*, 285.
13. *Opere*, ed. Marco Belpoliti (Turin: Einaudi, 1997), 2:1251.

14. Risa Sodi, "A Last Talk with Primo Levi," in *Jewish Profiles: The Best of Present Tense* (New York: Jacob Aronson, 1992).

15. From Stefano Jesurum, *Essere ebrei in Italia* (Milan: Longanesi, 1987), quoted in Anissimov, *Primo Levi*, 345.

16. Thomson, *Primo Levi*, 319.

17. Molinari, *La sinistra e gli ebrei in Italia, 1967–1993* (Milan: Corbaccio, 1995), 56–57.

18. Ibid., 57.

19. Ibid., 106. This manifesto elicits controversy even today, as evidenced by a July 1, 2007, interview at the Jerusalem Center for Public Affairs with Italian journalist Fiamma Nirenstein, "The Cynical Use of Israel in Italian Politics." Nirenstein accuses Levi and Ginzburg of "criminalizing Israel." While granting that Levi was "more ambivalent" than Ginzburg (who is quoted as saying, "To the sunburnt sabra, the Hebrew soldier with the weapons in his hand, I prefer the bent Jew who studies the Bible, the fragile, weak, and sick Jew") and admitting that Levi, through the Zionistic conclusion to *La tregua* (*The Reawakening*), showed "a great passion for Israel," she nonetheless states that Levi's position was "typical for many Italian Jewish postwar intellectuals" who continued to believe "the false idea to which I had succumbed after tens of years of propaganda that Judaism is leftist." See Jerusalem Center for Public Affairs, *Post-Holocaust and Anti-Semitism* 58, July 1, 2007.

20. Composed of members of the Israeli Supreme Court and the military and presided over by President of the Supreme Court Justice Yitzhak Kahan, the three-man commission was charged on September 28, 1982, with investigating the facts of Sabra and Chatilla. It delivered its report on February 8, 1983.

21. Poli and Calcagno, *Echi di una voce perduta*, 296. In Italian: "Sgomenti per l'infamia che macchia l'intero paese a angosciati per il suo futuro."

22. Interview with Giampaolo Pansa, "Io Primo Levi chiedo le dimissioni di Begin: Sharon, Begin, gli ebrei dicono basta," *La Repubblica*, September 24, 1982.

23. Primo Levi, "Chi ha il coraggio a Gerusalemma?" *La Stampa*, June 24, 1982; Alberto Stabile, "Sì, Israele ha passato il segno: Ma non è giusto parlare di nazismo," *La Repubblica*, June 28, 1982; Primo Levi, "Il pericolo viene dal militarismo," *La Repubblica*, February 11, 1983; cited in Poli and Calcagno, *Echi di una voce perduta*.

24. Thomson, *Primo Levi*, 402.

25. Vittorio Dan Segre, an Italian Jew who emigrated to Israel and the author of *Memoirs of a Fortunate Jew*, said this about his meeting with Levi in 1982, on the heels of the revelations about Sabra and Chatilla: "I found that

he had an extraordinary range of knowledge, very remote from politics, and extraordinarily ingenious and innocent. . . . The basic elements of the Israeli situation were unfamiliar to him. . . . He had done some reading but, in fact he was a stranger to Jewish culture. No experience, but great interest—a detached interest. He had landed on a Jewish planet in Auschwitz with no preparation and no Jewish upbringing, like many Italian Jews. I have always had the impression that his attitude toward the Jews was engage committed of his life but, as I say, detached" (Anissimov, *Primo Levi*, 351). See also Levi's review of Segre's book, "Se questo è un ebreo fortunato, ditelo voi," in *Opere* 2:1271–1273.

26. Gad Lerner, "Se questo è uno stato," *Espresso*, September 30, 1984; included in Belpoliti, *Conversazioni e interviste*.

27. These include a television interview denouncing the Chernobyl disaster (conducted by Alberto La Volpe, in May 1986; cited in Poli and Calcagno, *Echi di una voce perduta*, 331; Thomson, 466) and an interview criticizing the U.S. intervention against Libya ("L'intervento Americano in Libia non è giustificabile in alcun modo"); Francesco Ciafaloni, "Etica e politica," *Ex-Macchina* 4 (May–June 1986), cited in Belpoliti, *Conversazioni e interviste*, 314. In May 1986, Levi also wrote "La peste non ha frontiere" (The Plague Has No Borders), about the dangers of nuclear fallout, for *La Stampa*.

10. PRIMO LEVI'S STRUGGLE WITH THE SPIRIT OF KAFKA
Massimo Giuliani

1. Raniero M. Speelman, "Primo Levi's Short Stories: Modern Midrashim," in *The Legacy of Primo Levi*, ed. Stanislao G. Pugliese, 23–31 (New York: Palgrave, 2005).

2. Primo Levi, *Opere I*, ed. Marco Belpoliti (Turin: Einaudi, 1997), 566–567.

3. Ibid., 623.

4. Primo Levi, *Conversazioni e interviste 1963–1987*, ed. Marco Belpoliti (Turin: Einaudi 1997), 113.

5. Louis Ginzberg, *Le leggende degli ebrei* (Milan: Adelphi, 1995), 1:64–65.

6. See Moshe Idel, *Golem: Jewish Magical and Mystical Traditions on the Artificial Anthropoid* (Albany: State University of New York Press, 1990).

7. Levi, *Opere I*, 713.

8. Ibid., 710.

9. Ibid., 714.

10. Ibid., 716.

11. Ibid.

12. Ibid.

13. Ibid.

14. Primo Levi, *Opere II*, ed. Marco Belpoliti (Turin: Einaudi, 1998), 1208.

15. Ibid., 940.

16. The use of the neologism "salv-action" is explained in Massimo Giuliani, *A Centaur in Auschwitz: Reflections on Primo Levi's Thinking* (Lanham, Md.: Lexington Books, 2003), 55–64.

11. ETHICS AND LITERARY STRATEGIES
Sara Vandewaetere

1. Robert Gordon, *Primo Levi's Ordinary Virtues: From Testimony to Ethics* (Oxford: Oxford University Press, 2001).

2. Ibid., 39–54.

3. Primo Levi, *Se questo è un uomo*, in *Opere I*, ed. Marco Belpoliti (Turin: Einaudi, 1997), 101–102. All works of Levi are cited in the two-volume Italian edition *Opere*; translations into English are my own unless otherwise indicated.

4. Emmanuel Levinas, *Totalité et infini: Essai sur l'extériorité* (The Hague: Nijhoff, 1961).

5. Ibid., 103.

6. Martin Jay, *Downcast Eyes: The Denigration of Vision in Twentieth-Century French Thought* (Berkeley: University of California Press, 1993), 557.

7. Primo Levi, *L'altrui mestiere*, in *Opere II*, 673–675.

8. Primo Levi, *La tregua*, in *Opere I*, 392.

9. Primo Levi, *I sommersi e i salvati*, in *Opere II*, 1125.

10. Levinas, *Ethique et infini*, 91.

11. Levi, "Trattamento di quiescenza," *Storie Naturali*, in *Opere I*, 551.

12. Bessel A. Van Der Kolk and Onno Van der Hart, "The Intrusive Past: The Flexibility of Memory and the Engraving of Trauma," in *Trauma: Explorations in Memory*, ed. Cathy Caruth (Baltimore: Johns Hopkins University Press, 1995), 158–182.

13. Levi, *Il sistema periodico*, in *Opere I*, 924. "Ora, degli incontri fatti in quel mondo ormai remoto io conservo memorie di una precisione patologica."

14. Ezrahi Sidra Dekoven, "Representing Auschwitz," *History and Memory* 7, no. 2 (Fall/Winter 1996): 121–154.

15. Levi, *Se questo è un uomo*, 17.

16. Lorenzo Mondo, "Primo Levi e Dante," in *Primo Levi: Memoria e invenzione—Atti del convegno internazionale*, ed. Giovanna Ioli (Monferrato: Edizione della Biennale, 1995), 224–230.

17. Levi, *Se questo è un uomo*, 3.

18. Ibid., 10.

19. George Lakoff and Mark Johnson, *Metaphors We Live By* (Chicago: University of Chicago Press, 1980).

20. Levi, *L'altrui mestiere*, 642.

21. Primo Levi, *La chiave a stella*, in *Opere I*, 959.

22. Levi, *Se questo è un uomo*, 99.

23. Primo Levi, *The Periodic Table*, trans. R. Rosenthal (New York: Schocken Books, 1986).

24. Levi, *Ad ora incerta*, in *Opere II*, 568.

25. Levi, *Se questo è un uomo*, 3.

12. LITERARY ENCOUNTERS AND STORYTELLING TECHNIQUES
Elizabeth Scheiber

1. See, for example, Carole Angier's biography of Levi, *The Double Bond* (New York: Farrar, Straus and Giroux, 2002.)

2. Andrea Rondini's study of *Lilìt*, "La scrittura e la sfida: Una lettura di 'Lilìt' di Primo Levi" (*Studi novecenteschi* 59 [2002]: 239–276), is an exception. Rondini examines this collection as a unified whole to seek out Levi's thoughts on conflict and writing, crossing boundaries to find echoes of themes throughout the collection. However, Rondini does not take note of any organizational structure in the work. The translations from her study herein are my own.

3. Ross Chambers, *Story and Situation: Narrative Seduction and the Power of Fiction* (Minneapolis: University of Minnesota Press, 1984), 33.

4. "In Due Time." Other translations of the title could be "In the Fullness of Time," "All in Good Time," and "In Due Course." Unless credited otherwise, the translations from the Italian here and hereafter in this essay are my own.

13. PRIMO LEVI AND THE HISTORY OF RECEPTION
William McClellan

1. Editor's note: Reception history has been defined by Harold Marcuse of the Department of History at the University of California at Santa Barbara as "the history of the meanings that have been imputed to historical events. It traces the different ways in which participants, observers, historians and other retrospective interpreters have attempted to make sense of events both as they unfolded and over time since then, to make those events meaningful for the present in which they lived and live." http://www.history.ucsb.edu/faculty/marcuse/receptionhist.htm.

2. William McClellan, "Primo Levi, Giorgio Agamben, and the New Ethics of Reading," in *The Legacy of Primo Levi*, ed. Stanislao G. Pugliese (New York: Palgrave Macmillan, 2005), 147–152.

3. Giorgio Agamben, *Remnants of Auschwitz: The Witness and the Archive*, trans. D. Heller-Roazen (New York: Zone Books, 1999); *Homo Sacer: Sovereign Power and Bare Life*, trans. D. Heller-Roazen (Stanford: Stanford University Press, 1998).

4. Agamben, *Remnants of Auschwitz*, 69.

5. Dominick LaCapra, *History in Transit: Experience, Identity, Critical Theory* (Ithaca, N.Y.: Cornell University Press, 2004), 161. See also Esther Marion, "The Nazi Genocide and the Writing of the Holocaust Aporia: Ethics and Remnants of Auschwitz," *MLN* 121 (2006): 1009–1022.

6. Primo Levi, *Survival in Auschwitz* (New York: Touchstone, 1996), 90.

7. Agamben, *Remnants of Auschwitz*, 81, 82.

8. Ibid., 69.

9. Berel Lang, *Holocaust Representation: Art Within the Limits of History and Ethics* (Baltimore: Johns Hopkins University Press, 2000), 149.

10. Walter Benjamin, *The Arcades Project*, trans. H. Eiland and K. McLaughlin (Cambridge, Mass.: Harvard University Press, 1999), 463.

11. Giorgio Agamben, *The Time That Remains: A Commentary on the Letter to the Romans*, trans. P. Dailey (Stanford: Stanford University Press, 2005), 74. Agamben refers to Erich Auerbach's classic definition regarding the exegetical practice of typology in which figures of the Old and New Testaments are construed in relation to one another. See Auerbach, "Figura," in *Scenes from the Drama of European Literature* (Minneapolis: University of Minnesota Press, 1984), 1–79.

12. Auerbach, *Figura*, 53.

13. Agamben, *The Time That Remains*, 142.

14. Benjamin, *The Arcades Project*, 463.

15. Ibid.

16. Ibid., 462.

17. Agamben, *The Time That Remains*, 145.

18. Walter Benjamin, "Theses on the Philosophy of History, V," in *Illuminations*, ed. Hannah Arendt, trans. H. Zohn (New York: Schocken Books, 1969), 255.

19. Primo Levi, *Survival in Auschwitz*, trans. Stuart Woolf (New York: Simon & Schuster, 1996), 109–116. As Risa Sodi (in *A Dante of Our Time: Primo Levi and Auschwitz* [New York: Peter Lang, 1990]), and others have shown, Levi is deeply indebted to Dante in how he structures his memoir around figures and the themes he develops, such as witnessing and judgment.

20. Levi, *Survival in Auschwitz*, 113.

21. Enzo Traverso, *The Origins of Nazi Violence*, trans. J. Lloyd (New York: New Press, 2003).

14. AUTOBIOGRAPHY AND THE NARRATOR
Nancy Harrowitz

1. Primo Levi, *The Periodic Table*, trans. Raymond Rosenthal (New York: Schocken Books, 1984), 232–233. Interestingly enough, Levi wrote his college

thesis on the subject of the Walden inversion, a study of the asymmetry of the carbon atom.

2. Irving Howe, "Writing About the Holocaust," in *Writing and the Holocaust*, ed. Berel Lang (New York: Holmes and Meier, 1988), 175–199, at 186.

3. Cynthia Ozick, "Primo Levi's Suicide Note," in *Metaphor and Memory* (New York: Knopf, 1989), 37, 46.

4. Hayden White, "Figural Realism in Witness Literature," *Parallax* 10, no. 1 (2004): 113–124, at 115–116.

5. Primo Levi, *The Drowned and the Saved*, trans. Raymond Rosenthal (New York: Vintage, 1989).

6. Bryan Cheyette, "The Ethical Uncertainty of Primo Levi," *Judaism* (1999): 56–67, at 57.

7. Elizabeth Scheiber, "The Failure of Memory and Literature in Primo Levi's *Il sistema periodico*," *MLN* 121 (2006): 225–239.

8. In a description of *The Memory of the Offense*, a critical study of Levi by Judith Woolf, the following words appear as the reason that Woolf uses Levi's works to explicate *Survival in Auschwitz*: "in the absence of a definitive body of criticism, Levi remains the best explicator of his own work." http://www.troubador.co.uk/book_info.asp?bookid = 3.

9. Paul de Man, "Autobiography as De-facement," *MLN* 94, no. 5 (December 1979): 919–930, at 919.

10. Levi, *The Periodic Table*, 224.

11. Ibid., 5.

12. Alberto Cavaglion, *Notizie su Argon: Gli antenati di Primo Levi da Francesco Petrarca a Cesare Lombroso* (Turin: Instar Libri, 2006). Translation mine.

13. http://www.etimo.it.

14. Levi, *The Periodic Table*, 14.

15. Ibid., 18.

16. Pierre Nora, "Between Memory and History: Le Lieux de Mémoires," in *Theories of Memory*, ed. Michael Rossington and Anne Whitehead (Baltimore: Johns Hopkins University Press, 2007), 144–149.

17. De Man, "Autobiography as De-facement," 920.

18. Massimo Lollini, "Primo Levi and the Idea of Autobiography," in *Primo Levi: The Austere Humanist*, ed. Joseph Farrell (Peter Lang, 2003), 76–77.

19. Primo Levi, *The Periodic Table*, 48–49.

20. Primo Levi, *The Reawakening*, trans. Stuart Woolf (New York: Simon & Schuster, 1993), 26.

21. De Man, "Autobiography as De-facement," 930.

22. Ibid.

23. The issue of the relation between de Man's rhetorical theories and his wartime history of collaboration has been extensively discussed. For example, see *Responses: On Paul de Man's Wartime Journalism*, ed. Werner Hamacher, Neil Hertz, and Thomas Keenan (Lincoln: University of Nebraska Press, 1989).

24. Elie Wiesel, "A Plea for the Dead," from *Legends of Our Times* (New York: Avon, 1968), 73, 77.

25. Primo Levi, *Opere II*, ed. Marco Belpoliti (Turin: Einaudi, 1997), 1414.

15. WRITING AGAINST THE FASCIST SWORD
Fred Misurella

1. Alberto Moravia, *The Conformist*, trans. Tami Calliope (South Royalton, Vt.: Steerforth Italia, 1999), 313.

2. Alberto Moravia, *Two Women*, trans. Angus Davidson (South Royalton, Vt.: Steerforth Italia, 2001), 240.

3. Ibid., 329.

4. Ibid., 331.

5. Giorgio Bassani, *The Garden of the Finzi-Continis*, trans. William Weaver (New York: MJF Books, 1977), 200.

6. Primo Levi, *The Reawakening*, trans. Raymond Rosenthal (New York: Collier Books, 1987), 29.

7. Ibid.

8. Ibid., 32.

9. Ibid., 39.

10. Ibid., 110.

11. Primo Levi, *The Drowned and the Saved*, trans. Raymond Rosenthal (New York: Vintage International, 1989), 69.

12. Ibid., 97.

16. "*SINGOLI STIMOLI*": PRIMO LEVI'S POETRY
Nicholas Patruno

1. Primo Levi, *Ad ora incerta* (Milan: Garzanti, 1990). All quotes in Italian of Levi's poems will be taken from this volume; unless otherwise noted, all translations are my own. *Ad ora incerta* is also included in Levi's *Opere II* (Turin: Einaudi, 1988), 519–634.

2. Ibid., 7.

3. Primo Levi, *Il sistema periodico*, in *Opere I* (Turin: Einaudi, 1987), 546–547. English version: *The Periodic Table*, trans. Raymond Rosenthal (New York: Schocken Books, 1984), 128.

4. Giovanni Tesio, "Le occasioni? La memoria, un ponte, una ragnatela," *Tuttolibri*, November 17, 1984.

5. Massimo Lollini notes that the sinister image of the crow bringing news of death is already present in the closing pages of Levi's *If This Is a Man*. Lollini, "Primo Levi and the Idea of Autobiography," in *Primo Levi: The Austere Humanist*, ed. James Farrell (New York: Peter Lang, 2004), 71.

6. Nagant is a kind of gun, Suzuki a kind of motorbike.

7. "To a Young Reader" in *Other People's Trades*; Italian original in Primo Levi, *L'altrui mestiere* (Turin: Einaudi, 1985), 237.

8. Ibid., 236.

9. Ibid., 53.

10. Primo Levi, *La ricerca delle radici* (Turin: Einaudi, 1997), 211.

11. Levi, *L'altrui mestiere*, 49.

12. Primo Levi, *Terza pagina* (Turin: La Stampa, 1986), 115.

13. Ibid., 117.

14. In *Ad ora incerta*, 154. Raboni's article originally appeared in the newspaper *La Stampa* (November 17, 1984).

18. A NOTE ON THE PROBLEM OF TRANSLATION
Ann Goldstein

Editor's note: Ann Goldstein, along with Alessandra Bastagli, the translator of Levi's collection *A Tranquil Star* (New York: Norton, 2007), is editing new translations of Levi's entire oeuvre. The two-volume project, to be published by Norton, is scheduled to appear in 2012.

1. Here Levi was speaking of the stories collected in *Lilith*; quoted in Primo Levi, *A Tranquil Star* (New York: Norton, 2007), 16.

Adorno, Theodore. "Cultural Criticism and Society." Translated by Samuel and Shierry Weber. In *Prisms*, 17–34. Cambridge, Mass.: MIT Press, 1967 (1981).

———. *Negative Dialectics*. Translated by E. B. Ashton. New York: Seabury Press, 1973.

Agamben, Giorgio. *Homo Sacer: Sovereign Power and Bare Life*. Translated by Daniel Heller-Roazen. Stanford: Stanford University Press, 1998.

———. *Remnants of Auschwitz: The Witness and the Archive*. Translated by Daniel Heller-Roazen. New York: Zone Books, 1999.

———. *The Time That Remains: A Commentary on the Letter to the Romans*. Translated by P. Dailey. Stanford: Stanford University Press, 2005.

Améry, Jean. *At the Mind's Limits: Contemplations by a Survivor on Auschwitz and Its Realities*. Translated by Sidney Rosenfeld and Stella P. Rosenfeld. Bloomington: Indiana University Press, 1980.

———. *On Suicide: A Discourse on Voluntary Death*. Translated by John D. Barlow. Bloomington: Indiana University Press, 1999.

———. *Radical Humanism: Selected Essays*. Translated by Sidney and Stella P. Rosenfeld. Bloomington: Indiana University Press, 1984.

Anissimov, Myriam. *Primo Levi, or The Tragedy of An Optimist*. London: Aurum Press, 1998.

Arendt, Hannah. *Between Past and Future: Six Exercises in Political Thought*. New York: Viking Press, 1961.

———. "History and Immortality." *Partisan Review* 24 (Winter 1957): 11–35.

———. *The Jewish Writings*. Edited by Jerome Kohn and Ron H. Feldman. New York: Schocken Books, 2007.

Auerbach, Eric. "Figura." In *Scenes from the Drama of European Literature*, 11–78. Minneapolis: University of Minnesota Press, 1984.

Bartov, Omer. *Germany's War and the Holocaust: Disputed Histories*. Ithaca, N.Y.: Cornell University Press, 2003.

Bassani, Giorgio. *The Garden of the Finzi-Continis*. Translated by William Weaver. New York: MJF Books, 1977.

Bauer, Yehuda. *Rethinking the Holocaust*. New Haven: Yale University Press, 2001.

Belpoliti, Marco. *Opere di Primo Levi*. Turin: Einaudi, 1997.

———. *Primo Levi: Conversazioni e interviste: 1963–1987*. Turin: Einaudi, 1997.

Benjamin, Andrew, ed. *Walter Benjamin and History*. New York: Continuum, 2005.

Benjamin, Walter. *The Arcades Project*. Translated by H. Eiland and K. McLaughlin. Cambridge, Mass.: Harvard University Press, 1999.

———. *Selected Writings, 1938–1940*, volume 4. Edited by Howard Eiland and Michael W. Jennings; translated by Edmund Jephcott et al. Cambridge, Mass.: Harvard University Press, 2003.

———. "Theses on the Philosophy of History, V." In *Illuminations*, 253–264. New York: Schocken Books, 1969.

Berghahn, Volker R. *America and the Intellectual Cold Wars in Europe: Shepard Stone Between Philanthropy, Academy, and Diplomacy*. Princeton: Princeton University Press, 2001.

Berlin, Isaiah. "Notes on Prejudice." *New York Review of Books*, October 18, 2001.

Best, Steven, and Douglas Kellner. *Postmodern Theory: Critical Interrogations*. New York: Guilford Press, 1991.

Bianchini, Edoardo. *Invito alla lettura di Primo Levi*. Milan: Mursia, 2000.

Biasin, Gian Paolo. "Our Daily Bread." In *Primo Levi as Witness*, edited by Pietro Frassica, 1–20. Fiesole: Casalini, 1990.

Bigsby, Christopher. *Remembering and Imagining the Holocaust: The Chain of Memory*. Cambridge: Cambridge University Press, 2006.

Bons, Eberhart. "Vergangenes erinnern, um Drohendes zu bannen: Judenverfolgung und Partisanenkampf in Primo Levis Romanen." *Orientierung* 51 (1987): 134–136.

Brecht, Bertolt. *Bertolt Brecht: Poems, 1913–1956*. Edited by John Willett and Ralph Manheim; translated by Michael Hamburger et al. New York: Methuen, 1987.

Brison, Susan J. "Outliving Oneself: Trauma, Memory, and Personal Identity." In *Feminists Rethink the Self*, edited by Diana T. Meyers, 12–39. Boulder: Westview, 1997.

Browning, Christopher R. *Nazi Policy, Jewish Workers, German Killers*. New York: Cambridge University Press, 2000.

———. *Ordinary Men: Reserve Police Battalion 101 and the Final Solution in Poland*. New York: Harper Perennial, 1998.

———. *The Origins of the Final Solution: The Evolution of Nazi Jewish Policy, September 1939–March 1942*. Lincoln: University of Nebraska Press, 2004.

Buck-Morss, Susan. *The Dialectics of Seeing: Walter Benjamin and the Arcades Project*. Cambridge, Mass.: MIT Press, 1989.

Burke, Peter, ed. *New Perspectives on Historical Writing*. Cambridge: Polity Press, 1991.

Burke, T. E. *The Philosophy of Karl Popper*. Manchester: Manchester University Press, 1983.

Callan, Eamonn. "Patience and Courage." *Philosophy* 68, no. 266 (1983): 523–539.

Camon, Ferdinando. *Conversations with Primo Levi*. Translated by John Shepley. Marlboro, Vt.: Marlboro Press, 1989.

Camus, Albert. "La Nausée de Jean-Paul Sartre." In *Essais d'Albert Camus*, 1417–1419. Paris: Gallimard, 1965.

Cavaglion, Alberto. *Notizie su Argon: Gli antenati di Primo Levi da Francesco Petrarca a Cesare Lombroso*. Turin: Instar Libri, 2006.

Chambers, Ross. *Story and Situation: Narrative Seduction and the Power of Fiction*. Minneapolis: University of Minnesota Press, 1984.

Cheyette, Bryan. "The Ethical Uncertainty of Primo Levi." *Judaism* (Winter 1999): 56–67.

Chiampi, James T. "Testifying to His Text: Primo Levi and the Concentrationary Sublime." *Romanic Review* 92 (2001): 491–511.

Cicioni, Mirna. *Primo Levi: Bridges of Knowledge*. Washington, D.C.: Berg, 1995.

Citati, Piero. *Kafka*. Translated by Raymond Rosenthal. London: Minerva, 1991.

Corvi, Roberta. *An Introduction to the Thought of Karl Popper*. Translated by Patrick Camiller. London: Routledge, 1997.

Crossman, Richard H., ed. *The God That Failed: Six Studies in Communism*. New York: Columbia University Press, 2001.

Cutler, Bruce. *Seeing the Darkness*. Kansas City, Mo.: BkMk Press, 1998.

D'Amico, Robert. *Historicism and Knowledge*. New York: Routledge, 1989.

Dean, Martin. *Collaboration in the Holocaust: Crimes of the Local Police in Belorussia and Ukraine, 1941–44*. New York: St. Martin's Press, 2000.

De Felice, Renzo. *Storia degli ebrei italiani sotto il fascismo*. Turin: Einaudi, 1997. English translation: *The Jews in Fascist Italy: A History*. Translated by Robert L. Miller. New York: Enigma Books, 2001.

Dekoven, Ezrahi Sidra. "Representing Auschwitz." *History and Memory* 7, no. 2 (Fall/Winter 1996): 121–154.

de Man, Paul. "Autobiography as De-facement." *MLN* 94, no. 5 (December 1979): 919–930.

Des Pres, Terrence. *The Survivor: An Anatomy of Life in the Death Camps*. Oxford: Oxford University Press, 1976.

Donat, Alexander. *The Holocaust Kingdom*. Washington, D.C.: U.S. Holocaust Memorial Museum, 1999.

Druker, Jonathan. *Primo Levi and the Fate of Humanism After Auschwitz*. New York: Palgrave Macmillan, 2009.

Eagleton, Terry. *The Meaning of Life*. Oxford: Oxford University Press, 2007.

Eco, Umberto. "Ur-Fascism." *New York Review of Books*, June 22, 1995.

Edelheit, Abraham J., and Herschel Edelheit. *History of the Holocaust: A Handbook and Dictionary*. Boulder: Westview Press, 1994.

Fabre, Giorgio. *Mussolini razzista: Dal socialismo al fascismo—La formazione di un antisemita*. Milan: Garzanti, 2005.

Fackenheim, Emil L. *To Mend the World: Foundations of Post-Holocaust Jewish Thought*. Bloomington: Indiana University Press, 1994.

Farrell, James, ed. *Primo Levi, the Austere Humanist*. New York: Peter Lang, 2004.

Felman, Shoshana, and Dori Laub, eds. *Testimony: Crises of Witnessing in Literature, Psychoanalysis, and History*. New York: Routledge, 1992.

Ferris, David S., ed. *The Cambridge Companion to Walter Benjamin*. Cambridge: Cambridge University Press, 2004.

Foucault, Michel. *The Order of Things: An Archaeology of the Human Sciences*. New York: Pantheon Books, 1971.

———. "Right of Death and Power Over Life." In *The History of Sexuality, Volume I: An Introduction*, 133–160. New York: Vintage Books, 1990.

———. *"Society Must Be Defended": Lectures at the Collège de France, 1975–1976*. Edited by Mauro Bertani and Alessandro Fontana; translated by David Macey. New York: Picador, 2003.

Francovich, Carlo, ed. *Giustizia e libertà nella lotta antifascista*. Florence: La Nuova Italia, 1978.

Frassica, Pietro. "Invarianti dell'invocazione: 'Se non ora, quando?' di Primo Levi." *Prometeo* 3, no. 9 (1983): 20–32.

Frassica, Pietro, ed. *Primo Levi as Witness*. Fiesole: Casalini, 1990.

Frisby, David. *Fragments of Modernity: Theories of Modernity in the Work of Georg Simmel, Siegfried Kracauer, and Walter Benjamin*. Cambridge, Mass.: MIT Press, 1986.

Furet, François. *The Passing of an Illusion: The Idea of Communism in the Twentieth Century*. Translated by Deborah Furet. Chicago: University of Chicago Press, 1999.

Gambetta, Diego. "Primo Levi's Last Moments." *Boston Review*, Summer 1999.

Gilbert, Martin. *The Righteous: The Unsung Heroes of the Holocaust*. New York: Henry Holt, 2003.

Gilbert, Sander L. "To Quote Primo Levi: 'Redest keyn jiddisch, bist nit kejn jid' ['If you don't speak Yiddish, you're not a Jew']." *Prooftexts: A Journal of Jewish Literary History* 9, no. 2 (1989): 139–160.

Gilloch, Graeme. *Myth and Metropolis: Walter Benjamin and the City.* Cambridge: Polity Press, 1996.

Ginzberg, Louis. *Le leggende degli ebrei.* Milan: Adelphi, 1995.

Ginzburg, Carlo. "Microhistory: Two or Three Things That I Know About It." *Critical Inquiry* 20 (1993): 10–35.

Giuliani, Massimo. *A Centaur in Auschwitz: Reflections on Primo Levi's Thinking.* Lanham, Md.: Lexington Books, 2003.

Glass, James M. *Life Unworthy of Life.* New York: Basic Books, 1997.

Goetschel, Willi. "Models of Difference and Alterity: Moses Mendelssohn, Herman Cohen, Franz Rosenzweig, Martin Buber, and Hermann Levin Goldschmidt." In *The German-Jewish Dilemma: From the Enlightenment to the Shoah*, edited by Edward Timms and Andrea Hammel, 25–38. Lexington, Ky.: Mellen, 1999.

Goldhagen, Daniel J. *Hitler's Willing Executioners: Ordinary Germans and the Holocaust.* New York: Knopf, 1996.

Gordon, Robert S. C. "'Per mia fortuna . . .': Irony and Ethics in Primo Levi's Writing." *Modern Language Review* 92, no. 2 (1997): 337–347.

———. *Primo Levi's Ordinary Virtues: From Testimony to Ethics.* Oxford: Oxford University Press, 2001.

———. "Which Holocaust? Primo Levi and the Field of Holocaust Memory in Post-War Italy." *Italian Studies* 61, no. 1 (Spring 2006): 93.

Gross, Jan T. *Neighbors: The Destruction of the Jewish Community in Jedwabne, Poland.* New York: Penguin Books, 2002.

Gutting, Gary. "Michel Foucault." *Stanford Encyclopedia of Philosophy*, http://plato.stanford.edu/entries/foucault/#3.3.

Hacohen, Malachi Haim. *Karl Popper, The Formative Years, 1902–1945: Politics and Philosophy in Interwar Vienna.* Cambridge: Cambridge University Press, 2000.

Heidelberger-Leonard, Irene. *Jean Améry: Revolte in der Resignation.* Stuttgart: Klett-Cotta, 2004.

Henry, John. *Knowledge Is Power: Francis Bacon and the Method of Science.* Cambridge: Icon Books, 2002.

Hilberg, Raul. *Perpetrators, Victims, Bystanders: The Jewish Catastrophe, 1993–1945.* New York: HarperCollins, 1992.

Hoffman, Eva. *After Such Knowledge: Memory, History and the Legacy of the Holocaust.* New York: Public Affairs, 2004.

Horowitz, Sarah R. *Voicing the Void: Muteness and Memory in Holocaust Fiction.* Albany: State University of New York Press, 1997.

Hoss, Rudolf. *Death Dealer: The Memoirs of the SS Kommandant at Auschwitz.* Buffalo: Prometheus Books, 1992.

Howe, Irving. "Writing About the Holocaust." In *Writing and the Holocaust*, edited by Berel Lang, 175–199. New York: Holmes and Meier, 1988.

Hunter, Jefferson. "Troubles Overcome Are Good to Tell." *Hudson Review* 39, no. 2 (1986): 329–333.

Idel, Moshe. *Golem: Jewish Magical and Mystical Traditions on the Artificial Anthropoid*. Albany: State University of New York Press, 1990.

Iggers, Georg G. *Historiography in the Twentieth Century: From Scientific Objectivity to the Postmodern Challenge*. Middletown, Conn.: Wesleyan University Press, 2005.

James, William. *The Principles of Psychology*. Cambridge, Mass.: Harvard University Press, 1981.

Janicaud, Dominique. "The Theological Turn of French Phenomenology." In *Phenomenology and the "Theological Turn": The French Debate*, edited by Bernard G. Prusak, Jeffrey L. Kosky, and Thomas A. Carlson, 16–103. New York: Fordham University Press, 2000.

Jay, Martin. *Downcast Eyes, The Denigration of Vision in Twentieth-Century French Thought*. Berkeley: University of California Press, 1993.

Jesurum, Stefano. *Essere ebrei in Italia nella testimonianza di ventuno protagonisti*. Milan: Longanesi, 1987.

Jumonville, Neil. *Critical Crossings: The New York Intellectuals in Postwar America*. Berkeley: University of California Press, 1991.

Kaplan, Harold. *Conscience & Memory: Meditation in a Museum of the Holocaust*. Chicago: University of Chicago Press, 1994.

Kellner, Douglas. "Popular Culture and the Construction of Postmodern Identities." In *Modernity and Identity*, edited by Scott Lash and Jonathan Freidman, 141–167. Cambridge, Mass.: Basil Blackwell, 1992.

Kidd, Dustin. "The Aesthetics of Truth, The Aesthetics of Time: George Steiner and the Retreat from the World." http://xroads.virginia.edu/~ma99/kidd/resume/steiner.html

Kogon, Eugen. *The Theory and Practice of Hell: The German Concentration Camps and the System Behind Them*. Translated by Heinz Norden. New York: Farrar, Straus and Giroux, 2006.

Kramer, Lloyd, and Sarah Maza, eds. *A Companion to Western Historical Thought*. Oxford: Blackwell, 2002.

Kremer, Roberta S., ed. *Memory and Mastery: Primo Levi as Writer and Witness*. Albany: State University of New York Press, 2001.

LaCapra, Dominick. *History in Transit: Experience, Identity, Critical Theory*. Ithaca, N.Y.: Cornell University Press, 2004.

Lakoff, George, and Mark Johnson. *Metaphors We Live By*. Chicago: University of Chicago Press, 1980.

Lang, Berel. *Holocaust Representation: Art Within the Limits of History and Ethics*. Baltimore: Johns Hopkins University Press, 2000.

Lang, Berel, ed. *Writing and the Holocaust*. New York: Holmes and Meier, 1988.

Langbein, Hermann. *People in Auschwitz*. Translated by Harry Zohn. Chapel Hill: University of North Carolina Press, 2004.

Langer, Lawrence L. *Holocaust Testimonies: The Ruins of Memory*. New Haven: Yale University Press, 1991.

Lazzarin, Stefano: "'Fatti non foste a viver come bruti': A proposito di Primo Levi e del fantastico." *Testo: Studi di Teoria e Storia della Letteratura e della Critica* 22, no. 42 (2001): 67–90.

Lerner, Gad. "Se questo è uno stato." *L'Espresso*, September 30, 1984.

Levi, Carlo. *Christ Stopped at Eboli*. Translated by Frances Frenaye. New York: Farrar, Straus and Giroux, 2006.

———. *Paura della libertà*. Turin: Einaudi, 1946.

Levi della Torre, Stefano. "Primo Levi: Una stella tranquilla." In *Italienische Erzählungen des 20. Jahrhunderts in Einzelinterpretationen*, edited by Manfred Lentzen, 277–285. Berlin: Schmidt, 2003.

Levinas, Emmanuel. *Ethique et infini: Dialogues d'Emmanuel Levinas et Philippe Nemo*. Paris: Fayard, 1982.

———. *Totalité et infini: Essai sur l'extériorité*. The Hague: Nijhoff. 1961.

Lewinska, Pelagia. *Twenty Months at Auschwitz*. New York: Lyle Stuart, 1989.

Leys, Ruth. *From Guilt to Shame: Auschwitz and After*. Princeton: Princeton University Press, 2007.

Lifton, Robert Jay. *The Nazi Doctors: Medical Killing and the Psychology of Genocide*. New York: Basic Books, 1986.

Lollini, Massimo. "Primo Levi and the Idea of Autobiography." In *Primo Levi, the Austere Humanist*, edited by Joseph Farrell, 67–89. New York: Peter Lang, 2004.

Lorenz-Lindemann, Karin. "Wieviel Heimat braucht der Mensch? Aspects of Jewish Self-Determination in the Works of Jean Améry and Primo Levi." In *The Jewish Self-Portrait in European and American Literature*, edited by Hans-Jürgen Schrader, Elliott M. Simon, et al., 223–230. Tübingen: Niemeyer, 1996.

Lower, Wendy. *Nazi Empire Building and the Holocaust in Ukraine*. Chapel Hill: University of North Carolina Press, 2005.

Löwy, Michael. *Fire Alarm: Reading Walter Benjamin's "On the Concept of History."* Translated by Chris Turner. New York: Verso, 2005.

Mailer, Norman. *The Castle in the Forest*. New York: Random House, 2007.

Marcus, Laura, ed. *Modernity, Culture, and "the Jew."* Cambridge: Polity Press, 1998.

Marcus, Millicent. "Primo Levi: The Biographer's Challenge and the Reader's Double Bind." *Italica* 80, no. 1 (2003): 67–72.

Marion, Jean-Luc. *Being Given: Toward a Phenomenology of Givenness*. Translated by Jeffrey L. Kosky. Stanford: Stanford University Press, 2002.

————. *In Excess: Studies of Saturated Phenomena.* Translated by Robyn Horner and Vincent Berraud. New York: Fordham University Press, 2002.

Marsálek, Hans. *Die Geschichte des Konzentrationslagers Mauthausen: Dokumentation.* Vienna: Österreichischen Lagergemeinschaft, 1974.

McClellan, William. "Primo Levi, Giorgio Agamben and the New Ethics of Reading." In *The Legacy of Primo Levi*, edited by Stanislao G. Pugliese, 147–152. New York: Palgrave Macmillan, 2005.

Mertens, Bram. *Dark Images, Secret Hints: Walter Benjamin, Gershom Scholem, Franz Joseph Molitor and the Jewish Tradition.* New York: Peter Lang, 2007.

Miller, Arthur. "The Nazi Trials and the German Heart." In *Echoes Down the Corridor: Collected Essays, 1944–2000*, edited by Steven R. Centola, 62–68. London: Methuen, 2000.

Mitchell, Mitchell T. *Michael Polanyi: The Art of Knowing.* Wilmington, Del.: Intercollegiate Studies Institute, 2006.

Molinari, Maurizio. *La sinistra e gli ebrei in Italia, 1967–1993.* Milan: Corbaccio, 1995.

Mondo, Lorenzo. "Primo Levi e Dante." In *Primo Levi: Memoria e invenzione, Atti del convegno internazionale*, edited by Giovanna Ioli, 224–230. Monferrato: Edizione della Biennale, 1995.

Moravia, Alberto. *The Conformist.* Translated by Tami Calliope. South Royalton, Vt.: Steerforth Italia, 1999.

————. *Two Women.* Translated by Angus Davidson and Ann McCarrell. South Royalton, Vt.: Steerforth Italia, 2001.

Mulisch, Harry. *The Discovery of Heaven.* Translated by Paul Vincent. London: Penguin, 1996.

————. *Siegfried.* Translated by Paul Vincent. London: Allen Lane, 2003.

Muller, Jerry Z. *The Other God That Failed: Hans Freyer and the Deradicalization of German Conservatism.* Princeton: Princeton University Press, 1987.

Nirenstein, Fiamma. "The Cynical Use of Israel in Italian Politics." http://www.jcpa.org.

Nora, Pierre. "Between Memory and History: Le Lieux de Mémoires." In *Theories of Memory*, edited by Michael Rossington and Anne Whitehead, 144–150. Baltimore: Johns Hopkins University Press, 2007.

Nyiszli, Miklos. *Auschwitz: A Doctor's Eyewitness Account.* New York: Arcade, 1993.

Nystedt, Jane. "Lunghezza della frase e interpunzione: Mezzi stilistici in Primo Levi." *Studi Italiani di Linguistica Teorica e Applicata* 21, nos. 1–3 (1992): 85–106.

Oliner, Samuel P., and Pearl M. Oliner. *The Altruistic Personality.* New York: Free Press, 1992.

Ozick, Cynthia. "Primo Levi's Suicide Note." In *Metaphor and Memory*, 34–48. New York: Knopf, 1989.

———. "The Suicide Note." *New Republic*, March 21, 1988.

Patruno, Nicholas. *Understanding Primo Levi*. Columbia: University of South Carolina Press, 1995.

Piterberg, Gabriel. "Zion's Rebel Daughter: Hannah Arendt on Palestine and Jewish Politics." *New Left Review* 48 (2007): 48–53.

Polanyi, Michael. *The Logic of Liberty: Reflections and Rejoinders*. London: Routledge and Kegan Paul, 1951.

———. *Personal Knowledge: Toward a Post-Critical Philosophy*. Chicago: University of Chicago Press, 1958.

———. *Science, Faith, and Society*. Chicago: University of Chicago Press, 1946.

———. *The Tacit Dimension*. London: Routledge and Kegan Paul, 1967.

Poli, Gabriella, and Giorgio Calcagno. *Echi di una voce perduta*. Milan: Mursia, 1992.

Popper, Karl R. *Miseria dello storicismo*. Translated by Carlo Montaleone. Milan: Editrice l'industria, 1954.

———. *The Open Society and Its Enemies*. London: George Routledge and Sons, 1945.

———. *The Poverty of Historicism*. London: Routledge and Kegan Paul, 1957.

———. *Unended Quest: An Intellectual Autobiography*. London: Routledge, 1992.

Pugliese, Stanislao G. "The Antidote to Fascism." In *My Version of the Facts*, edited by Carla Pekelis, vii–xii. Evanston, Ill.: Marlboro Press/Northwestern University Press, 2004.

———. *Carlo Rosselli: Socialist Heretic and Antifascist Exile*. Cambridge, Mass.: Harvard University Press, 1999.

Pugliese, Stanislao G., ed. *Primo Levi*. New York: Palgrave Macmillan, 2005.

Rabinow, Paul, ed. *The Foucault Reader*. New York: Pantheon Books, 1984.

Rhodes, Richard. *Masters of Death: The SS-Einsatzgruppen and the Invention of the Holocaust*. New York: Vintage Books, 2003.

Rondini, Andrea. "La scrittura e la sfida: Una lettura di 'Lilìt' di Primo Levi." *Studi novecenteschi* 59 (2002): 239–276.

Rosen, Alan, ed. *Celebrating Elie Wiesel: Stories, Essays, Reflections*. Notre Dame, Ind.: University of Notre Dame Press, 1998.

Roubach, Sharon, and Dina Wardi. "Primo Levi in Israel." In *La manutenzione della memoria: Diffusione e conoscenza di Primo Levi nei paesi europei—Atti del convegno, Torino 9–10–11 ottobre 2003*, edited by Giovanni Tesio, 279–299. Turin: Centro Studi Piemontesi, 2005.

Rudolf, Anthony. *At an Uncertain Hour: Primo Levi's War Against Oblivion*. London: Menard Press, 1990.

Sarfatti, Michele. *La Shoah in Italia: La persecuzione degli ebrei sotto il fascismo*. Turin: Einaudi, 2005.

Scheiber, Elizabeth. "The Failure of Memory and Literature in Primo Levi's *Il sistema periodico*." *MLN* 121 (2006): 225–239.

Scholem, Gershom. "Walter Benjamin." *Leo Baeck Memorial Lecture* 8. New York: Leo Baeck Institute, 1965.

Schwann, Heribert, and Helgard Heindrichs. *Der SS-Mann: Josef Blösche—Leben und Sterben eines Mörders*. Munich: Droemersche Verlagsanstalt, 2003.

Scott, William Taussig, and Martin X. Moleski. *Michael Polanyi: Scientist and Philosopher*. New York: Oxford University Press, 2005.

Segre, Vittorio Dan. *Memoirs of a Fortunate Jew*. Bethesda, Md.: Adler & Adler, 1987.

Sereny, Gita. *Into That Darkness: An Examination of Conscience*. New York: Vintage Books, 1983.

Sodi, Risa. "A Last Talk with Primo Levi." *Present Tense*, May/June 1988.

Speelman, Raniero M. "Primo Levi's Short Stories: Modern Midrashim." In *The Legacy of Primo Levi*, edited by Stanislao G. Pugliese, 23–31. New York: Palgrave, 2005.

Spiegelman, Art. *Maus: A Survivor's Tale/My Father Bleeds History*. New York: Pantheon Books, 1986.

———. *Maus II: A Survivor's Tale/And Here My Troubles Began*. New York: Pantheon Books, 1991.

Stabile, Alberto. "Sì, Israele ha passato il segno: Ma non è giusto parlare di nazismo." *La Repubblica*, June 28, 1982.

Steiner, George. "The Idea of Europe." *The Liberal* 8 (July/August 2006), 9.

Tesio, Giovanni. "Le occasioni? La memoria, un ponte, una ragnatela." *Tuttolibri* 17 (November 1984).

Thomson, Ian. *Primo Levi*. London: Hutchinson, 2002.

Todorov, Tzvetan. *Facing the Extreme*. London: Weidenfeld and Nicolson, 1999.

———. *Imperfect Garden: The Legacy of Humanism*. Princeton: Princeton University Press, 2002.

Tosi, Giuseppe. "Dall'attesa alla storia-esilio: La memoria e l'identità in *Se non ora, quando?* di Primo Levi." *Annali d'Italianistica* 20 (2002): 285–305.

Traverso, Enzo. *The Origins of Nazi Violence*. Translated by J. Lloyd. New York: New Press, 2003.

Trevor-Roper, Hugh. *Hitler's Table Talk*. London: Allen Lane, 1953.

Van Der Kolk, Bessel A., and Onno Van der Hart. "The Intrusive Past: The Flexibility of Memory and the Engraving of Trauma." In *Trauma: Explorations in Memory*, edited by Cathy Caruth, 158–182. Baltimore: Johns Hopkins University Press, 1995.

Vattimo, Gianni. *After Christianity*. Translated by Luca D'Isanto. New York: Columbia University Press, 2002

————. *Belief*. Translated by Luca D'Isanto and David Webb. Stanford: Stanford University Press, 1999.

Von Lang, Jochen, and Claus Sibyll. *Eichmann Interrogated: Transcripts from the Archives of the Israeli Police*. New York: Da Capo Press, 1999.

Wachtel, Eleanor. *Original Minds*. Toronto: Harper Flamingo, 2003.

Westermann, Edward B. *Hitler's Police Battalions: Enforcing Racial War in the East*. Lawrence: University Press of Kansas, 2005.

White, Hayden. "Figural Realism in Witness Literature." *Parallax* 10, no. 1 (2004): 113–124.

Wiener, Philip P., ed. *Dictionary of the History of Ideas: Studies of Selected Pivotal Ideas*. New York: Scribner, 1973–74.

Wiesel, Elie. *Legends of Our Time*. Translated by Stephen Donadio. New York: Avon, 1970.

Wilson, Jonathan. "Primo Levi's Hybrid Texts." *Judaism: A Quarterly Journal of Jewish Life and Thought* 48 (Winter 1999): 67–72.

Wismann, Heinz, ed. *Walter Benjamin et Paris (Ecoles des hautes études en sciences sociales, colloque international, 27–29 juin 1983)*. Paris: Editions du Cerf, 1986.

Woolf, Stuart. "Primo Levi's Sense of History." *Journal of Modern Italian Studies* 3 (1998): 273–292.

Young-Bruehl, Elizabeth. *Hannah Arendt: For Love of the World*. New Haven: Yale University Press, 1982.

Zillmer, Eric A., Molly Harrower, Barry A. Ritzler, and Robert P. Archer. *The Quest for the Nazi Personality: A Psychological Investigation of Nazi War Criminals*. Mahwah, N.J.: Lawrence Erlbaum Associates, 1995.

Zuccotti, Susan. *The Italians and the Holocaust*. New York: Basic Books, 1987.

JOHAN ÅHR is Assistant Professor of History at Hofstra University, where he teaches courses on modern continental Europe, particularly Germany. He is currently publishing on the city of Berlin and the significance of the monument to historical debate and critical discourse. See his "Memory and Mourning in Berlin: On Peter Eisenman's *Holocaust-Mahnmal* (2005)," *Modern Judaism* 28 (2008), and "Hans Haacke Versus the Myth of *Volk*," *Journal of War and Culture Studies* (May 2010).

MARIE L. BAIRD is Associate Professor and Director of Graduate Studies in Theology at Duquesne University. Her research interests include the theology of suffering, the philosophies of Emmanuel Levinas and Eric Voegelin, spirituality and mysticism, and the role of ethics in theology and spirituality after the Holocaust. The title of her first book is *On the Side of the Angels: Ethics and Post-Holocaust Spirituality*. Her current research is focused on the phenomenology of bearing witness.

TERRI BOWMAN received a bachelor of arts degree from Hofstra University. As a student of history and fine arts, she created the charcoal drawings in the epilogue to this book while exploring both the writings of Primo Levi and the use of art as therapy throughout the Holocaust. She lives in Boston, where she is currently pursuing a career in art therapy and education.

JONATHAN DRUKER is Associate Professor of Italian at Illinois State University, where he also teaches Holocaust literature. He has contributed articles on Primo Levi to *Italica*, *Clio*, and *Italian Culture* and has written three essays for Modern Language Association publications on how to teach Levi's texts. He also coauthored an essay with Michael Rothberg on Levi's reception in the United States, published in *Shofar*. Druker's book *Primo Levi and Humanism after Auschwitz: Posthumanist Reflections* was published by Palgrave Macmillan in 2009. The essay in this collection is adapted from that book.

JOSEPH FARRELL is Professor of Italian Studies at the University of Strathclyde, in Glasgow, Scotland. His main research interests are in the fields of Sicilian culture and theater history. He is author of *Leonardo Sciascia* and *Dario Fo and Franca Rame: Harlequins of the Revolution*. *The History of Italian Theatre*, coedited with Paolo Puppa, was published by Cambridge University Press. In addition, he has edited volumes of essays on Carlo Goldoni, Dario Fo, Primo Levi, Carlo Levi and the Mafia. He has also produced editions of *Accidental Death of an Anarchist* and of *Six Characters in Search of an Author*.

MASSIMO GIULIANI is Professor of Jewish Studies and Philosophical Hermeneutics at the University of Trent, Italy. He received his PhD from the Hebrew University of Jerusalem and taught for several years in the United States. He is a member of the scientific boards of the Maimonides Foundation in Milan and the Museo dell'Ebraismo Italiano e della Shoah in Ferrara. Among his most recent books are *Theological Implications of the Shoah*, *A Centaur in Auschwitz: Reflections on Primo Levi's Thinking*, *Il pensiero ebraico contemporaneo*, *Le tende di Abramo. Ebraismo, cristianesimo, islam: interpretare un'eredità comune*, and *Eros in esilio. Letture teologico-politiche del Cantico dei cantici*. He regularly writes for a national Italian newspaper and the journals *Humanitas* and *Sefer*.

ANN GOLDSTEIN is an editor at *The New Yorker*. She has translated works by, among others, Primo Levi, Pier Paolo Pasolini, Alessandro Baricco, Elena Ferrante, and Roberto Calasso, and she is currently editing the *Complete Works of Primo Levi* in English for Norton. She has been the recipient of several prizes, including the PEN Renato Poggiolo Prize and an award from the Italian Ministry of Foreign Affairs.

NANCY HARROWITZ is Associate Professor in the Department of Romance Studies at Boston University. She has published widely on the topics of anti-Semitism and misogyny in the modern period, including *Antisemitism, Misogyny and The Logic of Cultural Difference: Cesare Lombroso and Matilde Serao* (1994), and two edited collections: *Tainted Greatness: Antisemitism and Cultural Heroes* (1994) and *Jews and Gender: Responses to Otto Weininger* (1995, coedited with Barbara Hyams). She is completing a book entitled *Primo Levi and the Identity of a Survivor*.

ILONA KLEIN is Associate Professor of Italian at Brigham Young University. Her scholarly interests and publications focus on Italian Romanticism, paleography, the Shoah, Primo Levi, and the personal memoirs of Jewish concentration camp prisoners.

WILLIAM MCCLELLAN is an Associate Professor of English at Baruch College, City University of New York. He has published articles on literary and cultural studies and is writing a book whose working title is *Reading Chaucer After Auschwitz.*

JAMES TASATO MELLONE is Associate Professor of Library, Social Sciences Librarian at Queens College, CUNY. He has served as an abstracter for *Historical Abstracts*, and he reviews books on modern Italian history for *History: Reviews of New Books.* His essay "An Edwardian's Search for Meaning: Trevelyan's *Garibaldi*" appeared in the *Journal of the Historical Society.* He is currently working on a book-length annotated bibliography of the scholarly writings on Primo Levi.

FRED MISURELLA has published *Lies to Live By: Stories*; *Short Time*, a novella; and *Understanding Milan Kundera: Public Events, Private Affairs.* His stories and nonfiction have appeared in *Partisan Review, Salmagundi, Kansas Quarterly, Voices in Italian Americana, L'Atelier du roman, The Christian Science Monitor, The Village Voice*, and the *New York Times Book Review.* His essay, "A Clear Eye on Life," appears in *The Legacy of Primo Levi.* He teaches writing and Italian-American Literature at East Stroudsburg University in Pennsylvania.

NICHOLAS PATRUNO is Emeritus Professor of Italian at Bryn Mawr College. He has done extensive research on the works of Primo Levi and, in addition to several articles, is the author of *Understanding Primo Levi.* He has also commented on Primo Levi's life and works for the American television program *Today.*

STANISLAO G. PUGLIESE is Professor of History and Queensboro Unico Distinguished Professor of Italian and Italian American Studies at Hofstra University. He is a former research fellow at the Italian Academy for Advanced Studies at Columbia University, the United States Holocaust Memorial Museum in Washington, D.C., Oxford University, and Harvard University. Pugliese is the author, editor, or translator of a dozen books on Italian and Italian American studies, including *The Most Ancient of Minorities: The Jews of Italy* and *The Legacy of Primo Levi.* His edition of Carlo Levi's *Fear of Freedom* was published by Columbia University Press in 2008. His latest book, *Bitter Spring: A Life of Ignazio Silone*, was awarded the Premio Flaiano in Italy and the Marraro Prize by the American Historical Association.

TIMOTHY PYTELL is Associate Professor of History and Director of Graduate Studies in Social and Behavioral Sciences at California State University

San Bernardino. He is the author of *Viktor Frankl: Das Ende eines Mythos?* and of numerous articles on Holocaust survivors.

ELIZABETH SCHEIBER is Associate Professor of French and Italian at Rider University in New Jersey. She has published articles on Primo Levi's *The Periodic Table* in *Modern Language Notes* and *Forum Italicum*, as well as on Charlotte Delbo's memoirs for *Dalhousie French Studies* and *Studies in Holocaust Literature*. She is interested in various aspects of representation in Holocaust literature, especially the use of symbol, analogy, and metaphor, and her current project focuses on Holocaust poetics. She is also the Coordinator of Commemorative Programs at the Koppelman Holocaust/ Genocide Resource Center.

AMY SIMON is a PhD candidate in the History Department at Indiana University with a minor in Jewish Studies. Her dissertation examines Jewish Holocaust victim perceptions of their perpetrators as represented in their Yiddish writings. She has taught classes on Holocaust history and American perceptions of the Holocaust and was a scholar in residence at the United States Holocaust Memorial Museum; she was also named a Kagan Claims Conference Fellow. In her research and in her teaching, she seeks to bridge the gap between literature and history.

RISA SODI is the Language Program Director and Senior Lector II in the Department of Italian Language and Literature at Yale University. She teaches and publishes on Jewish Italy, Italian-Jewish authors, including Primo Levi, and Italian Holocaust literature. She is the author of *A Dante of Our Time: Primo Levi and Auschwitz*, the first monograph in English on Primo Levi, and *Narrative and Imperative: The First Fifty Years of Italian Holocaust Literature, 1943–1993*. Her 1986 interview with Primo Levi was published in American journals and was republished in Italy and in Israel. She is coediting a volume of essays currently titled *New Reflections on Primo Levi: Before and After Auschwitz*.

IAN THOMSON is a journalist and writer from London whose work has appeared in the *Sunday Times Magazine*, *The Independent*, *Daily Telegraph*, *Spectator*, and *Times Literary Supplement*. His books include *Southern Italy*, *Bonjour Blanc: A Journey Through Haiti*, *Primo Levi: A Biography* and, most recently, *The Dead Yard: A Story of Modern Jamaica*.

SARA VANDEWAETERE received an MA in Italian literature at the University of Antwerp and a DEA (French MSc) degree in Italian culture and literature at the University of Paris X. She is currently completing her PhD at the University of Antwerp on the theme of the senses and sensations in Primo Levi's work.

JORAM WARMUND is Professor and Chair of the History Department and Coordinator of the Social Science Division at Long Island University, Brooklyn. He is is coeditor of and contributor to *Jackie Robinson: Race, Sports, and the American Dream*. A specialist in modern German and diplomatic history, he has recently developed a research interest in Holocaust studies, resulting in his authorship of "The Gray Zone Expanded" in *The Legacy of Primo Levi*. Warmund is a two-time recipient of the Fulbright Award, as well as the recipient of a DAAD (German Academic Exchange Service) award.